TWAIN'S FEAST

TWAIN'S FEAST

SEARCHING FOR AMERICA'S LOST FOODS

in the

FOOTSTEPS OF SAMUEL CLEMENS

ANDREW BEAHRS

THE PENGUIN PRESS

New York

2010

THE PENGUIN PRESS
Published by the Penguin Group
Penguin Group (USA) Inc., 375 Hudson Street, New York, New York 10014,
U.S.A. • Penguin Group (Canada), 90 Eglinton Avenue East, Suite 700, Toronto,
Ontario, Canada M4P 2Y3 (a division of Pearson Penguin Canada Inc.) •
Penguin Books Ltd, 80 Strand, London WC2R 0RL, England • Penguin Ireland,
25 St. Stephen's Green, Dublin 2, Ireland (a division of Penguin Books Ltd) •
Penguin Books Australia Ltd, 250 Camberwell Road, Camberwell,
Victoria 3124, Australia (a division of Pearson Australia Group Pty Ltd) •
Penguin Books India Pvt Ltd, 11 Community Centre, Panchsheel Park,
New Delhi–110 017, India • Penguin Group (NZ) 67 Apollo Drive, Rosedale,
North Shore 0632 New Zealand (a division of Pearson New Zealand Ltd) •
Penguin Books (South Africa) (Pty) Ltd, 24 Sturdee Avenue,
Rosebank, Johannesburg 2196, South Africa

Penguin Books Ltd, Registered Offices:
80 Strand, London WC2R 0RL, England

First published in 2010 by The Penguin Press
a member of Penguin Group (USA) Inc.

Library of Congress Cataloging-in-Publication Data

Beahrs, Andrew, 1973–
Twain's feast: searching for America's lost foods in the footsteps of
Samuel Clemens / Andrew Beahrs.
p. cm.
Includes bibliographical references and index.
ISBN 978-1-59420-259-9
1. Gastronomy. 2. Cookery, American. 3. Food habits—United States.
4. Twain, Mark, 1835–1910. I. Title.
TX633.B393   2010
394.1'20973—dc22   2009053444

Printed in the Unites States of America
1   3   5   7   9   10   8   6   4   2

DESIGNED BY AMANDA DEWEY

For Erik and Mio

IF I HAVE A TALENT IT IS FOR CONTRIBUTING VALUABLE
MATTER TO WORKS UPON COOKERY.

— *Mark Twain*

CONTENTS

INTRODUCTION   *1*

One

IT MAKES ME CRY TO THINK OF THEM
Prairie-Hens, from Illinois   15

Two

A BARREL OF ODDS AND ENDS
Possum and Raccoon   49

Three

MASTERPIECE OF THE UNIVERSE
Trout at Lake Tahoe   83

Four

HEAVEN ON THE HALF SHELL
Oysters and Mussels in San Francisco   113

Five

DINNER WAS LEISURELY SERVED
Philadelphia Terrapin 148

Six

THE MOST ABSORBING STORY IN THE WORLD
Sheep-Head and Croakers, from New Orleans 183

Seven

IT IS *MY* THANKSGIVING DAY
Cranberries 217

Eight

TWILIGHT
Maple Syrup 252

EPILOGUE 281

Acknowledgments 291

Notes 293

Selected Bibliography 309

Index 313

TWAIN'S FEAST

INTRODUCTION

FOR MY THIRTY-THIRD BIRTHDAY, I wanted breakfast with Mark Twain. I'd been preparing for more than a week—reading Twain's novels, digging through old cookbooks, shopping in a half dozen markets. Now a two-inch-thick, dry-aged porterhouse rested on my kitchen counter in a nest of brown butcher paper. Buckwheat batter and a tray of biscuits waited for the oven; dark maple syrup warmed in a small saucepan. In the living room, my wife had our three-year-old son pinned down (literally, I hoped). Beside me a deep, seasoned-to-black cast-iron fryer heated over the highest possible flame.

I owed my planned menu to Twain's painful homesickness. In the winter of 1879, he was more than a year into the European tour chronicled in *A Tramp Abroad*. Along the way he'd mocked the pretensions of Alpine expeditions, the absurdity of French duels, the awful German language—and the food, most of all the food. He *detested* the food. From watery coffee to decayed strawberries to chicken "as tasteless as paper," Twain thought European food monotonous, a hollow sham, a base counterfeit. "There is here and there an American who will say he can remember rising from a European table d'hôte perfectly satisfied," he wrote. "But we must not overlook the fact that there is also here and there an American who will lie."

So Twain dreamed of American dishes, from peach cobbler and

simply dressed tomatoes to oyster soup and roast beef. But he dreamed first of breakfast. He imagined an angel, "suddenly sweeping down out of a better land," and setting before an American exile "a mighty porterhouse steak an inch and a half thick, hot and sputtering from the griddle; dusted with fragrant pepper; enriched with little melting bits of butter of the most unimpeachable freshness and genuineness; . . . a great cup of American home-made coffee, with the cream a-froth on top, . . . some smoking hot biscuits, [and] a plate of hot buckwheat cakes, with transparent syrup." He concluded wistfully: "Could words describe the gratitude of this exile?"

I'd known at once that I'd make the breakfast; for me, cooking and reading blend like a chicken-fat roux. When Ishmael writes of savory clam and cod chowders, or of frying ships' biscuits in the try-pots, I linger; I return to "The Adventure of the Blue Carbuncle" (Sherlock Holmes finds a gem hidden in a roasting goose) and "Breakfast" (Steinbeck eats breakfast) more often than the stories deserve. After roasting a pig, I'll gnaw the tail and think of Laura Ingalls Wilder's autumn butchering. I've cooked snails from my backyard with butter, garlic, and prosciutto, raising the first from the broth to salute those that sent Italo Calvino's young Baron Cosimo into the trees (my wife threatened to follow his example). I've cooked prawns from Hemingway, steaks from Joseph Mitchell, and gumbo from Least Heat-Moon.

So it seemed inevitable, after reading *A Tramp Abroad,* that I'd cook Twain's breakfast. I'd make the first meal he thought of, when he thought of home.

———>●<———

Twain described his ideal steak as though he were mapping his own home country—he wrote of a county of beefsteak, of townships of fat, of districts separated by bone. When I looked at the meat on my counter, I could see why. This was no uniform, sterile cut; it had heft, authority, presence. The mottling of meat and fat declared that no two bites would be alike.

Wanting a steak as much as possible like those Twain enjoyed, I ordered a grass-fed, dry-aged porterhouse from a small local butcher. Raising cattle on grass makes both biological and environmental sense, requiring vastly less oil and water than is needed to grow enough grain for a large ruminant. More important for my purposes, Twain's steaks were invariably from cattle raised on pasture. Until cattle were forcibly moved to a diet of corn, the sometimes rich, sometimes gamy taste of beef fed exclusively on grass was simply what beef tasted like.

Similarly, it's likely that every steak Twain ever ate was dry-aged, hung in a cool, dry spot for the three to five weeks necessary for the proteins to begin to break down and the flavor to ripen. Wet aging—a cheaper, faster process that begins with packing meat in plastic—leaves the steak with more of its original weight; dry aging can give it an aroma as smooth as old wine.

I had an urge to brag. I imagined myself calling up relatives or knocking on neighbors' doors. Instead I rubbed the meat with a fistful of kosher salt. Soon it was sizzling in the pan; I'd finish it in a hot oven.

"Some smoking hot biscuits," Twain wrote. "Some real butter, firm and yellow and fresh." I was using a biscuit recipe given to me by an archaeology graduate student on the Virginia corn-and-peanut plantation where I excavated during college summers. The recipe always reminds me of a thunderstorm that turned the air purple and sent lightning crashing along the James River as we feasted, after a long week of digging out colonial bottles and pipe stems, on angel biscuits, blue crabs, and beer. I'd considered making beaten biscuits—slamming the dough with a rolling pin until it blistered and needed no leavening. But using the Virginia recipe instead was a sympathetic nod to Twain's nostalgia, which, by the time he wrote his fantasy menu, was both intense and introspective. He'd published the semiautobiographical *Tom Sawyer* only a few years prior, and had begun to draft *Huckleberry Finn;*

soon *Life on the Mississippi* would revisit his years of young manhood. Thinking of each well-loved place must have made him long for the foods he'd eaten there. I knew it did for me.

The butter was from a local farmers' market, churned and shaped into an irregular log only the day before. I dipped in the tip of a knife, touched it to my tongue, and . . . well, you know what's better than sweet, fresh butter? Not a whole lot. Fresh butter melting on a steak, maybe.

"A plate of hot buckwheat cakes, with transparent syrup." This was a harder one. Making flapjacks would complicate the timing of the steak, biscuits, and coffee, which I planned to brew in a French press at the last minute. I found a solution in *The Confederate Housewife,* a compilation of recipes printed in Southern newspapers during the Civil War. Though the buckwheat-cake recipe was serenely confident, concluding with a simple, imperious "try it," the truth is that the instructions seemed off, calling for neither leavening nor salt. Still, the cake had the advantage of being baked, instead of cooked on a griddle; I'd be able to finish the entire meal in the oven, making the timing immeasurably easier. Besides, I mostly wanted the cake to serve as a base for dark maple syrup.

Twain wanted his syrup "transparent," probably the grade called light amber, or "fancy." But I like maple syrup dark. One of my earliest memories—not just food memories but memories—is of boiling sap in a lean-to at my Connecticut-hippie nursery school. It's an intensely sensory memory of melting snows, and cold spring air swirling into the smoky boiling house, and steam pouring from a slowly sweetening kettle of syrup. Most of all it's a memory of maple—maple sipped from a wooden ladle, maple boiled until it seemed, to my four-year-old tongue, to be dark as night and sweet as the heart of the tree.

The hell with transparent syrup.

Steak, buckwheat cake, and biscuits went into the oven together. When the smells of baking breads and roasting meat began filling the kitchen, I turned to the coffee.

"A great cup of American home-made coffee, with the cream a-froth on top." I didn't go so far as to roast my own beans, which might have been what Twain meant by "home-made." But I did take care with my French press, pouring in water a few degrees below boiling, relishing the blooming of the fresh, coarse grounds. The beauty of a French press is that every bit of coffee spends precisely the same amount of time steeping as all the rest; in a drip machine, some grounds are wet long enough to go bitter while others stay dry until the very end, which isn't long enough for them to yield all their flavor. I stirred down the grounds and spent a happy ninety seconds inhaling the ever-richer steam. I wanted it strong, dark as earth, the antithesis of Twain's Recipe for German Coffee: "Take a barrel of water and bring it to a boil; rub a chicory berry against a coffee berry, then convey the former into the water. Continue the boiling and evaporation until the intensity of the flavor and aroma of the coffee and chicory has been diminished to a proper degree; then set aside to cool. . . . Mix the beverage in a cold cup, partake with moderation, and keep a wet rag around your head to guard against over-excitement."

But though the coffee was important, the cream was probably closer to Twain's heart. Throughout his trip he railed against European cream, calling it pale, sickly, and counterfeit. He suggested that the hotels made it by diluting single cans of condensed milk in the fifty-eight-thousand-gallon Great Tun of Heidelberg. And he viewed European cows with suspicion. Germans "work the cows in wagons—maybe they *can't* give good milk," he reflected in his journal. "I'd like to put one in a hydraulic press and *squeeze* her."

Today raw milk or cream is illegal in nearly half of the states, and European raw cheeses are legally required to be aged for more than sixty days before being imported. The overwhelming majority of American milk has been pasteurized at a temperature as high as 171 degrees Fahrenheit, a process that extends shelf life but also produces hydrogen sulfide gas, giving the milk a distinctive, slightly burned flavor. When raw milk can be found at all, its price reflects the difficulty of delivery and its short shelf life—I paid an insane fourteen dollars for half a pint, blowing my family's milk budget for the next two weeks. But the moment I opened the bottle, I remembered how Twain the young news-paperman had loved the cream served at San Francisco's Ocean House, "so rich and thick that you could hardly have strained it through a wire fence."

I coaxed the raw, almost clotted cream from the bottle with gentle taps, spreading it thickly on the bottoms of two cups with the back of a spoon. Then I let dark streams of coffee ripple under the cream's edge, raising it like a hot-air balloon's yellow silk. The steak sputtered; the biscuits and buckwheat cake steamed. Breakfast was ready.

———— ❧ ————

Among the German phrases Twain resolved to master:

"This tea isn't good."
"This coffee isn't good."
"This bread seems old."
"Isn't there a curious smell about . . ."
"Isn't that something in the butter?"

No wonder that his perfect breakfast revolved around fresh, hon-est, genuine flavors. My breakfast table, loaded down with ripping-hot steak and biscuits and coffee, with warm syrup and cool cream, gave humbling testimony to the depth and power of Twain's genius. Never again would I speak ill of *Tom Sawyer Abroad,* or of the last eleven chapters of *Huckleberry Finn.*

The steak was the color of well-oiled oak, and I knew from my first bite that it was the best piece of meat I'd ever had (much more a comment on the skills of the rancher and butcher, I stress, than on my cooking—in the hands of a professional, the steak might have killed me with joy). It tasted denser, more packed, than wet-aged steaks, which by comparison seem almost insubstantial. Though the aging gave the porterhouse a slightly gamy, almost smoky taste, the grass was distinctly present, giving even the painstakingly aged meat a contrasting suggestion of freshness. The biscuits were tall and hot, the butter clean as springwater.

Honesty compels me to record that the buckwheat cake sucked. Henceforth, "Do not doubt Mark Twain" would be my motto. When Twain called for buckwheat cakes, I would by God make buckwheat *cakes,* with batter properly salted and cooked to perfection in a bit of good butter, and no more of this Confederate buckwheat-cake claptrap. I contented myself with a sip of pure dark syrup.

The coffee was commandingly rich, the cream a revelation. Though the butter was vastly fresher and sweeter than what I was used to, it was still recognizably butter—a familiar taste, much improved. The cream was something altogether new to me, with a raw, immediate flavor that homogenized cream doesn't even aspire to. I understood Twain's anger at the thought of another cup of hotel coffee, topped with watery cream. *Insipid!* I imagined him spitting. *Counterfeit! Baptized!* Then I imagined his happiness at being handed the cup I held; I breathed in, and out. I sipped.

I tend to cook too much food, and I'd cooked too much that morning. But my wife and son and I tore in with appetites that would have done credit to Twain—cranky, ravenous, homesick Twain. Soon there was nothing left but plates of crumbs and a platter divided by a lonely border fence of bone.

I'd learned a lot while getting ready to cook, and more while cooking. I knew more about dry-aged meat than I had, and a little about what pasteurization does to the flavor of milk (consult your thesaurus: see "decimates"). I'd learned something about the grades of maple syrup, and when the Worcestershire I used in the butter-and-meat-juice gravy was invented (around 1840, reputedly when a keg of unpalatable sauce was discovered to have mellowed during its several years forgotten in a cellar; it is not known whether the first taster was drunk). Though it's impossible to exactly replicate the flavors of a meal dreamed up nearly 150 years ago, learning something about the history of the foods on the table—the difference between beaten and baking-powder biscuits, the way that feeding cattle on grass results in healthier fats—had been part of the pleasure of the breakfast. Knowing a little about the menu rooted it, and gave me a sense of real connection to Twain. It made the meal a conversation.

But Twain didn't stop with breakfast. He went on to list some eighty American foods, which he said he wanted served at a "modest, private affair," all to himself, the moment he stepped off his steamer:

> Radishes. Baked apples, with cream.
> Fried oysters; stewed oysters. Frogs.
> American coffee, with real cream.
> American butter.
> Fried chicken, Southern style.
> Porter-house steak.
> Saratoga potatoes.
> Broiled chicken, American style.
> Hot biscuits, Southern style.
> Hot wheat-bread, Southern style.
> Hot buckwheat cakes.
> American toast. Clear maple syrup.
> Virginia bacon, broiled.
> Blue points, on the half shell.
> Cherry-stone clams.
> San Francisco mussels, steamed.
> Oyster soup. Clam soup.
> Philadelphia Ter[r]apin soup.
> Bacon and greens, Southern style.
> Hominy. Boiled onions. Turnips.

Pumpkin. Squash. Asparagus.

Butter beans. Sweet potatoes.

Lettuce. Succotash. String beans.

Mashed potatoes. Catsup.

Boiled potatoes, in their skins.

New potatoes, minus the skins.

Early rose potatoes, roasted in the ashes, Southern style,
    served hot.

Sliced tomatoes, with sugar or vinegar. Stewed tomatoes.

Green corn, cut from the ear and served with butter and pepper.

Oysters roasted in shell—Northern style.

Soft-shell crabs. Connecticut shad.

Baltimore perch.

Brook trout, from Sierra Nevadas.

Lake trout, from Tahoe.

Sheep-head and croakers, from New Orleans.

Black bass from the Mississippi.

American roast beef.

Roast turkey, Thanksgiving style.

Cranberry sauce. Celery.

Roast wild turkey. Woodcock.

Canvas-back-duck, from Baltimore.

Prairie-hens, from Illinois.

Missouri partridges, broiled.

'Possum. Coon.

Boston bacon and beans.

Green corn, on the ear.

Hot corn-pone, with chitlings, Southern style.

Hot hoe-cake, Southern style.

Hot egg-bread, Southern style.

Hot light-bread, Southern style.

Buttermilk. Iced sweet milk.

Apple dumplings, with real cream.

Apple pie. Apple fritters.

Apple puffs, Southern style.

Peach cobbler, Southern style.

Peach pie. American mince pie.

Pumpkin pie. Squash pie.

All sorts of American pastry.

"Fresh American fruits of all sorts," he went on, "including straw-berries which are not to be doled out as if they were jewelry, but in a more liberal way." And "ice-water—not prepared in the ineffectual goblet, but in the sincere and capable refrigerator."

Now, *that* is a meal. Twain's wide-ranging enthusiasm extends even to properly fresh, cold ice water. At times he jumps around at random; at others he riffs for five or six lines on vegetables, game birds, or pie. When he lists corn pone, hoecake, egg bread, and light bread, all served Southern style, he's almost audibly excited. And his enthusiasm is not just due to hunger. If it were, surely he'd never have opened the menu with radishes. Radishes! I thought of a bowl of them, fresh and crisp, dipped in butter, sprinkled with salt. Peppery, refreshing radishes: wonderful, yes, but probably not the first thing most hungry men think of.

It was different reading the menu after I'd cooked breakfast. I understood better what Twain had meant when he used the words "earnest" and "generous," "genuine" and "real"; I understood better what he thought of when he thought of American food. Reading it again, with the dense, strong, fresh flavors of breakfast still lingering, the menu spoke to me.

I've always hated it when people say that America doesn't have a real cuisine, as though fast food were the only thing we can truly call our own. Granted, the growing national trend toward fresh, high-quality, local food is greatly inspired by the incredible depth of French and Italian cookery. But food is our most basic connection to the world, our fundamental means of sustaining ourselves on earth; it's always seemed intuitively wrong to me to say that America lacks rooted culinary traditions. Surely we have them, even if many have been buried beneath a sodden heap of McNuggets.

As I looked deeper, returning to Twain's other writings for more insight into his menu, I saw that when he thought of American food, he thought of anything but tired, clumsy, monotonous junk. Instead he thought of freshness and abundance. He thought of careful preparations. Most important, I realized, he thought of his own life.

The foods of the feast were necessarily fresh, the menu filled with local, seasonal flavors. Asparagus, butter beans, sliced tomatoes—none could have been eaten very long after harvest, at least without Twain's judging them "insipid" or "decayed," as he did European string beans and cherries. And in the 1840s America of Twain's childhood, it would have been simply impossible to eat a fish like "sheep-head, from New Orleans" very far from the Gulf of Mexico. Such things were purely local; he'd later write that though many fine dishes could be had at Buckingham Palace, such dishes as pompano, crayfish, "shrimps of choice quality," and "small soft-shell crabs of a most superior breed" could be had in "perfection only in New Orleans"—a testament both to the city's legendary cooking and to its thriving lake, bayou, Gulf, and Mississippi River fisheries.

The menu shouts of a joyous abundance. It testifies to a deep bond in Twain's mind between eating and tasting and celebrating, an association that went back to childhood. Twain remembered to the end of his life the cheapness and plenty of many of the foods in Florida, Missouri, the tiny village where he'd been born: apples and peaches, sweet and Irish potatoes, corn and chickens and butter, coffee and sugar and whiskey. "It makes me cry to think of them," he wrote of the meals his Uncle John Quarles served at his farm not far outside of Florida, meals that included biscuits, corn on the ear, fried chicken, succotash, tomatoes, buttermilk, apple dumplings, and many more foods he'd later yearn for in Europe. And there were more beloved dishes from Boston to San Francisco, from the highest Sierras to the deepest lakes. . . .

Of course, such good things demanded respectful attention. Twain took as firm a stand on questions of regional cookery as he did when he declared European-style butter a "sham" because it lacked salt or when he moaned that to carve a chicken in the German fashion one must "use a club, and avoid the joints." Concerning the meals on his uncle's farm, he declared that "the way that the things were cooked was perhaps the main splendor—particularly a certain few of the dishes. For instance, the corn bread, the hot biscuits and wheat bread and the fried chicken. These things have never been properly cooked in the North—in fact, no one there is able to learn the art, so far as my experience goes. The North thinks it knows how to make corn bread but this is gross superstition."

In journals, novels, and travelogues, Twain's love for a dish was inseparable from his love of life. "Open air sleeping, open air exercise, bathing, and a large ingredient of hunger" make freshwater fish incomparably delicious, he declared in *Tom Sawyer.* And he reflected after stagecoaching through the Rockies that "nothing helps scenery like ham and eggs. . . . Ham and eggs and scenery, a 'down grade,' a flying coach, a fragrant pipe and a contented heart—these make happiness. It is what all the ages have struggled for." When I read his travelogues, it seemed that he never had a bad meal when happy or a good one when miserable. Maybe he really didn't; it was very much like him either to love a moment utterly or to despise its every detail.

So of course he loved foods recalled from great times in his own life. He'd passed through Saratoga, New York, only a few days after the invention of Saratoga potatoes, now better known as potato chips. Doubtless he'd eaten turtle soup during his brief stint as a printer's assistant in Philadelphia. The menu included many of the foods from his uncle's farm. On, and on, and on, so that when I returned to the menu, I now saw a memoir, and a map. It was filled with memories, of all the things Sam Clemens had eaten in boyhood and during his wild travels from the New Orleans docks to the backstreets of San Francisco. No wonder that when Twain thought of food, he thought of the best of America, an America imagined as generous, full-hearted, and young.

———⊰⊷⊱———

James Fenimore Cooper on American food: "As a nation, their food is heavy, coarse, ill prepared and indigestible, while it is taken in the least [artful] forms that cookery will allow."

Twain on Cooper: "Cooper's eye was splendidly inaccurate."

———⊰⊷⊱———

Fresh. Local. Lovingly prepared. Intimately tied to the life of a place. These were Twain's standards, as they are for many food lovers today. I was amazed by the currency of the menu, at its relevance; Twain might have been writing a love letter to today's growers of native New Mexico peppers, makers of Creole cream cheese, and raisers of American Bronze turkeys: people dedicated to preserving the unique species and ingredients and recipes that have made American food special. He seemed to speak to all those who search for, and relish eating from, tables anchored on the land—and to share their longing.

Because the truth is that not even Twain's angel from a better land could assemble the entire feast today. To be sure, some are still with us. Whole books have been written about Southern-fried chicken, clam chowder, and many of Twain's pies; heritage gardeners raise Weeping Charley tomatoes, Long Scarlet radishes, and Cherokee White Eagle corn, varieties long since vanished from land given over to industrial-scale farming. Some of the specific preparations are still with us—American broiled chicken, Southern-style corn pone with chitlins, northern-style oysters roasted in the shell—though sometimes in renditions that would have Twain shouting, *Counterfeit!*

Many more are entirely gone. And with a pang I realized that many of those were the most purely local, rooted foods on Twain's menu, those that reminded him not only of his country but of a lake, a river, or a mountain. It was when Twain thought of wild things that he knew, precisely and without hesitation, both what he wanted and where it could best be had. *Sierra Nevada* brook trout. *San Francisco* mussels. Prairie hens *from Illinois*. These were the foods that defined American places in the days before cheap railroad transport blurred the culinary lines between New York City and Twain's boyhood home of Hannibal, Missouri. They spoke to Twain of special times, places, and people.

To me they spoke of prairies and marshes, of rivers and bays, of forests and mountains, of landscapes that once literally gave American life flavor. Now I read Twain's menu more carefully, and this time I was choosing—choosing foods rooted in the lands and waters he knew. I wanted to find out what had become of the prairie chickens near his uncle's farm, the mussels and oysters he feasted on in San Francisco, the trout he ate near Tahoe before accidentally setting the forest ablaze in a roaring conflagration. I wanted to know about the maple syrup and cranberries harvested near his Connecticut home—the former still a wild food, the latter only recently coaxed into cultivation. I'd find out what these foods meant to a single man during a life well and fully lived, a life that had taken him from the Mississippi's shoals and murky currents to Nevada's crazed shanties. I'd find out how each food once helped to make a place a place.

Once more I read through the menu. Croakers, from New Orleans. Philadelphia terrapin soup. Canvasback duck, from Baltimore.

I wanted to know what we still have. I wanted to know what we were losing, and what we might be getting back. I wanted to know what was gone.

One

IT MAKES ME CRY
TO THINK OF THEM

Prairie-Hens, from Illinois

MY WIFE, ELI, looks a bit wary when I bring up Twain. She's happy enough about some of my ideas, such as visiting Tahoe; when I start in with San Francisco mussels, at least it'll be close to home. But she fears that my first plan—to sit, at dawn, in a frozen Illinois cornfield and watch prairie chickens—could be the first step down the road toward serious Berkeley eccentricity. "I just don't want you to be 'that freaky Twain guy,'" she says. "There's enough of that here. One day you're reading about food, the next you're walking around campus shouting at the sun and random undergrads."

I laugh a little; she snorts a bit.

"I'm serious," she says. "You do know this is kind of weird, right?"

In fact, I do. And I'm grateful that Eli (rhymes with "Kelly") is just joking around, because right now I do want to go to Illinois and sit in a cold, bare field—in fact, I need to. So much of Twain's life was spent looking back at his own youth; exploring those memories inspired his best work. The weekend after his wedding at the age of thirty-four, he found himself in a kind of trance, seeing old faces, hearing old voices. "The fountains of the deep have broken up," he wrote to his longtime friend Will Bowen, who would later appear as Tom Sawyer's companion Joe Harper. For a day and more, Twain watched and listened. It was as though settling into married life had primed a fuse that a letter from Bowen then lit, returning him to a childhood he was thrilled to rediscover. And the earliest of his many memories, the first with real heft, color, and presence, were of the wonderful feasts on his Uncle John Quarles's prairie farm.

Every year the boy Sammy Clemens had spent several months on the farm, just four miles north of the hundred-person village of Florida, Missouri. Though Florida was a forest town, the farm abutted the prairie, "a level great prairie which was covered with wild strawberry plants, vividly starred with prairie pinks." The farm's five hundred acres were in a lucky country of grass, wood, and water, and all lent their bounty to the heavily laden table that Twain later remembered.

Ducks and geese, wild turkeys, venison, squirrel, rabbits, pheasants and partridge—when these wild things were served alongside garden-fresh corn, watermelons, cantaloupes, tomatoes, butter beans, and peas, and with the corn bread, fried chicken, and hot biscuits that Twain would later claim could never be properly cooked anywhere outside the South, the result was *rooted* food that would live forever in his memory. He'd remember its flavors, of course—but he'd remember, just as vividly, the way his uncle gathered and hunted and tended the foods, the way in which the meals sprang from a place he loved so dearly:

> I can call back the prairie, and its loneliness and peace, and a vast
> hawk hanging motionless in the sky, with his wings spread wide
> and the blue of the vault showing through the fringe of their end
> feathers. . . . I can see the blue clusters of wild grapes hanging

among the foliage of the saplings, and I remember the taste of them and the smell. I know how the wild blackberries looked, and how they tasted, and the same with the pawpaws, the hazelnuts, and the persimmons; and I can feel the thumping rain, upon my head, of hickory nuts and walnuts when we were out in the frosty dawn to scramble for them with the pigs. . . . I know the taste of maple sap, and when to gather it. . . . I know how a prize water-melon looks when it is sunning its fat rotundity among pumpkin vines and "simblins." . . . I know the look of green apples and peaches and pears on the trees, and I know how entertaining they are when they are inside of a person. I know how ripe ones look when they are piled in pyramids under the trees, and how pretty they are and how vivid the colors. . . . I know the look of an apple that is roasting and sizzling on a hearth on a winter's evening, and I know the comfort that comes of eating it hot, along with some sugar and a drench of cream.

I remember. I can remember. I know. I know. I know. Twain re-members; Twain chants. His memories bound together land and table, as surely as they joined Mark Twain with Sammy Clemens, the boy he once was.

Of all the incredible bounty of the Quarles table, roasted prairie chicken was perhaps the most rooted, the most fundamentally local. Where tallgrass prairie thrives, with its prairie pinks and "fragrant and fine" wild strawberries, prairie chickens thrive also; and when the grasses vanish, so do the birds. When Twain was a boy, there was still more than enough tallgrass to shelter the prairie chickens, and he re-membered well the mornings spent hunting them and other grassland creatures: "I remember . . . how we turned out, mornings, while it was still dark, to go on these expeditions, and how chilly and dismal it was, and how often I regretted that I was well enough to go." Once in the woods, the party "drifted silently after [the dogs] in the melancholy gloom. But presently the gray dawn stole over the world, the birds piped up, then the sun rose and poured light and comfort all around, everything was fresh and dewy and fragrant, and life was a boon again. After three hours of tramping we arrived back wholesomely tired, overladen with game, very hungry, and just in time for breakfast."

But when Twain wanted prairie hens in later years, he thought first of those from Illinois—Illinois, where there was little *but* prairie, where thousands of years of grass growing and burning and dying, then growing again, had left a bounty of soil among the deepest and blackest ever found, at any time, anywhere in the world. In 1861, when Twain left the Mississippi River for Nevada at the age of twenty-five, fleeing before either North or South could force him into service as a steamboat pilot, he knew that he was leaving behind the howl of the steam whistle, the splash of the paddlewheels, and the long journeys to New Orleans from Cairo, Illinois. He couldn't have known that there would never be more Illinois prairie chickens than there were at the moment he went west. The young pilot left behind a countryside that would soon be leached of some of its abundance; many would feel the loss, but few as powerfully as did the aging, elegiac, haunted Twain.

That, more or less, is what I tell Eli. She kisses me; she gets it. I kiss her back, and I'm off for Illinois.

PRAIRIE CHICKENS

Cut out all shot, wash thoroughly but quickly, using some soda in the water, rinse and dry, fill with dressing, sew up with cotton thread, and tie down the legs and wings; place in a steamer over hot water till done, remove to a dripping-pan, cover with butter, sprinkle with salt and pepper, dredge with flour, place in the

oven and baste with the melted butter until a nice brown; serve
with either apple-sauce, cranberries, or currant jelly.
—Mrs. Godard.

—ESTELLE WOODS WILCOX, *Buckeye Cookery and Practical
Housekeeping*, 1877

Newton, Illinois, has three thousand people and two power plants.
It has a motel with weekly rates for men who ignore the No Smoking
signs in their rooms, having driven from Carbondale and Vandalia and
Terre Haute to work in the plants for five days at a time. It has a bowling alley, the Parklane, that serves the only breakfast in town, eggs and
potatoes and biscuits and bacon. But the Parklane doesn't open until
5:00 A.M., which is still a half hour away when I drive off from the motel
and out into the country darkness.

On this April morning, it's twenty degrees in Newton. Outside
town a steady, freezing wind pulls across winter-naked soybean fields
and fields stubbled with ranks of cornstalks—stalks cut down to their
last spare inches, looking elastic after a winter under snow.

Scattered among the hundreds of thousands of farmed acres are
perhaps twelve hundred of broken-up prairie—a few acres here, twenty
there, a hundred more here, acquired piecemeal whenever money and
opportunity presented themselves. The plots of prairie are marked on
my map: small, irregular blocks covered in cross-hatching like braille.
But even to my untrained eye, even by the light of a two-thirds moon,
the grasses are obvious as I drive toward Prairie Ridge State Natural
Area. What seems a flat, featureless landscape will rise suddenly high
and ragged against the pale road, swelling beside my headlights like
surging water. It's vaguely discomfiting to see wild grasses carved into
such clean plots, as though a flock of flying starlings had formed into
perfectly even ranks.

Newton is a strange place to come in search of Twain's feast; as far as I know, Twain never heard of the place, let alone set foot in it. But there are only about three hundred prairie chickens left in all of Illinois, and all of them are here. So: the cornfields outside Newton.

Besides, I've already begun to understand that when it came to the foods of the feast, the simple fact is that Twain knew what he was talking about. What, for instance, is so special about canvasback ducks from Baltimore or, by extension, from Maryland? Why is it so certain that the birds living near that particular place were what Twain loved, rather than a single Baltimore restaurant's recipe? Here's why: the vast waters feeding into the Chesapeake Bay are replete with wild celery, an aquatic grass (unrelated to table celery) that canvasback ducks gorge on. Such is the greed of the ducks for the grass that they're named after it (wild celery is *Vallisneria americana;* canvasbacks are *Aythya valisineria*). When able to feed with abandon, as they are in the waters near Baltimore, the result is birds so fat that a contemporary of Twain described them as filled with their own gravy.

I learned my lesson with the buckwheat cakes: I will not doubt Twain.

That's why I'm soon trudging behind a Prairie Ridge guide named Bob across an icy field, flashlight in hand, toward a distant plywood blind. The freeze is recent, so in spite of the cold only a half inch of ice covers the wide, wintry puddles. This, I realize, explains why the one thing the taciturn Bob has said to me is, "Got rubber boots?" and why, when I said I didn't, Bob was much amused. To avoid breaking through and soaking my feet, I have to stay on top of the clumps of frozen grass, jumping clumsily as though I'm crossing mossy stepping-stones.

The wind blows over the bare fields and straight through the five-inch-high viewing slot that runs the length of the blind's front wall. I shiver on a long bench with a few dedicated birders, my arms tightly crossed, eyes squinted against the cold. The bench is long enough to hold six people, and it's cold enough that I wish we did have that last body squeezed in here. The mating ground—or "booming ground," or "lek"—is immediately in front of the blind, perhaps forty yards wide, a bit less than that deep. It was disked last fall, and the grass on it is as short as though mowed. But that's all I can make out; except for the moon, the only light comes from a pair of radio towers blinking steadily across the fields.

Twenty degrees is *cold*. When I called to reserve the blind, Bob told me that I wouldn't be allowed to leave it until the birds were done booming, which might be several hours. He insisted, Bob did, that I not drink coffee. At home I drink a lot of coffee. At home, right now, it is three in the morning. I've come a long way to hear the birds that even now, I remind myself, are stirring, figuratively clearing their throats, picking silently toward the dark lek. But the truth is that at this moment I would happily garrote a prairie chicken for an espresso. The wind through the viewing slot is picking up, icing my ears and nose. I have obeyed orders, I have drunk nothing, and yet I greatly desire to pee. I begin to suspect that coming to Illinois was actually sort of dumb— even dumber, maybe, than some of my friends thought, which was pretty dumb.

Then from behind the plywood blind comes a mournful, hollow cry, as though someone were blowing across the lip of a jug. At once it's answered from across the lek—it's a pair of male prairie chickens beginning to boom.

The booming ground is thirty or forty yards wide; the movement of the birds on the far side is just visible in the gray of the coming dawn. It's like trying to make out crabs scrabbling under murky water. I guess that there are about four cocks there, though it's difficult to tell; their calls blend into one long, low, lonely note. They boom steadily, each holding a sustained tone that sometimes rises a step for a moment or two. The intermittent rises give the whole a slowly throbbing quality, like the sound of UFOs descending in 1950s science-fiction movies.

The booms don't merely echo across the emptiness, they infuse it; what was bare and dismal is now pulsing, beating, full.

But still lonely. Later I'll try and fail to approximate the sound on a cello, guided by an 1893 *Science* article that suggested beginning with a low G. But strings have too much presence, too much vibrancy; when stringed instruments sound lonely, it's because of what they're playing. The prairie chickens can't sound any other way. "Some morning in the month of April," author T. A. Bereman exhorted in *Science* magazine, "when the sun rises clear and the air is crisp and frosty, go out upon the suburbs of a prairie town, away from the usual noises of the village, and listen."

Even the streaking shadow of a great horned owl can't stop the cocks for long; they press themselves flat on the lek or flee into taller grass, but rise or return almost as soon as the predator is past. Now at least six of the large, black-and-white grouse scratch and stamp and turn. Raised pinnae feathers jut from their brows like horns. Spotted tail feathers fan and flare as they stamp their feet in rapid staccato, their stout, black-striped bodies level with the ground. Though their bodies are rounded and soft-looking, their tail feathers are stiff and straight. Every wing is locked tightly back.

People who have handled prairie chickens describe them as among the wildest of animals—wilder than badgers, than bald or golden eagles. Some of that explosive force is on display here. Though one cock stands entirely still except for an orange timpani sac ballooning at his throat, most rush fiercely at their counterparts, stamping as they square off. Sometimes they burst into the air, nearly chest to chest. One flips backward, landing awkwardly on the dust and short grass.

The booming rises, rises. Now, in their excitement, the cocks entirely ignore the northern harriers and short-eared owls hunting in the tall grass beyond the lek. At last the booms are answered by the high, sharp caw of an approaching hen. As one of the ornithology students whispers, it doesn't sound like an American thing; it makes me think of a jungle more than a patch of low grass beside an Illinois cornfield.

It also makes me really hungry. A confession: watching almost any animal for long enough makes me wonder how it tastes. Eli is like this, too. We'll wander the Monterey Bay Aquarium, watching awestruck as sleek tuna, graceful sea turtles, and sevengill sharks cruise through shimmering blue water and forests of kelp. Then we'll go for sushi. This is a large part of what drew me to Twain's feast in the first place; it's when we use all our senses that we're most powerfully alive, most engaged with the world that feeds and sustains us. Primed by Twain's description of early-morning hunts, I naturally start thinking about making a meal of these rare, beautiful birds.

Of course that isn't about to happen; I'll almost certainly never taste prairie chicken. To do so I'd have to move to Minnesota, one of the few places with a healthy population, and enter a lottery to win one of the something like two hundred licenses that would allow me to shoot a brace of birds. Still, a number of historical descriptions let me imagine how it would have been to sit down to a plate of prairie chicken on John Quarles's farm.

First off, the meat is dark. Just about everyone, from William Clark of Lewis and Clark fame to the author of a guide to America's urban markets, calls it dark; the one chef who doesn't, Charles Ranhofer of New York's legendary Victorian restaurant Delmonico's, calls it "black." Prairie chicken is a species of large grouse, and so other grouse, like sage hens, probably offer the most analogous flavor (though Clark clearly preferred prairie chicken, finding sage hen by comparison "only tolerable in point of flavor," probably due to the latter's winter diet of pungent sagebrush). Ranhofer's recipes use grouse and prairie chicken interchangeably and describe partridge as relatively light.

How best to cook this dark, rich meat? The short answer is "add fat."* Naturalist Frances Hamerstrom, who studied the birds in Wisconsin for decades, always resented having to stuff their skins for use as specimens rather than using them to enrich the meat while roasting.

---

*Not bad general cooking advice, when you think about it. Drizzle roasted vegetables with olive oil; sauté almost anything in butter; fry pastries. Figure out what kind of fat to add, and how much, and how to do it: this will bring you joy.

Ranhofer dipped his in butter or oil before broiling, or he served the roasted birds with gravy, fried bread crumbs, and applesauce, or he prepared them "a la Tzarina," which meant including a forcemeat of game and cream. On occasion he indulged in baroque, Gilded Age productions involving molding prairie-chicken breasts with jelly before garnishing with truffles, cock's combs, mushrooms, and poached chicken kidneys.

Twain, I like to think, would have wanted his simply roasted in a hot oven, quickly enough that the meat wouldn't go dry. True, in later years the dinners served at his Hartford home owed a great deal to the rich, elevated food served at Delmonico's—considered the finest restaurant in America from the time of its founding in 1827 through the end of the nineteenth century—and other dining palaces. It is, regretfully, necessary to report that one 1887 dinner at Twain's house involved creamed asparagus, creamed sweetbreads, and creamed shad sauce over shad-roe balls, and that the tomatoes were molded into jelly, with mayonnaise on the side (afterward came ice cream sculpted into flowers). But Twain was a man of many contradictions, and the fact is that when he thought of his favorite things, he thought first of ingredients instead of preparations, tastes instead of recipes. His most impassioned food writing is about basic things, roasted meats and fried chicken and freshly picked vegetables. The prairie chickens he remembered and wanted again, I believe, were those he'd helped to hunt and ate simply roasted.

With the rising sun, the booming ground in front of me has come fully alive. The cocks pace and charge and fly; the two hens stroll, seeming to ignore the mock combats. One cock hangs at the lek's eastern edge, strutting as enthusiastically as any but never approaching the other birds. Eventually the larger group works its way toward him. The lone cock waits for his chance; suddenly he strides forward, swiftly cuts a hen away from the others, and hurriedly escorts her into a patch of tall grass. Everyone in my blind wants to adopt him. When he returns to the lek, we give soft group cheers. Vivid yellow meadowlarks sing a few feet in front of the blind; owls and northern harriers stalk the tall grass behind the lek. But behind all that, behind the grasses, the corn ground is quiet and gray. The lek is a jungle island in an acid sea.

It's literally awesome to think of the scale of the old prairies. Lewis and Clark started crossing them in May, at the very beginning of their transcontinental journey; they came to the far edge of the grasslands in June *of the following year*. Imagine the labor it took to cross that vast distance and it's easy to understand why the first European explorers—men who knew what crossing the Atlantic meant— used words like "ocean" and "sea" when they spoke of the grass.

It's humbling to imagine those thousands of miles, and what filled them. Nowadays people think of prairies as empty and monotonous. But what they're really thinking of is the cornfields that replaced the tallgrass. Corn ground is acre upon acre upon acre of row after row after row, all planted in one variety, of one thing, all at the same time. Corn ground is more a growing medium than it is soil, having been drenched in enough pesticide and herbicide to kill all the microbes that let the soil live. In *The Omnivore's Dilemma,* Michael Pollan calls such land "food deserts"—producers of a volume of calories that must be processed by industry or used to feed livestock prior to human consumption. Anything growing on corn ground—except for corn—is a mistake.

Prairie is this: Twelve-foot-high big bluestem. Blazing stars. Sky blue aster. Purple coneflower, also called echinacea. Poppy mallow and downy gentian. It's 230 species crowded onto a tiny, remnant "postage stamp" prairie. A prairie is marshes, filled with crayfish and ornate box turtles. It's a silent sky, exploding with a flight of grouse. It's dust tossed in billows by wallowing bison. It's prairie fire sending smoke to redden, then blacken, the summer sun; it's snow in drifts that can bind and kill entire herds of elk. Though the early explorers described what they saw as an ocean, their word "prairie" came from the French or Belgian name for a park or a grassy orchard. *That's* a prairie—a place that invokes both ocean and garden, both the wildest place and the tamest. And that's what Twain remembered—a lonely place, but also one replete and bounteous, a place whose sounds and smells and tastes remained with him all through his life.

Today prairie is also, very often—too often—much like what's in front of me at the moment: a display, nearly a zoo. This tiny patch of grassland, acquired and maintained for the express purpose of preserving the prairie chickens, needs constant human care and attention. Without periodic burns and occasional grazing by hired local cattle to replicate prairie fires and bison, short invasive grasses could, and would, overwhelm Prairie Ridge. Keeping this place "natural" is damned hard work.

Still, for an observer like me, there is one great difference between the booming ground and a true zoo, and that is the sky. Even through the thin viewing slot, the sky is a palpable presence, stretching vast and blue over this postage stamp of teeming, wakeful grassland. When grass ruled, reaching this open land was a true shock, a moment of almost terrifying emergence after hundreds of miles of dark eastern forests. Twain himself remembered the suddenness of the change: "Beyond the road," he wrote, "where the snakes sunned themselves was a dense young thicket, and through it a dim-lighted path . . . ; then out of the dimness one emerged abruptly upon a level great prairie."

He recalled the prairie's loneliness; he recalled its peace. And doubtless it was peaceful, especially to a boy of seven or eight, who could view it at his leisure before retreating to a forest-hemmed farmhouse. But, ironically, the quiet of the prairie was an early sign of sickness, the cough before the fever.

A healthy prairie is a living, breathing, and extraordinarily dangerous place—a place of malarial wetlands and brutal storms. Most of all it's a place of fire. Tallgrass like big bluestem *needs* fire; fire is how a prairie breathes. Without periodic burns, the eight-foot-tall stems begin to choke on themselves, creating a wall of grass that a horse can vanish behind, far too thick for prairie chickens to nest on. Burning fertilizes the earth and allows light and water to reach the soil, all without damaging the roots that remain safe in the dark, cool earth.

Looking at the old tallgrass land today, it can be difficult to imagine the force and peril of a prairie fire. Prairie fire could move as fast as the wind, make its own weather, kill anything on the surface that couldn't burrow or fly. In 1836 an eight-mile-wide blaze tore through more than sixty miles of grass in six hours before the Rock River halted it. This kind of terrifying burn was once an annual event.

No longer, of course. Beyond the grassy lek, the ground is bare; corn is harvested before the stalks are as explosively dry as grass. But Native Americans understood the relationship between fire and prairie; the Illinois nation used the same word, *sce-tay,* to refer to both. In fact, Native Americans were probably the single biggest source of prairie fires (the second was lightning). Fire softened and prepared bottomland for planting, promoted green growth to attract bison, or simply burned away dry growth, making the land around a village or a camp safe. Precontact Native Americans of the plains were gardeners of grass.

Burning helped to sculpt the prairies and the great societies that lived on them. In A.D. 1200, thirty thousand people lived at Cahokia, the mound city in the prairies a hundred miles west of Newton. Thirty thousand people—that's more than there were in London at the time, just fifteen years before the Magna Carta. Thirty thousand people hearing the prairie chickens boom at dawn in the surrounding cornfields, feasting on the meat of hunted birds, then adorning themselves with bones and barred feathers and quills. Later the Blackfoot and Shoshone and Sioux and Cheyenne all danced prairie-chicken dances in praise of approaching spring, celebrating as the booming echoed over black, newly burned grasslands. In 1805 William Clark wrote of "a Cloudy morning & Smokey all Day from the burning of the plains, which was Set on fire by the Minetarries for an early crop of Grass." It was a common experience for newcomers. The birds were always deeply American, dependent on a land the first nations helped make with fire.

That the young Sammy Clemens never directly confronted a prairie fire, a wall of flame advancing as fast as a horse, was all to the good as far as his safety and that of his uncle's farm were concerned. But by damping down the burns, the settlers were ending an ancient pattern of destruction and renewal, a pattern that animals like the prairie chickens depended upon to create the blend of grasses they used for nesting and the open ground they needed to mate.

Mating, after all, is why the chickens boom and call, and I've been hoping to see a pair coupling.* But they never do, at least out in the open. Each hen typically spends five days on the grounds, moving through stages of indifference, awareness, flirtatiousness, seduction, and reception. Though the season as a whole is winding down, I'm probably seeing these particular birds on one of their first days; they still feign disinterest, like seventh-graders at their first dance.

One by one the remaining hens fly off. When the last is gone, the booming soon fades. The cocks sink onto the grass. Lying on the lek, pinnae and tails lowered, orange throat sacs deflated and invisible, they seem like entirely different birds—diminished, depleted, and humble.

The last hen is gone; we're free to leave without fear of disturbing them. When I shuffle out and swing the plywood door closed, the sky seems vast and bright and open. Though the puddles have frozen thicker since dawn, as I make my way along the path toward the Prairie Ridge offices I stay on clumps of icy bunchgrasses to avoid the deepest.

As I crunch from clump to clump, the booming still fills my head. I've seen something strange, a flamboyant performance that couldn't be seen anywhere in the state save for our quiet, frozen blind. And it brings me low to think how sad that is. I reach the Parklane Bowling Alley very hungry, and just in time for the last of breakfast.

---

*I do have a life, I swear to God.

PRAIRIE CHICKENS STEWED WHOLE

Skin the birds, cut off the head and feet, draw them without breaking the intestines, and truss them so that they will be short and plump. Put them into a large saucepan with sufficient butter to prevent burning, and brown them; when the birds are brown, add for each one a tablespoonful of dry flour, and stir them about until the flour is brown. Then put in a gill of tomato-catsup for each bird, enough boiling water to cover them, and a palatable seasoning of salt and pepper, and cook them slowly for two hours, or until they are tender. Serve the birds with their sauce and plain boiled potatoes.

—JULIET CORSON, *Practical American Cookery and Household Management*, 1886

Late in boyhood, years after leaving his uncle's farm for the last time, Twain finally, reluctantly, abandoned his dreams of piracy and joining the circus. One "permanent ambition," however, he clung to—that of piloting a steamboat on the Mississippi River. In the five years that he lived his greatest and longest-lasting childhood dream, surely Twain often heard the booming of prairie chickens in grasslands along the shore, thrumming in the silence after the howl of the steam and the splashing of the great paddlewheels were stilled. It must have sounded like the moaning of the earth.

Because, amazingly, there were more prairie chickens in Illinois during Twain's piloting tenure than at any time before or since. The booms I heard at Prairie Ridge were made by twelve cocks, give or take. As Twain piloted his way up and down the Mississippi River, some *14 million* of the birds lived amid the Illinois tallgrass. No wonder that in

Moby-Dick, Melville used them as a symbol of ingrained permanence, writing that the Nantucketer "lives on the sea, as prairie cocks in the prairie."

Still, the ideal habitat for prairie chickens is a blend of native tall-grass and cultivated ground, a combination that provides the birds with shelter and an easy supply of corn for food. Years later, heading west to the Nevada Territory and California, Twain would describe the transition from grass to agriculture: "the land was rolling . . . like the stately heave and swell of the ocean's bosom after a storm. And everywhere were cornfields, accenting with squares of deeper green, this expanse of grassy land."

For a few decades after the arrival of white farmers, it had seemed that corn farming would never take hold on the vast upper prairies; the defiant, incredibly dense tallgrass roots stopped traditional iron plows as suddenly as though they'd struck bedrock. Cahokians and other Native American farmers had always clustered in the bottomlands along the Missouri and Knife rivers, where gardeners like the famous Buffalo Bird Woman (subject of a 1917 book and herself a member of the Hidatsa tribe's Prairie Chicken clan) used sticks to break out small clumps of sod they then beat free of topsoil. A month of this brutal labor might ready a small garden plot, enough for a single family—and this was ground that Buffalo Bird Woman called "soft and easy to work."

White farmers were slow to realize that the world's best soil lay under an armor of sod. Some even assumed that land where no trees would grow must be worthless; James Monroe once wrote to Thomas Jefferson that "a great part [of northern Illinois] is miserably poor. . . . that upon the Illinois [River] consists of plains which have not had . . . and will not have a single bush on them for ages." Even when farmers began to understand the quality of the black soils, the knotted tallgrass roots defied anything less than fourteen oxen pulling a hundred-pound plow. Sod would cling to the plowshare like glue, forcing a halt every few feet to scrape the iron clean with a wooden paddle. The work was known as "breaking" the prairie; even with the massive oxen teams, attacking the roots must have felt like swinging a sledgehammer at a mile-thick wall.

Then, in 1837, just two years after Twain's birth, John Deere invented the self-scouring steel plow. Nobody knew it at the time, but the day the first steel plow left Deere's workshop marked the end of the wild American tallgrass. The time of the prairie farmer had come. Now a homesteader with a single pair of horses could break grassland by himself, quickly tearing through the dense sod to reach the unbelievably fertile soils below. And so, for the next fifty years, row by row and field by field, farmers broke the Illinois prairies for corn ground, creating a patchwork of food and shelter. For those fifty years, Illinois was prairie-chicken heaven; their numbers doubled, tripled, quadrupled.

Those fifty years happened to correspond almost exactly with the first great expansion of America's railways. Chicago's first train appeared in 1848; by 1860, just before Twain went west, the city was serviced by more than a hundred daily trains from eleven different railroads. The nation's total miles of track more than tripled, from nine thousand miles in 1850 to thirty thousand miles by the decade's end. The simultaneous growth in railroads and the prairie-chicken population meant that the birds would be one of the first fresh, inherently local foods to be eaten thousands of miles from where they were hunted.

Now, eating local, seasonal foods often makes both culinary and environmental sense. When you eat something grown in season, close to your home, you get something fresh that also took far less gasoline to transport than something grown a continent or an ocean away. Still, my local supermarket has shrimp from Thailand, apples from Chile, lamb from New Zealand, and this is deeply strange; from a historical perspective, it's just completely bizarre that eating locally takes any effort at all.

Of course, transporting food long distances has been going on for millennia. But the Egyptian wheat that fed Rome, the spices of medieval Europe, and the cod that sustained the Iberian empires were all important precisely because they were easily preserved. Eating dried or salted foods is very different from eating a banana picked five thousand miles away. When you eat fresh meats or fruits or vegetables raised or grown more than a few miles from your home, you're doing something that makes you different from nearly all other people who have ever lived; today we have to struggle to *avoid* doing it. Through most of history, when it came to fresh food, eating locally and seasonally was just what humans did.

By the mid–nineteenth century, technologies that could carry game and produce to distant markets ever more quickly, ever more reliably, were transforming America's tables—and its landscapes. As author Ann Vileisis points out, America's foodsheds—the areas that produce a given community's food, just as a watershed provides its water—were rapidly expanding and overlapping. The foodsheds of major eastern cities saw particularly dramatic change. The Erie Canal had already opened the Midwest; soon steamboats would carry Southern vegetables from converted cotton plantations. After the Civil War, the spreading spiderweb of railroads carried game like prairie chickens fresh to markets hundreds, or even thousands, of miles from the grasslands the birds needed to live. In Twain's boyhood the foodshed of the Quarles farm had included the surrounding prairie, forests, and fields. Now, as transportation technology radically expanded, New York City's foodshed included the same places; it included, in effect, the Quarles farm.

We take this kind of thing for granted. But in Twain's day it was a huge novelty, and novelty sells. So, for a few decades, Illinois was heaven not only for prairie chickens but also for prairie-chicken hunters. Thomas De Voe, author of a magisterial 1867 guide to New York, Boston, and Philadelphia foodstuffs called *The Market Assistant,* recalled that in 1821 a pair of aged prairie chickens had sold in New York for the spectacular price of five dollars (they might have been prized as a substitute for the quickly vanishing Long Island grouse). By the time Twain wrote the menu for his feast, prairie chickens were hunted by the literal trainload. Chicago markets measured them by the cord and ton, to the tune of some six hundred thousand birds every year. As early as 1861 in New

York, the five dollars per pair had fallen to fifty cents; by 1867 enough birds regularly appeared between October and April to glut the city's market. Some people even credited the first development of insulated shipping barrels and techniques of carrying frozen food to the hunger for prairie chicken. What's more, a private "chicken hunting culture" was developing, with railroads offering special rates to parties of hunters; specially equipped wagons were sold complete with gun racks, dog kennels, and iceboxes.

One Illinois newspaper, recognizing that the birds had become emblems, named itself the *Prairie-Chicken.* The paper, declared the editors, would be "rich, spicy, popular, cheap and wholesome." But not long after, *Science* magazine noted that most people could hope to encounter a prairie chicken only once it had been killed and shipped to market. The prairie chicken was beginning to vanish; soon it would again be a local dish, until it disappeared entirely from restaurant and even home tables.

However strongly he associated prairie chickens with their native grasslands, Twain wasn't immune to the charm of eating them hundreds of miles away. In 1879 he wrote a letter noting that a friend of his was "in the habit of sending . . . a Christmas present of prairie chickens" to his home in Hartford. That year, he concluded happily, "those chickens were fine & came just in time for Christmas dinner."

PRAIRIE CHICKENS

Clean and wash thoroughly in water in which you have put a little soda. Rinse in clear water several times, and if time allows, let them lay in water half an hour or more. Then wipe dry and fill with a good dressing. Tie down the wings and legs with a

cord and stew, closely covered, with plenty of butter, or steam
over hot water in a steamer until tender and then place them in a
pan with a little butter, and brown. Serve with a tart jelly and
garnish with parsley.

—*"Aunt Babette's" Cook Book* (one of America's first Jewish
   cookbooks), 1889

Springfield, Illinois, is the home of Abraham Lincoln and the
"horseshoe." A horseshoe is two thick, side-by-side pieces of sourdough
toast, heaped with ground beef, mounded with fries, and finally
drowned under cheese sauce. When I sample one at D'Arcy's Pint, I'm
ravenous—I haven't eaten since the night before, and I've spent the
morning walking all over Goose Lake Prairie, the state's largest surviving grassland—and I scarf that sucker down.

It doesn't taste much like any of its constituent foods: beef, potatoes, cheese. But it hits all the basic pleasure centers, the desires for salt
and meat and fat and gooeyness and crunch. Humans evolved on grasslands; our gigantic brains, as well as our bipedalism, may have developed to aid us in foraging and hunting for food over large distances in
a region given to paralyzing seasonal droughts. Somewhere deep in my
own brain, there still resides the notion that I might soon need to head
out there across the fields with a sharpened stick and hunt me down
some elk, or wrestle a baboon for groundnuts. These activities, it stands
to reason, will demand a store of protein and fat: they will require a
horseshoe.

But even as my ape mind drives me to gulp down the horseshoe, a
different part of my brain recognizes that it's garbage. This is the part
that, when it hears that horseshoes have never spread far beyond Springfield, asks, *And what does that tell you?* For in truth the bread and fries
and ground beef and cheese necessary to a horseshoe are not difficult

to procure elsewhere in this land of ours. Maybe the fact that the horseshoe technically qualifies as "local" to Springfield testifies only to the great good sense of people not living in Springfield.

That's the part of my brain that understands that the grasslands, cradle and driver of human evolution, are gone from this part of the world mostly because of the kind of foul concoction that I am, at this moment, eating as though it's my job. When an animal was once hunted by the millions, it's natural to assume that that is why it isn't exactly blotting out the sun anymore. But in the case of the prairie chickens, the real culprit was habitat loss. Once that wonderful checkerboard of corn and grass gave way to corn and soybeans, and nothing but corn and soybeans, there was no place for the birds to seek shelter for their nests.

And in 1947, just over a century after the invention of the plow that broke the prairies, another innovation appeared that would further transform the land, making it even more uniform—at once more productive and more sterile. That was the year that farmers began applying ammonium nitrate from World War II–era munitions plants to their cornfields. Now corn could be grown even on the poorer "gray" prairies of southern Illinois, where cultivated redtop grass (grown for use making dye) had sheltered a good-size remnant of prairie chickens. Once the redtop was gone, only birds on refuges like Prairie Ridge could survive.

Even more important, the new fertilizer destroyed the ancient rhythms of corn agriculture; the idea of land going "corn sick" and being left fallow for a few seasons to recover became a historical curiosity, as did the use of most winter cover crops. Growing corn on ammonium nitrate meant that the land could be left bare for half the year. And across much of the tallgrass country, where roots once literally locked soil into place, bare land was suddenly defenseless before rain, and wind, and melting snow.

Now, erosion is nothing new on the Mississippi; erosion, in fact, is one of the things that Twain loved about it. In *The Adventures of*

Huckleberry Finn, Huck eavesdrops on a party of river men arguing "about differences betwixt clear-water rivers and muddy-water ones. The man they called Ed said the muddy Mississippi water was wholesomer to drink than the clear water of the Ohio; he said if you let a pint of this yaller Mississippi water settle, you would have about a half to three-quarters of an inch of mud in the bottom. . . . The Child of Calamity said that was so; he said there was nutritiousness in the mud, and a man that drunk Mississippi water could grow corn in his stomach if he wanted to." And in *Life on the Mississippi,* Twain claimed to have seen a steamboat so thickly coated with windblown dirt that "her hurricane deck would be worth a hundred and fifty dollars an acre" in New England. "The soil on her forecastle," he wrote, "was quite good—the new crop of wheat was already springing from the cracks in protected places. The companionway was of a dry sandy character, and would have been well suited for grapes. . . . The soil on the boiler-deck was thin and rocky, but good enough for grazing purposes."

But the affection of Twain and his characters notwithstanding, the best soil is soil that stays where it is. And destroying the old root systems meant that more soil went sliding down the muddier Mississippi than ever before. Today Iowa can lose as much as six bushels of earth for every bushel of corn produced; an equivalent amount of prairie would lose only one-eighth as much, while simultaneously adding a great deal more to the loam from its own constantly dying and regrowing root system. Since the beginning of corn's reign, Iowa's fabulously rich black topsoil has shrunk to about two feet deep—still thick by worldwide standards but about half of what it probably was when prairie grass held the loam in place. In the Great Plains, tiny "postage stamp" prairies sometimes tower as much as three feet above contiguous plowed land, pedestal monuments to the scars left by the plow.

Twain wanted corn bread, and "green corn, on the ear," and corn "cut from the ear and served with butter and pepper." He also wanted the prairie chickens that those foods displaced. When I think about this, I start to feel that Twain's feast is at war with itself. But that's actually wrong; the sad truth is that modern, industrial corn has almost nothing in common with the sweet corn Twain loved. In fact, the vast majority of corn grown in this country is completely inedible to humans. When it does appear in our food chain, it's indirectly, after being fed to cows or pigs or processed into soda or Twinkies or a thousand other things that look and taste nothing like corn.

So corn and prairie chickens don't have to be completely mutually exclusive, as the long decades of prairie chickens thriving alongside cornfields showed. But having a truly diversified landscape requires a deep shifting of priorities—beginning with the decision to grow . . . you know, *food,* instead of something that can be ground and bleached and manipulated into something that looks like it might be food, if you hold it just so in exactly the right light.

When it comes to the prairies, the effect of America's subsidizing of industrial corn has been nuclear, reducing thousands of species to one, or at best a handful. Strikingly, even our modern monocultures still shadow the old ecosystems, the ancient patterns of grass. A single tall grass, corn, has replaced the thick tallgrass prairies of Illinois and Iowa; the mixed prairies of Nebraska and Kansas now hold winter wheat; the western, shortgrass Great Plains, where millions of bison once grazed, have been made over as cattle ground. But these shadows are only that. To an extent that was once literally unimaginable, we've extricated ourselves from nature's seasonal constraints (at least temporarily, at least as long as the oil flows). It's an impressive achievement in its own terms, but it also means the sharp amputation of nature's rhythms, subtleties, and joys.

When, after many years away, Twain returned to Illinois on an 1874 promotional tour, he promptly ordered a roasted prairie chicken from room service in a small-town hotel. The African-American boy who served him was amazed that he meant to eat the whole bird himself, which led to an evening-long chat. Twain later immortalized their talk in the essay "Sociable Jimmy," an essay that, Twain scholar Shelley Fisher Fishkin argues, contains the first seeds of Huckleberry Finn's voice. Surely it's only a coincidence that it was prairie chicken that set off the conversation. But, at the same time, it's appropriate that a meal bound so inextricably to the land and to Twain's memories helped to spark his greatest work of American life and speech.

After leaving Springfield, I drive through mile after mile of corn-fields, across the Mississippi and into Missouri, across a contrastingly grassy country all the way out to the site of John Quarles's old spread near the town of Florida—the place that fixed itself so deeply into Twain's heart. Today it's easy to miss. In fact, I miss it twice, zooming past its nondescript, lopsided trailer and a matching pair of tool sheds. Then, beside a barbed-wire-rimmed culvert—maybe even Twain's "divine place for wading" with swimming pools "which were forbidden to us and therefore much frequented by us"—I see a tilting mailbox of rusty steel, marked with the kind of block-lettered sticky squares that kids use to put their names on bedroom doors:

MARK TWAIN'S
'THE FARM'
23651 HWY 107

TO CHOOSE A YOUNG PRAIRIE CHICKEN

Bend the under bill. If it is tender, the chicken is young.

—MARY NEWTON FOOTE HENDERSON, *Practical Cooking and Dinner Giving*, 1877

On the day after Easter, I'm on Frank Oberle's land in Missouri's Adair County, a hundred miles north of Florida, waiting for Frank to burn a prairie.

Frank can concentrate *hard*. His thick, strong frame hunches over a small bunch of grass; he seems to use it to gauge all the hundreds of acres in the wide prairie bowl before us. Over a salt-and-pepper mustache, Frank's eyes are intent as a scope. The intensity may come from his decades as a photojournalist, during which he took some of the best shots of bald eagles you'll ever see. Or it may simply be that the day's work requires this level of concentration—without it, a shift in the high wind could send his planned fire ripping the wrong way, throwing flames across the two-lane road, with nothing to stop it until the river some eight miles away. The only hope then would be setting a hurried, even frantic, burn along the road, hoping to make a blackened firebreak before the main blaze came on with all the force of the wind behind it.

Whatever its source, Frank's focus makes me feel scattered and flighty, though Frank himself couldn't be friendlier or more welcoming— at least in between tasks that require his full, almost unnerving, attention. "I've promised myself that when I burn, I'll never, ever hurry," he says without looking up.

Until Frank and his wife, Judy, bought these eight hundred acres of northern Missouri pasture, the land had been owned by the same family since the prairie on it was first broken in 1854. Now it's home to their Pure Air Native Seed Company, which sells native grass and brome seeds to jump-start prairie restorations of all sizes. If prairie chickens are ever going to return in numbers to Illinois, it will be because of the work of Frank and others like him; it will be because people care enough to raise the seed that once grew wild from skyline to skyline.

Frank fell in love with this land while driving through on his way to photo shoots in Minnesota and the Dakotas. After decades spending as many as eight months of every year on assignment, he realized that his work was becoming more of a job than a passion, and he and Judy began looking for a farm with potential. "It's kind of a gem in the rough," he told me. "This morning there was a dozen turkeys along the road, deer over in the meadow there, geese down there setting on eggs. We had pelicans here, I think twenty-four last week." He still takes huge numbers of photos, but now only on their own land. "I could do a book just on this farm, the flowers and butterflies and bees and groundhogs, badgers and deer and bobcats and coyotes. If you had a four-hundred-page book, you could fill each page with something totally different."

Where once there was nothing but relatively uniform dairy pasture, now the bottoms wait for row crops of blue wild indigo, coreopsis, Indian paintbrush, foxglove beardtongue, and dozens of other prairie flowers. The surrounding hills are covered with grasses, all high and wild and dry at this time of year. "Up there we take whatever she gives us," Frank says of the grasslands. But his seeming nonchalance disguises the brutally hard work needed to replicate the dramatic processes of the natural prairies: "Growing for seeds is a young man's sport. Hard work, weeding and harvesting and clearing." Someday he'd love to have it as an outreach and education spot, maybe set up some cabins—have people come out "for a week, or until they *get* weak."

Until then he's lucky in his workers. One of the first things that Frank told me was not to photograph the faces of the three lanky teenagers in plain blue work clothes, who moved quietly and without eye contact as they readied the farm vehicles for the coming burn. Naturally, I agreed to keep my camera pointed away, learning only later that the three come from an Old Order Amish community and would consider photos to be forbidden graven images.

They're hard, hard workers; by the time Frank picks them up at 8:00 A.M. for a full day's work, they'll already have put in two hours in their own dairy barns. But it's difficult for me to figure out what, exactly, they're allowed to do. They can't drive cars (Frank has to drive them forty miles twice a day), which seems straightforward enough—no machinery allowed, except for the horse-powered implements they use on their own land. Then I find that they can operate his tractor, so apparently *owning* the machine is what matters. But no, they can't drive the quick, tough little camo Kawasaki Prairie four-wheeler. Evidently, the fact that it has handlebars instead of a steering wheel puts it off-limits. This one I never figure out.

Two of the Amish silently push the Kawasaki from the barn, while the third fires up the tractor so Frank can check the rear sprayers. The worst thing that could happen today would be not to have enough water in the right place at the right time. At last it's done, and Frank invites me into the house for coffee while the others fuel up the machinery.

Frank's connections to this mixed and rolling country run deep. His mother's side of the family arrived from France in the 1700s and prospered for well over a century as fur traders. "In fact, I grew up in a French-speaking household. I'm the last generation to have heard that, listening to my grandmother and my grandpa's sister speaking French the whole time they were baking bread on Tuesdays, there along the river." As the fur bearers grew scarcer, the family turned to truck farming. "But I had that sense of wonderment from my grandmother. She'd say, 'We only use this land. When the river needs it, we move.' In my family it's almost a disgrace to talk about getting government money when the floods come. You know when you're planting in that ground that the river owns it. So our mentality is that we only use it." Frank talks about a century ago and this morning in the same present tense, using "we" to speak of things he likely only ever heard about. "We use the land when she lets us. When she needs it, we go up to the hills. We come back when it's dry." The river would flood from March until May; if his family planted in June, sometimes there was still time to get a crop out.

It's a powerful combination, this willingness to work so hard to bring something from the land while still accepting the earth's primacy. It's of a piece with his and Judy's work here, which requires both constant labor and an acceptance that the prairie will offer what it wants to.

"Prairie is the rarest ecosystem in North America," Frank says, increasingly animated. "'Cause where it's good, it's being eyed for four-dollar corn. Seven-dollar beans. That'll jeopardize a lot. But for now Missouri has more flat, native prairie than anywhere else in North America. It's mostly still here for cultural and traditional reasons, kind of an ingrained thing with some English mentality, or Scottish, or Irish. You plow some up, but you *never* plow it all. That'll save you in dry years, because you'll get a hay crop off those fifteen-foot roots. It's not like Illinois, with the flat land and good drainage. Here you need some insurance to feed your livestock, feed your milk cows. If you keep the prairie, then in drought years you'll always have something. And I'm afraid we're going to lose all that."

He pauses and cups his hands around his mouth; prairie-chicken booms and cackles fill the living room, as though a flock has taken to the rafters. "There are black prairies not far from here that should be a national landmark," Frank says. "I go out there, hear the booming. But the guy who owns them says it's too much work to keep it in pasture, and the government will only subsidize row crops—never pasture ground."

I ask about the Department of Agriculture's Conservation Reserve Program, or CRP, intended to allow the conversion of some cropland back into prairie. Frank shakes his head. "I feel that conservation is the worm put on a hook to get dollars, and only crumbs get to the conservation it's trying to attract. Look, all Americans have a soft spot in their hearts for conservation. We owe the wildlife, and we owe the landscape for the benefits we've had from it. But I believe the bureaucracy feels inconvenienced by the necessity for conservation, so they administer conservation programs without the passion that makes taxpayers willing to be charged in the first place.

"If it was me, I'd have people signing up for programs only on the basis of performance. There shouldn't be money just for a practice; it should be for the *quality* of that practice. Some of the landowners we sell seed to because they want money from CRP . . . well, I know for a fact that they just go through the motions. We got guys throwing seeds on the bare ground and coming in with receipts that say they planted it. Some of what the government pays for is just wrongheaded. We got a million and a half acres in fescue and brome. But fescue's a noxious weed! It *inhibits* growth. We were better off when we had small farms row cropping."

Frank sighs, somewhat spent, and drags two fingers along his mustache. "It's like love and *love*," he says after a long moment. "True love is the personality being driven forward by the will. Then there's the love that's just a kind of flat emotional response—you know, I *looove* my four-wheeler. Agencies can't have the right kind of love. They don't have the will necessary for it. If we had the will and determination and passion, we could turn the whole thing with prairie chickens around right away. But you know what it is—it's when you go into a government office, they look at you like there's a tattoo on your head that says 'Work.' *Results* don't come into it."

PRAIRIE-CHICKEN OR GROUSE ROASTED

Epicures think that grouse (in fact, all game) should not be too fresh. Do not wash them. Do not wash any kind of game or meat. If proper care be taken in dressing them they will be quite clean, and one could easily wash out all their blood and flavor. Put plenty of butter inside each chicken: this is necessary to keep it moist. Roast the grouse half an hour and longer, if liked thoroughly done; baste them constantly with butter. When nearly done, sprinkle over a little flour and plenty of butter to froth them. After having boiled the liver of the grouse, mince and pound it, with a little butter, pepper, and salt, until it is like a paste; then spread it over hot buttered toast. Serve the grouse on the toast, surrounded with water-cresses.

—MARY NEWTON FOOTE HENDERSON, *Practical Cooking and Dinner Giving*, 1877

On such a windy day, the only safe course is to begin the burn very, very slowly, and Frank keeps his promise not to hurry. He carries a drip can, which is like a combination oilcan and blowtorch, and with the pull of a trigger drips a burning diesel blend onto the dry grass. I join Chris, one of the Amish teens, in an ATV equipped with spray bottles (and, I notice—feeling like an insider—a steering wheel). The others follow Frank as he begins setting a long, narrow fire beside the road, downwind from the three hundred acres he intends to set on fire today. The wind is so strong that the smoke stays plastered to the ground for perhaps ten feet before finally rising and unraveling like a flag left too long in a gale.

What would happen if the wind changed? "It's happened before," Chris says. "Frank'd have to just get on the four-wheeler and try to circle around as fast as it would go, setting the fire behind him the whole way." As it is, the fire creeps slowly downslope and into the wind, kept from spreading by the sprayers on the tractor and in the hands of the Amish. It will take hours to burn a firebreak thirty feet across and maybe a mile long, big enough that the fire can then have its way with the land.

I realize there's no chance I'm making my flight home. In the scant twenty minutes it takes to change my ticket, the wind begins to shift, sending a black band of burning far to the south. If it gets too far and the wind shifts again, the fire could shoot down and across the bottom of the grassy bowl with enough force to jump the road. Frank is worried, returning to that first state of almost eerie concentration. "It's tenuous right now." He pulls up some of the dry grass that's been pressed flat beside the road, waits for it to burn in a quick flash, then pulls up another beside it. He hands me one of the rakes and takes off on his four-wheeler, wanting to be sure he has enough fuel in the drip can to set the long fire he'll need if this one gets out of control.

My first couple of efforts smoke and die. "He makes it look easy," I say to Chris. Then I see that Chris makes it look easy, too; in fact, I'm probably the only person within a hundred miles who really stinks at this. But I eventually improve, and soon we're moving at a pretty good pace, extending the fire line about ten feet per minute.

As I work, I think back to my talk with Frank, finding it difficult to pinpoint how he felt about the utter transformation of the land. He was visibly angered by bureaucratic cynicism, which he thought led to the failure of programs meant to bring back some of what we lost by transforming the land. But when he talked about development, about the incredible capacity of riverboats and barges compared with trains, there was a genuine excitement in his voice, an enthusiasm about the ability to *do*.

Twain once wrote scornfully that seeing humanity as the pinnacle of Creation was like imagining that the Eiffel Tower had been built to hold up the skin of paint covering its tip. I doubt Frank would make that mistake. "We owe the wildlife," he'd said. "And we owe the landscape for the benefits we've had from it." Maybe that was the key; he didn't think it was wrong to take from the land, only to see nothing in what it gives but the product of our own hands. Soon I have a chance to watch him put that balance into practice—the winds fade and turn back to a safe course. Frank heads for the opposite ridge, drip can in hand, and begins burning in earnest.

———◈———

There is one fire; there are many fires. They break and split and merge, running red up slopes, filling the sky with smoke. As long as I stay on burned ground, it's safe. Now the fire is approaching from two directions, each blaze about knee-high. As they draw closer, they rise slowly to my waist, then my chest, before at last reaching an invisible, crucial point, some precisely correct combination of wind and heat and fuel; the fires inhale, smoke and air sweeping up between them as into a chimney. In seconds the flames triple in height, roaring overhead. I feel instantly sunburned. There's a sound like a thousand thin glass rods shattering, as the stiff cells in the grassy stalks explode. The wind had been blowing smoke into my face, but now air passes me, in a rush, from behind. It's like a wave drawing water into itself before crashing forward, a sensation so familiar from bodysurfing that I recoil, instinctively expecting a massive blowing back of flame. But the fires hold behind the wind they've shifted. Hawks wheel beside the scorching thermal; behind me fire tornadoes dance, sassy whirlwinds of smoke and dust that spit along the burned ground at skipping-stone cadence, pulling black ash swirling up their chutes.

The fires meet with a roar; their lines shift, again moving with the prevailing wind, a bright, hundred-yard-long line stalking through dead grasses. I imagine prairie chickens fleeing from the burn like ghosts, their flight among the fastest of all birds. I run far up a slope and then down, behind the fire now, following it on the black, smoking ground. The smoke from the main blaze is black and gray, orange and yellow. It is towers and curtains, and it pours before the sun, so thickly that when I snap a photo the flash goes off.

I had thought that with the fire so high the ground behind it would be like a forest floor after a fire—glowing, blanketed with embers, surely unbearably hot. But, in fact, the only thing that keeps me from approaching closer to the burn is the heat off the ten-foot flames. The grasses burn too quickly to warm the ground even slightly; the potash cools almost as soon as the fire is gone. I creep closer, until I have to hold a hand to shield my eyebrows. Even so close to the blaze, the ground is cool enough for me to place a palm flat against the earth; the grass stubs are scratchy as a two-day beard.

Around me ribbons of smoke trail up from still-burning clumps of grass, and from tufts twisted into wicks like volcanoes. Sometimes I see what look like glowing orange snakes that, when kicked, burst apart into dry, dead grass and sudden fire. But other than that, there is the lethal fire and then the ground it already touched and so made safe, and little or no border between them.

After an hour the flames have cleared great reaches of grass. Then I find myself in what feels like the most wildly open place I've ever been.

I've been on salt flats and on the open ocean, but this is different; the speed of the transformation from impassably thick grass into clean and ashy slope leaves me exhilarated, with an uncontrollable urge to run. So I do, striding out down one hill and up the next. The ground is spongy, packed with living roots. Smoke blows into my face, and then clear air. I send a surprised hawk flying; I kick the glowing snakes. I'm alone out here, and free to do what I want, and that simple fact is oddly new to me. I've gotten used to the notion that you can hurt a natural landscape by so much as looking at it the wrong way. But there is nothing I can do to this land that the fire hasn't done already. There are no trails here, or guardrails, or signposts—just the rolling, blackened land and the hawks flying, and me, on the run.

"This is savanna," Frank says. We're on top of a rise with grass and trees intermingled, one of the rarest prairie ecosystems. Though this kind of land impressed early explorers of Illinois like Louis Jolliet, today there are about eighty-four acres left in the state. For us, right now, it's simply the best place to watch the remaining burn. My boot soles have melted; tonight my nose will blow black. The fire will go on for a few more days, little spots popping up around wood coals burned from the stands of trees.

"There are flowers in here that survived hundreds of years of grazing. It's a special place," Frank says with unabashed affection. Then he stoops and sets one of those flower survivors on fire. It's an odd, necessary way of showing love; Frank knows about this land, and its grasses, and the destruction it needs. But he won't burn whatever doesn't burn on its own. He likes to leave some spots as hideouts, mimicking the way that trees and grass can take passive shelter from a wildfire in the lee of a lake.

"The red, running buffalo," Frank says as the flame makes its way toward a copse of burr oak. "That's what the Indians called it. And we do the same thing they would, letting the red buffalo run." I ask how they would have stayed clear of burns set by others, or by lightning. "They pretty much held to the river courses," he says. "But listen to that now." Again the fierce crinkling, like breaking glass. "You'd have heard that coming on the wind. If I hear that coming, I got matches with me. And I'm dropping a match and following my own fire out."

Soon the fire is roaring down the slope, pulled higher and hotter by its own wind. Red-tailed hawks circle before the fire line, hoping for rabbits or quail to dash from the blaze and onto exposed ground.

Behind us the ground is black, and smoking, and clean. It's ready to grow.

Two

A Barrel of Odds
and Ends

Possum and Raccoon

BERKELEY RACCOONS ARE BIG, fearless, sewer-swimming bastards. One has begun sneaking in through our supposedly impregnable, magnetically locked cat door; once he left muddy footprints next to Erik's bed. My latest confrontation with the raccoon ended with me, naked, brandishing a Maglite in one hand and an umbrella in the other, as the foul beast ate a bowl of our cat's food. I bellowed—I swung the umbrella like a sword.

The raccoon yawned. It looked better than three feet from nose to tail. When it yawned, I saw its teeth. I must say again—really, I find, I can't stress this particular point enough—that I was naked. What's more, I *felt* naked, like I'd never in my life worn clothes. It came to me, then, that I did not greatly desire to fight the raccoon, or to do anything that would increase, even marginally, the chances of my fighting the raccoon. Maybe I was being rude. I shone the flashlight on the floor, so he could eat in peace. It didn't seem to make any difference either way; the raccoon ate calmly, picking up cat kibbles individually or by the pawful, leaving, in its own leisurely good time, with a final, disdainful slam of the plastic cat door.

It was a scandal: a disgrace. For a few days, we considered repellents, motion-detecting sprinklers, even a dog.

For some reason it did not immediately occur to us to try eating him. But there it is! Right there on the menu—"coon," tucked neatly between "'possum" and "Boston bacon and beans."

Eli says, "No."

I hadn't asked. But she knows that there's a chance I'll try to follow through; though I've eaten neither raccoon nor opossum, I have eaten muskrat, and after muskrat, raccoon sounds like freakin' pumpkin pie. When I was cooking Twain's breakfast biscuits, I used a recipe given to me by archaeology grad student Alison Bell on Flowerdew Hundred Plantation, deep in the Virginia Tidewater. The plantation is named for an early colonist, Temperance Flowerdew Yeardley ("Hundred" was a way of implying, falsely, that the settlement could support a hundred men-at-arms); through the centuries it's been the site of both Native American and English palisades, a colonial tavern, and the pontoon bridge that carried Grant's army as he tried to outflank Lee near Petersburg.

When I worked on excavations at Flowerdew during my college summers, it was home to country ham and angel biscuits and Rabelaisian breakfast spreads and brutally hot weather relieved by hammering James River thunderstorms. The professor who ran the dig was a guy named Jim Deetz, a native Marylander who looked (speaking conservatively) forty years older than his actual sixty-five and who thought of his years spent at UC Berkeley as an eon of exile. For one month a year, Flowerdew was a place for him to drink Rebel Yell bourbon, and play horseshoes and his beaten banjo.

Though it was best known as the site of the first windmill in

English America, Jim thought the farm might be the site of another, far more important, first—that it might be the literal birthplace of African America. In 1625 a muster of the plantation's people included the simple entry "NEGRO WOMAN and a young Child of hers." The first Africans in what would one day be the United States had arrived in 1619, when a Dutch ship brought slaves to Jamestown. Five years later there were still only some thirty in the whole Virginia colony, which wouldn't adopt truly large-scale slavery for decades. That's an awfully small window—if the "young Child" wasn't the first person of African descent to be born in what would become the United States, he or she was certainly among the first. Flowerdew Hundred, on the bank of the James, might be the best place in America to raise a monument to a small, unnamed child.

Anyway, Jim hated Berkeley and, I believe, California in general. So when he was back in the Tidewater, he wanted to eat *Southern,* reveling in properly cured slab bacon, blue crabs, and stone-ground hominy grits. And up at the local store, there was a big chest freezer filled, Jim discovered, with skinned and gutted muskrats; and there, atop the freezer, was a hand-lettered sign affirming that eight of said muskrats could be had for the price of seven. So he came back with a sack of the things and wanged one down on a picnic table like a shovel, right in the middle of a particularly heated game of Spoons. The muskrats had their heads on, and their teeth were really long, their noses wrinkled up as though in disgust. We wrinkled our own noses in completely genuine disgust; some of us, I recall, swore. "Dinner, you assholes," said Jim.

The cook at Flowerdew that year was frankly astonishing. Archaeology food usually slants toward cold cereal, peanut butter and jelly, and mushy spaghetti with jarred sauce—hot dogs, if you're lucky. But Eric put together unbelievable spreads, breakfasts that included biscuits, real-deal home fries, country ham, Virginia bacon, pork chops, fresh fruit, blintzes, and omelets cooked to order; one night we had homemade dim sum. He did all this in an open pavilion overlooking some thousand acres of corn and peanut fields and a cypress swamp where bald eagles nested. The story was that Eric had worked for a time at Chez Panisse, but I never knew if that was true—the path from the Berkeley Gourmet Ghetto to a Prince George County peanut field seemed a strange one, but Flowerdew did have a way of collecting wanderers. Whatever the truth was, Eric seemed like a fine person to trust with a platter of whole, semiaquatic rodents. He butchered the muskrats, soaked them in a salt-and-vinegar solution overnight, and fried the pieces up like chicken.

It didn't work. Perhaps Eric simply approached it wrong; maybe muskrat is a delicate and subtle thing, to be approached with the fine hand of a sushi artist touching his knife to fugu. Whatever: what we ended with, that day, was a platter of chicken-fried meat so dark as to be almost purple, which tasted like a cross between beef liver and sea mussels. Beef liver with sea mussels, let it be known, does not rank with truffled eggs among the world's great natural taste combinations. I don't think of myself as a tentative eater; as I write this, a whole pig's head is simmering on my stove. I'll fry the slivered ears with joy and strip the snout and tongue for brawn. But I've never again sought out muskrat.

Raccoon has a much better reputation. So does possum. You come across recipes for either more frequently than with muskrat, up to and including *Joy of Cooking;* the encyclopedic *L.L. Bean Game and Fish Cookbook* says that raccoon meat is "just as tasty as squirrel, and better than rabbit." People *like* raccoon, it seems, and anyway, I wouldn't be cooking the ones from our backyard, which clambered from Berkeley's antique, redwood storm drains after foraging for unspeakable things. The ones I'd eat would be clean raccoons, woodland raccoons, *sanitary* raccoons, the kind that spend hours scrubbing acorns in fresh mountain streams.

Eli says, "No."

Reluctantly, I agree. And when I have time to think about it, I realize that the most important thing Twain wrote about raccoon wasn't even about the taste. It was about how he got the meat in the first place, hunting it in the woods beyond his uncle's hazelnuts and persimmons, among the wild trees filled with the "far-off hammering of woodpeckers and the muffled drumming of wood pheasants in the remoteness of the forest." And the most important thing of all was who he hunted with:

> I remember the 'coon and 'possum hunts, nights, with the negroes, and the long marches through the black gloom of the woods, and the excitement which fired everybody when the bay of an experienced dog announced that the game was treed; then the wild scramblings and stumblings through briers and bushes and over roots to get to the spot; then the lighting of a fire and the felling of the tree, the joyful frenzy of the dogs and the negroes, and the weird picture it all made in the red glare—I remember it all well, and the delight that everyone got out of it, except the 'coon.

Such hunts could be exhausting; Thomas De Voe went on one (his "first and last") that left him "hungry, thirsty, tired, hoarse, and used-up generally" and "unable to speak aloud for several days." But they were popular, especially in the South—and on the Quarles farm, as was common elsewhere, they were often led by slaves.

Thinking about Twain's feast means thinking about the people who grew, caught, gathered, and prepared the foods he later longed for. The farm was known as the Quarles farm, but the fifteen people enslaved there were the ones leading hunts, harvesting corn, and tending the garden with its butter beans, tomatoes, muskmelons, sweet potatoes, and peas. They were the ones cooking the hot batter cakes, venison, roasted pig, apple dumplings, and peach cobbler—it was their cooking that, as Twain put it, gave the farm's food its "main splendor."

Understanding a little about what they did and made means thinking about differences. But it also means thinking about things that

whites and blacks shared—the things that, after generations of influ-
ences from Africans, Europeans, and Native Americans, were on their
way to being simply Southern. And on the Quarles farm, as Twain remembered all his life, that included the hunting, cooking, and eating of
raccoon.

※

Raccoons are in-between animals—border dwellers that thrive where
fields and woods and marshland meet. They'll eat almost anything, but
the bulk of their wild diet is made up of creatures that can survive in
both air and water, that creep from stream to bog: turtles, newts, mussels, crawfish, salamanders. Their dexterity is legendary, so that their
Algonquin name, *aroughcun*, means "one who scratches with his hands."
That dexterity only improves under their preferred, between-places conditions; as a raccoon gropes in shallow, standing water for food, the skin
on its paws softens, and it can better detect the kind of minute details
that let one dismantle my cat door with the fantastically annoying
aplomb of a furred Houdini. If raccoons had opposable thumbs, I suspect they might one day rule the earth.

A tapetum lucidum, or "bright carpet," at the back of their eyes
collects light and gives them good night vision (less fortunately for raccoons, their shining eyes also provide targets to hunters who don't want
to injure a pelt). But they're also exceptionally nearsighted; their vision
is less important than their sense of smell and a tremendous sensitivity
to vibration. When researchers tagged one blind raccoon with a radio
collar, they found that it could still follow its normal routines, traveling
easily over eight square miles of snowy countryside.

Raccoons are terrific climbers, able nearly to run up trees with
their powerful hind legs and gripping forepaws. Once there, they're
tough to dislodge; in the 1950s one two-hundred-pound hunter reported
hanging from a raccoon's tail as the animal clung to the inside of a hollow tree. They can swim across swift rivers well over a hundred feet

wide. A person would have little or no chance of chasing down a moti-vated raccoon; there's a reason that they're hunted with dogs.

Unlike prairie chickens, which are forever tied to a single natural habitat, raccoons are fantastic generalists. Raccoons don't disappear when their territory is plowed up or clear-cut; much as deer multiply when suburban lawns push into the woods or rock pigeons thrive on the overhangs of stone and brick buildings, raccoon populations often explode near human sprawl. The Humane Society estimates that *twenty times* as many raccoons can live in an urban environment as in a com-parable rural area; prehistoric Berkeley didn't have anything like the numbers of raccoons that its fruit trees, storm drains, open trash bins, and attics support today. There's no shortage of raccoons, no single place to go look at them.

But looking for places that serve roasted raccoon is a different story. And if you want to meet people for whom eating the meat is a yearly event—who gather, a thousand strong, to feast on raccoon in the local high-school gym—your options narrow still further. They narrow, in fact, to one.

———

In January 1988, Governor Bill Clinton's plane slid off the end of an icy agricultural runway in the Arkansas rice country, sending up a cloud of white powder as it skidded through a blizzard. The plane ended up nose down in a snowbank; Clinton and his companion, Senator Dale Bumpers, were both fine. They climbed into a waiting car and began driving south. Fourteen miles later—still a bit pale, townspeople recall—they pulled into the high-school parking lot in Gillett, population eight hundred: "Home of Friendly People and the Coon Supper."

The run-up to Gillett's annual supper may be your one chance to hear someone say, without irony, that they're cooking only six hundred pounds of coon this year. The supper began in the 1930s, when a few local hunters decided to get together and cook up the meat they had left over after skinning out their take. By 1947 it had evolved into an annual early-January fund-raiser for the Gillett High School football team, a team that, like most of the downtown—two of three motels, four of five small grocers, the lone hardware store—has now vanished.

Gillett is on the Grand Prairie of Arkansas, and it's rice farming country. It's also almost entirely white. That's unusual for a rice-growing town in the American South, and can largely be explained by the fact that rice wasn't planted here until the first decade of the twentieth century; in Louisiana and the Carolinas, by contrast, slaves grew rice for over 150 years before abolition. Actually, saying that the slaves planted rice doesn't go far enough; for a time enslaved Africans—especially those from the French Company of the Indies' Senegal Concession— probably knew more about growing rice than anyone else in their respective colonies.

For hundreds of years, farmers in the Senegal Concession (which stretched from Mauritania to Sierra Leone) had painstakingly constructed earthen dams and bulwarks, holding and diverting water as they cultivated wet rice. The farmers pierced each earthwork with a valve made from a hollowed-out tree trunk, allowing rains to flood rice paddies while keeping seawater out. As early as 1594, a Portuguese trader out of Cape Verde described how residents were "growing their crops on the riverain deposits, and by a system of dikes had harnessed the tides to their own advantage," a system nearly identical to the one slaves eventually built in South Carolina. White planters clearly recognized the African farmers' expertise; in the decade after 1719, when French ships carried seed rice from Whydah (modern Benin) to Louisiana, more than half the slaves brought to the territory were from the Senegal Concession. In 1785 newspapers still advertised newly arrived slaves "who have been accustomed to the planting of rice." Much of America's early rice history is African: African in conception, African in design, and African-labor built.

Which is why Gillett is mostly white. The wet, granular Delta soils just south of the Arkansas River—where the towns are mostly African American—were just what early rice-growing slave owners wanted. But until 1909 the land around Gillett was prairie—and, in the town's historical memory anyway, *poor* prairie, where German Americans from the Midwest struggled to raise cattle on sage grass. The relatively thin prairie soils overlay a hardpan of packed clay, which eventually proved to be a blessing. The hardpan, it turned out, could trap water nearly as effectively as plastic sheeting; if you built levees and pumped in water, the earth would flood—holding the water, ready for rice.

Soil, here, is demographic destiny. Still, the farmers of Gillett owe a genuine debt to those of the Gambia and Niger rivers—if not for the establishment of rice around Gillett proper, then for the existence of an American rice industry at all. It's a debt not lessened in the slightest by the fact that it goes unacknowledged.

At the edge of town, a black-and-white sign has a picture of a startled-looking raccoon and the town slogan: GILLETT: HOME OF FRIENDLY PEOPLE & THE COON SUPPER. It's a rice-growing town. But it's the Coon Supper that brought Clinton, and decades of governors and Miss Arkansases, and it's what brings me.

The Quarles farm was in the region called Little Dixie. Flanking the Missouri River, Little Dixie was settled, in the plurality, by white farmers from slaveholding states like Virginia, Kentucky, and Tennessee. Many of the farmers brought enslaved men and women with them from their home states and grew corn, tobacco, and hemp to ship downriver to New Orleans. By reputation at least, Little Dixie was not as brutal as the worst cotton- or rice-growing regions, and there's no record of physical cruelty on John Quarles's part (except, of course, for the raw fact of forced bondage). He was typical of the region, having arrived from Tennessee in the 1830s with the intent of setting up as a tobacco farmer.

During his childhood summers, the boy Sammy Clemens spent weeks with the slaves—playing with the children, tagging along with the adults. He believed that one of them, Aunt Hannah, was old enough to have talked to Moses; another, Uncle Dan'l, was a potent figure who would live on vividly in the mind of Mark Twain. "We had a faithful and affectionate good friend, ally and advisor in 'Uncle Dan'l,'" he wrote in his *Autobiography*, "whose sympathies were wide and warm. . . . It was on the farm that I got my strong liking for his race and my appreciation of certain of its fine qualities. This feeling and this estimate have stood the test of sixty years and more and have suffered no impairment. The black face is as welcome to me now as it was then."

But even as a child, he understood that truly good and honest friendship wasn't possible under the divide of slavery; he later wrote that "all the negroes were friends of ours, and with those of our own age we were in effect comrades. I say in effect, using the phrase as a modification. We were comrades and yet not comrades; color and condition interposed a subtle line which both parties were conscious of and which rendered complete fusion impossible." Of course, it's not taking any kind of leap to say that the "subtle line" looked considerably less subtle to the boys standing on the other side of it; there's no doubt that the farm that Twain remembered so clearly and so well had many secret pathways, many places hidden to him.

Twain loved secret places. His literary double, Tom Sawyer, thrived on them, as when Tom "entered a dense wood, picked his pathless way to the center of it, and sat down on a mossy spot under a spreading oak. . . . Nature lay in a trance that was broken by no sound but the occasional far-off hammering of a wood-pecker, and this seemed to render the pervading silence and sense of loneliness the more profound." But Tom's routes were those of play, as he flung himself through woods to Robin Hood's lair, discovered the dens of robbers and the haunts of pirates, and learned the infinite interworkings of the cave south of town "as well as anyone." Slaves had their own vitally important mental maps, ways of doing what they wanted to do—or had to do—without being seen and stopped.

What Tom Sawyer (and Twain) found a fun midnight lark might be, to a slave, a dangerous expedition requiring courage and skill, a way of supplementing inadequate rations of corn and low-quality meat. Maria Franklin, once a graduate student at Flowerdew, now professor at Texas-Austin, points out that in Virginia "blacks understood the advantage of familiarizing themselves with their untamed surroundings—landscapes that remained wooded and natural—for they facilitated secrecy and anonymity. Before long, enslaved Virginians acquired an in-depth knowledge of their environment, and the flora and fauna sustained by it." That's one reason that raccoon and possum, as relished by Twain as muskrat was by Jim Deetz, eventually gained a reputation among some whites as slave foods. Raccoons are night creatures, emerging at dusk from their dens—perfect prey for people who had to hunt and trap and fish for what they could in the few unwatched hours they had.

Maryland and South Carolina slave Charles Bell found that secretly trapping and hunting game in a nearby swamp was the best way of ensuring his family's health. Bell worked hard to "procure supplies of such things as were not allowed me by my master," first among which was meat. By walking several miles through the woods after dark, he managed to catch enough raccoons, opossums, and rabbits for two or three meals a week; he scorned men like the head of family who, having come in from the fields, "seldom thought of leaving his cabin again before morning." In the spring, when the raccoons were thin and worthless, Bell turned to fishing, working to feed his loved ones however the season best permitted. It's not surprising at all that so many plantation raccoon hunts, like that on the modest Quarles farm, were led by slaves: people whose days were not their own, for whom a successful nighttime hunt could mean more meat than they'd be rationed in a week.

Of course, eating raccoon wasn't restricted to the South; in his 1839 *A Diary in America,* visiting Englishman Frederick Marryat noted the

profusion of "rackoon" in the New York game market, and in 1867 De
Voe occasionally saw it sold there "both alive and dead." But the growing white perception of raccoon as slave food could be self-fulfilling;
once the stereotype took hold, some whites who had enjoyed the meat
might refuse to eat it. At Virginia's Rich Neck Plantation, for instance,
black households ate four times as much raccoon after 1765 as they had
before, while the species vanished almost entirely from white tables.
Whites may have abandoned the food because of its racial associations,
with poor whites in particular coming to see eating raccoon as a kind of
symbolic barrier between themselves and enslaved African Americans.

   None of this is to say that slaves hunted raccoon only when forced
to by hunger. Early European travelers to West Africa were often amazed
at the variety of wild game eaten there; Francis Moore of the Royal
West Africa Company wrote that "there is scarce anything [the people]
do not eat: large snakes, guanas, monkeys, pelicans, bald-eagles, alligators, and sea-horses [hippos] are excellent food." Once in America, the
long experience of many Africans with hunting and eating a variety of
game may have helped them to see the potential food value of raccoon
and other wild species. Benin, for example, has an obvious raccoon
analogue called the grasscutter (or greater cane rat), which is two feet
long, prefers wet areas like riverbanks, will happily take to a new plantation cut into the forest, and is popular enough to eat to be raised in
cages for sale. It's sometimes served with yam porridge, or *teligbo*, par-
alleling the matching of dark, shredded meat with sweet potatoes that
culinary historian John Martin Taylor says is common throughout the
African diaspora. To West Africans used to eating grasscutters and
other nocturnal mammals, eating raccoon and possum with sweet potatoes may have been familiar, even comforting.

   Certainly some ex-slaves thought of both raccoon and possum
with affection. "Oh! I was fond of 'possums, sprinkled with butter and
pepper and baked down 'till de gravy was good and brown," one remembered. Another, Anthony Dawson, had liked raccoon better:
"Sometimes de boys would go down in the woods and get a possum. I

love possum and sweet-taters, but de coon meat more delicate and de hair don't stink up de meat." But whether they preferred possum or raccoon, it's impossible to know how the slaves on the Quarles farm felt about the hunts they led. Did they resent the loss of sleep? Did they feel the excitement Twain had? Sammy liked and admired some of the slaves; but of course he'd never be their confidant. They had their own secrets, their own paths.

Among the paths Twain couldn't see was the one leading back to the source of many of his favorite Southern foods. The roots of the slaves on the Quarles farm can't be traced as easily as can those of people living on the rice plantations of South Carolina or Louisiana, many of whom were enslaved and brought from specific rice-growing areas; some of those on the Quarles farm had probably lived in America for three or more generations. But whatever the ancestry and origin of the slaves there, by the time Sammy came to the farm they were cooking a thoroughly creolized cuisine—one with perhaps its deepest and most important roots among the incredibly diverse cultures of Africa.

POSSUM ROASTED

Chill thoroughly after scraping and drawing. Save all the inside fat, let it soak in weak salt water until cooking time, then rinse it well, and partly try it out in the pan before putting in the possum. Unless he is huge, leave him whole, skewering him flat, and laying him skin side up in the pan. Set in a hot oven and cook until crisply tender, taking care there is no scorching. Roast a dozen good sized sweet potatoes—in ashes if possible, if not, bake them covered in a deep pan. Peel when done, and lay while hot around the possum, turning them over and over in the abundant gravy. He should have been lightly salted when hung up, and fully seasoned, with salt, pepper, and a trifle of mustard, when put down to cook. Dish him in a big platter, lay the potatoes, which should be partly browned, around him, add a little boiling water to the pan, shake well around, and pour the gravy over everything. Hot corn bread, strong black coffee, or else sharp cider, and very hot sharp pickles are the things to serve with him.

—MARTHA MCCULLOCH-WILLIAMS, *Dishes & Beverages of the Old South*, 1913

Frank Wolfe has been growing rice in Gillett for more than forty years; he's been attending Coon Suppers for even longer. By 6:30 A.M., when Frank drives me out to the Harris place from the Rice Paddy Motel where I'm staying, about a third of this year's six hundred pounds of cut-up raccoon is already boiling furiously in huge outdoor pots. The sky is clear, and it's cold but not freezing—lucky, since the supper goes on rain or shine, and the only real question is how miserable the cooks will get during the next two days. Beyond the kettles the rice fields lie green and dormant.

The pots are just outside a thirty-yard-long, sheet-steel-covered farm shop. There are fifteen members of the Gillett Farmers' and Businessmen's Club here, aged twenty to probably eighty; whatever their ages, they wear tan coveralls and hats reading RICELAND (a farmers' co-op up north in Stuttgart) or MARTIN FLYING SERVICE (a spraying operation— Frank openly snorts when I ask about growing organic). They stand around the kettles or make runs into the farm shed, returning with shovels and dripping sieves.

Except for a stretch in the army and the winters he spent making a few extra dollars drilling water wells in Haiti and Bangladesh, Frank has lived here for most of his seventy years. He's been to almost every Coon Supper since their official 1947 inception. For decades, some of the meat for the supper was procured during a single communal hunt; families gathered around bonfires while men and the older boys headed into the woods. One of the men was Frank's father, who'd worked on the Arkansas River levees during the Depression. "He'd tie up his hounds while he was working," Frank says. "When he was done, he'd just hunt his way back home. If he could get a coon or two in a week, that'd just about double his salary." It says something about how hard times were then that the pelts were thought worth the trouble—the fur of Arkansas raccoons is much thinner and less valuable than that of those farther north, which have to contend with brutal winters.

Now Frank smiles mischievously. "Stomach feeling strong?"

"Sure," I say, and follow Frank into the farm shop. Inside, not far from a dusty 1947 Ford truck, surrounded by white molded-plastic chairs, are a pair of metal cattle-watering troughs. Each trough is lined with a sheet of white plastic; each is halfway full of a slurry of brine and raccoon meat and blood. The sheets keep the salty brine from eating into the aluminum, but my immediate concern is how very brightly red they make the blood look. The liquid is actually probably mostly brine—still, it's brine that's gone extremely and thoroughly crimson.

I force a smile and a "Well, would you look at that," or something similarly lame, and make myself step closer to where Scott Plaice—this year's head cook and an absolutely enormous man—is loading cut-up raccoon into a sieve by the shovelful. The shovel blade has been drilled with holes (your kitchen probably has slotted spoons; these guys have slotted shovels), and as Scott shovels the meat, the smell of blood is rank and just *everywhere*. The breakfast special at the Paddy was scrambled eggs, bacon, and toast slathered in margarine—they threw in a couple of sausage patties just to be kind—and right now I'm feeling every bite of it.

If I didn't already know what the cut-up meat is, I'd be hard-pressed to guess. It's a perfect example of how modern butchering distances us from the animals we eat. Cutting up meat with an ax, as most Americans did before the late eighteenth century, left identifiable pieces of animal—a haunch, a flank, even a head. When you looked in a pot, it was obvious what was simmering there. Butchering with knives or saws, on the other hand, produces cutlets and fillets—pork and beef, instead of pig and cow. There's a big difference, both visually and conceptually, between roasting a freshly killed raccoon over the coals and simmering a kettle of nearly unidentifiable segments.

So though the hunters skin, gut, and behead each raccoon before sale, Scott and Frank and the rest insist that they leave on at least one paw. "We gotta check, just to make sure they're not comin' in with kitty cats or something," Scott says. Once the animal's identity is confirmed, they cut up the raccoons in such a way that (if you can put aside the sight of the brining tank) the meat *looks* pretty good. But it sure smells bad.

I retreat outside, stepping across a bloody little rivulet and into what I think will be blessedly clear air, but I at once make the mistake of wandering over to Frank, who—a brief cross-draft masks this fact at first—is immediately downwind from the cooking kettles. Three of the four pots were made by welding sheet steel over sections of three-foot pipe. The fourth, the story goes, was once a Confederate cookpot (or maybe a washbasin), found buried under someone's grandmother's front porch and identified by an elderly black woman named Bessie Lee. They used to use all iron pots and wooden paddles. But the health department got interested, forcing the move to stainless-steel implements. (The other point of contention was the homemade pies once served for dessert at the supper. The department has declared that Gillett can serve up six hundred pounds of raccoon at a sitting, but the citizenry is forever safe from the ravages that homemade peach cobbler and huckleberry pie might visit upon them.)

The steam from the kettles is furious, bathing me and Frank in a thick, gray blanket that I feel it would be somehow dishonorable to flee from; I just stand there and use the time to practice breathing through my mouth. I'd imagined that even if the smell of two big vats of raw meat was nauseating, the smell of that same meat cooking in a broth of onions, celery, carrots, and black pepper might be appetizing. But no, I'm soon feeling sick again. *Smells like coon,* the farmers here will say. *That's it.* And that's right, raccoon smells exactly like raccoon, a smell like nothing I've smelled before but which I'll now recognize until I die (not, I hope, as a result of eating raccoon).

For the record, though: it's a smell that's trying its damnedest to smell good, as would any combination of aromatic vegetables and fatty meat. I keep wanting to offer a compliment, to say how it smells delicious, but always before I can form the words I'm arrested by an iron ballast of Paddy breakfast and a whiff of the pungent, bubbling pots. Probably a small leak in the propane line adds to the funk.

But mostly, everyone agrees, it's the fat. Raccoon fat is pretty awful stuff. "End of the day, that pot'll be about half coon grease. Dogs won't eat it," Scott says, and Heath Long throws in "that there is the one thing a man'll eat that a dog won't touch," and a third farmer muses, "If I live fifty years, I might could think of something to do with the fat." When I get too close to look at one of the bubbling cauldrons, a last guy observes that if I let that shit splatter me, I'll stink all day.

Sometimes the scorn extends to the meat itself. Very early in the day, these members of the Gillett Farmers' and Businessmen's Club started cooking up Boston butts and chicken in a homemade smoker with rotating grills, which affords ample chances to compare and contrast the raccoon with other meat: "Yeah, we're gonna eat real well, but . . . "—laughing, nodding toward the kettles—"it won't be comin' out of *there*." Yes, the Coon Supper is a sixty-three-year tradition, in a shrinking town that's only 104 years old to begin with. Still, some of the men will conclude, disdainfully, that the meat's local importance during the Depression only proves that people were real hungry back then. In this they're a bit like chef Homaro Cantu at Chicago's Moto restaurant, who served raccoon with a yellow stripe across the plate to make it look like roadkill ("disdain" may be too strong a word—Cantu would probably vote for "playful"—but there was at least as much irony on the plates as there was actual food).

Then there's Heath's father, Billy, who declares that he's going to just eat holy hell out of the raccoon. Most people in Gillett seem to like the flavor; they're closer in spirit to customers of the semiunderground raccoon trade in Illinois, where a single dealer can sell 250 carcasses in a week, or to those who buy raccoon, possum, muskrat, and beaver from a stall at the Soulard Farmer's Market in St. Louis. Still, the days of hunting raccoon as a completely integral part of Gillett life, whether for the money from pelts, or a simple meal, are mostly over.

Gillett isn't a big place, but you have to drive to hunt raccoon—you can't just walk out your front door with a hound and a .22 and start working the woods. There are miles of rice fields between the kettles and the beginning of the trees. So most of the raccoons are hunted by truly rural people, people whose lawns end in forest or marsh instead of the neighbor's mowed grass. Besides, raccoon hunts take time, effort, and money, especially when you factor in a good dog or two. Dogs are both necessary and legally required—you can be fined or arrested for hunting after dark without a hound (according to the Arkansas Game & Fish Commission, it's otherwise just impossible to find the raccoon).

John Cover is Gillett's self-appointed local historian (he edited a volume of essays on the town for its 2006 centenary), and he has a deep appreciation for the tradition of the supper. He shows me a picture of him and his wife, Linda, at a supper exactly fifty years ago; his father was out hunting raccoon at the precise moment he was born. Over a dinner of Linda's ham-and-cheese sandwiches, John tells me that he isn't happy about how hunting raccoon is fading. "You just have to travel too much now," he says. "Plus, there's too much on TV, too many distractions. Video games. Too much to keep the kids from wanting to head out and play baseball or football or go hunting."

When townspeople do hunt, it's usually for the newly plentiful deer; Frank Wolfe says it used to be an occasion to see as much as a track, whereas hunters will now sometimes take a doe just so they don't have a tag left over at season's end. Others guide out-of-towners hunting the ducks that stop to feed on waste rice along the Mississippi flyway (some say the hunting was better when they harvested rice with binders, which left stalks to dry in easily raided sheaves instead of efficient modern combines). Raccoon hunting just isn't as central to the town's life anymore.

Still, they sell their thousand tickets, each and every year (this, I repeat, in a town of eight hundred). And it's clear that if Gillett abandoned raccoon tomorrow, governor after governor wouldn't keep driving into town to feast on baked chicken or ham. The supper is completely wrapped up in the place; it's a natural successor to the Polk County Possum Club in the thirties, which a WPA writer called "Arkansas' outstanding ceremonial feast" and "characteristically Arkansan in its background and color," and which drew five hundred people from senators to backwoodsmen. Frank Wolfe and Heath Long and the rest of the farmers can poke fun at the supper, claiming to dislike the annual work and the raccoon meat itself. But there's a certain inherent rightness to their collective decision to make the Coon Supper Gillett's public face— the supper makes Gillett different, makes it stand out from other small, struggling, or even dying farm towns. The football team it supported is gone now, but lots of towns have football teams. A Coon Supper is something else.

In some ways the annual gathering may be getting more important as the town's troubles grow. A few years back, Governor Mike Huckabee sponsored legislation saying that any high school with fewer than 350 people had to consolidate with other schools or close down. Gillett, of course, didn't come close, and there was some hurried and intense debate over whether to absorb the closest school, a poor, mostly black one in the delta across the Arkansas River. The town took the second option, which was to become a satellite campus of DeWitt (where Clin-

ton's plane crashed); part of the deal was losing the football team—
until then a major focus of town life—to the northern school. Now
there's a lot of worry ahead of another upcoming school-consolidation
vote, which could mean losing the high school altogether—losing one
more thing that binds the young people to town, connects them with
local traditions, and gives them a reason to build a life here.

Pretty much anyone who's heard of Gillett has heard of it because
of the supper. I hear it again and again: *He knows where Gillett is.* They
say it about Clinton, and Dale Bumpers, and Mike Huckabee (a somewhat detested figure in Gillett now, given his role in the whole DeWitt
situation). It can be applied to a couple decades' worth of Miss Arkansases, and any number of congressmen, judges, and attorneys general. It's interspersed with talk about fuel prices, which the farmers can
recite like baseball stats; it comes up as they talk about a neighbor's new
equipment, and a recent Alexander Hamilton biography, and the an-
noyance of having a girlfriend insisting on trying to text you when
you're out on the tractor. *He knows where Gillett is.*

STUFFING FOR A SUCKLING PIG AND 'POSSUM

Put two tablespoonfuls of finely chopped onions into a saucepan
with one teaspoon of oil. Toss them over the fire for five or six
minutes, add eight ounces of rice boil[ed] in stock, an equal
quantity of sausage meat, four or five ounces of butter, a small
quantity of mince parsley, and pepper and salt to taste. Turn the
mixture into a basin and add three eggs to make the whole into
a stiff paste. It is then ready for use.

—RUFUS ESTES, *Good Things to Eat, as Suggested by Rufus,* 1911

Hot egg-bread, Southern style. Hot light-bread, Southern style. Hot corn-pone, with chitlings, Southern style. Early rose potatoes, roasted in the ashes, served hot. Fried chicken. Peach cobbler. Bacon and greens. Apple puffs. Hoe-cake. Wheat-bread.

Southern style. Twain lived in New York and New England for as long as he did in the South. Still, he remained nearly nationalistic about Southern cooking. His menu included far more dishes cooked Southern style than any other; he wrote about those cooked at the Quarles farm with passion and love:

> The way that the things were cooked was perhaps the main splendor—particularly a certain few of the dishes. For instance, the corn bread, the hot biscuits and wheat bread and fried chicken. These things have never been properly cooked in the North—in fact, no one there is able to learn the art, so far as my experience goes. The North thinks it knows how to make corn bread but this is gross superstition. Perhaps no bread in the world is quite so good as Southern corn bread and perhaps no bread in the world is quite so bad as the Northern imitation of it. The North seldom tries to fry chicken and this is well; the art cannot be learned north of the line of Mason and Dixon, not anywhere in Europe. This is not hearsay; it is experience that is speaking.

Like most of his contemporaries, Twain probably didn't think much about the dishes' origins; the very fact that they seemed so natural to the place might have prevented that. He didn't write at any length about who exactly was doing the cooking, who it was that gave them their "main splendor." And he didn't muse about why it was, exactly, that these particular foods were cooked so well in the slaveholding states—and, Twain insisted, *only* there. He didn't name the enslaved women who worked in the log kitchen, connected to the main house by a "big broad, open, but roofed passage," or in the smokehouse behind that.

Though these women were almost certainly several generations removed from Africa, their skills—and those of millions of women like them—were anchored in the cooking and customs of their great-grandmothers' homelands, as surely as much of their spoken English reflected the cadences and grammar of Fulani, Ibo, Kongo, and other African languages. Rice farmers carried the knowledge of how to build dams and master coastal floods; cooks knew how to fry in oil, how to bake in ashes, how to make vegetables savory by stewing them with a little meat. Their understanding of food—the ways they used it to strengthen, comfort, and sustain their families—made Southern food splendid.

It's hard to give a brief description of West African food without annoying people who truly know the subject. My archaeologist friend Cameron Monroe, taking me to school, says flatly that "there's no such place as Africa." And he's right, in the sense that talking about "Africa" forces you to make broad and sometimes empty generalizations. Africa is just unbelievably huge; you could pretty well lose the lower forty-eight states in the Sahara, and early Portuguese, English, and Italian mapmakers used to do amazing conceptual backflips to make the continent look like something less than nearly triple the size of Europe.

Still, the cultures of sub-Saharan Western Africa share some broad culinary tendencies, just as those of Northern Europe do. These tendencies and customs were probably especially important to the first generations of enslaved Africans, who had been thrown together without sharing a language, or possibly a religion—without sharing very much at all. Cooking food in a way familiar to all those present could have signaled that they shared at least some widely dispersed customs and practices; it could have hinted at the start of a community.

Of course, the food choices of slaves were often terribly limited; the familiar would always be welcome, but it might not always be attainable. Even in rice-growing states, where the primary grain was known and loved by many recently enslaved farmers, most were given rations of less expensive corn. Where Africans had yams, there might be sweet potatoes; for millet, substitute wheat. What's more, social conditions varied widely by region—even from one plantation to the next—so one family of slaves might have access to very different foods than those eaten by another only a few miles distant. Slaves might be given only tough, cheap cuts of meat, or else whole animals might be shared throughout the entire quarter; they might be allowed fowling pieces, or nets and traps, or forbidden from hunting at all.

But whatever they were given as provisions, whatever else they grew or trapped or hunted or scavenged, the slaves cooked food as they understood food should be cooked. And just as a language can quickly adopt new words within a slowly changing grammatical structure, particular ingredients were naturally cooked using familiar, traditional, durable skills. The fact that many West Africans made vegetable relishes—using meat more as a flavoring than a primary ingredient—then served them over cooked starches, may have been more important than whether the starch was corn, as on the Gold Coast, or yams, as among the Ibo. West African gardeners and cooks knew millet, rice, corn, yams, and manioc; they knew eggplant, peppers, okra, black-eyed peas, cowpeas, onions, and a variety of greens. Now, no matter what there was to fill it, the stewpot would keep on simmering—whether there were yams or white potatoes, roots baked on the hearth.

West Africans shared six major cooking techniques: boiling in water, steaming in leaves, frying in deep oil, toasting beside the fire, roasting over the fire, and baking in ashes. Like specific ingredients such as sesame, many of these techniques became important in the emerging food culture of the American South—a culture that drew on African and European roots and used many ingredients grown for generations by Native Americans. Within that food culture, there could still be many distinctions between place and class and race. But just as the African banjos became the heart of bluegrass music and Yoruba *to-gun* ("place of assembly") buildings were adapted as the shotgun houses common through the Mississippi Delta, African elements were simply included, without comment, among the foundations of Southern food.

The cooking on the Quarles farm was creolized to the point that both whites and blacks may have seen it, simply, as *cooking*.

Twain's menu is full of dishes with African roots. His fried chicken (perhaps the region's single most famous dish) was cooked in deep fat, a technique used in Scotland but perhaps more common in Western Africa, where the cooking fat would have been palm oil. What's more, the chicken was so familiar to many Africans, who raised the birds in open yards (a practice common through much of the South), that enslaved women eventually displaced white women as Virginia's main chicken vendors. A pot of bacon and greens would be prepared more or less identically to the meat-flavored vegetable relishes of Western Africa, though with new ingredients substituted—salt pork, for instance, replacing the dried shrimp common in some African regions. Twain's "early rose potatoes, roasted in the ashes, served hot," also used one of the region's most common cooking techniques. Corn pone could be substituted for simmered sorghum or millet—or might not represent a substitution at all, since maize was well known in regions like the Gold Coast (modern Ghana). And chitlins were deeply associated with slave cooking, especially after the late eighteenth century, when planters increasingly offered poor cuts instead of whole animals to be divided.

The slaves on the Quarles place might have cooked very differently than did those in other states or regions. They probably didn't make hoppin' John, the Carolina classic of cowpeas and rice simmered with a seasoning bone of smoked ham, possibly brought from the West Indies as *pois pigeon* (say it out loud). They wouldn't have made gumbo like that cooked by black and white Louisianans (*gombo* was the Bantu word for the okra stewing with chicken and shrimp and spices and ground sassafras leaves). They couldn't have cooked diamondback terrapins, like the ones roasted in the shell by slaves living close to brackish coastal marshes. They probably didn't have Guinea hens, the African fowl still found near old Virginia and Maryland plantations, or cook much with peanuts, calling them "goobers" in a corruption of the Kongo word *nguba*.

Still, many of their meals came from the same deep, African-American culinary grammar as these dishes, and that later inspired the free black cooks of Virginia's Freetown (Edna Lewis's evocation of Freetown in *The Taste of Country Cooking* is one of the most flatly gorgeous, inspiring visions ever written about what American food can be). Dipping a wooden spoon into a pot of savory greens, stirring up the bits of bacon and fatback, smelling to judge the "pot likker";* whether cooking for themselves or for the Quarleses, the slave cooks helped to define a place over which they seemed to have little control, shaping it with their sensibilities and desires and tastes. For both blacks and whites—and certainly for Twain—their skills helped to make the South the South.

In *Was Huck Black?* Shelley Fisher Fishkin makes what is, to me, a completely convincing argument that Huck's talk owed more to Southern black dialects than to the white, "backwoods Missouri" speech Twain mentions in the introduction to *The Adventures of Huckleberry Finn*. Food is much less important to the novel than is speech; still, Twain uses it both to mark Huck's class and to give him a cultural bond with Jim, though it's a bond that Huck only gradually recognizes.

In *The Adventures of Tom Sawyer*, Huck had told Tom about a slave named Uncle Jake, ending with, "Sometimes I've set right down and eat *with* him. But you needn't tell that. A body's got to do things when he's awful hungry he wouldn't want to do as a steady thing." Still, the foods Huck loves best are also those of the slaves. His own eponymous novel opens with him pining for a "barrel of odds and ends" in which "the things get mixed up, and the juice kinds of swaps around, and the things go better," a cooking style that sounds a lot like the single-pot stews preferred by slaves throughout the South (the low-fired clay colono-ware pots made by some slaves were most appropriate for a slow simmer). By the book's midpoint, his reluctance to eat with a black man is

---

*For fellow Yankees: pot liquor (or "likker") is the delicious, smoky, salty, bitter brew you get from simmering greens with a hock of good ham.

completely gone. When Huck returns to the raft after escaping the stunning, casual bloodlust of the Shepherdson-Grangerford feud, it's when
he shares a meal with Jim that Huck knows he's well and truly away—
that he's safe. "I hadn't had a bite to eat since yesterday," he says, "so Jim
he got out some corn-dodgers, and buttermilk, and pork and cabbage,
and greens—there ain't nothing in the world so good when it's cooked
right—and whilst I eat my supper we talked and had a good time."

It almost went without saying that Jim knew how to cook it right.
Huck is enjoying a meal completely typical among both Southern African Americans and poorer whites: vegetables flavored with meat, served
over or alongside a simmered or baked corn dish. Even with monumental social divisions, and great variations in ingredients and cooking technique, Southern food now had a grammar that often crossed racial
lines.

The overall culinary situation on the Quarles farm was complicated—in fact, given the forces at work, it's kind of amazing how natural it
seemed to those involved. Borrowings, lendings, bleedings-together, from
people originating on different continents and migrating from various
regions of the country. Twain himself migrated an entire farm, when in
Huckleberry Finn (a novel of motion, travel, and escapes) he lifted up the
entire Quarles place, moved it a few hundred miles, and dropped it, now
a cotton plantation, in Arkansas.

———————

All through the day in Gillett, I get sized up; there's a kind of basically
good-natured circling that usually ends with an assertion that I stand
out like . . . well, like a guy from Berkeley hanging around four boiling
kettles of raccoon. Heath Long asks where I'm from by asserting that
it has to be somewhere else: "I *know* you're not from around here." And
when I start to do the list, saying I'm from Connecticut but then
California and then Virginia and California again, I get no further than
Connecticut before he's breaking in again, dryly, "Never would have

guessed." Later I think I've scored: a farmer looks me up and down, considers, spits, and offers, "I *know* you're not from L.A." That's something, I think. "Los Angeles," I imagine, is shorthand for the farthest away you can get without leaving the continental United States; there are limits to how out of place I am here.

Then it hits me: L.A. = Lower Arkansas. Ah.

Every fifteen minutes Scott Plaice leans over a kettle, raising a piece of raccoon on a two-pronged fork. Once the meat barely slips from the bone under its own weight, the men shovel forty pounds of it into gigantic, flat-bottomed, homemade colanders. In the farm shop, Heath and his father, Billy Long, dump the steaming, diminutive shins and flanks and hindquarters across two plastic-covered tables. The men line up, pull on disposable blue gloves, and grab steak and paring knives. Then it's all business. They hunch silently over the tables, seizing piece after piece, cutting off every bit of visible fat.

One thing is clear: they're not laboring to bring out the essence of raccoon, highlighting its unique flavor; raccoon is not something to be sliced thin and served as carpaccio. The cooks have already boiled the hell out of the meat. And now, by cutting away the pungent fat, they're also stripping off most of what would probably taste really distinctive. Fat is a terrific carrier of flavor; one reason that many lean meats tend to "taste like chicken" is that when you compare, say, alligator tail and chicken breast, what you're mostly comparing is the taste of unadorned lean proteins. In this case unadorned lean protein is the goal; the fat of swamp foragers like muskrat and raccoon isn't usually classed with that of bacon.

Possum is a different story. De Voe wrote that the animal was usually "scalded like a pig," only the hair removed with the skin left intact. And Paul Laurence Dunbar, an African-American poet and the son of slaves, wrote in his tongue-in-cheek 1905 poem "Possum":

Ef dey's anyt'ing dat riles me . . .
Hit's to see some ign'ant white man

'Mittin' dat owdacious sin—
W'en he want to cook a possum
Tekin' off de possum's skin. . . .

Possum skin is jes' lak shoat skin;
Jes' you swinge an' scrope it down,
Tek a good sha'p knife an' sco' it,
Den you bake it good an' brown. . . .

White folks t'ink dey know 'bout eatin',
An' I reckon dat dey do
Sometimes git a little idee
Of a middlin' dish er two;

But dey ain't a t'ing dey knows of
Dat I reckon cain't be beat
W'en we set down at de table
To an unskun possum's meat!

But raccoon tastes much stronger, and in Gillett they've insisted for decades on trimming it. "Yeah, the recipe changes *real* slow," Frank says with a laugh.

"And you're dead ten years before they take you off a committee," Scott puts in.

"Hell—we got *servers* been dead five."

I pull on gloves, pick out a paring knife, and find an empty space beside a table. Once boiled, it develops, raccoon fat is gluey enough to resist cutting. The trick is to get in under it and peel it off, almost like cutting the rind off an orange, removing as little of the dark meat as possible. We work through sieve after sieve, tossing stripped pieces of raccoon into aluminum roasting trays, the fat and vegetables into a big heap in the table's center. When a pile is done, the men assume identical positions, feet firmly planted, arms straight, fingers stretched out an even eight inches from their coveralls as they face the bright opening of the farm shop, waiting for the next colander.

After the raccoon is stripped and put into the refrigerated trailer until tomorrow, and the pots and plastic sheets have been blasted with a high-pressure hose, out comes smoked pork and chicken, french fries from an outdoor fryer, and barbecue rice—the latter a much-loved local concoction of rice cooked with margarine, liquid smoke, chicken broth, and condensed chicken soup. We sit around the farm shop and eat, the farmers showing what seems a surprising level of concern about the cholesterol in the pork; a lot of these guys eat at the Paddy every morning, and frankly, having eaten at the Paddy, I wouldn't put the pork in the top ten of local lipid concerns. Anyway, the pork would be delicious if my nostrils weren't tainted by raccoon steam, which they are; but it's good all the same, and the hospitality is better.

COON SUPPER

For a Friday supper:
Save six hundred pounds of raccoon, buying from local hunters, freezing as necessary. On Wednesday before the supper, cut up your frozen coon; place in saltwater vats to thaw.

Very early Thursday morning—just after daylight—fire your cooking pots. Wash the coon, then boil with carrots, onions, celery, and black pepper. At each pot station a chief cook, preferably with years of experience, to stir and test the meat for state of readiness. When the meat slips from the bone, remove to tables and trim all excess fat. Place in barbecue trays and refrigerate.

Friday morning, place in smokers that you fired before dawn. Pour chicken broth over. When the meat is dark and fully

smoked, apply barbecue sauce, place in coon warmer, and
remove to banquet site.

—paraphrased from JOHN COVER

The football field of Gillett High School is a dead, January gray,
the scoreboard standing but dark for years. Inside, the high-school gym
is decked out and looking sharp, filled with long rows of white-clothed
tables. Each setting has a souvenir plastic cup, a hat donated by a Little
Rock businessman, and a plate already filled with candied sweet potatoes and barbecue rice. Along the tables' center lines are paper platters
of ham; beside each platter is a foil-lined paper bucket overflowing with
raccoon.

First thing this morning, the trays of boiled raccoon went into a
pair of giant, converted-propane-tank smokers not far from the farm
shed. Along with the meat, each tray held an inch of Swanson's chicken
broth (which, as Heath put it, has about as much chicken in it as if a
bird walked through water). Nearby, a bonfire roared on a girder-and-
tire-rim frame that looked a bit like Fred Flintstone's car. As embers fell
to the ground, cooks shoveled them into the smoker, leaving them to
smolder under the meat. After a couple of hours, the cooks drained the
trays and poured over Little Pig barbecue sauce, a tomato-based concoction with a healthy dollop of vinegar. Then it all went into the coon
warmer (a giant tank that once held red phosphate).

The crowd has been lining up in the January chill for better than
thirty minutes; many of the men wear suits. There's a sextet of young
women from Little Rock wearing vibrant purple hats with dangling
raccoon tails. One kid wears full coonskin regalia; his hat still has a
face. There are women in evening dress or jeans, men in camouflage
jackets and hunter's orange. Lots of people have name tags left over

from Blue Dog congressman Marion Berry's pre–Coon Supper party (the local Methodist minister, Preacher Chuck, was good enough to bring me along, so I'm already half full of broiled wild mallard duck breasts with jalapeño peppers, cream cheese, and bacon, upon which I went to town). The seats are preassigned; once inside, everyone sits and eats without ceremony.

The only guy who ever suggests to me that raccoon tastes like anything else is emcee and self-described "Cajun coon-ass" Phil English. Raccoon, Phil says, tastes like eagle, which I'm almost sure he's kidding about (for the record, an early expedition of the *Mayflower* passengers said that eagle was "hardly to be discerned from mutton"). Other than Phil, everyone just gives me a kind of sideways glance and says, "Tastes like *coon*," or "Sure as hell not like chicken." The women in particular are likely to announce, unprompted, that they've never tried it and never will. I sit and pick a leg out of a bucket.

To be honest, after the brining, boiling, smoking, and saucing, it's tough to get at the raccoon's real flavor. Much as I hate to admit it, the first thing that comes to mind is chicken. Not chicken breast, the dreaded, flavorless, protein-patty white meat—they've cooked the raccoon a lot, but they could have stewed it since September and not ended up with that. What it tastes like is an elusively gamy version of the super-dark and moist meat alongside a chicken's spine. It has the texture of pot roast (or, I suppose, mutton), but bland pot roast, without any of beef fat's unctuousness; again, there's a gamier undertaste that I can't quite bring to the front. When Eric cooked muskrat at Flowerdew, you tasted nothing but muskrat, absolute and pure; here there are layers of barbecue sauce and broth before you get to the meat. In the supper's early days, the cooks would smoke it in skimmed broth from the stewpots instead of Swanson's, and I wish they still did—if you're gonna eat raccoon, you might as well taste the raccoon. "Bear I abominate," Marryat wrote, but "rackoon is pretty good." I agree enough to eat three pieces.

The Coon Supper program is much like that of any small-town athletic dinner; there are brief, four- to five-sentence testimonials to each kid, each with the same mix of joshing and flattery that brings me back to my own Connecticut high school's football dinner circa 1990. The basketball coach takes the joshing further—too far, really, ripping into some of the kids with the stated intent of getting each to "play like he can." In fact, the basketball coach is on fire, comparing himself twice to David and a minimum of three times to Custer (this, apparently, because other schools had the temerity to appear at athletic contests, as scheduled, with the intention of fielding a team). The anger makes more sense when he turns it on the assembled dignitaries, making a call to "any politician in earshot" to stand up for what's right for the school.

Miss Arkansas follows, and is just a flat-out silver-tiaraed pro, speaking the perfect ergonomic and enunciatory distance from the microphone, obviously feeling that the coach went too far as she talks about how everyone just loves these kids to death. Then she plays an aria from *Carmen* on the flute—and does so pretty well, I think, considering the echoing and hollow PA system. Soon afterward a kid receives an over-under shotgun as a sportsmanship award; it's given in honor of students killed in a traffic accident, recently enough that emotions in the room are still palpably raw. Then Governor Mike Beebe stands, pledging to fight for Gillett, but I don't really totally believe him. The fire-spitting attorney general follows, endorsing the individual right to bear arms and the notion that the presidential oath of office should include "so help me God," getting by far the loudest applause of the night.

Back in 2005 or 2006, there was an Internet campaign to stop the supper. You can still see one of the petitions at thepetitionsite.com, and the comments there make for interesting reading; one woman claims that raccoons are smarter than her college-honor-student daughter, several assume that the raccoons are raised in tiny cages, and a good

portion—maybe one in ten—are actually in favor of the supper's continuing as an annual tradition. Unsurprisingly, the people in Gillett are
dismissive or scornful of the protesters, usually taking it for granted
that they drew up their plans over a mighty platter of T-bone steaks.
John Cover says that "you probably couldn't find a person in this
community that thinks of it as an event harmful to animals," while
emcee Phil English goes further: "If you're a Christian, you have to
think of these things as put here for sustenance. When I drive along the
levy and I see a coon there, skinny, got the mange, I ask, are we doing
right by that animal? Any piece of land got its own carrying capacity—
you get past that, all you have is hungry animals, starving animals,
dying slow."

Well, I'm not a Christian, or not in the sense in which I think Phil
means the term, and (as Phil himself might suspect) I don't believe that
anything was put here exclusively for our sustenance. On this I stand
with Twain when he compared humanity to the paint on the Eiffel
Tower's tip.

But even if I come at it from a very different direction, I agree with
Phil's broad point. You can't separate hunting from the health of the
population being hunted, and to me it seems dogmatic and shallow and
blind to oppose all hunting, everywhere, as inherently cruel, without
considering what the actual real-world results are of *not* hunting. These
can include overpopulation and associated malnutrition—as Phil put
it, "starving animals, dying slow." Besides, if I'm going to eat meat, it
matters to me that the animal it comes from was raised as humanely
as possible. The raccoons served at the supper lived fully wild lives
until being killed; that, it seems to me, is going way beyond cage-free
chickens.

At last the supper tapers off; Phil offers a last thank-you. I grab a
few souvenir cups and follow the crowd flowing from the gym; one of
the first houses we pass boasts a spotlighted raccoon sign beside a fully
lit Christmas tree. The after party starts now (an ad in the local paper

describes the Coon Supper as the "biggest party weekend in Arkansas County"). The Hideout, the lone bar left on Main Street, will be jammed until three, people dancing to a band covering "Suspicious Minds," and "Maggie May," and "Keep Your Hands to Yourself."

It's time to go home. But I know where Gillett is.

Three

MASTERPIECE OF
THE UNIVERSE

Trout at Lake Tahoe

I N SEPTEMBER OF 1861, Twain lay facedown on the thwart of a skiff, looking farther into Lake Tahoe than he'd dreamed you could see into water. He could see rocks and trout eighty feet below, so clearly that he felt he was in flight—he and his partner, John Kinney, had immediately dubbed their boat trips "balloon voyages." But the water here was deeper than that; his vision ended in a blue at once dark and translucent. He found it strange to drift over perfect transparency and yet see nothing; he peered, trying contentedly to make out anything at all, his vision wavering only when he let his fingers trail along the surface. This was a week before he set the forest on fire.

Twain was now a lanky young man of twenty-five, who compared his own dancing to that of a kangaroo. He was far from home, and from any need for propriety in dress or manners; he wore a broken slouch hat over a mop of curly red hair, a blue woolen shirt, and rough pants stuffed into the tops of work boots still dusty from the long walk to Tahoe. He and Kinney had been told that the lake lay a mere eleven miles from their starting point in Carson City, capital of the Nevada Territory. But those miles, it turned out, were nearly vertical. "[We] toiled laboriously up a mountain about a thousand miles high and looked over," Twain later remembered. "No lake there. We descended on the other side, crossed the valley and toiled up another mountain three or four thousand miles high. . . . No lake yet. We sat down tired and perspiring, and hired a couple of Chinamen to curse those people who had beguiled us." But when they did finally crest the mountain and look down on the lake, Twain was enchanted. "As it lay there with the shadows of the mountains brilliantly photographed upon its still surface," he said, "I thought it must surely be the fairest picture the whole earth affords."

When they at last reached the lakeside, they raided three friends' cache of provisions for bacon and coffee. Then they rowed across the still water to a fine, unclaimed stand of yellow pine, its trees a hundred feet tall and as much as five feet around. On the shore they boiled coffee, fried bacon, and warmed the bread they'd brought from Carson City. "It was a delicious supper," Twain declared. "It was a delicious solitude we were in, too. Three miles away was a saw-mill and some workmen, but there were not fifteen other human beings throughout the wide circumference of the lake." This was one of the fortunate moments that Twain would experience throughout his life, a moment intensely lived, lodged in his memory by all his senses together. There was silence here, and the sight of a mountain-girdled lake; there was hope of a fortune, the smell of pines, the taste of a hot meal after a long journey.

Twain's first fine supper at Tahoe avoided the normal pitfalls of mining or trail food: the hard bread, indifferent canned beans, rancid bacon, and horrific tea substitute called slumgullion (which had "too much dish-rag, and sand, and old bacon-rind in it to deceive the intelligent traveler"). But he had yet to taste the food he'd later remember best—lake trout from the water before him, and brook trout from the hemming Sierra Nevadas. When Twain took to the water he could see the giant fish below him, drifting under a clear cushion of cold water. They were there "by the thousand," he claimed, "winging about in the emptiness, or sleeping in shoals on the bottom."

The clarity must have been doubly astonishing for Twain, who was only a few months removed from a career as a Mississippi River pilot. He'd been known as a man who could read water and judge it by its surface, who could intuit obscure depths, who had memorized a thousand miles of bends and shoals in a river that sometimes seemed equal parts soil and water. The Mississippi had been a welter of snags and shallows—here overtaking a woodland, there abandoning a prosperous riverside village and leaving it helplessly inland. Twain understood *that* water well—its dangers, its opacity.

Tahoe was different. It was a place of clarity and vision. The place enraptured him: this bright air, this clear water full of fish. He and Kinney allowed themselves to drift until nightfall. "As the great darkness closed down," he wrote, "and the stars came out and spangled the great mirror with jewels, we smoked meditatively in the solemn hush and forgot our troubles and our pains."

Troubles and pains. Before starting to read about Twain in earnest, I'd never realized how much of both he'd seen in childhood. I grew up on *Tom Sawyer*, falling completely in love with the way its genuine and imaginary adventures bled together (*Huckleberry Finn*'s opening revelation that Tom hadn't, in fact, become a successful bandit left me slightly crushed). But the truth is that the sequel's dark currents were as much a part of Twain's childhood as were Tom's fantasies. By the time Twain reached Nevada, he'd seen a slave murdered on a whim with a chunk of iron and discovered the beaten corpse of another in the Mississippi. He'd watched a third man gunned down in the street (an event later dramatized in *Huckleberry Finn* as Colonel Sherburn's shooting of Boggs). He'd spied on his own father's autopsy. He'd given matches to a drunken tramp, who later accidentally burned himself to death in a jail cell.

Worst of all had been the death of his younger brother, Henry, in the explosion of a steamboat Twain himself had left only the week before. Henry's death haunted his dreams for decades; he told the story in letters, memoirs, and at last in his *Autobiography*. Each time he told the story, Henry lived a little longer. In each telling he was more heroic; in each he came closer to survival.

Still, piloting had been a deliriously happy time for Twain. Receiving his license had been the one "permanent ambition" of his childhood, outlasting even his dreams of piracy. Now the Civil War had cut his career short; Twain himself had been a passenger on board the last commercial boat heading north from New Orleans, watching as Union cannonballs slammed through one of the smokestacks. With war overtaking the Mississippi, he'd become a valuable commodity to both North and South; conquering or defending the nation's central artery would take pilots. It was flee or be forced to fight. For a short time, he joined a small troop of irregular Confederate infantry roaming the Missouri countryside;* the group disbanded and scattered after accidentally gunning down a civilian. When his older brother, Orion, was offered the secretaryship of the Nevada Territory, the choice was clear for Sam: he ran.

Years later, in *Roughing It,* he wrote that the decision to go west was a romantic one, driven by dreams of silver mines and Indians. But the truth is that his presence in Washoe was forced and unwilling. At times what he saw as barren land made him deeply uncomfortable; soon after arriving, he wrote to his mother that "it never rains here, and the dew never falls. No flowers grow here, and no green thing gladdens the eye. The birds that fly over the land carry their provisions with them. Only the crow and the raven tarry with us."

---

*It's an enduring mystery why Twain's Confederate service never annoyed his Northern readers, while his deserting the Confederate army never alienated the South. In part it's probably because the man could charm a statue: on one occasion he blamed his desertion on the weather, and in his *Autobiography* he explained that he'd become "incapacitated by fatigue" after two weeks of persistent retreating.

Early the next year, he'd write her again: "I wish I was back there piloting up & down the river again. Verily, all is vanity and little worth—save piloting." He'd steered some eighteen great boats from St. Louis to New Orleans. He'd reveled in the languages of the river and in the markets of New Orleans—its coffee and hot rolls, its pyramids of plantains, pineapples, and figs. But all that was closed to him now. Back home his beloved river was a battlefield.

So here he was. And now, he found, he had come at last to the great good place. Below him were trout in their thousands, the difficulty of catching them only adding to his sense of a place entirely at peace with itself. Even the fish here were sated. When he looked up, the lake surface was painted in clouds; Twain floated on a liquid diamond a thousand feet thick.

This, he thought, was the masterpiece of the universe.

FRIED TROUT

Clean, wash, and dry small trout; season them with pepper and salt; roll them in dry flour, and then plunge them into enough smoking-hot fat to entirely cover them. As soon as they rise to the surface of the fat, and are light brown, take them up with a skimmer, lay them for a moment on brown paper to free them from fat, and then serve them at once.

In the country, trout are usually fried with salt pork.

—JULIET CORSON, *Practical American Cookery and Household Management*, 1886

Throughout Twain's life the simple phrase "trout dinner" was synonymous with simple enjoyment, with pleasure at once luxurious and comforting. Whether he was in Germany or stagecoaching across the

Nevada flats, when Twain wrote something to the effect that "we had a trout supper," you can be sure that whatever had happened before, he ended the day contented.

But Twain didn't include German trout on his menu, or trout from Missouri, or brook trout from back east, where mills and dams now dirtied the water and blocked once famous spawning runs. He didn't ask for trout smothered in cream sauce, stewed with mushroom catsup, or preserved in a pot sealed with clarified butter. What he wanted was lake trout from Tahoe and brook trout from the Sierra Nevada range—fish he remembered frying with bacon fat and eating on the shore.

Twain was in Tahoe before prospectors spread rainbow trout throughout the Sierras and hatcheries began introducing fish from other waterways, states, and even continents. In 1872 fishery managers would introduce eastern brook trout from Pennsylvania to the mountains; in 1889 others released lake trout into Tahoe. During the next decade, they'd seed brown trout—hatched from eggs carried in iced moss from Europe—throughout the surrounding range. But when Twain was there, cutthroat trout remained what they'd been for centuries, even millennia: the true western trout, the only trout found from the crest of the Rockies to the Sierras' eastern slope. His "lake trout, from Tahoe," and "brook trout, from Sierra Nevadas" were actually a single subspecies, the Lahontan cutthroat.

This seems like a pretty big mistake to make, but it's actually often hard to define different trout species. Many of the world's trout, in fact, aren't even trout: eastern brookies are char, and Lake Pontchartrain's famed spotted trout are weakfish. On the other hand, Europe's eleven historically recognized species of trout are all local varieties of browns. In the American West, fishermen distinguished among Sierra trout, Tahoe lake trout, Tahoe silver trout, Rocky Mountain trout, and so on—all one species, though they sometimes looked as distinct as oysters and mussels. Twain's brook trout were mottled golden and brown—just right for life in a sunny stream—while those in Tahoe's deeper waters had the silver-and-gray coloration of lake dwellers. It wasn't until 1884 that a writer for *American Angler* named all cutthroat for the red stripe below the jaw.

Whatever he called them, the trout that Twain ate at Tahoe had been in the lake only minutes before hitting the frying pan. Years later he wrote about the taste of such fresh fish when the boys hide out on Jackson's Island in *Tom Sawyer:* "They fried the fish with the bacon and were astonished; for no fish had ever seemed so delicious before. They did not know that the quicker a fresh water fish is on the fire after he is caught the better he is; and they reflected little upon what a sauce open air sleeping, open air exercise, bathing, and a large ingredient of hunger makes, too." That last bit sounds like a pretty fair description of life at Tahoe, right down to cooking with bacon fat, which Twain and Kinney had a good supply of after raiding their friends' cache.

The fish themselves were remarkable, even astonishing. You might confuse the local varieties of Lahontan cutthroat, but you'd never mistake one for a comparatively puny eastern fish: comparing a brook trout to a Lahontan is like comparing a fish stick to a barracuda. More than forty years earlier, Thomas De Voe had reported that brook trout sold in New York ranged from half a pound to four pounds, and he made special mention of one "mammoth" fish, "one of the largest brook trout perhaps ever known in this country," which weighed in at seven pounds two ounces. Cutthroats, by contrast, were simply colossal—the record catch in Tahoe, in 1911, weighed better than thirty-one pounds. Twain joked about the difficulty of catching trout in the lake, saying that they averaged less than a fish a week—but even if that's true, that one might have fed them until their next take. If he'd seen one of Tahoe's larger specimens, only his experience with Mississippi River catfish (he called a six-foot, 250-pounder a "roaring demon") might have muted his amazement.

Good fish come from good water—and even in 1861 good water wasn't a given in America, especially close to the cities. In 1734 the nation's first fishing regulation had restricted fishers working Manhattan's Collect Pond (today a very dry park, not far from Chinatown) to

hooks and lines. Now, many fish were failing in New York City's pol-
luted water, which also imparted an awful, muddy taste; a friend of De
Voe's who caught eels in the Hudson afterward "supposed the gas-
works or refuse from that place cast into the river had affected them, as
he found the taste much as the gas-tar smelled."

Tahoe's water wasn't just clear compared to the Mississippi or the
Hudson; it was one of the world's most transparent large bodies of
water. Even today, with visibility diminished by more than twenty feet
from what it was in Twain's day, it's a challenge to stay oriented while
scuba diving. Without floating sediment to orient you, you feel like
you're hovering perfectly still as you sink down, and down, and finally
bounce off a boulder. That clarity may be one reason Twain had such
a hard time catching the trout—he thought it was an advantage to see
the trout but didn't consider that they could also see him.

Light bends when it enters water; this means that outside a given
ring—known as Snell's window—a floating object can't be seen from
below. Beyond Snell's window, which gets wider and wider the deeper
the viewer sinks, the surface looks more like a mirror. But the cutthroats
in Tahoe were very deep indeed and could have seen Twain's boat row-
ing around for a good long while before it came to rest straight overhead
(which was, of course, exactly the easiest place to be seen). What's
more, light slows in water, so Twain looked much closer to the trout
than they did to him. Finally, the eyes of trout continue to grow along
with their overall body size, and larger eyes mean more cones (and thus
sharper vision). Twain knew that trout might detect his line, but he
didn't realize that the bigger fish could probably have counted the hairs
on his knuckles. He just wasn't a wily angler.

The trout in Tahoe lived in water famous for clarity and purity and
were fresh as any fish could be; they probably tasted especially delicious
considering that a lot of frontier food was awful. Twain later enjoyed
the beer, cheese, and mustard of Virginia City, whose ten thousand
tents, dugouts, cabins, and frame houses (he described them as "'pa-

pered' inside with flour-sacks sewed together" and decorated with engravings from *Harper's*) were serviced by fifteen restaurants and fifty-one saloons. He at least respected the spartan cooking of the prospectors, whom he described as "young men who made their own bacon and beans." He'd relished a ham-and-egg breakfast on board a stagecoach. But these were exceptions.

Most food on the trails west was dried, burned, or borderline rotten; butter could take nearly a year to reach Washoe or California. It was also monotonous; 1870s Dakota settler Annie Tallent remembered trail menus of "for breakfast, hot biscuit, fried bacon, and black coffee; for dinner, cold biscuit, cold baked beans, and black coffee; for supper, black coffee, hot biscuit, and baked beans warmed over." Sometimes canned goods were an option (the two big early booms in the canning industry came with the Gold Rush and the Civil War), or even a necessity—Twain might as well have crossed an ocean to reach Washoe from Missouri, jolting for over a month across prairie and uncertain desert. But useful as they could be on long journeys, the cans usually held gray meat or limp, pale vegetables. Too often the contents had spoiled; until 1895, canners believed that it was the lack of air that sterilized the cans, and sometimes they failed to boil them long enough to kill off bacteria.

Twain did get used to trail food, once describing fried bacon, bread, molasses, and black coffee as part of "earthly luxury." But most meals he remembered were those that provided a break from what were basically shipboard provisions—long-lasting, easily carried stuff. Put fried lake trout—wonderful in its own right—beside that spread of dried, rotten, or indifferently packed food and it's easy to see why Twain would remember it decades later. And though the taste of perfectly fresh fish had a lot to do with Twain's love for it, I think it also had a lot to do with the place and the heady memory of those roving, exploratory days when he was on the verge of discovering his voice—discovering, in a real sense, just who he'd be for the rest of his life.

Twain did make one rare aesthetic misstep at the lake; he preferred the name "Lake Bigler" to Tahoe, which was a corruption of the Washoe Indian word for "water in a high place."* In the September 4, 1862, *Virginia City Territorial Enterprise* (he often wrote for the paper under the wince-inducing, double-entendre pen name "Josh") Twain wrote that though "of course Indian names are more fitting than any others for our beautiful lakes and rivers, which knew their race ages ago, perhaps, in the morning of creation," he wanted nothing "so repulsive to the ear as 'Tahoe' for the beautiful relic of fairy-land forgotten and left asleep in the snowy Sierras when the little elves fled from their ancient haunts and quitted the earth."

Why "Bigler" should beat out "Tahoe" as the name of a beautiful relic of forgotten fairyland is, to put it gently, unclear. The only upside to "Bigler" is that, unlike "Tahoe," it can't easily be slapped on a Chevy (though admittedly that's a pretty serious upside). But whatever he called it, Twain's love for the lake was pure and absolute. I imagine him cresting that last, "three thousand mile high" mountain, gasping and exhausted, the blue basin suddenly visible below; I imagine his breath catching in his throat. Twain wrote about Tahoe so lovingly that it's difficult to pick out any one passage—it even feels like slighting him to try. Still, there is this:

> If there is any life that is happier than the life we led on our tim-
> ber ranch for the next two or three weeks, it must be a sort of life
> which I have not read of in books or experienced in person. We
> did not see a human being but ourselves during this time, or hear
> any sounds but those that were made by the wind and the waves,
> the sighing of the pines, and now and then the far-off thunder of

*The original name had been given in honor of former California governor (and Confederate sympathizer) John Bigler; after the Civil War broke out, Union-friendly Washoe adopted the name Tahoe (weirdly, no one got around to changing the name officially for the better part of a century; the lake known on maps as Tahoe was officially Lake Bigler until 1945). We can be grateful at least that Twain didn't argue for the other early alternative, Lake Bonpland.

an avalanche. The forest about us was dense and cool, the sky above us was cloudless and brilliant with sunshine, the broad lake before us was glassy and clear, or rippled and breezy, or black and storm-tossed, according to Nature's mood; and its circling border of mountain domes, clothed with forests, scarred with land-slides, cloven by cañons and valleys, and helmeted by glittering snow, fitly framed and finished the noble picture. The view was always fascinating, bewitching, entrancing. The eye was never tired of gazing, night or day, in calm or storm; it suffered but one grief, and that was that it could not look always, but must close sometimes in sleep.

And this:

While smoking the pipe of peace after breakfast we watched the sentinel peaks put on the glory of the sun, and followed the con-quering light as it swept down among the shadows, and set the captive crags and forests free. We watched the tinted pictures grow and brighten upon the water till every little detail of forest, preci-pice and pinnacle was wrought in and finished, and the miracle of the enchanter complete.

And also this, years later, while standing before the Sea of Galilee:

When we come to speak of beauty, [the sea] is no more to be com-pared to Tahoe than a meridian of longitude is to a rainbow. The dim waters of this pool cannot suggest the limpid brilliancy of Tahoe; . . . when the still surface is belted like a rainbow with broad bars of blue and green and white; . . . when [a man's] boat drifts shoreward to the white water, and he lolls over the gunwale and gazes by the hour down through the crystal depths and notes the colors of the pebbles and reviews the finny armies gliding in procession a hundred feet below. . . . The tranquil interest that was born with the morning deepens and deepens, by sure degrees, till it culminates at last in resistless fascination!

And then dinner. *This* is why Twain loved Tahoe trout; this is why I take the menu seriously. On one level the menu is a joke, sure—it certainly began that way. But these things, these places, mattered to Twain. He wasn't a conservationist in the classic sense—he'd come to the lake, after all, with the intention of cutting down as many trees as he could. But his love of place is still moving; it can still inspire. His memory of the lake helped to mark out his life; it returned him to life when he was a young man just fled from war, trailing fingers in cold water.

In his 1825 *Physiology of Taste,* the great gastronome Jean Anthelme Brillat-Savarin described the experience of a man eating a peach. First he "is agreeably struck by the perfume which it exhales; he puts a piece of it into his mouth, and enjoys a sensation of tart freshness," then swallows and experiences the full aroma. But "it is not until it has been swallowed that the man, considering what he has just experienced, will say to himself, 'Now there is something really delicious!'" Memory, for Brillat-Savarin, was not simply the recollection of a taste; memory was *part* of taste, the means to understanding and holding the fullness of a flavor.

Surely it's true that memory is what makes taste something more than a momentary sensation. Memory is how a flavor becomes part of our lives. Remembering a taste, a smell—even the sound of cooking, of fresh fish sizzling in bacon fat—can summon vanished landscapes, aspirations, hopes. It can remind you of who you were, and help you see your present life more clearly.

Years later, in *A Tramp Abroad,* Twain would rant about seeing a modern house in the Alps, a "prim, hideous, straight-up-and-down thing, . . . so stiff, and formal, and ugly and forbidding, and so deaf and dumb to the poetry of its surroundings, that it suggests an undertaker at a picnic, a corpse at a wedding, a Puritan in Paradise." I wish we had him to comment on Tahoe's casinos, which are, objectively, some of the worst places in the world and which brag on billboards about how completely their food doesn't belong, their lakeshore restaurants serving Maine lobster and Chilean sea bass and other seafood from half a world away. It's true that some of the world's best chefs have set up shop in Las Vegas casinos (even the Vegas egg cooks are legendary, to the point that scientists have done studies on their preternatural timing and control). I just really hate casinos—for me, eating food created by Mario Batali within a stone's throw of the slots would be like spotting a rainbow in the Port Authority men's room. And it's worse when you're in a place like the Tahoe lakeshore, which the casinos just utterly deform.

When Twain knew Tahoe, nothing was out of place, nothing other than exactly as it should be. And Tahoe trout, cooked over a campfire, was not something borne on sweltering ships, hauled by stagecoach, or packed over mountains. Trout belonged.

CREAM TROUT

Having prepared the trout very nicely, and cut off the heads and tails, put the fish into boiling water that has been slightly salted, and simmer them for five minutes. Then take them out, and lay them to drain. Put them into a stew-pan, and season them well with powdered mace, nutmeg, and a little cayenne, all mixed together. Put in as much rich cream as will cover the fish, adding some bits of the fresh yellow rind of a small lemon. Keep the pan covered, and let the fish stew for about ten minutes after it has begun to simmer. Then dish the fish, and keep them hot till you have finished the sauce. Mix, very smoothly, a small tea-spoonful of arrow-root with a little milk, and stir it into the cream. Then add the juice of the lemon. Pour the sauce over the fish, and then send them to table.

—ELIZA LESLIE, *The Lady's Receipt-Book,* 1847

I'd like to pause, briefly, to praise ice water. Twain was devoted to the stuff. The very last item on his feast menu was "ice-water—not prepared in the ineffectual goblet, but in the sincere and capable refrigerator." He conceded that the European term, "*iced* water," was at least more accurate than the American, which described water made from melted ice. Nevertheless, he said, most European water was "flat and insipid beyond the power of words to describe," and that most hotels "merely give you a tumbler of ice to soak your water in, and that only modifies its hotness, doesn't make it cold. Water can only be made cold enough for summer comfort by being prepared in a refrigerator or a closed ice-pitcher." So when, on a blazing afternoon, he came to a pool of the "pure and limpid ice-water" flowing from a glacier, he stretched himself out, dipped his face in, and "drank till [his] teeth ached." He scoffed at the European notion that ice water hurt digestion. "How do they know? They never drink any."

Years later he told an audience, "I think that there is but a single specialty with us, only one thing that can be called by the wide name 'American.' That is the national devotion to ice-water. All Germans drink beer, but the British nation drinks beer, too; so neither of those peoples is the beer-drinking nation. I suppose we do stand alone in having a drink that nobody likes but ourselves." Americans, devotees of the refrigerator and the "cold ice-pitcher," were also devotees of ice. In Massachusetts, or even Virginia, ice cut from frozen winter ponds could be packed in sawdust and stored in icehouses, to be brought out in the hottest days of August. But New Orleans and Atlanta had to look farther away; ice was probably never more prized than during a Southern summer's swelter.

The keys, as with so much else, were the steamships and railroads, which carried ice to cool rooms, frost drinks—and, of course, to preserve and ship food. By 1842 railroads were experimenting with using ice-filled cars to ship fish. Exactly twenty-five years later, one J. B. Sutherland received a patent for a refrigerated train car; cold air sank from huge overhead ice blocks, driving out warm air and cooling the contents (the same basic idea had been used in home refrigerators since the 1820s). Ice let prairie chickens reach New York in frozen barrels and oysters reach most everywhere. It brought fresh milk to cities from the countryside—replacing that from urban "swill dairies" where cows had been fed on whiskey mash—and enabled large-scale brewing of beer. Maybe the biggest changes were to beef; after Gustavus Swift built a line of icehouses to supply refrigerated cars, beef butchered and packed at the Chicago stockyards replaced the bruised, battered meat from live cattle that had endured the long trip from the Midwest. By 1885 Swift was shipping some 292 million pounds of beef along the Grand Trunk Railroad.

Until the advent of large-scale ice factories, all this ice came from winter or the mountains, and one of the first things the Virginia & Truckee Railroad shipped after its 1872 completion was "Sierra ice." Cut from the Sierras' ponds and lakes and loaded into cars just north of Tahoe, much of the ice was used in the Washoe mines, lowered to the bottoms of shafts that could otherwise reach 140 degrees. But much more of it cooled refrigerated train cars, allowing the shipment of trout, game, and—most important—produce back east. Sierra ice helped to shape California; without it the state's Central Valley might not have become a dominant source for lettuce and other vegetables until decades later than it did.

Much of the ice was for shipping food; more ended in champagne buckets from Chicago to New Orleans (ice, in Louisiana, was as much a long-distance product as a California orange). But I absolutely love the fact that the only drink Twain lists on his menu is ice water, America's "single specialty." Thinking of him drinking until sated, then drinking for sheer pleasure until his throat went numb, makes me feel nostalgic—weirdly nostalgic, considering it's for something a century before I was born. It's just nice to remember that sometimes ice water, on a hot day, is as good a drink as there is.

HOW TO MIX ABSINTHE IN EVERY STYLE

Plain absinthe: half a sherry glass of absinthe; plenty of fine ice, with about two wineglassfuls of water. Put in the water, drop by drop, on top of absinthe and ice; stir well, but slowly. It takes time to make it good.

—LAFCADIO HEARN, *La Cuisine Creole*, 1885

In the decades after Twain left Tahoe dams sealed off mountain spawning runs, and surrounding rivers and lakes went murky from mining and logging runoff; in the 1920s pathogens from newly introduced species of trout caused huge die-offs. The last Lahontan cutthroats disappeared from the lake by 1940, and they aren't likely to return anytime soon; in 2003, the UC Davis Tahoe Research Group said it would be more effective to concentrate restoration efforts on lakes with less human impact. Today Lahontan cutthroats are nearly gone from the waters that once froze into clear Sierra ice.

But north of Carson City, across sixty miles of what Twain believed to be a desert of only the "purest, . . . most unadulterated, and uncompromising *sand*," lay Pyramid Lake, a body of water nearly as large as Tahoe. And Pyramid Lake's *tomoo agai*—the Paiute name for the Lahontan cutthroat's winter run—were the biggest trout in the world, bigger even than Tahoe's titans. Before the Truckee River was straightened, its flow dammed, trout from Pyramid followed it through a hundred miles of desert and mountain, climbing thousands of feet until they came at last to Tahoe and its inlet tributaries. In Twain's day some of the trout in Tahoe came there only to spawn; some hatchlings remained in the surrounding streams only long enough to attain a safe size before returning to Pyramid. Before the dams, the lakes were linked. If I want to find out what's happened to Lahontan cutthroat trout in the last hundred years, the Paiute hatcheries at Pyramid Lake are a good place to start.

Driving north from Reno, you come on Pyramid Lake all at once—you've been hauling through the desert, leaving behind the casinos and tract homes as you pass the dust cloud of the Bureau of Land Management's mustang-adoption corrals. Then there's only stony hills and sagebrush, the occasional ranch house or American-flag-draped fence, thirty miles of desert until you cross the final ridge, and the lake is there: sandbound, turquoise in late afternoon. It's wide, bright, and almost painfully inviting.

It's also hugely and invisibly diminished; the lake covers more than five hundred square miles, held entirely within the Pyramid Lake Paiute Reservation, but that's a last spare remnant of the water that once spread over most of northern Nevada. Twelve thousand years ago, Lake Lahontan was as big as Lake Erie; Pyramid lies in its ancient low point. The high desert here once lay under nine hundred feet of water.

Today, as Twain wrote to his mother, this is dry, dry country. The Sierras create a dramatic rain shadow, stealing clouds that approach from the west; the summit of Wheeler Peak might get fifty inches of rain annually, the Great Basin only five. Living here seems, to the unfamiliar eye, like an impossible challenge. But twelve thousand years ago, the Paiute's genius forerunners realized just how much the seemingly bare hills and alkali flats actually held.

"There's this misperception, 'Oh, those poor Indians, how did they survive?'" says Paiute Cultural Resource Manager Ben Aleck. Ben's been dealing with such attitudes for a long time, and as he talks about them, he's both patient and audibly weary. "Some places that's true, sure, where northern hunters were moved to bad land and told to farm. You know—cow-and-plow. But this is our historic land. We know how to live here, and how to keep the land and water healthy, too." Part of what that meant was respecting the land's natural contours, the water's natural course. "The river used to meander, and you'd have cottonwood groves along the bends, cooling the water. The fish needed that. But the Army Corps of Engineers came in here and straightened it all out."

Twain, sad to say, might have shared the corps's misunderstanding of the Truckee—he described another desert river, the Carson, as "so villainously rapid and crooked, that it looks like it had wandered into the country without intending it, and had run about in a bewildered way and got lost in its hurry to get out again before some thirsty man came along and drank it up." The Nevada desert is one landscape he doesn't seem to have had an eye for. Now, Ben says, putting the Truckee's curves back could be a $12 million project. "You've got the corps coming back in, talking to tribal people, saying, 'What did the river look like, what plants were here, where were the bends?' It's been a hundred years, but that information's been passed on."

Though most visiting anglers come to Pyramid Lake after cutthroat trout, historically the most important fish for the Paiute has been the giant suckerfish called the cui-ui. "There's a piece of boneless fillet in there from the back of the head to the dorsal fins," Ben tells me, holding his fingers to show a chunk the size of a cereal bowl. "*This* big. Tastes real good, too. That's what our band is named for—we're the Kuyui Dokado, or 'Cui-Ui Eaters.' In the old days, when the river was running free, the mouth of the river would just run black at spawning time." There's no fishing for cui-ui anymore, but the fish hasn't vanished entirely from the local diet—every year researchers catch fish, remove the opercular bone, and pass the remainder on to the band membership. The people called the Cui-Ui Eaters are, once again, the only people who eat cui-ui.

Of course the cutthroats were always important as well. "There'd have been fish out there twenty, thirty pounds, even more than that," Ben says. "Just one would feed a lot of people. And this was a good, healthy lake—we still consider it healthy, but those cottonwood groves along the river and the streams running to it would have supported a lot more game back then. We still have people go out for deer, antelope . . . we've got rabbits, ducks, geese. Everything the lake will support has been here for thousands of years." There were buckberries, desert parsley, bitterroot, and pine nuts—pine nuts most of all. Every year some Pyramid Lake Paiute still go and gather the nuts; it's become a challenge, with much of the good mountain land now controlled by uncooperative private landowners, but they can still gather with one of the other Paiute bands or with the Western Shoshone.

Long before there were people along its now shrunken shoreline, Lake Lahontan was the incubator of the Lahontan cutthroats. Their progenitors originated along the Pacific coast, making their way up the Columbia River before heading south via a network of now mostly vanished lakes. Sixty-thousand-year-old fossils of the old fish have been found in what's now a dangerously dry, alkaline basin. Among the region's lakes, only Pyramid still has the old array of ecological relationships—including the only large predator, the cutthroat trout, which here sometimes approached the size of oceangoing salmon (the trout's great size helped them feed on the tui-chub, a still-abundant fifteen-inch fish).

I sleep in a pup tent on the shore of Pyramid (the Paiute's lone camping regulation, wonderfully, is to keep twenty-five feet back from the waterline; Ben made it clear that they don't believe in fencing off the lake). As the sun sets, the tufa formations go red, deep purple, and finally gray; at the lake's far edge, close to the namesake tufa pyramid, something shimmers on the water like heat from off the desert. It takes

binoculars to see that the shimmer is pelicans—white pelicans by the
hundreds or thousands, flown from as far away as Mexico. There's far
more life in this desert than my unpracticed eye can make out; in this
I'm like Twain, who saw little in the sand of Washoe but sagebrush,
which he said smelled like a compromise between magnolia and polecat. As the pelicans fade into the evening, the stars emerge, gleaming,
filling the Big Dipper's cup. I go to sleep hugely satisfied after a dinner
of beef jerky and almonds and whiskey, feeling peaceful and surprisingly at home until a midnight bathroom break, when the scuffle of an
approaching tumbleweed scares me nearly into an early grave.

In the morning I'm creakingly sore, and I make cowboy coffee,
throwing a handful of grounds directly into boiling water. I didn't use
water from the lake; Twain called coffee made from alkaline water
(the lake is about a sixth as salty as the sea) "the meanest compound
man has yet devised." Even with decent water, the coffee is bitter
enough that I understand why sugar was a standard provision in wagon
trains.

Interestingly, though, the alkaline water may be why many people
thought that Pyramid Lake cutthroats were among the best eating fish.
In 1844 a group of Paiute brought a cutthroat to John C. Frémont, the
first white explorer to see the lake. Having "had the inexpressible sat-
isfaction to find [that it] was a salmon-trout," Frémont judged the flavor of the trout "excellent—superior, in fact, to that of any other fish
I have ever known" (seeing his delight, the Paiute brought more cutthroats up to four feet long, fully stocking the camp). Frémont may have
been noticing the effects of Pyramid's alkaline water; though it makes
terrible coffee, it also makes fish taste particularly rich. The dire desert
that Twain detested had flavors of its own.

Soon I'm heading along the shore toward Sutcliffe, whose twelve
hundred people make up about half the reservation's population. The
first step in maintaining Pyramid's Lahontan cutthroats takes place
at the town's Lake Operations, a few nondescript tan buildings and

garages surrounded by round, fifteen-foot-wide tanks. When I arrive, Lake Operations Supervisor Robert Eagle is leaning easily against an outside wall, watching what looks like a culverted stream flow past the building and down to the lake. The stream, it turns out, is an artificial channel, dry unless they pump in water; doing so in the spring attracts trout desperate to head upstream. Now dozens of huge dark fish drift easily in submerged cages, all facing against the flow.

"There's nothing smaller than seventeen inches in there," Robert says. "Some go seven, eight, ten pounds—we take them all trying to spawn." Historically, of course, most fish would have preferred the Truckee, both because of size and because it enters Pyramid from the east; cutthroats still have a genetic memory of the ocean and instinctively try to head in the direction their spawning ancestors followed from the Pacific. But these fish were released here soon after hatching, and this is their natural point of return.

Robert and the workers have already separated out fifty males and fifty females; the latter are ripe, ready to shed their eggs. They're big fish, drifting gigantic and gentle in the holding tanks. This many females will produce about a hundred fifty thousand eggs, which is all the hatchery's trays and tanks can handle until the renovations on the Numana hatchery are complete. "But that's nothing against what we'd have had before the whole lake basically got fished out," Robert says. "The original cutthroat would head up the Truckee up to the vista, way up in the mountain area into the cold water from the spring snowmelt, and there were so many that they'd say the river would turn black. But at the time there was a commercial fishery right alongside the people fishing for sport—they were taking them left and right, and there was no program to replenish it."

At its peak the fishery at Pyramid Lake was taking out up to two hundred thousand pounds of trout a year with traps and gill nets, the equivalent of twenty thousand ten-pound fish. And that's only the fish that were shipped by Wells Fargo—the numbers don't include any sold locally or caught for personal use. The combination of Sierra ice and the speed of the Virginia & Truckee Railroad meant that trout could be eaten as far away as Chicago. Such shipments were becoming a national habit; in the decades after the Civil War, ice and railroads let Americans get used to eating fish caught hundreds of miles away (on the day New York's Fulton Fish Market first opened in 1882, it offered trout from Vermont, Quebec, and Long Island, along with hatchery-raised brook trout, rainbows, two kinds of bass, and landlocked salmon). "Fresh" and "local" were no longer synonymous.

"There used to be a railroad right up there—they were taking the trout out through Fernley, sending them all over the place," Robert says, "and with the agricultural dams there was no way for them to recover. It got to the point that there was no fishery at all."

When Robert said there was no program to replenish the trout, he was actually understating how bad things got—in fact, the programs that *were* in place couldn't have done more damage to the local cut-throat if they'd been designed to. The worst of these was the Derby Dam. The Derby was the Bureau of Reclamation's very first project (literally Specification Number 1, Drawing Number 1), and when completed as part of the 1905 Newlands Project it instantly sealed off the trout's historic spawning channels. The day the dam closed for the first time, hundreds of trout were left flopping in what little water remained downstream; onlookers rushed into the channel and clubbed them to take home. Meanwhile the agricultural diversions—which removed some quarter million acre-feet of water a year from the river, mostly to grow cantaloupes on land better suited for growing native pasture and other low-value crops—promptly dropped the level of Pyramid Lake some eighty feet. Though the Nevada Fish Commissioners complained loudly about the lack of adequate fish ladders, Frederick Newell, the bureau's first commissioner, said outright that "fish have no rights in water law," with Senator Newlands, the project's namesake, adding that "Pyramid Lake exists solely to satisfy the thirsting sun."

That attitude, Ben said, is still a problem. "People say, 'Do you want water for people in Reno, or a suckerfish in Pyramid Lake?' It's all about development. They don't realize that when you start chipping away bits and pieces of the ecosystem, you get problems in the food chain. We've done all right in the court system—we were here first, our water claims have priority. But it's hard to make people, politicians, understand— water is sacred. It's for *all* life. Fish and Game, Reclamation . . . they all tend to separate it out. But if the tiniest creature—the frog, the fish— gets in trouble, the problems just head right up the line."

The last spawning run of the original Pyramid cutthroat strain was in 1938. Tahoe's last run was the same year; though Tahoe's commercial fishery had been banned in 1917, Lahontan cutthroats had been declining since the 1880s. Before that time some seventy thousand pounds of fish were caught annually for long-distance sale, some with traps and nets that captured entire spawning runs. By the time twenty-two thousand pounds were shipped in 1904, the population was nearing collapse— when disease struck in force twenty years later, it was too much for the diminished numbers to handle. Tahoe's cutthroats have never returned; most of Pyramid's are a strain collected in Summit Lake in the seventies, maintained today only by the Paiute's rigorous stocking program.

In the hatchery's main room, fifteen men and women gather around a long wooden table with three round holes down its centerline. The flopping, stranded fish below Derby Dam were twenty or even thirty pounds, numbers I understood only intellectually; it's when Steve Samson picks out a female trout, handing her through the window to Kia Blindman, that I realize how big even an eight-pounder is. She's colored a dark olive, shining as though glazed, and like any fish straight from the water she looks vivid—in shockingly sharp focus. She's big enough that Kia has to hug her against his rubber-aproned chest: this is a serious fish, over two feet long. The world hook-and-line record for trout is for a forty-three-pound Lahontan cutthroat caught here by Paiute John Skimmerhorn in 1925; there were unconfirmed reports, back in 1912, of a fish weighing in at a colossal sixty-two. Elizabeth Thomas, who works just up the hill with the cui-ui at the Dunn Hatchery, says that "a ten-pounder'll kick us around pretty good," and that's clearly true. A *sixty-two*-pounder? Bring a harpoon.

Big as the trout at the hatchery today are, they don't approach the size of the old ones. A lot of what made Pyramid Lake Lahontan cutthroat special was completely local, below subspecies level; the bigger the predatory lake dwellers got, the better they were at hunting tui-chub. The prospectors and settlers who seemingly called the trout of every mountain by a different name actually had a point; you can't preserve what's beautiful and unique about a species by maintaining it in one place. The challenge, and the hard work, comes in seeing the differences *within* a species, to see that even what seems like a single kind of fish can mold itself to the world—and the world to it—in a hundred different ways. Today there are Lahontan cutthroat trout *in* Pyramid Lake, but the largest trout in recorded history were the Lahontan cutthroat trout *of* Pyramid Lake. Those are gone.

Or so everyone thought. At some point (no one knows when) somebody (no one knows who) carried Lahontan cutthroat trout to Pilot Peak in Utah, depositing them in Morrison Creek. Genetically identical to the original Pyramid Lahontan cutthroats, the trout are now raised at the Fish and Wildlife Service's National Lahontan Fish Hatchery; in 2004 over thirteen thousand fish were returned to Pyramid Lake, each with a coded tag that allows them to be separated from the Summit Lake stock during spawning. Lisa Heki, the project leader, is optimistic about the fish's prospects with the right combination of stocking and dam breaches; she's said that "twenty years down the road, we could have twenty- to thirty-pound cutthroat trout running the river right through downtown Reno." Others—Robert is one—are less hopeful, feeling that the river's obstructions and degraded water quality won't allow that kind of comeback. Whatever happens, it's a tremendous irony that the kind of haphazard transfer of species that helped doom the original trout of Pyramid and Tahoe has made their return possible.

Small stainless-steel bowls are set in the holes along the table. Kia holds his trout firmly with one arm and centers her over a bowl. With the other hand, he takes a sturdy grip just behind and below the pectoral fins, drawing steadily toward the tail; at once a continuous stream of what looks like orange liquid shoots out and into the bowl. When it tapers off, the bowl is a third full of beautiful, brightly colored eggs the size of tapioca. Kia tosses the trout—out of the water for less than a minute, but now looking concave and insulted and squished— into a hole in the wall, where she slips down a slick pipe and back into the lake.

I'm bemused. They just *squeeze* the fish? Apparently they do. Apparently this isn't an unusual talent on Kia's part, like being able to flip flapjacks in midair or write with his toes—another man is already squeezing a second fish over the same bowl. This time the fish is a male, dripping sperm onto the orange eggs. Michelle Moore picks up the bowl, unceremoniously mixing the contents with her fingers as she disappears into the next room. Soon there's a respectable assembly line going: fish wrestled from the water, fish squeezed over the bowls, bowls mixed and moved to the next room as soon as they're ready.

The process, the only reason there are any trout in the lake at all, seems amazingly straightforward and low-tech—enough so that I ask Kia for permission to help. The idea is to mix the eggs with your bare fingers, then ladle in some numbingly cold water from the hatchery farther up the hill. You mix this cold biological soup for exactly one minute, which seems too short until you consider that under natural conditions this mixing would all be taking place in nearly open, flowing water, with only a small depression, called a redd, to keep the eggs from washing away. After the eggs are fertilized, they need to be cleaned of any worms or mud or lake weed, so you ladle in several changes of water, swirling the eggs as though rinsing starch from white rice; the water gets dumped out through the grated floor. "The dud eggs are the most important to get out," Kia says. "Those white ones—they'll rot and kind of cottonball, spread fungus all over the rest of the eggs and smother them." But this part of the process is simple and also, when I think about it, amazing: I'm helping to *grow fish*.

In 1864 market fisherman Seth Green, frustrated with trying to fill orders for wild fish hurt by logging and overfishing, opened his first hatchery in Caledonia, New York. Within two decades the U.S. Fish Commission was hatching salmon in California and shad in New England; it brought in European brown trout to replace the failing eastern brookies. Though hatcheries sometimes helped to supplement healthy fisheries, they were more often responding to a collapse, as the Paiute hatcheries did. Today the Pyramid Lake cutthroat trout are entirely dependent on the descendants of people who once largely depended on them.

More ironically, some of the rivers the trout once spawned in are now being slowly, laboriously twisted back into their proper knots by the same army corps that once carved them sterile and straight. Twain mocked the twisting desert rivers, but their cottonwood-shaded bends sheltered the redds of the trout he loved. Though their beauty wasn't as obvious to him as Tahoe's, or that of the Sierra mountains, all were bound together—all helped make the others what they were.

TROUT PIE

Clean, wash, and scale them, lard them with pieces of a silver eel rolled up in spice and sweet herbs, with bay leaves powdered; lay on and between them the bottoms of sliced artichokes, mushrooms, oysters, capers, and sliced lemon; lay on butter, and close the pie.

—SUSANNAH CARTER, *The Frugal Housewife,* 1803

Tahoe's peace touched Twain. But it wasn't like him to stay calm and quiet for long; his Tahoe idyll ended when he set the mountain on fire. He'd set a blaze to burn down into coals for supper, heading down to the skiff for a frying pan. But a shout from Kinney interrupted him—when he looked back, the fire "was galloping all over the premises."

The forests around Tahoe needed fire almost as much as the great prairies did. Fifteen years before Twain came to Tahoe, a member of the Mormon Battalion descending along the Carson River said that "the mountains seem to be all on fire and the valley full of smoke. . . . At night we could see as it were a hundred fires in the California mountains made no doubt by Indians." Washoe Indians would often set fires intentionally, helping to clear out undergrowth and encourage the growth of mule's ears, a sort of sunflower the Native Americans harvested for seeds. They burned most often during spring's first thaws, when the remaining snows created natural firebreaks. "By this means," the admiring traveler and poet Joaquin Miller wrote in 1887, "the Indians always kept their forest open, pure and fruitful, and conflagrations were unknown." Other fires could have been set by lightning (Forest Service land in California can receive seventeen hundred strikes per year).

Whether people or lightning had caused the earlier blazes, Twain's fire wasn't nearly as intense as it would be today, when a policy of stopping all burns as quickly as possible has left behind a century's worth of dry, tangled growth. Still, the burn was spectacular and terrifying. Now the fishing boat became a means of escape, as the young men pulled offshore and away from the blaze. In *Roughing It,* Twain recalled that

> Within half an hour all before us was a tossing, blinding tempest of flame! It went surging up the adjacent ridges—surmounted them and disappeared in the cañons beyond—burst into view upon higher and farther ridges, presently—shed a grander illumination abroad, and dove again—flamed out again, directly, higher

and still higher up the mountain side—threw out skirmishing parties of fire here and there, and sent them trailing their crimson spirals away among remote ramparts and ribs and gorges, till as far as the eye could reach the lofty mountain-fronts were webbed as it were with a tangled net-work of red lava streams.* Away across the water the crags and domes were lit with a ruddy glare, and the firmament above was a reflected hell!

But the lake was there—always the lake. Even when watching a mountain inferno, Twain couldn't draw his eyes from the water for more than a few moments:

> Every feature of the spectacle was repeated in the glowing mirror of the lake! Both pictures were sublime, both were beautiful; but that in the lake had a bewildering richness about it that enchanted the eye and held it with the stronger fascination.

They watched for four hours. By that time they looked like "*lava* men, covered as we were with ashes, and begrimed with smoke." With the fire miles away, "hunger asserted itself," Twain remembered, "but there was nothing to eat. The provisions were all cooked, no doubt, but we did not go to see."

There are a few theories about the location of Twain's timber claim, but one convincing idea places it near Stateline Point, on Tahoe's northern edge. That would mean a south-facing slope, vulnerable to burns as it dried and warmed during the sun's long passage. What's more, south faces in Tahoe are favored by ponderosa pines, which leave the ground "deeply carpeted with dry pine needles" just as Twain later remembered. Add in the fact that any slope will increase the speed and

---

*By the time Twain wrote this, he'd have known what lava streams looked like, having seen volcanoes in the Sandwich Islands (Hawaii) in 1866.

intensity of a blaze and you have a recipe for a genuinely impressive, if not particularly dangerous, burn.

In a letter to his mother a week after returning to Carson City, Twain described the "standard-bearers, as we called the tall dead trees, wrapped in fire, and waving their blazing banners a hundred feet in the air." That probably means that the main forest never caught—the fire was restricted to clearing out dead and extremely dry growth, such as the "dense growth of manzanita chaparral." Such clearing burns are, after all, exactly what forest species have evolved to expect—even to want. There was intense heat, surely, but evidently not so much as to make living trees explode with flame.

So Twain's fire probably left the trees of the timber claim mostly untouched, even if the ground was charred and smoking. Still, cutting the wood down, then milling and transporting it, was harder than Twain had guessed, and he decided to return to Nevada and take up something he was sure would be easier: milling quartz to find trace amounts of silver. After a week he asked his employer for a raise: "He said he was paying me ten dollars a week, and thought it a good round sum. How much did I want? I said about four hundred thousand dollars a month, and board, was about all I could reasonably ask, considering the hard times." That disappointment (and several prospecting failures) would lead to something momentous: his first regular writing job, at the *Virginia City Territorial Enterprise*.

But for now that was in the future. Twain and Kinney packed up their surviving belongings, rowed across a wide cove, and began trudging back to Carson City. On the way to Washoe, Twain had dropped a leaf on either side of the Continental Divide, imagining the easternmost going on a long, familiar journey, past the wharves of St. Louis and the canefields of Louisiana and finally into "the bosom of the tropic sea." Now, as he walked toward the tumultuous silver towns, another divide lay behind him, behind Tahoe and its necklace of stream-cut mountains. A leaf dropped on the Sierras' western face would drift through the ponderosa pines and sugar pines, the balsam and yellow firs, past the prospectors with their pans and rockers and sluices and wing dams, down and down and into a maze of wetland delta—until, at last, it reached a blue bay, and San Francisco, and the roar of the world-spanning Pacific.

four

HEAVEN ON THE
HALF SHELL

Oysters and Mussels in San Francisco

ORMA'S RESTAURANT, in New York's Le Parker Meridien Hotel, will, if you desire, sell you an omelet for a thousand dollars. Possibly to distract from the actual price, Norma's calls the omelet the Zillion Dollar Lobster Frittata. Now, expensive though lobster is, a thousand dollars will get you a mighty pile, even in New York, even at Norma's (the standard lobster omelet costs twenty-eight bucks); the real cost of the Zillion Dollar Frittata is in the ten ounces of sevruga caviar cupped within the folded eggs.

Hangtown fry was the Zillion Dollar Frittata of Gold Rush California. Though it consisted of a humble-sounding scramble of eggs, bacon, and fried oysters, the real point of the fry was the price; all the stories about its invention stress the rarity and expense of the ingredients. One version says that a newly wealthy prospector strutted into a restaurant in Hangtown (now, disappointingly, called Placerville) and demanded the most expensive meal they could cook. Another claims that a condemned man ordered the rarest ingredients possible in order to delay his execution.

Today oysters are by far the most expensive part of a Hangtown fry. But in the early Gold Rush days, though oysters could be expensive in the mining country, the real cost was in the eggs. Oysters could be packed into barrels and hauled in wagons to the mining towns, but there just weren't many chickens in California yet—certainly not nearly enough to meet the demand for fresh, homey eggs. Soon a thriving business in seabird eggs developed; eggers would sail across thirty miles of dangerous currents to the rocky spires of the Farallon Islands, where hundreds of thousands of murres nested. Robbing murres' nests for eggs to sell in San Francisco and the mining towns was so profitable that rival egging parties had bloody fights over the best grounds, culminating in a deadly shootout on the islands the year before Twain came to town. But murre eggs, while decent baked, were apparently appalling when fried. For Hangtown fry you needed chicken eggs, and people would pay dearly for a plate.

I made my first Hangtown fry soon after Erik was born. Eli wanted something rich, nourishing, and memorable—a comfort food we'd never tried before. I spent much more on eggs than I had to, thinking as I did so of a fantastic rant by one Mr. Flood, a New Yorker who, by the time he turned seventy, had given up eating anything but seafood. "When I was a boy on Staten Island," Flood recalled in 1944, "hens ate grit and grasshoppers and scraps from the table and whatever they could scratch out of the ground, and a platter of scrambled eggs was a delight. Then the scientists developed a special egg-laying mash made of old corncobs and sterilized buttermilk, and nowadays you order scrambled eggs and you get a platter of yellow glue." Eggs from Vacaville's Soul Food Farm obviously have full access to grasshoppers and grit and whatever they can scratch from the ground; if he could have tried them, Flood might have danced. Their yolks are a deep gold, approaching amber; recently five Soul Food Farm yolks survived over a minute of whisking by Erik, which any parent of a four-year-old will recognize as evidence of almost metaphysical strength. By comparison a factory-farmed egg is tasteless and watery and insipid.

I rolled eight jarred but sweet and fat oysters in cracker crumbs, then fried them golden in butter. When they were nearly done, I poured six lightly beaten eggs over them; in a second pan, thick-cut slab bacon sizzled and spat. When everything was done, I laid a cross-hatching of bacon on each plate, and spooned eggs and oysters over it. The first plate went on a blanket laid over Eli's lap. Erik, blessedly, was asleep.

The eggs tasted so endearingly rich that Eli asked if I'd added cheese; the raw, briny centers of the crisp oysters were an unexpectedly perfect complement. Below them the bacon made a salty, smoky foundation. Erik breathed quietly; Eli took another bite, closing her eyes to taste.

Hangtown fry may have started as an extravagance, but now it's more of a straightforward comfort—something to make on rainy winter mornings or for dinner when you just want to curl up on the couch. That's not, probably, how the prospectors saw it (and we didn't wash it down with whiskey, which might change things). But Hangtown fry is good enough that it doesn't really matter whether it shows off your newfound wealth or just gives simple comfort to your family, when your family is a family for the first time.

OYSTER OMELET

Add to a half cup of cream six eggs beaten very light, season with pepper and salt, and pour into a frying-pan with a tablespoon of butter; drop in a dozen large oysters cut in halves, or chopped fine with parsley, and fry until a light brown. Double it over, and serve immediately.

—ESTELLE WOODS WILCOX, *Buckeye Cookery and Practical Housekeeping*, 1877

"I began to get tired of staying in one place so long," Twain wrote in *Roughing It*. "I wanted to see San Francisco. I wanted to go somewhere. I wanted—I did not know *what* I wanted. I had the 'spring fever' and wanted a change, principally, no doubt."

That's just about all that Twain had to say about his reasons for leaving Nevada and heading off to San Francisco. And what more, really, did he need to say? *The road!* The American road, vast and singing and open; the road, ready and waiting for his quick and popping tread. The road: our national poem, tangled and eternal and in this case kind of a crock.

Because in his brief explanation, Twain neglected to mention several salient points. The first was that duels were common in the boomtowns near the Comstock Lode's massive silver deposits, and these fights, between men with guns, did not always prove so amusing as he sometimes claimed.* Second, that in the boomtowns it was seen as a mark of highest honor to have "killed your man." A third, closely related point was that it was—understandably enough—considered less desirable to *be* someone's man. And finally, in light of the foregoing, that the May 1864 declaration by rival Virginia City newspaperman James Laird of his intention to kill Mark Twain was, to put it gently, worrisome.

The fight began over a sack of flour. For nearly a year, one Reuel Gridley (coincidentally, a former Hannibal classmate of Twain's) had been hauling the sack from one Washoe town to the next. At each stop, Gridley jokingly auctioned off the sack to benefit the Sanitary Commission, the charity for Union soldiers that later evolved into the Red Cross. The winner of the auction never took the flour; it was just a novel way of raising money to help wounded soldiers.

---

*Once he was up against a newspaper deadline, with two empty columns to fill, when he got word of a murder; Twain later wrote that he'd told the killer, "Sir, you are a stranger to me, but you have done me a kindness this day which I can never forget. If whole years of gratitude can be to you any slight compensation, they shall be yours. I was in trouble and you have relieved me nobly and at a time when all seemed dark and drear. Count me your friend from this time forth, for I am not a man to forget a favor."

When Gridley's flour sack came to Virginia City, Laird's *Virginia City Union* bid a hundred dollars. But Laird refused to pay—or so Twain claimed in the *Territorial Enterprise*. In retaliation Laird published an angry assault on Twain's manhood. Twain demanded a retraction, in terms amounting to a challenge to a duel. Laird refused to apologize. After a few more increasingly hostile back-and-forths, Twain ran. Probably it was his first smart move during the whole business.

He'd visited San Francisco the year before, but this time he'd come to live. The city suited him perfectly, for though he described the homes as wooden and "old fashioned," the truth is that they were anything but old. San Francisco was, in fact, the newest of cities, built on sand hills and crazed, seldom realized dreams of instant fortune. Before 1848, when gold was found near the Sierra settlement of Sutter's Mill, maybe 850 people had lived in ramshackle houses among the dunes. Now there were over 56,000, a number that would again double by the end of the decade. San Francisco was a young, mostly male place, with so few women that the birthrate couldn't maintain the population. Virtually everyone there was from somewhere else (and often very far indeed—the first, lesser-known wave of '48ers hailed from Hawaii and Peru as often as from the far-off states of the Union, the nearest of which was Texas). New, wild, transient, irreverent—in many ways San Francisco was Twain's spiritual hometown.

"I fell in love with the most cordial and sociable city in the Union," he recalled. Virginia City, where he'd taken up with a terrific group of newspapermen and writers at the *Territorial Enterprise,* had treated him very well. Still, he wrote, "after the sage-brush and alkali deserts of Washoe, San Francisco was Paradise to me. I lived at the best hotel, exhibited my clothes in the most conspicuous places, [and] infested the opera."

The "best hotel," in Twain's opinion, was the Occidental. The Occidental was becoming the unofficial meeting place of an early San Franciscan bohemia—Charles Henry Webb, Adah Menken, Ada Clare, and more had left behind Pfaff's Cellar (and Walt Whitman) in New

York to make a new home out west. Twain took a room at the Occidental with his great friend Dan De Quille,* furnished with "a huge double bed, piles of bedding, splendid carpets and fine fittings of all kinds." De Quille later wrote that "Mark and I agreed well as room-mates. Both wanted to read and smoke about the same length of time after getting into bed, and when one got hungry and got up to go down town for oysters the other also became hungry and turned out."

By this time cooks had followed the prospectors (or else disappointed prospectors had become cooks); the city boasted dozens of restaurants staffed by Americans, English, French, Germans, Dutch, Pacific Islanders, Mexicans, Chileans, Chinese, and more. But when Twain and De Quille got hungry, they were probably going to an oyster house. Oyster houses were hugely popular places for men to gather, and eat, and (not incidentally) have a smoke and a drink or ten while standing about on a sawdust-covered floor. They'd remain vastly popular throughout the century until, in 1892, Americans would eat 197,639,000 pounds of oysters—and that's *dressed* weight, counting only meat. It was the age of the oyster house . . . and of oyster cellars, stalls, and counters.

But if they weren't in the mood to go out, Twain and De Quille could have just tumbled downstairs. Though Twain loved the hotel's rooms and companionship, he wrote most enthusiastically about the food. As he reported in the *Golden Era* (one of the several local journals he wrote for), the Occidental's proprietor relied heavily on locally caught fish and game, especially the beds of shellfish spread out among the eelgrass and clean bay water:

---

*Let us pause here to praise Clemens's choice of alias. *Mark Twain*—short, sharp, sounds like a name. It works. Compare it with his friends' pseudonyms: *Old Blow, Yellow Bird, Amigo, Dan De Quille*. Tough to imagine Hemingway saying, "All modern American literature comes from one book by Amigo," as he did about Twain and *Huck Finn*.

To a Christian who has toiled months and months in Washoe, . . . whose soul is caked with a cement of alkali dust, . . . [whose] contrite heart finds joy and peace only in Limburger cheese and lager beer—unto such a Christian, verily the Occidental Hotel is Heaven on the half shell. He may even secretly consider it to be Heaven on the entire shell, but his religion teaches a sound Washoe Christian that it would be sacrilege to say it.

Here you are expected to breakfast on salmon, fried oysters and other substantials from 6 till half-past 12; you are required to lunch on cold fowl and so forth, from half-past 12 until 3; you are obliged to skirmish through a dinner comprising such edibles as the world produces, and keep it up, from 3 until half-past 7; you are then compelled to lay siege to the tea-table from half-past 7 until 9 o'clock, at which hour, if you refuse to move upon the supper works and destroy oysters gotten up in all kinds of seductive styles until 12 o'clock, the landlord will certainly be offended, and you might as well move your trunk to some other establishment. (It is a pleasure to me to observe, incidentally, that I am on good terms with the landlord yet.)

San Franciscans eagerly awaited the fowl—Twain noted in the *Morning Call* that the Occidental served quails at 6:00 A.M. on the opening day of hunting season (he praised the enterprise of the hunter before concluding, dryly, that "it would be wrong to suspect him of having captured the quails the day before"). But the main glory of the Occidental was the shellfish—mussels, no doubt, and clams, and oyster after seductive oyster.

Twain liked his mussels steamed. That's simple (and good) enough: scrub the beards from black, glistening, tightly closed shells. Simmer wine; melt in a knob of butter. Slip in the mussels. Leave them just long enough to open, turning hot wine into an ocean of sauce. Serve in wide, steaming bowls, with a platter of bread. In San Francisco, in Twain's day, bread always meant sourdough—even prospectors were proud of their spontaneously leavened starter, so that some would splurge on whiskey while refusing to pay for loaves. Then as now, steamed mussels went great with a drink, and Twain had plenty of those: "We returned drunk, but not disorderly," was one typical report.

But if it's easy to imagine what "San Francisco mussels, steamed" meant, oysters done up in "all kinds of seductive styles" leaves much more leeway. Oysters were one of the most popular foods in nineteenth-century America, often enjoyed dozens or hundreds of miles from the coast. The same things that let an oyster live for hours when the tide receded—a clamping adductor muscle to retain seawater, an ability to slow the metabolism to nearly nothing, even a curved lower shell that helped hold moisture—made it perfectly suited for long trips overland. By 1887, when some hundred fifty thousand miles of rail spiderwebbed across the country, the Ohio cookbook *Buckeye Cookery* could include some fifteen oyster recipes—including at least one for raw oysters served simply with lemon, vinegar, and horseradish. "Oysters in the shell must be kept in a cool cellar," the authors recommended, "and occasionally sprinkled with salt water."

But even in 1857, before railroads truly dominated American land and Americans' tables (there were less than a fifth as many miles of rail as there would be thirty years later), canned oysters would allow an Indiana cook to declare a sauce made from nothing more than oysters, butter, and flour "the most delicious sauce in the whole catalogue of culinary compounds." Americans ate oysters whenever, wherever, and however they could; they simmered them in soups, stuffed them into turkeys, froze them in ice cream, and baked them in shortbread and pies. In San Francisco, where oysters were cheap, "seductive styles" must have covered a lot of ground.

Twain doubtless reveled in the variety; he was known to be able to do tremendous damage to a spread of shellfish. "I never saw a more used-up, hungrier man, than Clemens," a Boston friend would write years later. "It was something fearful to see him eat escalloped oysters." Surely oysters were scalloped at the Occidental, baked with a sprinkling of sourdough bread crumbs and butter. A later cookbook author would credit the popular Manning's Oyster House with inventing the salt roast (which has nothing to do with seasoning the oysters but rather with roasting them on the half shell on a bed of hot rock salt). And there was Hangtown fry, of course; I like to think of Twain—who still held some reasonably valuable silver-mine stock—indulging in something like it, reveling in being young and feeling rich. Fried oysters might also have been packed into a hollowed-out loaf of sourdough bread, the local version of an oyster loaf or "peacemaker." Oysters were served in soups, stews, gumbos, and croquettes; they were broiled, deviled, stuffed into fish, and used to garnish chicken (and wild ducks and geese, especially in San Francisco, where wetlands still vastly outnumbered farms).

Then there were raw oysters: the real thing. Twain had eaten them before, of course; New Orleans, then as now, was legendary for its spreads of fat eastern oysters, fresh from the Gulf. And even the relatively limited rail networks sometimes brought oysters far from the coast. The year before Twain moved to San Francisco, the French government sent one P. de Broca to report on the American oyster industry; de Broca reported that "this delicious article of food has become so necessary with every class of the population that scarcely a town in the whole country can be found without its regular supply. By means of railroads and water channels, oysters in the shell, or out of the shell, preserved in ice, in pickle, or canned, are carried even to the remotest parts of the United States." But there's a big difference between live, iced oysters and oysters pickled or canned; and the farther you got from the ocean, the more likely the latter became. Twain later recalled that champagne and pickled-oyster stew had been "incredible luxuries" in Washoe. And the reverence accorded to Hangtown fry suggests how expensive hauling oysters over the mountains in barrels of seawater made them (as much as a dollar each by the time they reached Reno).

Now the Washoe desert was behind Twain. In San Francisco the oysters were fresh (and champagne so plentiful in the city's brothels that vintners were known to bail out prostitutes). Here the snap of seawater replaced the tang of pickling brine or the tired and limp flavor of live oysters jounced over hundreds of miles of road. Raw oysters are more than fresh—they're still alive, waiting in a curve of cupped shell, their minuscule hearts still beating a liquor of briny blood. That's the purest way to eat an oyster; a pan roast can be great, but raw oysters make for rhapsody.

For Twain, youth and the taste of shellfish were a heady combination. Sure, San Francisco oysters and mussels were exquisitely fresh in their own right. But how wonderful for him to eat them late at night in the bayside city, a writer among writers as he honed his sardonic, uproarious voice.

"My boy," said Old Mr. Flood as he turned his attention from eggs to shellfish, "people who are unaccustomed to oysters sometimes behave real queer after putting away a few dozen." He told of a group of Brooklyn boys, "weevily fellows, pale, stoop-shouldered, and clerky looking, three runts, no life in them at all," who were given permission to eat all the oysters they could hold. Later that afternoon, said Flood, "those Brooklyn boys were laughing and shouting and wrestling and throwing each other's hats in the water. They were flinging themselves head over heels. The air was full of Brooklyn boys."

The air was full of him: that's how I think of Twain in San Francisco. He'd fled Washoe disgraced and fearing for his life. Now he was in a city of delights, part of a circle of young writers running over rooftops, and betting shellfish dinners on bowling matches, and drinking until dawn. A city of steamed sea mussels and of oysters by the bushel, of whiskey and Chinatown, of gold prospectors and Emperor Norton, of champagne and gas lamps and fog. Yeah.

OYSTER LOAVES

Cut out a piece of the size of a quarter of a dollar from the top of half a dozen buns, scoop out most of the crumb, put a portion of the latter with a good bit of butter, and about two dozen fresh oysters into a frying pan and fry all together for five minutes, add a little cream or milk and seasoning. Then fill the loaves, allowing four oysters to each; replace the pieces of crust on the tops, butter the outsides, and place them for a short time in an oven to get crisp. Serve them hot or cold.

—JANE CUNNINGHAM CROLY, *Jennie June's American Cookery Book,* 1870

There are few things as liable to start an argument about food as oysters. You can argue about species: the relative merits, for example, of New York's eastern *Crassostrea virginica* and France's flat *Ostrea edulis* (Frederick Marryat wrote a classic takedown of America's eastern oysters, saying that "as the Americans assert that the English and French oysters taste of copper. . . . I presume they do; and that's the reason why we do not like the American oysters, copper being better than no flavour at all"). Or you can argue about region; Thomas De Voe said that "the Northern oyster has a broad, thin, tough shell, with a pleasant smell, savoring of the odor of marine plants, while the Southern oyster has a thick, spongy, soft shell, and [is] of less flavor." You can even debate marine microclimates—whether oysters from the north cove of a given bay have a brinier snap than those farther south (if there's a river to the south, they probably do). If Twain's near duel had been about oysters instead of flour, it might have seemed almost reasonable.

Opinions about oysters are passionate for a simple reason: oysters are rabid filter feeders. With each oyster filtering thirty gallons of water a day, the character of the surrounding water—temperature, clarity, mineral content, salinity—completely infuses the flesh. Whether you prefer your oysters coppery or briny, meaty or smoky, or with a note of cucumber or celery salt, the ones you love are best from a particular spot. The prizewinning Sweetwaters from Hog Island Oyster Company take their name from the stream that empties near the fattening beds, which, as one oyster aficionado put it, "balances the saltiness of the oyster liquor with a smoky sweetness." The Armoricaines of Locmari-aquer, which author Eleanor Clarke insisted had "no relation at all to the taste, if there is one, of the usual U.S. restaurant oyster," made her feel that she was "eating the sea, . . . only the sensation of a gulp of sea water [had] been wafted out of it by some sorcery" (she thought of mermaids, and poems, and the smell of kelp during ebb tide). Oysters from Cape Breton grow slow and briny, those from off Louisiana rapidly and mild. And oysters change flavor *fast*, fast enough to qualify as truly seasonal; the Hog Island Sweetwaters, for example, are brinier during California's dry summer months, when the fresh stream flowing to the fattening beds becomes a mere trickle.

Terroir is the French word for the way a flavor can contain and express the essence of a place. Oysters have *terroir*. Do you ever sit around thinking about the salinity and temperature and nutrients and currents and clarity of local waters? Probably not—but eat a dozen oysters with a group of informed oyster lovers and you probably will. Arguments about oysters are really arguments about place, about the merits of home, whether home is New York or South Carolina or San Francisco.

Now, San Francisco Bay isn't actually a bay. It's an estuary. And though this might seem semantic, it actually makes all the difference in the world. A bay simply holds water; an estuary mixes it. It's the difference between a glass of neat gin and a dry martini—gin is well and good, but dry martinis are holy, and though bays are useful, estuaries are explosive creators of life. In an estuary, fresh and salt waters come

together, mixing and churning, creating a state of change and utter confusion that is one of the most literally lively conditions on the planet.

It's a situation as rare as it is precious, at least on the scale of the
San Francisco estuary. Think, for a moment, of a hopeful '49er taking
a ship around Cape Horn (maybe he was worried enough about malaria
to avoid the land crossing at Panama). He'd sail north past Chile, and
Peru, and Ecuador, and Colombia, and past the Darien gap and along
the sweeping curve of Mexico and then the whole lower California
coast, and after all that time and distance his first encounter with a
major estuary would be when he sailed through the nearly invisible
narrow mouth of the Golden Gate and into the tidal maze beyond.

You tell the story of an estuary through water flow—where it
comes from, how long it stays, what it carries, where it goes. In the San
Francisco Bay, the story was complex and ever-changing. Every day the
San Joaquin and Sacramento rivers carried some 24 billion gallons of
fresh water to meet the more than 200 billion gallons of cold, salty,
ocean water sluicing in and out the Golden Gate. More streams, creeks,
and winter rivulets ran through three hundred square miles of brackish
bay wetlands, as well as the Sacramento Delta's five hundred square
miles of "reeds and rivers." Leaves, reeds, and dead wetland plants
drifted downstream, rotting into rich nutrients; plankton fed on them,
bloomed, and in turn died and sank to the bottom of the bay. There, in
the mud, the filter feeders waited, oysters and mussels and clams ready
for the slow, steady rain of nutrients.

Call it a bay or an estuary, it suffused San Francisco. Sand dunes
loomed above the "old-fashioned" frame houses; below them piers
probed the bright water like fingers. People bathed in the bay, at least
until (or so Twain claimed) the owner of a new North Beach bathing
house fed pork to a shark, cut it open on the dock, and exclaimed in
horror that the fiendish beast had eaten human flesh.* Twain could

---

*Speaking of bathing houses: it can't be confirmed, but a recurrent rumor has it that Mark
Twain met, in a Turkish bath on the Montgomery Block, where the Transamerica Pyramid now
stands, a San Francisco firefighter named Tom Sawyer. Submitted without comment.

walk to the docks, passing Abe Warner's Cobweb Palace with its mounds of scrimshaw and New England–style clam and crab dishes; there he could watch fishermen sail in with salmon and flatfish, and eggers unload baskets of murre eggs from the shark-haunted Farallons. Afterward he sometimes boarded a touring sailboat for a cruise to Oakland, or San Leandro, or Alameda. Along the way he doubtless saw wide beds of eelgrass hissing under the incoming tide, and flanking reefs of native oysters. There'd have been trawlers, feluccas with brightly colored square sails, even Chinese junks heading for the shrimping beds. Flights of pelicans tracing long lines in the water with their wing tips. Sea otters. Maybe a whale.

And he'd have seen, along with native oyster reefs, the sticks and stakes of submerged oyster holding pens. It's hugely surprising how few of the oysters eaten in San Francisco in Twain's day were true bay natives; hundreds of shell mounds flank the bay, after all. Oysters have fed people here for centuries. Still, within a few years into the Gold Rush, the great majority of oysters eaten in San Francisco came from somewhere else. Specifically, they came from Shoalwater Bay, Washington, on the Olympic Peninsula—came in such quantities that San Franciscans soon called all native western oysters "Olys" (they're still called Olympias—the scientific name is *Ostrea conchaphila*).

The main complaint about native San Francisco oysters was their size. Clarence Edwords's 1914 restaurant guide and cookbook *Bohemian San Francisco* has a recipe for oyster omelets, calling for six eggs . . . and *one hundred* native oysters. Ed Ricketts (the model for Doc in Steinbeck's *Cannery Row*) later estimated that it would take between sixteen hundred and two thousand shucked natives to make a single gallon. Small oysters are great—you make the mistake of bypassing them in favor of the big ones at Hog Island only once, and even the landlocked *Buckeye Cookery* says simply that "the small-shelled oysters have the finest flavor"—but this is pretty extreme. What's more, both Edwords and Ricketts are probably talking about imported Olys, which were about 50 percent larger than those native to San Francisco Bay. Newcomers accustomed to the larger, lighter eastern oysters began looking elsewhere—even to the small oysters of Oregon and Washington—from very early on. The first shipment of some six hundred bushels of Shoalwater Olympias arrived from Washington in 1850. For the next twenty years, they were the majority of the oysters eaten in the city (and 90 percent of imports). In 1859 some thirty-five thousand thirty-two-pound baskets were imported—over 1.1 million pounds, if you include the shells. Most went into holding tanks close to the city, fenced off against foraging bat rays. Even the fact that Olys couldn't spawn in the cool bay waters had its advantages, since they could be taken from the pens and served on the half shell all year long; San Francisco didn't have a "no oysters in months without r's" rule.

Olys were San Francisco's major oyster even before 1861, when huge floods flushed the bay with fresh water and killed many of the local shellfish. Still, they probably tasted much like the oysters that had been eaten in the region for thousands of years. Like all Olympia oysters, Shoalwater Bay Olys absorbed minerals quickly, which gave the dark meat a distinctly coppery taste, unlike the brinier (and more widely known) easterns. As soon as they reached the city's holding tanks, they promptly began their relentless, untiring filter feeding; they must have quickly taken on some of the qualities of the even darker local oysters. An oyster didn't have to have been spawned in San Francisco to be a San Francisco oyster.

Twain was very much aware of where his oysters came from—and his partisanship shifted, at different times, between several sources. When one Mr. Scoofy brought in a shipment of oysters from his Mexican shellfish farm, Twain declared them fine, fat, and "far superior to the poor little insipid things we are accustomed to here." Scoofy, he rejoiced, would "hereafter endeavor to keep this market supplied with his delicious marine fruit." The Mexican market never came to much (a steamer took thirteen days from Mazatlán, while a sailboat could arrive from Washington in less than a week). But did Olympia oysters, whether true natives or Washington imports, really suffer as much by comparison as Twain claimed?

If he was talking about size . . . well, shucking a hundred Olys to make a single omelet would be a true labor of love. Still, many people loved Olympias; an 1877 *Scribner's* article said that "in San Francisco you earn the confidence of the Californian by praising his little coppery oysters and saying that . . . after all the true taste of the 'natives' is only acquired where there is an excess of copper in suspension." And Edwords obviously loved the labor-intensive oyster omelets, writing that "the slightly coppery taste of the California oysters gives a piquancy to the flavor of the omelet that can be obtained in no other way, and those who once ate of Arbogast's California oyster omelet, invariably called for it again and again." Recent European arrivals like Marryat, loving intense Belons, might have preferred Olympias to bluepoints.

Here's the definition of a good day of research: house-made potato chips, beer, and an oyster happy hour. Berkeley's Sea Salt restaurant serves, among its many oysters, Olympias from Taylor Shellfish's Skookum Inlet farms, brought from Washington, just like Twain's were (though his were from extensive wild beds). Before my dozen arrive on the table, I know to expect something small and coppery-tasting, and that's exactly what I get—the shells are as small as a doll's dishes. And coppery? They're coppery like a pulped penny is coppery. Yet I don't mean to make them sound bad. In fact, they're terrific with an IPA, the beer cleansing the nearly bloody taste and leaving only a memory of a full and unforgettable flavor. Olys are oysters to lean into; I'm just glad, considering their size, that someone else did the shucking.

Maybe it's appropriate that Twain, a man who lived in and identified with so many American places, never took a firm and final position on which sort, or which preparation, was best. Beyond his praise for the half shells of San Francisco, his menu included fried oysters, stewed oysters, bluepoints on the half shell, oyster soup, and oysters roasted in the shell "Northern style." He ate them in all their varieties and in all styles; given how ebullient he was when praising fresh fruit, and his savagery in blasting tired meat, I'm guessing he enjoyed talking about oysters as much as eating them.

As to the pressing question of whether he thought that Olys were poor and insipid, I have to think that he was sucking up to Scoofy. There were, it seems to me, few men that Twain would have wanted to know more than the owner of literal shiploads of oysters; publicly praising Scoofy's "delicious marine fruit" would have been one way to get in good. In this case, however, the young writer's calculations backfired badly. After a night of debauchery by Twain, his friend Amigo reported in *Gold Hill News* that Twain "had abused the Scoofy oysters served in McDonald's Saloon," claiming hellish vomiting and diarrhea. Amigo declared the oysters wholesome, pointing out (reasonably enough) that "where there is a barrel of whiskey and only a half bushel of oysters, it is hardly fair to assume that the poison is *all* in the said oysters." He added that "the next time Mark gets poisoned, the police propose to have him ripped open and analyzed at once by a practical chemist."

As to the charges that Twain had feigned illness to avoid paying the bill . . . well, you couldn't really expect him to come up with the money. After all, Amigo concluded, the man was a bohemian.

ROAST OYSTERS IN THE SHELL

Select the large ones, those usually termed "Saddle Rocks," formerly known as a distinct variety, but which are now but the large oysters selected from any beds; wash and wipe them, and place with the upper or deep shell down, to catch the juice, over or on live coals. When they open their shells, remove the shallow one, being careful to save all the juice in the other; place them, shells and all, on a hot platter, and send to table hot, to be seasoned by each person with butter and pepper to taste. If the oysters are fine, and they are just cooked enough and served all hot, this is, *par excellence,* the style.

—Fanny Lemira Gillette, *White House Cook Book,* 1887

Mussels are less controversial than oysters—less prone to lead to violence. This may be because they're eaten raw far less often; Twain, specifying steaming, was firmly among the majority. When you steam something in wine, then dip it in butter (and Lord knows I'm in favor of doing both), you're getting a ways away from the immediate and pure experience of eating it raw. There are better mussels and worse mussels, for sure, but the differences simply don't inspire the same kind of intense, nearly bloody debate as with oysters.

Still, all mussels are very much of a particular place. In Twain's day, in fact, they were even more so than oysters—thin-shelled mussels didn't ship nearly as well and couldn't live as long without ice. In the waters around San Francisco, their huge beds caked any available substrate, growing even on oyster reefs. Beyond the Golden Gate, they colonized ocean rocks where nothing else could take hold. They thrived in the cold summer waters that welled up from the deep sea—waters that gave San Francisco its famous fogs, like the one that chilled Twain on the day he drank what may have been the greatest cup of coffee of his life.

If any food ever truly affronted Twain, leaving him stammering with agitation, groping about for a properly demeaning insult, it was watery European hotel coffee. "After a few months' acquaintance with European 'coffee,'" he wrote, "one's mind weakens, and his faith with it, and he begins to wonder if the rich beverage of home, with its clotted layer of yellow cream on top of it is not a mere dream, after all, and a thing which never existed." He had found that ideal cup in San Francisco. By the summer of 1863, riding out to the grand Cliff and Ocean houses before dawn had become a minor fad; Twain did it exactly once and swore never to do it again—the cold fog, he said, was so thick that he could scarcely see his horse. Afterward he wrote that

> we could scarcely see the sportive seals out on the rocks, writhing and squirming like exaggerated maggots, and there was nothing soothing in their discordant barking, to a spirit so depressed as mine was. . . .
>
> We were human icicles when we reached the Ocean House, and there was no fire there, either. I banished all hope, then, and succumbed to despair; I went back on my religion, and sought surcease of sorrow in soothing blasphemy. I am sorry I did it, now, but it was a great comfort to me, then. We could have had breakfast at the Ocean House, but we did not want it; can statues of ice feel hunger? But we adjourned to a private room and ordered red-hot coffee, and it was a sort of balm to my troubled mind to observe that the man who brought it was as cold, and as silent, and as solemn as the grave itself.

Then, the Miracle:

> That coffee did the business for us. It was made by a master-artist, and it had not a fault; and the cream that came with it was so rich and thick that you could hardly have strained it through a wire fence. As the generous beverage flowed down our frigid throats, our blood grew warm again, our muscles relaxed, our torpid bodies awoke to life and feeling, anger and uncharitableness departed from us and we were cheerful once more. We got good cigars, also, at the Ocean House, and drove into town over a smooth road lighted by sun and unclouded by fog.

Coffee so good that the earth seemed to smile. And at that moment, all along the coast, mussels were gorging.

San Francisco's cold summer fogs and its abundant ocean life are both gifts of offshore upwelling. As the California Current—a gigantic, six-mile-wide, invisible river in the sea—flows from Alaska to Mexico, the turning of the earth draws it steadily, constantly offshore. All this water is replaced by a gigantic upwelling from thousands of feet below, much as hot smoke rising through a chimney can pull a cold draft of air through an open door. And when this cold water touches warm summer air, the ocean breathes fog thick as a wet, gray blanket, the kind that Twain rode through cursing, swearing that he could "not see the horse at all, and [was] obliged to steer by his ears, which stood up dimly out of the dense white mist that enveloped him."

The cold, upwelled water that makes the fogs is full of detritus, decomposed fish, rotted plankton, and whatever else has drifted to the ocean bottom—all now broken down into particles fine enough to billow back to the surface on a rising current. When these nutrients combine with sunlight, the ocean explodes with plankton; if you scuba dive in the upper reaches of an upwelling zone, you can barely see your hand through the green, almost greasy water. And plankton is everything—plankton is it. Upwelled nutrients, and the plankton they support, are the foundation of all California marine life, from fish to whales to the Farallon Islands murres whose nests were once so busily robbed.

And mussels, for sure. Mussels spin strong thread, knitting themselves to rock in beds up to fifteen inches thick. The waves that break on the beds carry upwelled nutrients; as each wave draws, foaming, back, the mussels filter and feed. Mussels live on surfaces the ocean wants to shear clean—it's a triumph of life. And though the beds look pretty monotonous—just wads of sharp black shell slathered on rocks—they also allow other animals to live on wave-crushed stone. They shelter worms, anemones, crabs, and brittle stars, expanding the territory of dozens of species. What's more, the threads that bind the mussels down also act as spiderwebs, trapping tiny bits of detritus that feed the hidden hangers-on. Prairie chickens depend on grass for their habitat—but mussels *are* habitat, letting a kaleidoscope of life hold to what would otherwise be bare rock. Twain's mussels made their own forest, netting sustenance for an entire subtidal ecosystem, until they ended in city restaurants—in bowls rich with butter, heady with wine.

TO STEW OYSTERS OR MUSCLES

Plump them in their own liquor; then, having drained off the liquor, wash them clean in fair water. Set the liquor drained from the oysters, or as much as necessary (with the addition of an equal quantity of water or white wine, a little whole pepper, and a blade of mace,) over the fire, and boil it well. Then put in the oysters, and let them just boil up, and thicken with a piece of butter and flour: some will add the yolk of an egg. Serve them up with sippets and the liquor, and garnish the dish with grated bread or sliced lemon.

—SUSANNAH CARTER, *The Frugal Housewife*, 1803

The parking lot marking the old Berkeley shoreline belongs to Spenger's, a venerable, much beloved, extremely crappy fish restaurant (the onion rings used to be good; other than that, drink or go home). Beneath the parking lot lie remnants of a monumental mound of millions of oyster and mussel and abalone shells left by generations of Ohlone Native Americans. Four hundred such shell mounds once circled the bay, some of them forty feet tall and the size of a football field at the base; the Ohlone valued the sites for spiritual as well as physical sustenance, with one site including five hundred nearby burials. Shellfish gave the Ohlone stability in a world of change, allowing them to stay as a community year round, rather than dispersing into the hills when the fresh waters of winter dwindled and died.

But then, and for centuries after, oysters and mussels were only one part of the bay's grand treasury of fish. A day's haul at Fisherman's Wharf could include "fine, fat" crabs, sand dabs "but an hour or two from the water," smelt, herring, flounder, sole, shrimp sold "alive and active," crayfish, clams, squid, and more. Fishermen cooked breakfasts of fish and coffee on charcoal braziers set out on the decks while passersby bought fish straight from the boats. Into at least the 1870s, the catch sold so quickly that fishermen never used ice; the Vesuvius Italian restaurant was just one that would send a cook's helper to the Clay Street Market for a "still flapping" fish as soon as it was ordered. Sometimes the abundance bordered on parody: once, when a fishing boat was hauled into dry dock, some fifty large anchovies were found dangling underneath. The fish had gone pecking for algae among the mussels that encrusted the hull and been trapped when the shells snapped down tight (this sounds like an exaggeration, but mussels have been known to take off the toes of passing clapper rails). The bay was chockfull of life, everything eating everything else.

For many decades San Francisco was not only a city *by* the bay, it was a city *of* the bay and of the ocean beyond. The abundance that Twain knew, much of which lasted until midway into the twentieth century, was a pulsing expression of the water that gave the city its name (originally called Yerba Buena, the city was renamed after the San Francisco Bay, not the other way around). There may have been no better place in America to experience the blend of wild and domestic foods that distinguished his menu; a lavish testimonial dinner in the city might include venison, bear, and five varieties of duck, alongside veal tartare, calves' head, ice cream, nuts, raisins, and cake—things from both the vast nearby wetlands and quickly expanding tilled fields.

But even in Twain's day, the filling of the bay had already begun.

As he sailed south past holding tanks and reefs of native oysters and beds of eelgrass, he must also have seen the hulks of abandoned ships littering the bay, teetering or foundered in the muck; some were burned to the waterline, others beginning to rot. The boats were the face of the early Gold Rush, when gold fever was so intense that a newly arrived crew would often walk off the job and head for the Sierras—it would have been a huge problem for captains and shipowners, if they weren't just as likely to have called it quits.

And so, until swift new California Clippers began winging gold hunters around the tip of South America, Yerba Buena Cove (the city's major anchorage) filled up with the hulks of unwanted ships. As early as 1851, a majority of the nearly eight hundred ships in the cove were derelicts. The abandoned ships were so thick, in fact, that when the city really began pushing at the boundaries, stretching out over the bay on increasingly elaborate platforms, nobody bothered to move the abandoned boats—they just poured in sand until the hulls were effectively sitting on dry land. Later someone might build a superstructure on the deck and call it a hotel, or throw in an oven and open a restaurant. Ships became jails, theaters, homes.* Today the five blocks of infill between the bay and the old San Francisco shoreline still hold the remains of dozens of Gold Rush–era ships; sometimes a transit tunnel or the foundation of a new office building will run smack into one, and the world gets to look again at the *Rome* or the *Lydia* or the *William Gray*.

Still, beyond the city the old shoreline more or less held. Though farmers had begun diking the upper freshwater marshes, wetlands still spread for hundreds of square miles. The immediate problem was not yet infill, but silt that was beginning to smother the oyster holding

---

*One of the town's first Italian restaurants began in a ship owned by a man named Giuseppe Bazzurro, who may well have brought cioppino to San Francisco. He'd emigrated from Genoa, home of a fish stew known in the Genoan dialect as *cioppin* (possibly after the Chiappa fish market). If he *was* the primary importer, Giuseppe Bazzurro was a great man; there should be statues of him everywhere.

pens—silt sent down to the bay by the very prospectors who thought that a plate of fried bay oysters with bacon and eggs was the height of luxury.

Much of the Gold Rush consisted of guys figuring out increasingly efficient (and increasingly destructive) ways of washing gold out of riverside gravel and dirt. Though the typical image of a '49er is that of a rugged individualist kneeling beside a stream with a wide pan, that's really accurate only for the first months of the rush. Squatting on the stream banks soon gave the prospectors ruggedly thrown-out backs and individually blasted knees; most detested their pans, and ditched them as soon as they could. By the time Twain came to California, they were using cast-iron nozzles to blast away entire hillsides—undercutting bluffs by as much as three hundred feet, then sluicing out the collapsed gravel and sand. When it came to tearing up the landscape, the move from washbasins to hydraulic mining was like switching from trained ants to giant, angry boars. And the unromantic truth is that there were a lot more of the boars, for a lot longer.

But the hills, of course, did not simply vanish. They washed downstream. All in all, the prospectors blasted out some 1.5 *billion* cubic yards of sand and gravel and soil. To put it in perspective, the largest Egyptian pyramid is about 2.5 million cubic yards; if you made a pyramid out of all the washed-out Gold Rush dirt, it would be a mile on every side and another mile to the top, utterly dwarfing the ones at Giza.

Much of this enormous pile of sludge was full of mercury, which prospectors used to separate gold from earth (mercury could be made into an amalgam with the specks of gold, then separated out at leisure). Today the mercury might charitably be termed a problem. Back then, although the phrase "mad as a hatter" had been coined to describe people losing their minds from the mercury used to make hats, prospectors used the metal blithely and without much fear of consequence (Twain himself got sick during his short week in the quartz mill, possibly from exposure to the "quantity of quicksilver" kept on hand).

But at the time people worried less about mercury than about the hyperspeed erosion destroying all the waterways downstream. Erosion so damaged local agriculture that an 1884 lawsuit finally stopped hydraulic mining altogether. The suit came too late, however, to stop that monster pyramid of toxic sediment from poisoning and burying many of the shellfish; by the time of the court decision, the once omnipresent oyster holding pens around the city were gone.

They'd been replaced by fattening beds far to the south. Though people had tried for decades to bring big, light, mild eastern oysters to California, none ever survived the long ocean voyage. So when the transcontinental railroad was completed, oystermen wasted no time. The rails were finished in May 1869; the first shipment of easterns arrived in October (about as early as possible, given the summer spawning season). The new arrivals had some big advantages as aquaculture stock, among them a thin ostium tube that made them hugely efficient feeders, allowing them to grow four inches in four years, compared to an Olympia's two. Besides, San Francisco was a city of newcomers, many of them eager to eat oysters they remembered from Long Island or the Gulf of Mexico or the Carolina Tidewater. By 1875 the growers were ready to invest in earnest, ordering 167 train-car loads of inch-long seed oysters from the beds of New York and northern New Jersey.

Oysters thrived in the briny water of the southern bay, which received only 10 percent as much fresh water as the north. In the peak year of 1899, San Francisco Bay would produce 2.5 million pounds of oyster meat—nearly 80 percent of all oyster meat produced on the West Coast (in 1995, California produced about 1.5 million pounds). But having the farms far from the worst of the sediment left them vulnerable to a new threat: oyster pirates.

Most of the beds were separated from dry ground by a wide wetland; a quiet boatload of desperate poachers (balanced, I like to think, on peg legs and trying to clutch long knives between their teeth as they simultaneously rolled their *r*'s) could steal a load of oysters and be gone long before anyone suspected. Jack London's "A Raid on the Oyster Pirates" in *Tales of the Fish Patrol* gives a vivid picture of the South Bay beds and of the extent of the surrounding wetlands as late as 1906:

> Mr. Taft's beds were three miles away, and for a long time we rowed silently, . . . once in a while grounding and our oar blades constantly striking bottom. At last we came upon soft mud covered with not more than two inches of water—not enough to float the boats. But the pirates at once were over the side, and pushing and pulling on the flat-bottomed skiffs, we moved steadily along.
>
> After half a mile of the mud, we came upon a deep channel, up which we rowed, with dead oyster shoals looming high and dry on either side. At last we reached the picking grounds. . . . We hauled the noses of the boats up on the shore side of a big shoal, and all hands, with sacks, spread out and began picking.

Broad wetlands, shallow waters, old reefs, deep channels; the South Bay remained part of San Francisco's harvest horn for centuries. Eventually, though, sedimentation and pollution destroyed the beds there as well, just as the true Washington Olympias would one day fail during the advent of pulp mills on Puget Sound.

The bad news is that we're never going to get back a bay as clean as the one Twain knew, one bursting with an active shellfish fishery. We'll never eat oysters or mussels from the bay in any quantity; the mercury just lasts too long. And there are no longer salmon in anything like the numbers that supported a catch of two hundred thousand fish in 1857. The bay fishery for crabs was in trouble by 1890, sturgeon by 1901; market hunters stopped going for ducks and geese by 1917. When you consider that nearly half the land area of California (and whatever oils and chemicals are dumped on it) drains into the estuary, it's easy to despair. Maybe the bay will always be what it looks like from the air: postcard pretty in the middle, ringed by pavement and salt ponds the color of rust.

But some fisheries do survive, mostly herring and bay shrimp. The bay is a nursery for Dungeness crab, sole, and other fish; it still feeds the city, even if the days of eating bottom-dwelling filter feeders are gone. And healing the bay further—bringing back more birds, more salmon, more crab, more life—will mean, among a hundred other jobs, bringing back oysters: the pulsing, filtering, feeding reefs.

OYSTER SOUP

Wash and drain two quarts of oysters, put them on with three quarts of water, three onions chopped up, two or three slices of lean ham, pepper and salt; boil it till reduced one-half, strain it through a sieve, return the liquid into the pot, put in one quart of fresh oysters, boil it till they are sufficiently done, and thicken the soup with four spoonsful of flour, two gills of rich cream, and the yolks of six new laid eggs beaten well; boil it a few minutes after the thickening is put in. Take care that it does not curdle, and that the flour is not in lumps; serve it up with the last oysters that were put in. If the flavour of thyme be agreeable, you may put in a little, but take care that it does not boil in it long enough to discolour the soup.

OYSTER [ICE] CREAM

Make a rich soup, (see directions for oyster soup,) strain it from the oysters, and freeze it.

—MARY RANDOLPH, *The Virginia Housewife*, 1838

One of my mottos, seldom stated yet assiduously observed, is "I will not jump into a mudflat in winter." Today I volunteered to do it.

I clamber down the rocks beneath the Marin Rod & Gun Club, which consists of a nondescript clubhouse and a pier near the northern end of the Richmond Bridge. We're just across the peninsula from San Quentin Point, which commands a spectacular view of the city (and was once the site of some of the earliest oyster pens) but is now much to be avoided, there being a gigantic prison there and all. Marin Rod & Gun is a throwback, a place for older men to come and play checkers and have a drink or else head out on the pier to pull in a striper or bat ray. It owns twenty acres of waterfront property and forty more under-water (much to my surprise, most of the submerged bay, other than the shipping channels, is privately owned), and when I first arrived was catering to exactly three old guys playing cards.

Just north of the pier are three long, narrow grids of bamboo stakes: the site of what will become the biggest native oyster reef in modern San Francisco Bay.

My wet suit is meant for ocean diving, with a hood and two thick pieces that overlap all around my trunk, so I'm slow, clumsy, and in-creasingly sweaty even on such a cool and misty day. To keep me from bobbing around once I'm in deeper water, I'm wearing a twenty-pound weight belt, and it drives me better than knee-deep into the mud. Even with the bridge traffic roaring to the south, my steps are one of the loudest things out here—*Slurp . . . pop! Slurp . . . pop!* There are already a half dozen volunteers by the stakes, two more struggling out with me. More work from a dock on the other side of the main pier, handing sacks of shell into a pair of motorboats. There are eight pallets of sacks, each loaded chin-high—this could take a while.

The mud I'm in probably isn't Gold Rush mud. That's deeper, bur-ied under a century of additional sediment. But whatever this is, it stinks, and is fine as dust; later I'll try to rinse out my suit in a half dozen changes of water. In the end the silt will defeat me—the next time I dive, I imagine, I'll look like a squid shooting ink.

Bud Abbott, a fisheries expert at the health and environmental consultancy Environ, played a big role in getting the work here started; he calls efforts like this one "the largest social movement in the world that no one saw coming." There are, he'll tell me later, literally thousands of nongovernmental organizations helping to defend local waterways. Friends of a creek, friends of a pond, friends of the bay. "Every mud hole has its friends now," he says with a grin. "I mean, how in the world did we get a hundred volunteers?"

Rena Obernolte, Bud's partner and project director, chimes in. "A hundred and fifty."

"A hundred fifty, right. They're eager to get in there. It's dirty work, but they all want to help Mother Nature. Everyone's looking to help. Some come once, some are real fixtures—we see them every time we put out a call."

"It's a real community-based organization," Rena says. "That's the only way we can do it, with volunteers helping to put out mounds of shell, bagging up new shell, monitoring, all of that." It's clear what she means. This seems a large-scale project, especially after the slow, quiet, individual monitoring at the stations circling the bay, but in the end it's the accumulation of small acts by individuals. That's how the project started in the first place: Todd Mayer of Marin Rod & Gun gave Bud a call, Bud took a look at the site, Save the Bay started monitoring, grad students from San Francisco State and other schools joined in, Natalie Cosentino-Manning from the National Oceanic and Atmospheric Administration got involved, the call went out for community help—lots of people deserve credit, but in the end there isn't an easy story to tell, or any kind of fixed hierarchy. It's a bunch of concerned people with a common goal, doing what they can to heal the water they live beside.

We gather by the bamboo stakes, shin-deep in mud, chest-deep in water, as the first boat churns toward us. When it arrives, those on board hand down mesh bags of oyster shell contributed by Drake's Bay Oyster Farm. Each bag is a few feet long, maybe a foot across. We drop ten bags around each stake, holding them in mounds with our legs as we pin them with a piece of rebar through the mesh and into the mud. It's simple but clumsy work.

I blink away chips of oyster shell, soon learning not to look straight up at the bag I'm reaching for. The smells of salt and powdered shell and bare tidal mud overwhelm the bridge-traffic exhaust; the bags splash into the water like crab pots. Something is tickling my scalp, and I brush it from my hair into the water. Ah. An earwig. I'm about to ignore it when I feel more in my hair. When I shake my head, two more fall out. There are like two dozen of the earwigs twisting on the water, all around me—looking, I imagine, for a nice, cozy ear to dig into. Around them are all these bubbles, hundreds of minuscule yellow bubbles and . . .

Jesus. Are those earwig *eggs*?

Twain liked hot toddies. Dan De Quille even quoted him about it: "Methinks a toddy, piping hot, would rid this breast of the woes planted by our skulking enemies!" I could go for a toddy right about now. Instead I stop standing under the bags when I take them and generally try not to think about ears or wigs or anything but building the reefs.

The work is surprisingly straightforward, surprisingly mechanical. When we retrofitted our house against earthquakes, it was odd to realize how basic the work was. You bolt the house to the foundations. You hammer in some plywood. You clip the tops of the crawl space's beams to the floorboards. This feels something like that: after all the monitoring, the questions about where the oysters were, what happened to them, and where they are today, in the end the restoration comes down to stuffing bags of shell together in what seems a likely pattern—open enough for spat to drift through, dense enough for them to take hold—and hoping a reef starts to form. It's systematic and deliberate, but there's no real secret sauce here, just a groping, silent dialogue with the oysters to find out what the best shape for substrate might be.

If a large number of oysters do grow, the benefits could be huge. Mussels filter a lot of water—thirty liters per animal per day. But in the same time, an oyster can filter between twenty and fifty *gallons*. True, a reef like this one might not mean much for the bay as a whole—over 200 billion gallons, remember, sweep in and out with the tides every twenty-four hours. Even in the sailing lake near Shoreline Amphitheatre, where Rena found as many as 10 million native oysters—the largest known population in North America—they form only a thin ring, like a hatband, not nearly enough to keep the water really clean. For that you need acre upon acre of reefs.

Still, you have to start somewhere, and filtering is only one benefit of an oyster reef, which also makes a terrific habitat for herring, crabs, shrimp, and gobies (the last are a major food source for birds and fish). Plus, when oysters filter the water, they "repackage" some of the nutrients, leaving them behind as little packets that are later scavenged by crabs and other bottom feeders. And long before it affects the bay as a whole, their constant filtration does help to clean up small inlets and harbors. Clean water promotes eelgrass, which in turn transforms bare mudflats into something much more complex. Helping to restore some of the bay's complexity is really the heart of what we're doing—and "complexity," here, is just another word for opulence, abundance, and life.

These volunteers understand that. That's why they work, despite knowing that we won't be able to eat bay oysters in our lifetime—though the old mining sludge is finally starting to work its way out to sea, there's just too much mercury in what's left. So the volunteers are here out of a basic sense of caring, a desire to secure the bay's future. "The grants we got all required some social outreach," Bud tells me later, "but we didn't expect it to be at the heart of what we'd be doing. Quite unconsciously, we tapped into this need to get in, to get dirty, to help Mother Nature."

We work through the morning and into the afternoon, stacking bag after bag, staking them to the mud with rebar, telling bad jokes while we wait for the boat. "I don't consider this working," Rena says, and after I mentally partition the searing horror of the earwigs, neither do I. The sound of the traffic recedes; we're making a secret here, a little pocket of life that only the volunteers will know about, and that's enough.

There's no guarantee that the reef construction will work, or even that it's a good idea to do it this way at all. There's debate on every point. Would shell scatters be better? They might mirror natural conditions, but tend to vanish into the mud. And maybe dry shell isn't a good idea at all, since it could bring in more invasive plants and animals. How about chicken wire dipped in concrete, then? The open mesh might not get buried under the silt, but it would still mean dumping more metal into the water. One thought that Bud and Rena have is to try perforated concrete domes, with the concrete made only from materials dredged or dug from the bay. They've already bought the mold; maybe next year.

Whatever the ideal conditions, by the end of the day there's a new reef in San Francisco Bay. With the tide getting high, the water looks exactly like it did before we started, just a few rows of bamboo stakes projecting from the water. But who knows what's happening down there? Who knows what might be grateful? In 1870 Twain wrote a piece in the *Galaxy* claiming that he'd been fired by an agricultural paper for describing oyster beds under the heading of "landscape gardening." But really, this *is* a kind of gardening: the reefs are living things that need planting and tending.

Back on the pier, Rena squints through a microscope at an oyster from one of the test bags laid out the summer before. Suddenly she smiles, leans back, one hand paused in her hair. "I see larvae," she says. "It's working."

TO BOIL A SHOULDER OF MUTTON WITH OYSTERS

Hang it some days, then salt it well for two days, bone it, and sprinkle it with pepper and a bit of mace pounded; lay some oysters over it, roll the meat up tight, and tie it. Stew it in a small quantity of water, with an onion and a few pepper-corns, till quite tender. Have ready a little good gravy, and some oysters stewed in it; thicken this with flour and butter, and pour over the mutton when the tape is taken off. The stew-pan should be kept close covered.

—ESTHER ALLEN HOWLAND, *The New England Economical Housekeeper*, 1845

Nearly a year after helping build the reefs, I meet Rena and Bud for Korean spicy chicken and vermicelli at the Emeryville food court on, appropriately enough, Shellmound Street (once site of the region's largest mound, now a stone's throw from Trader Joe's, a massive multiplex, and the Pixar studios). It's been an exciting eleven months up at Marin Rod & Gun; an average of twenty spat have settled onto each shell in the sacks. That's an enormous number, hundreds of thousands of new oysters in all, and it's inspired a whole new phase in the restoration project. Native oysters, it seems clear, *can* be brought back, at least sometimes and in some places. The next step is to figure out what that means for the rest of the bay.

If there's one kind of seafood that brings out the protective Mama Bear in Northern Californians, it's salmon, with Dungeness crab a close second. Both salmon and crab depend on the bay, the former as a road to a spawning ground, the latter as the spawning ground itself. Bud and Rena are taking advantage of that, piggybacking on a salmon-monitoring project upstream. They plan to monitor the fish as they pass through the bay, thus discovering whether the oyster reefs can help to feed and support the shrinking population.

"The problem now," Bud says, "is that when salmon leave the bay, there's nothing in their stomachs. There used to be all kinds of channels through the flats, and they'd stay there, feeding. Now they still stay for a good while, poking around, trying to find food, but their body-fat content goes *way* down."

"So we're putting monitors out there," Rena says. "A control monitor near the eelgrass, another close to the oyster reefs, just to see how long the fish stay in each place."

What's the perfect result? Bud drums his fingers. "Ideally, we'd be able to salmon-tag steelhead, sturgeon, and sharks. You'd see them come to the mudflats, but just in and out—bing, bing, gone. But if you saw them stay near the reefs for hours . . ."

"Even six or seven minutes would be great!" Rena says.

Bud chuckles and nods. "Yeah, six, seven minutes . . . man, that's when I'd be jumping up and down."

It's a hugely expensive proposition (the tags are hundreds of dollars, the monitors fifteen hundred), especially given that they're going to strap most of the equipment to fish and toss the fish into a river. But it's also a hugely exciting one. When Twain was in San Francisco, oysters were an end in themselves, a food to be gathered or farmed, then served by the bushel on the city's tables. Now bay oysters are a tool, a means to restoring the healthy bay that San Franciscans once took for granted. Oysters mean cleaner water, and more eelgrass, and food, and all of that means birds—migrating birds by the millions. It could mean more salmon, before they're gone for good.

And the new efforts might be happening at just the right moment; for the first time since the Gold Rush, the bay is getting deeper. "It was only in 1999, or maybe 2000, that more sediment started leaving the bay than entering," Rena says. "It's that recent. And it was right then that we started seeing more eelgrass, more oysters. . . . Something's happening out there. It is. I just can't say *what*."

After some early Christmas shopping, I drive home on the highway alongside the bay. The sun is setting behind San Francisco; orange light plays through broken clouds onto the swells. I think of the light slanting down through the water—dying in the murk before it reaches the bottom, where bat rays cruise past tunicates clustered on glass bottles, discarded iron, and dumped brick. Before, all I would see out there was water, sunlight, and waves. Now I imagine necks and narrows, a play of salt and fresh water. I see invisible currents and millions of microscopic creatures riding them. The currents are there, and the plankton, and the birds and fish that come to feed. I've lived near the bay for a decade, but I'm only just now starting to see it.

five

DINNER WAS LEISURELY SERVED

Philadelphia Terrapin

LOBSTER, that prized and luxurious food, was once literally dirt cheap; in the 1850s, Canadians used the crustaceans to fertilize potato fields. Twenty years later, Nova Scotians still fed boiled lobster to their pigs and saw shells piled near a house as "signs of poverty and degradation." Like other "trash" fish, lobsters were often used as bait; when he needed more, a cod fisherman could simply send a kid to the shore with a pronged spear, confident that he'd return with a sack. Lobster meat was less an indulgence than a common, inexpensive protein—good for a cheap meal, or for compost, or for catching more expensive and desirable fish.

Until canneries began shipping them nationwide, lobsters remained an almost entirely coastal food. This was largely because they were much more difficult to keep alive during shipment than oysters; in 1842 the first lobster sent from New York to Chicago died in Cleveland.

The lack of extensive demand meant that early canneries used huge lobsters; in the 1870s it took the meat from only two average lobsters to fill a one-pound can. But within a few decades, as the larger specimens were fished out, as many as eight lobsters were needed to pack the same container. Soon they were too rare and expensive to be sold like Sunkist tuna. Lobsters grew scarce because they were an elite and desirable food, but they also became an elite and desirable food because they were scarce.

By the time I was growing up in Connecticut in the eighties, you got lobster by either paying through the nose or catching it yourself. I was lucky—my family had a small string of five traps in Long Island Sound. That meant, when everything was going well, all the lobster I could eat. It also meant that I came to see the shocked, rubber-banded creatures in seafood shops' holding tanks as belonging nearly to a different species from the snapping, flapping, furious bugs crowded into a trap's corners. Lobster meant dunking slick claw and robust tail meat into butter; it meant picking out tiny troves from the body and legs. But it also meant the smell of bony bunker fish strung on a coat hanger as bait and the splash as a wooden trap dropped onto a swell—an oddly plural splash, as ten slats hit the water all at once. And, regrettably, it meant the sound of lobsters clanking in the steamer as they died, a sound that drove my eight-year-old sister to two years of vegetarianism and wearing nothing but black.

Obviously, we were just hobbyists, heading out a few times a week to pull our traps on flat, safe water. There wasn't any physical or financial peril. Still, when the lobsters were nearly wiped out—killed by the runoff from mosquito spray after an outbreak of West Nile virus—it was heartbreaking, like learning that a childhood home had burned down.

Like lobsters, diamondback terrapins began the nineteenth century as a common food; like lobsters, they ended it among its elite. And, unsurprisingly, the more expensive and rarefied terrapin became, the less likely a given eater was to know the first thing about the source of the semiaquatic turtle in his soup bowl. Twain knew prairie chickens, trout, oysters, mussels, raccoons, and possums well; he'd lived on the same land, drunk and swum the same waters, breathed the same wild air, even chased them through their forest haunts. Philadelphia terrapin soup was different. Though he loved a particular mode of cooking them, Twain, I think, was as distant from terrapins and their salt marshes as most modern Americans are from New England lobster—which is to say completely distant. Just as some people today are surprised to learn that lobsters aren't actually bright red while crawling around the ocean bottom, I'm not sure that Twain could have picked a live diamondback terrapin out of a turtle lineup. He probably knew very little about how they lived, or were caught or shipped.

Though Twain had spent some time in Philadelphia as a printer's apprentice in 1853, Philadelphia isn't *of* the Chesapeake, or the salt marsh, in anything like the same way that San Francisco is *of* its bay. For Twain, terrapin soup was, in the end, a city thing. Though it was often a food of the poor, he probably ate it most often from the kinds of silver dishes that led an 1880 *Washington Post* reporter to declare terrapin essential to any dinner "laying claim to being a pretentious affair" (which was, at the time, apparently a compliment).

So to me it seems totally appropriate (in a way, almost inevitable) that Mark Twain, of Hannibal, Missouri, ate stewed terrapin soup in Boston on the night he tried to join the ranks of America's literary elite—the night that proved the most humiliating of his life.

TERRAPIN CLEAR SOUP

Save the water used in boiling the terrapin, and after they are dressed put their shells, broken up, into the water, and boil them for six hours; then add enough stock of bouillon or consommé to doubly cover them, and again boil them until they begin to soften. After that cool and clarify the broth thus made, season with salt, cayenne, and Madeira, and serve it clear.

—JULIET CORSON, *Practical American Cookery and Household Management*, 1886

Diamondback terrapins rule the eastern salt marshes. They have no competition at all from other turtles, which lack salt glands; the ability to purge salt from moderately salty drinking water gives terrapins exclusive title to all the prime brackish wetland real estate. They're carnivores and will eat almost anything else that swims or scrabbles: oysters, clams, snails, shrimp, mussels, barnacles, fish. They'll eat a crab's leg, tearing it off from behind and fleeing from the claws. In turn, crabs raid their nests, as do foxes, crows, and eagles; the turtles are themselves eaten by raccoons.

And by men. "Terrapin" is a corruption of the Algonquin *torope*, the Abenaki *turepe*, and the Delaware *turpen*, all of which mean "edible turtle"; Native Americans, and later white colonists and enslaved Africans, defined the animal by its value as food. Terrapins have been trapped, snatched up barehanded, rutted out from the mud, caught by children with hand nets, and unceremoniously dredged from their winter hiding spots. North Carolinians tracked nesting terrapins with dogs or set fire to marsh grasses in winter in hopes the warmth would tempt them from hibernation (the *New York Times* called both methods "barbaric"). More often men waded chest-deep in the autumn Chesapeake, probing the muddy bottom with pronged poles, hoping to prod a hibernating turtle's shell.

The same 1880 *Washington Post* article that declared terrapin essential to pretentious dinners also described the most "primitive" style of cooking one: laying it on its back, alive, among the coals or in a hot oven. After it was cooked, the cook removed the gall bag and ate the rest directly from the shell, possibly with a dressing of sherry and butter. Cooking terrapin this way (without the dressing, of course) was common among Chesapeake tribes such as the Delaware, who buried turtles alive in hot embers.

Terrapin stew also has deep roots among African Americans, such as those who made Louisiana's soupe à la tortue for French and Spanish Creole planters, or Baltimore's best French-trained turtle cooks (many had fled to the city from the Haitian Revolution). In 1880 the *New York Times* claimed that "there is an art about making terrapin soup which a professional cook has to acquire, but which seems to come natural to a Virginian negro" and a decade later praised "the terrapin dressed by the great original bandana-crowned negro cook." Meanwhile, New York socialite and dedicated snob Ward McAllister wrote that no Frenchman could make the soup, which "require[d] the native born culinary genius of the African." Putting aside "bandana-crowned" and that kind of garbage, terrapin was clearly something unusual: a dish with African-American origins that were openly acknowledged by the Victorian upper class.

That's not to say that wealthy whites were giving *all* the credit to poor or enslaved African Americans for inventing their beloved terrapin soup. It was common, for instance, to say that the turtles were "given" or "fed to" slaves—a typical example is the story that slaves once "raised their voices in loud complaint because their masters insisted on feeding them diamondback terrapin twice a week." Though turtles were sometimes provided by slave owners, African Americans were surely also supplementing poor rations by catching terrapin, much as they did with raccoon and opossum. After they took a necessity and made it art, stewed terrapin was—in a class sense—both humble and elevated, both high and low.

Once a simple, poor man's soup, terrapin became a luxurious dish; Washington and Lafayette are said to have eaten it the night before the

Battle of Yorktown, and Lafayette's love for the dish is supposed to have
helped draw him back to the States. John Adams ate it at least four
times during the Continental Congresses, with one meal including
"Turttle, and every other Thing—Flummery, Jellies, Sweetmeats of 20
sorts, Trifles, Whip'd Syllabubbs, floating Islands, fools—&c., and then
a Desert of Fruits, Raisins, Almonds, Pears, Peaches."

The "turttle" may well have been cooked with expensive Madeira
like that Adams drank during the same meal "at a great Rate and found
no Inconvenience in." Such Madeira or good sherry was, from very
early on, always used in upper-class terrapin recipes, which both added
to and symbolized a stew's exclusivity. An 1881 New York cooking class
taught by Juliet Corson, one of America's first cooking teachers, froze
up momentarily when the students realized that she was about to add
such a "precious cordial," a "treasure-trove" that could be found in only
two of the city's clubs. One student openly protested, asking whether
"such divine wine [was] to be amalgamated with a terrapin," and class
continued only after another argued that "noble food requires a royal
dressing." Terrapins, the author judged, were the Athenians of the fish
world, especially compared with helots like the skate.

Corson's students seem to have known everything about terrapin—
biology, history, price, where to find and eat the best—except for how
to cook it. The greatest distance the coastal specialty of terrapin soup
traveled was not east to west but down to up: from the iron stewpots of
poor blacks and whites to the silver tureens of the elite. And it was a
rare man who could make the same trip.

STEWED TERRAPIN, WITH CREAM

Place in a sauce-pan, two heaping tablespoonfuls of butter and
one of dry flour; stir it over the fire until it bubbles; then

gradually stir in a pint of cream, a teaspoonful of salt, a quarter
of a teaspoonful of white pepper, the same of grated nutmeg,
and a very small pinch of cayenne. Next, put in a pint of
terrapin meat and stir all until it is scalding hot. Move the
sauce-pan to the back part of the stove or range, where the
contents will keep hot but not boil: then stir in four well-beaten
yolks of eggs; do not allow the terrapin to boil after adding the
eggs, but pour it immediately into a tureen containing a gill of
good Madeira and a tablespoonful of lemon juice. Serve hot.

—FANNY LEMIRA GILLETTE, *White House Cook Book,* 1887

In 1866 Twain had left San Francisco for New York.* His short
story "The Celebrated Jumping Frog of Calaveras County" had already made him unexpectedly famous. But it was his next voyage that
would establish him firmly and finally among the country's most popular writers; in New York he boarded the steamer *Quaker City,* joining
the first organized touring cruise in American history. He'd visit Europe
and the Holy Land, traveling all the while with a party of mostly pious
and respectable fellow passengers.

Along the way Twain and a few like-minded friends mocked the
"pilgrims" mercilessly; they played cards, drank, and ran free through
Paris and Italy and the ruins of Greece. Twain's portrayal of the staid
pilgrims would be among the first of awkward, humorless American
tourists. It would also be among the most popular—during his lifetime
The Innocents Abroad was his best-selling book.

But for a short while, en route to the Middle East, he'd become
preoccupied with something smaller and more personal. A fellow trav-

---

*He'd only recently returned from a trip to Hawaii, where he surfed; it is for such things as this
that I love him.

eler had opened a locket, revealing a picture of his sister. Twain was enchanted. The picture was "something more than a human likeness," he proclaimed. The girl's name was Olivia Langdon; within a year of Twain's return in 1867, he and Livy were engaged.

Now, in 1877, the couple lived in Hartford with their young daughters Susy and Clara. But though these were happy years for Twain, he found himself increasingly absorbed by memories of his rustic childhood. He'd just published the semiautobiographical *The Adventures of Tom Sawyer;* a year before that had come the wonderfully vivid sketch of piloting life serialized in the *Atlantic Monthly* as "Old Times on the Mississippi." But he was writing, he knew, of vanished lives. He would never live in a steamboat's cabin again, or a Washoe tent, or even a modest house in Hannibal, Missouri. His home now was a fabulous "steamboat Gothic" mansion on Nook Farm, a Hartford community that included artists, social reformers, and writers such as Harriet Beecher Stowe; the house and its surroundings were perfect symbols of Twain's new social aspirations.

So by December 1877, Twain was deeply torn. Memories of childhood and the frontier dominated his creative life. But he also hoped that writing about those memories would allow him to break from them, to join the elevated reaches of the eastern literary high society. Stories such as "The Facts Concerning the Recent Carnival of Crime in Connecticut" and "The Personal Habits of Siamese Twins" told of doubles and alter egos. Earlier in the year he even published a straightforward travelogue of Bermuda under the name Sam Clemens; he struggled to find the right balance between the raw, powerful language that made him famous and what he hoped would be greater respect from America's best-known literary writers.

An invitation to speak at a birthday dinner for abolitionist poet John Greenleaf Whittier seemed a terrific opportunity. The roster of the guests was stunning: Henry Wadsworth Longfellow, Ralph Waldo Emerson, and Oliver Wendell Holmes, all assembled like a "row of venerable and still active volcanoes" at Boston's Brunswick Hotel, along with less famous (but, in an immediate career sense, just as important) luminaries from the *Atlantic Monthly*. Twain planned to begin in his normal rustic style, pivoting at last into lavish praise of the three famous writers. But the event, he later reported, was a disaster; and when Mark Twain, one of history's gutsiest public speakers, says he bombed, you know that something went really hair-raisingly wrong.

As he waited to speak, Twain ate and drank for over three hours. It was a banquet in high Victorian style, and it's easy to imagine the scene: the elaborate floral centerpieces, the blue-and-white china, the polished silver and shining glass. An enthusiastic reporter from the *Boston Daily Globe* recorded the evening's menu:

OYSTERS ON SHELL ❧ *Sauterne*

Soups.

PUREE OF TOMATOES AU CROUTONS.

CONSOMMÉ PRINTANIER ROYAL ❧ *Sherry*

Fish.

BOILED CHICKEN, HALIBUT À LA NAVARINE.

POTATOES À LA HOLLANDAISE.

SMELTS PANNE, SAUCE TARTAR ❧ *Chablis*

Removes.

CAPON À L'ANGLAISE.

RICE.

CAULIFLOWER.

SADDLE OF ENGLISH MUTTON À LA PONTOISE.

STRING BEANS.

TURNIPS.

Champagne.

MUMM'S DRY VERZENAY.

ROEDERER IMPERIAL.

Entrees.

FILET OF BEEF, LARDED, SAUCE FINANCIÈRE.

ÉPINARDS VELOUTÉES.

VOL-AU-VENT OF OYSTERS À L'AMÉRICAINE.

SQUABS EN COMPOTE À LA FRANCAISE, TOMATOES.

SAUTÉES.

TERRAPIN STEWED, MARYLAND STYLE.

SORBET AU KIRSCH ❧ *Claret*

Game.

BROILED PARTRIDGES ON TOAST. CANVASBACK DUCKS.

WATER CRESSES, SWEET POTATOES,

DRESSED LETTUCE ❧ *Burgundy*

Pastry.

CHARLOTTE RUSSE. GELÉE AU CHAMPAGNE.

GÂTEAUX VARIÉS.

CONFECTIONERY.

FRUIT. DESSERT.

COFFEE.

Twain was a long way from Hannibal—its raccoon and greens and corn pone, its hoecake and simply fried fish. At the Whittier dinner, course after course was accompanied by its own specialized silver;

it was an era deeply in love with ice-cream knives and fish cutters, orange cups and banana bowls. Oyster forks had been around for decades; now there were asparagus tongs, grape shears, insulated water pitchers for making proper, Twain-approved ice water—everything, I think, but strawberry seeders, and I might be wrong about that. Before sitting back replete (and a bit drunk), Twain had gorged on seven courses, including a Maryland-style terrapin soup: turtle meat and hard-boiled terrapin eggs floating in a clear, buttery, sherry-infused broth. He likely ate with a formal terrapin fork, each of its three broad tines like a curved, frozen, silver flame.

Guest after guest rose in praise of the Volcanoes. Whittier, Longfellow, Emerson, and Holmes were giants who knew themselves to be giants, and it was an era completely unembarrassed by lavish flattery; soon the accumulated pomposity threatened to inflate the Brunswick Hotel and float it high over Boston. Then it was Twain's turn. He ascended to the podium, paused, and launched into a tall tale of his days in the Nevada country, when he'd come upon a miner recently besieged by three impostors pretending to be Longfellow, Emerson, and Holmes. "Mr. Emerson was a seedy little bit of a chap, red-headed," Twain recalled the miner reporting. "Mr. Holmes was as fat as a balloon. He weighed as much as three hundred and had double chins all the way down to his stomach. Mr. Longfellow was built like a prize fighter. . . . They had been drinking, I could see that." Twain thought it was clear enough that the three were impostors; his plan was for the Twain of the story to slam them as pitiful impersonators of the "gracious singers to whom we and the world pay loving reverence and homage." But he took too long to reach that point—and by the time he had, the literary fellowship gathered at the Brunswick Hotel was severely unamused.

"I didn't know enough to give it up and sit down," Twain recalled almost thirty years later. "I was too new to public speaking." But the truth is that he'd been lecturing for more than a decade and was a flabbergastingly daring speaker. He once told a packed house the same dull anecdote six times in a row, until they saw the "delicate satire" and erupted. Another time he walked onstage and stood, smoking, saying nothing, *for over ten minutes,* until finally the room exploded with laughter and applause. In public-speaking terms, that's Super Bowl MVP stuff. The man knew how to work a crowd, how to read it, how to make uncomfortable silences work *for* him—to draw out pauses until they were primed to hold whatever he wanted to fill them with.

But at the Whittier dinner his instincts failed him. He looked out over the silent ruins of a fine Victorian banquet, the white table-cloths now stained and rumpled, covered with crumbs and coffee cups. The guests wore black vests; they sat in long, quiet rows. Someone toyed with a pastry fork; someone drained a last minuscule drop of claret. After a "frightful, . . . awful, . . . desolating silence," the next speaker had to get up. The poor hopeful is now remembered only as Bishop—the author of a recent well-received novel, who (in Twain's telling at least) was about to walk into the public-speaking equivalent of a chain saw:

> Bishop was away up in the public favor, and he was an object of high interest, consequently there was a sort of national expectancy in the air; we may say our American millions were standing, from Maine to Texas and from Alaska to Florida, holding their breath, their lips parted, their hands ready to applaud, when Bishop should get up on that occasion and for the first time in his life speak in public. . . .
>
> I had spoken several times before, and that is the reason why I was able to go on without dying in my tracks, as I ought to have done—but Bishop had had no experience. He was up facing those awful deities—facing those other people, those strangers, facing human beings for the first time in his life, with a speech to utter. . . . He didn't last long. It was not many sentences after his first before he began to hesitate, and break, and lose his grip, and totter, and wobble, and at last he slumped down in a limp and mushy pile.

It's not clear whether or not Bishop had to be hospitalized. *Atlantic Monthly* editor William Dean Howells pulled Twain from the room, then twisted the knife: "Consider what you have done for Bishop. It is bad enough in your case, you deserve to suffer. You have committed this crime, and you deserve to have all you are going to get. But here is an innocent man. Bishop had never done you any harm, and see what you have done to him. He can never hold his head up again. The world can never look upon Bishop as being a live person. He is a corpse."

Twain was mortified. One paper called his speech a "high-flavored Nevada delirium tremens," tossing him straight back to the western deserts he'd tried to escape. Twain wrote to Howells that "I feel my misfortune has injured me all over the country; therefore it will be best that I retire from the public at present." Less than four months later, Twain and his family left for Europe: they would be gone for more than a year.

MARYLAND TERRAPINS

A young one will boil tender in half an hour. They are done when the shell is easily removed. Be careful not to cut off the heads before boiling, as it will make them watery. In picking them, be careful not to break the gall or waste the liquor. The small bones are often left in the terrapin—if they are Diamondbacks. Be careful not to break the eggs. When picked, add the liquor, and to three medium sized terrapins, three-fourths pound of butter, salt and pepper (cayenne) to taste. Let them stew for a short time, but be careful not to stir them more than is absolutely necessary. If you wish, one-half pint of good wine can be added just before serving.

Another way to dress terrapin is to add to the liquor of three terrapins, three-fourths pound of butter thickened with browned flour, cayenne pepper and salt. Spices or onions are never used in Maryland to dress terrapins. —Mrs. William Reed.

—Carrie V. Shuman, *Favorite Dishes*, 1893

Baltimore and Philadelphia were both famous for terrapin soup; by including the Philadelphia version on his menu, Twain joined a debate that, Ward McAllister said in 1890, had "been agitated for thirty years or more." The major point of contention was cream. Philadelphians added a lot of cream, while Baltimoreans favored a butter-infused broth like that served at the Whittier dinner. The difference prompted long-running, passionate disputes, like the one over whether Manhattan clam chowder, lacking cream, is potentially good clam chowder, or even chowder at all (it's not).*

Given Twain's affectionate relationship with cream, it's no surprise that he sided with the Philadelphians. Colonel John Forney, once a member of Lincoln's cabinet, would have agreed, arguing that "terrapin is essentially a Philadelphia dish. Baltimore delights in it, Washington eats it, New York knows it; but in Philadelphia it approaches a crime not to be passionately fond of it." However, in 1893 two clubs met before an impartial jury to decide once and for all which soup deserved primacy. Twain was not on the jury; Baltimore won.

The stew wasn't always named after a city. There was also Southern style, sometimes attributed to Savannah or Charleston, which the *New Yorker*'s Joseph Mitchell gorged on in 1939 and which "contained

*And it's actually from Rhode Island; "Manhattan" is an insult, originally levied by right-thinking citizens of chowder-loving Massachusetts.

the meat, hearts and livers of two diamondbacks killed early that day, eight yolks of hard-boiled eggs that had been pounded up and passed through a sieve, a half pound of yellow country butter, two pints of thick cream, a little flour, a pinch of salt, a dash of nutmeg, and a glass and a half of amontillado." This recipe, like most others, included nutmeg; others added mace, or cayenne.

Many recipes called for liver, a holdout from a more all-inclusive era; Amelia Simmons had begun her 1796 recipe with detailed instructions on handling the entrails, lungs, blood, and liver, all added to the back and belly meat (each dish was then infused with Madeira and sweet herbs, covered with beaten eggs and parsley, and baked). But by the time of the 1887 *White House Cook Book,* entrails were "no longer used in cooking terrapins for the best tables." Boiled turtle eggs, on the other hand, were common—and usually taken from the female terrapin being cooked. Baltimore's Hotel Rennert (which kept hundreds of live terrapins penned in the cellar) also included the blood along with the liver, cream, and whole turtle eggs.

The normal accompaniment for terrapin soup was roasted canvasback ducks from the Chesapeake; canvasbacks headed up the game course as far away as the Whittier dinner in Boston, which probably made Twain happy. He once wrote a letter to Livy describing a "marvel" of a dinner he'd eaten in New York, beginning with individual quarts of champagne in a silver cooler. After a first course of "very small raw oysters—just that moment opened, and swimming in their own sea water," had come terrapin stew "in dainty little covered pots, with curious little gold-&-silver terrapin spoons from Tiffany's. Sublime," he wrote. "There never was such terrapin before. It was unspeakable." Finally, "before *each* man was set an entire canvass-back duck, red hot from the oven, & on his plate was laid a carving knife and fork.—he must do his own carving. These ducks were just simply divine. So ended the dinner. . . . Five skeletons represented the ducks; 6 empty bottles represented the champagne."

The best canvasbacks, as Twain noted on his menu, were from Baltimore, or at least the Chesapeake—by fall these had grown so fat on wild celery that they were said to include their own gravy. "There is no need to prepare a gravy," went typical instructions. "Immediately they are cut they will fill the dish with the richest gravy that ever was tasted." This regional quality is why they were so often paired with terrapin; McAllister said that "terrapin is with us as national a dish as canvasback," while in 1839 Frederick Marryat ate them together so frequently that he thought it natural to compare them directly, writing that "the great delicacies in America are the terrapin, and the canvas-back ducks. To like the former I consider rather an acquired taste, but the canvas-back duck is certainly well worthy of its reputation." He was unusual in strongly preferring one over the other; both delicacies, the *New York Times* said in 1888, were "necessary to a very swell dinner."

However it was prepared, whatever the accompaniments, terrapin meat was usually described as elevated, even delicate. Joseph Mitchell compared it to baby mushrooms. A recent *Baltimore Sun* article dissented considerably, saying that the word most often applied lately is "gamy"—and that it was even a bit like muskrat. This, I'd suggest, was written by someone who has never eaten muskrat—or else descriptions of tasty turtle soup were monstrous put-ons, massive acts of collective self-delusion. Besides, in Twain's day cooks agreed that the best analogue to terrapin was calf's head; recipes for mock turtle soup almost always began with simmering a head until the cheeks and tongue fall apart.

A lot of terrapin recipes sound delicious. Still, I can't get as enthusiastic about terrapin soup as about Twain's other foods, for the simple reason that before any cooking could begin, the terrapin had to be dead. Obviously that's true for the raccoons, trout, prairie chickens, and so on. The difference is that, like lobster today, terrapins were almost always sold live; you killed them in the kitchen.

After my semitough talk about killing lobsters resolutely and without regret, the descriptions of killing turtles remind me why I should never talk tough. Terrapins are cute. I wish terrapins well. And though, in an era of truly abundant terrapin, I can imagine killing one with a single swift stroke of the cleaver, nearly every recipe begins with something along the lines of "plunge the live turtle into boiling water." That I don't think I could do, or ask to have done on my behalf. And it strikes me that the necessity of killing and cleaning a turtle on the spot was probably a big part of its elite appeal; cooking terrapin was messy and difficult, but not so much if you had a full-time kitchen staff. (Suddenly the upper classes acknowledging the African-American origins of terrapin makes a bit more sense—they often referred to blacks *cooking* terrapin, rather than *inventing* the recipe. When it comes to maintaining race and class boundaries, that makes all the difference in the world; instead of crediting African Americans with creative cooking, the well-heeled were bragging about their servants' skills.)

Even in Twain's day, the death of the turtle could prompt serious angst among unpracticed cooks. An observer at the Corson cooking class admitted to hating the thought of the turtle's "martyrdom" and rationalized that "if there was a better way of taking away her life, humanity would have dictated that method," before finally giving way to practicality: "to decapitate a turtle by saying 'Dilly! Dilly!' to him or her does not always succeed in getting them to show their heads." Meanwhile, a souvenir cookbook from the 1893 World's Columbian Exposition argued that boiling or roasting them alive was preferable in any case and warned home cooks to "be careful not to cut off their heads before boiling, since it will make them watery." Putting aside the question of exactly how careful you have to be to avoid cutting off a turtle's head, even if it left the meat as watery as water I think I'd chant *Dilly! Dilly!* all day before I'd drop a *live goddamn turtle* into a boiling kettle.

Of course, my attitude here marks me as a person who can afford to make that kind of decision. If I don't eat turtle tonight, then tonight will be like every other night of my life; I can always call Lanesplitter Pizza and order a large Garbage Special. A few centuries ago, the Delaware wouldn't have had the luxury of turning down an available protein source, especially one that could be pried from marsh mud in winter; many enslaved Africans certainly did not. What's more, Native American earthenwares couldn't sustain a hot and furious boil. If the easiest way of cooking an animal that could retract into its shell was to put the whole, live animal into the coals, then that's what most people were going to do. Having a direct relationship with wild foods can mean respecting them, treating their sources with care. But it also means that they're *foods,* things needed and sought for a person's immediate sustenance.

After killing a turtle came preparing it for the stewpot; since gall or sand would spoil the meat, the big challenge was cutting out the gallbladder and sand bag whole. If the killing had been a matter for some angst, cutting it up inspired grandiose wariness, as though approaching the bladder were like stalking a grizzly. "Even a pinprick of gall will spoil the whole thing," quailed the *Post*. The *Times* reporter failed to man up: "Here was your terrapin, almost ready to give a foretaste of bliss, and only a puncture of the gall bladder between what was supremely excellent and what was horribly nasty! The class was serious at once, and looked on, breathless" (the successful extraction of the bladder led to "mutual hand-shaking" all around). Statesman and gourmet Sam Ward struck a Hemingwayesque, sentimental-tough-guy stance: "A little gall does not impair the flavor, . . . but the sand bag requires the skillful touch of a surgeon, the heart of a lion, the eye of an eagle, and the hand of a lady."

Terrapin stew retained its local reputation even after long-distance shipment became common (the ideal Maryland winter dinner, the *Post* said in 1880, included turtle, roasted canvasback ducks, oysters, and crab salad, along with potatoes, vegetables, fried hominy cakes, and celery). At its best, terrapin could be a revelation to a newcomer, a symbol of the region's delights. Corson's New York cooking class ended with a midwestern student eating turtle for the first time: "After his second spoonful instantaneous measures were mooted by him either for the introduction of the chelonian to Illinois or his migration, with his wife and family, to this, the land of the terrapin."

Four months after the Whittier dinner, Twain was as far from the Land of the Terrapin as he could reasonably get, his whole family—Livy, Susy, and Clara—in tow. Boarding the steamer, Twain had been full of anticipation, eager to return to the continent he'd loved exploring with his friends on the *Quaker City* a decade before. "One feels so cowed, at home, so unindependent, so deferential to all sorts of clerks & little officials," he wrote just before departure, "that it is good to go & breathe the free air of Europe & lay in a stock of self-respect & independence."

But as he traveled through Europe, his excitement faded. European manners, he came to believe, were often a mere cover—a polished disguise for aristocratic decadence. "It will not do for me to find merit in American manners," he began, with deadpan affect, "for are they not the standing butt for the jests of critical and polished Europe? Still I must venture to claim one little matter of superiority in our manners"— namely, that ladies could walk wherever they wanted, whenever they wanted; in London, Twain claimed, they would swiftly be approached and insulted by so-called gentlemen. In America, he said, a woman might "encounter less polish than she would in the old world, but [would] run across enough humanity to make up for it." Even artists were wildly overrated, especially the revered old masters. "There are artists in Arkansas to-day," he declared, "who would not have had to paint signs for a living if they had had the luck to live in the time of the old masters."

All of which says something about his mood when he sat down in an Italian hotel room, toward the end of his travels, and wrote his menu. European *home* food, Twain readily confessed, was often excellent—he called dinner with a Venetian family "a luxury which very seldom fell to our lot on the continent." But food in European *hotels,* where he ate most meals, was "a sorrowful business. A man accustomed to American food and American domestic cookery would not starve to death suddenly in Europe," he judged; "but I think he would gradually waste away, and eventually die."

Again and again the food in hotels and way stations left him frustrated. After breakfast one morning, he reported that he had "made a rare & valuable addition to my bric-a-brac collection. . . . It was an egg. There was a something about it which satisfied me that it was an antique." He decided that the best way to tell Rhine wine from vinegar was to consult the label. Even German beer could play false: "We bought a bottle or so of beer," he wrote; "at any rate they called it beer, but I knew by the price that it was dissolved jewelry, and I perceived by the taste that dissolved jewelry is not good stuff to drink."

He remained, of course, a man open to pleasure where he found it; he didn't close his eyes or mind to what was good. He loved Emmentaler cheese, and *Faschiertes* beefsteak with yellow of egg (minced or ground beef; probably it was bound together with egg yolk before cooking). He called green, egg-size plums the "pleasantest fruit in Germany," thinking them "better than oranges"; that, he mused, "is why the plum, which is with us a worthless fruit, holds such a place in [German] literature." When he could get good ones, away from the hotel's decayed specimens, he liked German pears, cherries, raspberries, apples, peaches, and strawberries, as well as broiled salmon, Wolfsbrunnen trout, and duck.

Sometimes food and life joined with a savor as intense as on the shores of Tahoe, or in the San Franciscan night. In Switzerland, Twain recalled,

> we had such a beautiful day, and such endless pictures of limpid lakes, and green hills and valleys, and majestic mountains, and milky cataracts dancing down the steeps and gleaming in the sun, that we could not help feeling sweet toward all the world; so we tried to drink all the milk, and eat all the grapes and apricots and

berries, and buy all the bouquets of wild flowers which the little peasant children had for sale; but we had to retire from this contract, for it was too heavy.

Another time, during a rafting trip, he stepped ashore at noon and bought bottles of beer and roasted chicken, immediately setting out again with the cold drinks and hot food. "There is no pleasanter place for such a meal," he said, "than a raft that is gliding down the winding Neckar past green meadows and wooded hills, and slumbering villages, and craggy heights graced with crumbling towers and battlements."

But these were the exceptions, the times when he broke out of his role as a visitor—a stranger—and ate the best of local produce. More typical were the first-class hotels that seemed "to use poor cheap 2d hand meats and veg[etables] because [they were] cheap," that bought "strawberries when they [had] been 2 full months in market," and then only the oldest and worst. He was sarcastically grateful for new potatoes, offered once and once only; Europe was not his home. "Short visits to Europe are better for us than long ones," he reflected. "The former preserve us from becoming Europeanized; they keep our pride of country intact, and at the same time they intensify our affection for our country and our people."

He scorned blind, political patriotism; but he did feel affection—love—for his home. Now he wanted the genuine, the honest, the real. "Ah for a hot biscuit," he longed in his journal, and "coffee, *real* coffee, with *real* cream.—& *real* potatoes. Fried chicken, corn bread, *real* butter, *real* beefsteak, *good* roast beef with *taste* to it." The menu began as a tribute to all his favorite foods, wherever in the world he'd eaten them; the first draft, in his journal, included chickens and hard-boiled eggs from Palestine, raisins and figs from Smyrna, Egyptian dates and pomegranates, South Island flying fish, and turtle steak (probably eaten in Hawaii, then called the Sandwich Islands), as well as complimentary nods to Roquefort cheese, German trout, English turtle soup, whitebait sole, and mutton. But as he went on—as he went deeper—the memory of American foods drew him back, and back, and back.

Maybe the Boston humiliation helped Twain to see American food in a different way; maybe his menu was, in some small, unconscious way, an act of defiance. It was at least the product of a defiant mood. Had the elite rejected his plain humor and language? Here, then, was his celebration of simple, honest, genuine American flavors. Here were things he loved without reservation or apology. He knew the country that produced them; it was, he thought, plainspoken, vibrant, straightforward, generous, and young . . . and perhaps too brash for the sophisticates who had wounded him to appreciate.

The Whittier dinner had gloried in consommé printanier royal, capon à l'anglaise, smelts panne, squabs en compote à la francaise. . . .

Game on.

"Radishes," he wrote. "Baked apples, with cream. Fried oysters; stewed oysters. Frogs. . . ."

CALF'S HEAD À LA TERRAPIN

Wash and clean a calf's head, and cook until tender in boiling water to cover. Cool and cut meat from cheek in small cubes. To two cups meat dice add one cup sauce made of two tablespoons butter, two tablespoons flour, and one cup White Stock, seasoned with one-half teaspoon salt, one-eighth teaspoon pepper, and few grains cayenne. Add one-half cup cream and yolks of two eggs slightly beaten; cook two minutes and add two tablespoons Madeira wine.

—Fannie Merritt Farmer, *The Boston Cooking-School Cook Book*, 1896

It's been over two hundred years since John Adams ate terrapin during the Continental Congresses. It's been ninety-one since sherry, the essential ingredient, temporarily disappeared during Prohibition (a lull that probably saved the terrapin from extinction). And it's been more than eighty since terrapin soup, by then rare enough to be eaten only by the wealthy, formed the first course of the first Academy Awards dinner. Now Marguerite Whilden roots three gentle fingers into a backyard patch of sand in Neavitt, Maryland, searching for a clutch of diamondback eggs.

The ideal terrapin habitat combines soft sand for nesting, thick marsh grasses where hatchlings can hide, and estuaries filled with oysters, snails, and clams. Even more than prairie chickens in their mosaic of grass and corn, or raccoons in their marshes and woods and lawns, terrapins need the border places—the margins, where the energies of different places wrestle and merge. The intertidal zone is among the greatest of such places, where swelling water carries nutrients to grasses and shellfish twice every day. That's where terrapins often feed; that's where they thrive.

But the terrapin nest Marguerite is digging up is in anything but a natural, sandy shoreline. Marguerite, sometimes known as "the Turtle Lady" since budget cuts at the Maryland Department of Natural Resources prompted an early retirement and full-time dedication to terrapin restoration, has dumped ten tons of sand into a three-foot-deep, fifteen-foot-long, ten-foot-wide oval in the center of an acre of Eastern Shore lawn. A quarter of Marguerite's "beach" is fenced, a safe place for terrapins to nest. The remainder is planted with native marsh plants: spartina, bayberry, cordgrass.

This time my whole family (Eli, Erik, and our newborn daughter, Mio) has come with me. Eli grew up in Virginia—we met in archaeology grad school in Charlottesville—and of all the things we miss living in California, the greatest is the vibrant sense of a landscape *alive:* of puddles that harbor huddling frogs, vines overtaking gas stations, cicada screams and fireflies muddling humid summer air. When we walk down to the dock, within moments we'll see tiny garfish, a pair of water snakes, crab moltings, jellyfish, gulls, and a bald eagle. Birdsong here is insistent and omnipresent. It's a very different feeling from that of the drier, statelier lands out west, where lack of water means life has to spread and space itself. Near the Chesapeake a thousand things want to live; here oysters once piled so high as to become navigational threats, a Swiss visitor writing in 1701 that "there are whole banks of them so that the ships must avoid them. . . . [A sloop] struck an oyster bed, where we had to wait about two hours for the tide." The shellfish grew so big, he recalled, that he had to cut them in two. This is a place that cries out to be crammed.

Near the house, flanked by containers where Marguerite grows tomatoes and basil, are three big plastic tanks of diamondbacks: ten-inch females, six-inch males, tiny hatchlings. The turtles are an odd combination of stoic and social, crawling slowly up to and over one another, bumping gently against the sides with a sound like the start of rain. When held they regard us calmly. Many have distinct "diamond" points along the midline of their upper carapace. Each scute plate is whorled, like the central few lines of a fingerprint, or the stretched view of the mission staircase in *Vertigo*.

When we boarded the plane, two small kids in tow, people eyed us as though we were guiding wolverines. But Mio is, at this stage of her life, basically a purse. And we were able to keep Erik happy by alternating chants of "We're gonna see turtles, right, man? Turtles! Yeah, turtles!" with the funktastic colors and sounds of an *Electric Company* DVD. Now we've made it, and Erik is on all fours, completely absorbed by finding eggs buried in the fenced laying area. He peers so closely into the hole that I have to crane to see the eggs emerge from the sand. One, two, three . . . each egg is half the size of a Ping-Pong ball, each dented and somewhat squished (they're hard as hens' eggs now, but when first laid the shells were soft as leather). This clutch has ten in all, several fewer than average; amazingly, though laid all at once by a single female, it might have more than one father—a female can store sperm for up to four years. Carefully, keeping them upright, Marguerite places each egg into a bucket full of sand.

Though she started out leasing a small portion of a wildlife refuge along the South River in Annapolis, where she worked to protect terrapins from litter, campfires, and boats, Marguerite chose Neavitt deliberately. This part of the Eastern Shore, she says, has a strong conservation ethic, and there are still some large farms left amid houses on land that once grew pink tomatoes and sweet corn. "There's a reason we don't do heart transplants in ninety-year-olds," she says. "You have to focus on the good bets, the things you can save for the long term."

Terrapins used to be vulnerable to upper-class appetites. Today, with their commercial catch and sale banned, they're more vulnerable to upper-class summer homes—the developments that eat up modest old houses and farms, replace meadows with lawns, and block routes to nesting grounds with banks of broken-stone riprap meant to slow the shore's erosion. But Neavitt, which was at the heart of the old terrapin fishery, is still intimately connected to the water. The public pier is filled with working boats, barnacled and beaten and sturdy-looking. There's a crab-shedding operation around the corner, holding blue crabs until they molt and become softshells; Marguerite's cottage was once a modest lodge for canvasback-duck hunters. Her immediate neighbor, Joe Jones, worked as a waterman for thirty years—hauling crab pots at 4:00 A.M., switching to oysters at 10:00 (Joe says he starts feeling homesick as soon as he passes Bozman, six miles up the road). A high spring tide will flood the sharp, salt-loving spartina grass, and then twenty feet of Joe's mowed lawn; the water wants this land.

Marguerite is tall and strawberry-haired, with a ready smile and an open, generous face—much more so than I'd expected, to be honest, even for someone whose notion of being "completely self-serving" includes dedicating thousands of hours to protecting a single shy species. When we spoke on the phone before the visit, Marguerite's voice tightened as she talked about the problems terrapins face; she clipped her sentences angrily, and I pictured someone with sharp, maybe even aggressive features. Her anger peaked when talking about Rodney Lewis, a local man who made a short-lived attempt to farm terrapin a few years back.

"I'm not PETA," Marguerite said. "And my issue isn't with Rodney personally. It's always easier to vilify one guy—I even called him after one article came out about his farm. It had quoted me, and I wanted to clear the air. But he should never have been given permission to do what he did—the permit was atrocious, absolutely outrageous. He was allowed to collect three thousand of every species! Diamondbacks, snappers, sliders, red-bellies. No investment at all on his part, just pulling animals from the wild and putting them in a shallow dugout on an old inland hog farm. Those thousands of eggs he says he found? No way. The turtles were gravid [carrying eggs] when he found them.

"The [Department of Natural Resources] had every chance to stop him; they *say* they care about the animals. The old terrapin pounds dealers used were these big brick tanks, usually close down to the water where they'd be cleansed by the tidal flow. They'd store their catch there for a while, before eventually packing them up and sending them off to hotels and restaurants. But what you had here was basically a cesspool with ridiculous turtle densities. Deer and geese were using it as a watering hole—no question it was a disease risk. The oversight just wasn't there."

Eggs collected, we go to the hatchery: a small side room—almost a lean-to—warmed by Marguerite's hot-water heater. Glass cages hold minuscule hatchlings (you could fit four in your palm) and larger, three-inch turtles, the latter ready to be passed on to local classrooms. It's a humble successor to the old fenced terrapin pounds, which held hundreds of turtles and grew more valuable as the terrapin grew scarce. In 1902 the *Washington Post* observed that

> one may commit murder, steal a horse, or run away with another man's wife on the Eastern Shore and stand some chance of coming clear, but woe betide the hapless one who is caught poaching about

the pounds, interfering with the eggs or taking terrapin out of
season. For he is as certain of punishment as the sun is to rise. The
pounds are jealously guarded night and day. . . . A pound full of
diamondbacks is as good as a gold mine any day.

Marguerite's head-starting project has its opponents. Among the
watermen, of course (though they have less of a stake one way or the
other now that harvesting terrapin has been banned—I left several
messages at the Maryland Watermen's Society office and never heard
back), but also among state wildlife officials. She defends herself
fiercely, though; she thinks that there's too much bureaucratic territo-
riality, too many people wanting to study instead of move forward with
genuine preservation efforts. When she's accused of releasing turtles in
the wrong places, mixing historically distinct populations, she scoffs:
"Where are these pristine populations supposed to be? Hotels would
release their extras, going way back. Just recently some Buddhists in
New York let a bunch go in the wetlands there. It's frustrating, like it's
more important to do a genetic study than to actually help the species
survive."

Marguerite started taking the protection of terrapin personally
when eight of the animals she'd bought, tagged, and released turned up
in a Chinese market in Albany.* "This was back when I was just getting
started," she says. "I didn't even have my number on the tags. The only
reason I heard about the turtles was that someone I'd recently met saw
them and called to see if they might be mine. So I called the market
and said, 'Those are my animals. I paid for them, I expect them back.'
They started arguing, and I said 'Look, it's real simple. I have a bill of
sale for the animals, and I'm claiming ownership. It's no different than
if my dog walked across state lines—it's still my dog. I paid for these
turtles. That's how they've made their contribution to the economy,

---

*At the time it was still legal to catch and sell terrapin; Asian markets remain the most common
destination for poached animals.

and now they're mine.' But it's hard. There's no gentleman's agreement, no rules people are willing to follow. If someone wants to take tagged animals out of the wild, and out of my research, all I can say is shame on them."

Albany seems like one of the last places you'd look for live terrapin being sold as food; it's like finding raw oysters at a hot-dog stand (or a good hot dog at a raw bar). But long-distance transport of terrapin is nothing new. When packed into well-aerated, straw-lined barrels, hibernating turtles can live for weeks or even months, long enough that in 1897 one Maryland woman could lay confident plans to send them to Italy's Queen Margaret. And the sad truth is that the Chesapeake population was eventually hunted to near extinction, to the point that even restaurants in Washington, Baltimore, and Philadelphia—cities with easy access to the bay, the nation's greatest natural incubator of turtles—usually served terrapin from hundreds or thousands of miles away.

Eventually the names of the various recipes were often the most local thing about them.

I've been talking about diamondback terrapin as if there's only a single homogeneous species from Cape Cod all the way to Texas. But of course that's not true; there are six distinct subspecies, defined by genetics or behavior or both. Admittedly, if you're like me, the list of their individual characteristics (northern diamondbacks lack knobs on the median keel; the posterior margins of Carolina diamondback shells curl upward; the median keel of the ornate terrapin has bulbous knobs) can make your eyes glaze a bit. They seem sort of trifling, only worth the attention of serious turtle junkies.

But the differences matter. In Twain's day terrapin eaters thought that they mattered a great deal—as much, certainly, as the difference between San Francisco's coppery native oysters and the fat, delicious, doomed shellfish of Blue Point. The best-tasting, most expensive turtles were northern diamondbacks; among them, aficionados would call for Long Islands, Delawares, or, most commonly, Chesapeakes. In

1897 one reporter wrote that northern diamondbacks had the "only flesh known which one can crush in his mouth with his tongue without the aid of his teeth." Since northern diamondbacks hibernate for longer than their southern cousins, he thought, their meat was naturally more tender and delicate. Whatever the reason, by 1894 northern diamondbacks from the Chesapeake commanded ninety dollars a dozen; turtles from farther south cost a buck apiece.

But Chesapeakes were becoming scarce. The official 1891 harvest was 89,000 pounds; by 1901 it had dropped to 1,583. To make up the difference, local dealers began shipping in terrapin from Texas and (even worse, gourmands believed) the Carolinas. Baltimore's Hotel Rennert insisted that it bought only genuine Chesapeakes, and some other restaurants were honest about the source of their turtles. But given the scarcity of Chesapeakes and the lower price of Carolinas, there was every incentive in the world to lie.

Just as round pieces of skate wing will sometimes pass as sea scallops, the change from Chesapeakes to their less-desirable cousins often went unnoticed. But the introduction of freshwater turtles from Illinois was the final straw for one well-known Baltimore gourmet, who began insisting on seeing a live northern diamondback in the dining room before he'd order terrapin. Maybe others should have followed his example; the *Times* warned in 1888 that when the proprietor of a cheap restaurant served terrapin, he often served his patrons "with a delusion and a snare in the shape of red-legged turtles which come from the flats of New Jersey." One local Maryland dealer said in 1898 that of the half million dollars spent by Baltimoreans on terrapin that year, no more than fifteen thousand went to buy genuine local Chesapeakes.

Not everyone thought that was a problem. The same dealer, who was himself bringing in "golden diamond-backs" as a substitute for Chesapeakes, claimed that "there ain't nobody in a hundred . . . what can tell the difference between these here goldens and the diamonds. There's a lot of people with a barrel of money who think they know, but I know they don't." Not even purchasers from wealthy clubs had noticed that they were paying top dollar for Carolina terrapin. "If the real terrapin dies out," the man went on, "he won't be so badly missed. There are lots of others just as good, as far as the epicur[e] is concerned." As long as there was *something* that could be sold to make Baltimore or Philadelphia terrapin soup, where it came from and where the original population had gone were both beside the point.

But a few years earlier, another dealer had been troubled by what he saw happening. It's so rare to find someone speaking openly against his own wallet that I want to let him speak for himself:

> I am constantly surprised . . . that no one has pointed out the alarming decrease in the choicest food products of this country. I remember very well that when Dr. Brooks of Johns Hopkins University used the extirpation of the buffalo on the Western plains to illustrate the diminution of the oyster supply along the Atlantic coast, everybody laughed as if it were a huge joke. . . . But we are living to see that it is the literal truth. At one time there were oysters in plenty all along the New-England coast, but the Pilgrim fathers and their descendants caught them so thoroughly that not an oyster can now be found north of Long Island Sound. In Long Island Sound they are very largely the result of transplantings from Maryland. On the Jersey coast and in the Delaware Bay the bottoms produce nothing like the quantities they used to yield. In the Chesapeake Bay, which has more natural oyster ground than all the rest of the world, the crop this year will not be 5,000,000 bushels, against 17,000,000 bushels twelve years ago. What is the result? The oyster is no longer the poor man's food, and the prices will continue to increase. In Europe, oysters have gone up so that they are now cultivating mussels, because they can be sold cheaper.

And what else was at risk, a *Times* reporter asked him? "Canvasback ducks, red-head ducks, and the better kinds of game. All are in-

creasing in price and decreasing in quantity. How will it all end? The
buffalo was exterminated. Why not the oyster and the terrapin and the
canvas-back duck and the other things that are worth living for?"

Substituting one wild food for another is just one way of breaking the bonds between food and place, one step on the road from eating backyard chicken on Sunday to the KFC Double Down Sandwich
(currently being test-marketed and consisting, as God is my witness, of
bacon, two kinds of cheese, and special sauce between two fried chicken
breasts). Wild foods have natural, undeniable *terroir*. Eating them is an
opportunity—if one that's too often missed—to think about a piece of
the world: its tides, its winds, its land, its limits. But substitution does
exactly the opposite. It creates an illusion of eternal plenty, blinding
eaters to how their choices shape the world.

Genuine bluepoint oysters from native beds on the south shore of
Long Island, for example, went extinct in the 1860s; even though he
included them on his menu, it's entirely possible that Twain never ate a
native oyster from Blue Point. Dealers simply sold new varieties, seeded
from Chesapeake stock, as the genuine article. But this did more than
cheat an eater; it encouraged in him an almost childish belief that he
could eat whatever he wanted, forever—that he could have everything,
all the time. The evidence on the plate said that surely there were still
massive reefs of oysters at Blue Point. And surely you could still have
Chesapeake canvasback ducks, fattened on wild celery and rich with
their own gravy; surely those weren't mallards or redheads (only Delmonico's, the *Times* claimed in 1888, was consistently honest about the
replacement).

It's a pattern that's been repeated again and again; in her wonderful *Kitchen Literacy*, Ann Vileisis describes some of the many substitutions. Shad shipped from Florida masked diminished Connecticut River
runs. Maine's Kennebec River salmon gave way to fish from the Columbia, and later Alaska. Before prairie chickens were shipped from grasslands by the millions, the occasional specimen substituted for Long
Island grouse. More recently, in California, failing to distinguish be-

tween subspecies of abalone (each of which grows to a different size, lives at a different depth, and reproduces at its own distinct rate) hid the fact that previous favorites had already been fished almost to extinction. The sudden collapse of the abalone fishery wasn't actually as sharp as it appeared; instead, people were seeing the last collapse in a line of collapses, as one subspecies after another vanished.

Of course, eating wild food can be done right. Maine's lobsters and Alaskan salmon are examples of wild seafood that thrive under intelligent management plans; both help make their homes places that are distinctively different. But when a wild food stops being a true feature of place—something that's harvested locally, eaten locally, and, most important, understood locally—it's in serious trouble. Eating wild foods has to mean respecting them, the land and water they come from, and their natural limits; most wild stocks simply can't survive becoming long-distance novelties. When they do, they're likely to vanish—and to prompt a new long-distance trade to fill the local gap. Then, instead of a great local tradition, you're left with a fossilized habit like an Upper Midwest fish fry serving only Atlantic haddock, or a Maryland crab house serving crab cakes that begin with opening a Chinese can.

Terrapins were luckier than Maine salmon or black abalone; before overharvest could wipe them out entirely, Prohibition banned the sherry and wine always used in the most popular recipes. Not long after, the Depression led many wealthy Americans to cut back on the kitchen staffs formerly tasked with killing the turtles. Together the two events probably saved northern diamondbacks from extinction. The next major hunting threat would come from China, but even that ended in 2006 with a law banning intentional harvest. Today, though poaching remains an issue, the biggest problem is shoreline development. With fewer sandy beaches around the bay, paths and driveways make tempting spots for a terrapin eager to return to the water.

That's probably why Erik finds a nest, one humid Maryland summer morning, in the packed-gravel path of the Neavitt playground. The only sign of the nest is a shallow depression. But Marguerite was a good teacher, and Erik spots it right away, calling to her at the edge of the grassy field where she's been picking honeysuckle. The hard, gray gravel is nothing like a prime nesting spot—but now that the sandy shores are often piled with jagged riprap, it's the best the turtle could find. Marguerite kneels, pointing out a few shell fragments—torn, lonely-looking remnants left by a raiding crow. Then Erik digs with the Turtle Lady, scraping through stone and sand, down to the three surviving eggs.

Neavitt isn't a waterman's paradise anymore, but it's still a Chesapeake place. It's as lovely and wounded as the bay.

ANOTHER WAY WITH TURTLE SOUP

Receive one can Bookbinder's Snapper Soup from the Turtle Lady. Open can and heat in saucepan, with addition of several tablespoons sherry. While heating, note that on the list of ingredients, "snapper turtle" falls behind water, tomato puree, cooked egg white, and sherry wine, which isn't overly discouraging, but also behind margarine and cornstarch, which is. Eat soup, attempting to find and taste turtle. Fail.

Twain dropped some terrific things between writing the list of favorite foods in his journal and the final menu he published in *A Tramp Abroad*. A lot of them were inexplicable—a man who forgets to include "lobsters boiled & deviled" on a list of great American foods can maybe be forgiven, but a man who lists them, then edits them out, is a man who has made a serious mistake. Fried onions, for some reason, failed to make the cut. So did hot eggs, pot liquor, cabbage boiled with pork, scalloped oysters, shrimps, pine nuts, catfish, hard crabs, potato salad, celery salad, lima beans, smelts and sturgeon from San Francisco, and rib of beef. I regret each and every one of these exclusions, except the celery salad, raw celery being one food I've never been able to champion.

Still, Twain was on a roll. In his *Autobiography* he'd rant that including too many details in a story made it into a "tangled, inextricable confusion," leaving it "intolerably wearisome to the listener." So on his menu, he pared dishes to their simplest essence. He listed ingredients rather than recipes; he wanted good things, simply prepared. Yes, he was strutting a bit—Twain was in an ostentatiously American mood, like Ben Franklin as he strolled through Paris in a coonskin cap. Still, the menu was a real cache, a trove of what the great writer saw as the best of his country's food; even the porterhouse steak he wanted for breakfast was an American cut, never produced by European butchers.

True, at home things were changing. Railroads and cans had already transformed the food of Twain's youth, increasing choice and availability but also disconnecting the food that made Americans *Americans* from the land that made America *America*. Michael Pollan makes the wise observation that a culture that treats foods as medicines can't be said to have a real cuisine at all; now dietary reformers like John Harvey Kellogg, Eliza Leslie, and Mary Mann were arguing that the health of one's bowels was more important than flavor, that inner purity should take precedence over taste. For Kellogg, Leslie, Mann, and more, proper food was a sign of physical and even moral virtue.

But though the idea that food should be something other than food was beginning to be a problem in Twain's day, it was never a problem for Twain. He scoffed at the whey-and-grape diets he saw offered to invalids; he demanded fried chicken, fresh butter, and hot rolls; he reflected that "it is a pity that the world should throw away so many good things merely because they are unwholesome." Food, for Twain, was most often about pleasure—pleasure in taste, pleasure in company, pleasure in remembering where a thing was from.

He had his dour moments. He had a store of dark bitterness that, later in life, would threaten to overwhelm him. But, man, nobody did joy like Twain.

When Livy wrote a letter to a friend, he had yet to actually write down his menu. Still, he added a postscript: "Dear Mrs. H—If I have a talent it is for contributing valuable matter to works upon cookery."

Six

THE MOST ABSORBING
STORY IN THE WORLD

Sheep-Head and Croakers, from New Orleans

WHEN TWAIN LEFT NEW ORLEANS in 1857 at the age of twenty-one, he left as an apprentice Mississippi River steamboat pilot. But he'd come looking for cocaine.

Brazilian cocaine. While working as a printer's apprentice in Keokuk, Iowa, Twain had read a book about Amazonian expeditions, which along with wild stories of alligators and monkeys "told an astonishing tale of *coca,* a vegetable product of miraculous powers . . . so nourishing and so strength-giving that the native of the mountains of the Madeira region would tramp up-hill and down all day on a pinch of powdered coca and require no other sustenance." Believing it to be "the concentrated bread & meat of the tribes . . . about the headwaters of the Amazon," Twain was inspired "to open up a trade in coca with all the world."

Upon arriving in New Orleans, though, he asked when a ship might be leaving for Brazil and "discovered that there weren't any and

learned that there probably wouldn't be any during that century." What
was more, the nine or ten dollars he had left in his pocket "would not
suffice for so imposing an expedition as [he] had planned." The disappointed Twain found himself unable to score coke in New Orleans.

Still, he was there, and that was saying a great deal. It was his
first visit to New Orleans, then the great metropolis of the South: cross-
roads between river and ocean, between the Caribbean and the Lower
Midwest—America's one West Indian city. The French Market, in particular, bustled with an incredible array of nationalities wandering
through "pretty pyramids of fresh fruit" and other delicacies. "I thought
I had seen all kinds of markets before," Twain wrote home, "but this
was a grave mistake—this being a place such as I had never dreamed of
before":

> Oranges, lemons, pineapples, bananas, figs, plantains, watermel-
> ons, blackberries, raspberries, plums, and various other fruits were
> to be seen on one table, while the next one bore a load of radishes,
> onions, squashes, peas, beans, sweet potatoes—well, everything
> imaginable in the vegetable line—and still further on were lob-
> sters, oysters, clams—then milk, cheese, cakes, coffee, tea, nuts,
> apples, hot rolls, butter, etc.—then the various kinds of meat and
> poultry.

New Orleans's famous cuisine relied on this kind of bounty. But it
owed just as much to the market's crowd of "men, women, and children
of every age, color and nation." There were Natchez, Houma, and
Chitimacha Indians, French and Spanish Creole planters, blacks from
the West Indies and the American South, Germans, Italians, and Chinese, along with rural Cajuns come to the city from the bayou. In the
market, black women fried hot calas—rice cakes—while Choctaw Indians sold filé made from powdered sassafras. Twain might have seen
Croatian oystermen, Cajun butchers, even Isleños—the Castilian-
speaking descendants of Canary Islanders—come to town to sell fish.

But of all the people he saw cooking and buying and selling and eating, the ones he admired most were the steamboat pilots.

As a young child, the fact that another boy had merely ridden on a steamboat to St. Louis left Sammy dying with jealousy. Now, begging, pleading—Lord knows how—he persuaded the pilot Horace Bixby to take him on as an apprentice. For years after, New Orleans would be a polestar for Twain: the final destination of the paddle wheelers racing currents or braving shallows down all the winding, treacherous lower river south of Cairo, Illinois.

It was the golden age of steamboating. When Twain was born in 1835, there had been some two hundred steamers on the river; when he began his apprenticeship in 1857 there were close to a thousand. With their churning wheels, towering Texas decks, and howling whistles, the ships were hugely impressive. Far more impressive, in fact, than they were durable or safe—their ornate superstructures floated on flat, fragile, amazingly shallow hulls that sometimes drew only a few feet of water.* The average steamboat lasted only five years. Still, they were by far the fastest means of long-range transport between the Midwest and the Gulf, so vital that they could earn back the cost of their construction within six months.

The only men able to maneuver these fragile but imposing craft were the pilots. While his steamboat was under way, a river pilot had authority even over the captain, who might set destination, cargo, and schedule but was legally bound to defer to the pilot in matters of navigation. A river pilot, Twain thought, was "the only unfettered and entirely independent human being that lived in the earth." Kings, by comparison, were underlings; writers were "manacled servants of the public." Twain would look back on this time as the happiest of his working life, when he commanded his howling, splashing dreams, his days and nights all in motion.

The river, Twain thought, was "a wonderful book . . . which told

---

*When he measured a safe depth of two fathoms, a leadsman would call out "mark twain."

its mind to me without reserve, delivering its most cherished secrets as clearly as if it uttered them with a voice." And it was "not a book to be read once and thrown aside, for it had a new story to tell every day." The river seemed to change shape in the night; it transformed under the stars and in pitch-blackness, in gray mist and by the light of a multitude of moons. His hulking paddle wheeler slid between shoals and sandbars, over blind crossings, and past hidden snags; charts were nonexistent, the water opaque as a wall. Twain had to memorize the river, steering by the constantly revised shape in his head; it was a job few could do at all, and fewer still could do well.

Change always fascinated Twain; calling a person or a story "monotonous" was an expression of intense disdain. Now he watched the varied light on the river's surface; the Mississippi was always in flux—always rending and re-forming the world around. The mud it carried built a maze of channels and sandbars. Currents lodged dead trees like hidden spears or washed all away in a night. When pilots came together, they would talk always, and only, about the river: how high it was running, how they'd run the crossings themselves, where bars and shoals had risen, which landmarks—dead trees, woodpiles, old barns—were gone.

The same changes that made the Mississippi fascinating, that made it beautiful, also made it deadly. "My nightmares, to this day," Twain wrote in 1883, "take the form of running down into an overshadowing bluff, with a steamboat. . . . My earliest dread made the strongest impression on me." Accidents and disasters were amazingly common; between 1811 and 1841, nearly a thousand boats crashed, exploded, or had their bottoms ripped out by a snag. Ten of the fifteen boats Twain piloted were destroyed on the river—none, fortunately, while he was piloting, though in 1860 he did back into the New Orleans levee—with two more blown up to avoid capture by Union troops. "The muddy Mississippi" is a cliché today, but its murk once made it genuinely dangerous—and made pilots essential. It took a skilled and experienced man to read the riffles and currents and swirls, to sense what was caused by wind and what signified a submerged trunk that could destroy a boat.

During a two-year apprenticeship, and then a two-year career as a licensed pilot, Twain mastered the river's language. It was a great achievement—but one that carried its own losses. While still a young cub pilot, he remembered, he had watched a sunset in a "speechless rapture":

> A broad expanse of the river was turned to blood; in the middle distance the red hue brightened into gold, through which a solitary log came floating, black and conspicuous; in one place a long, slanting mark lay sparkling upon the water; in another the surface was broken by boiling, tumbling rings, that were as many-tinted as an opal; where the ruddy flush was faintest, was a smooth spot that was covered with graceful circles and radiating lines, ever so delicately traced; the shore on our left was densely wooded, and the somber shadow that fell from this forest was broken in one place by a long, ruffled trail that shone like silver; and high above the forest wall a clean-stemmed dead tree waved a single leafy bough that glowed like a flame in the unobstructed splendor that was flowing from the sun.

Once he'd become a full-fledged pilot, he mourned, his educated eyes could no longer see the river's grace and beauty. Now the sun signaled wind, the floating log a rising river. The dark and silver marks on the water meant sandbars, reefs, and snags; the tall, dead tree was a useful landmark that he worried would not last long. "I had lost something," he wrote, "which could never be restored to me while I lived."

Still, he'd gained a lot. He had gained his independence and a sense of who he was. He would stay on the river his whole life, he believed, until one day he died at the wheel.

New Orleans was as far as Twain's steamers went, so arriving there often meant a break from the four-hours-on, four-hours-off schedule he kept during the long Mississippi passage. Characteristically, Twain didn't make much use of the rest time. "Yesterday I had many things to do," he once wrote to his brother Orion, "but Bixby and I got with the pilots of two other boats and went off dissipating on a ten dollar dinner at a French restaurant—breathe it not unto Ma!—where we ate Sheep-head fish with mushrooms, shrimps and oysters—birds—coffee with burnt brandy in it, &c &c,—ate, drank & smoked, from 1 P.M. until 5 o'clock, and then—then—the day was too far gone to do anything."

Sheepsheads, shrimp, oysters, and game birds: Twain's was the perfect languorous New Orleans luncheon. Gigantic, brackish Lake Pontchartrain bounded one side of the city, America's largest river the other. All around were swamps, crowded with bald cypress; nearer to the coast, the blend of salty Gulf water and fresh flows from the Mississippi's countless distributaries nourished an eternity of grassy wetlands. From the start, New Orleans was built on soaked land, utterly surrounded by water, sinking by the year—a horribly vulnerable position. But also an incredibly bountiful one; the swamps and wetlands, so thick and menacing to unfamiliar eyes, were the breeding grounds for the foundations of Creole and Cajun seafood cookery.

Juvenile redfish, red drum, black drum, pompano, speckled trout, black bass, red snapper, flounder, and dozens of other fish—all sheltered among the maidencane and giant cutgrass, along with incredible numbers of blue crab and literally trillions of shrimp (if all of Louisiana's shrimp survived to reproduce, in less than two years they would approach the volume of the sun). Decomposing leaves, grasses, detritus, and dead fish nourished the state's incomparable oyster beds. Oysters and shrimp; ducks and deer; crab-eating, prong-toothed sheepsheads; even bony Atlantic croakers—New Orleans knew how to use them all.

Twain loved the city as much as he did its incomparable food. In another breathless letter, this one to his sister Pamela, Twain wrote, "I think that I may say that an American has not seen the United States until he has seen Mardi Gras in New Orleans." He'd paraded with revelers dressed as giants and Indians and knights, danced with living playing cards and chess pieces and the queen of fairies. Watching Santa Claus march with genii "grotesque, hideous & beautiful in turn" to the music of drums, trumpets, clarinets, and fiddles, led him to the almost subdued observation that "certainly New Orleans seldom does things by halves."

In 1861 Twain had left New Orleans as the city prepared for war; he'd fled west rather than pilot a Union or Confederate steamboat. Now, in 1882, his days of piloting and exploration were long over; now he was a famous writer, back in his country after an unwilling year abroad. It was time for Twain to loosen his manacles and return, for a while, to the site of his realized childhood dreams. It was time to go downriver once more—this time as a passenger.

BAKED SHEEPSHEAD
Casburgot au Gratin

Clean and wash a 3-pound Sheepshead. Chop one large onion fine and rub the fish with salt and black pepper. Take a large and deep kitchen pan, place within a tablespoonful of butter, the chopped onion, bay leaf and thyme. Place the fish on top and pour over a half bottle of white wine. Cover with another close pan and put the whole on top of the oven. Bake from the bottom. When it begins to boil from below, turn the fish over carefully without breaking, and let it bake on the other side.

In a saucepan, brown without burning a tablespoonful of butter and two tablespoonfuls of flour. Add six fresh tomatoes, skinned and chopped fine, or a half can. Add two dozen cleaned and scalded Lake Shrimp, a half can of mushrooms, salt and pepper to taste. Cook for about five minutes and then water with the gravy in which the fish has been cooking. Mix well and cover the fish with it. Place fish in serving dish and surround with one dozen parboiled oysters on diced toast. Cover the fish with the shrimp. Sprinkle with cracker crumbs, parsley, and small bits of butter. Bake in oven with a quick fire until brown and serve immediately.

This preparation is an exclusive conception of our Creole cuisinieres and cannot be too highly recommended.

—condensed from *The Picayune's Creole Cook Book*, 1901

On my first day in New Orleans, I find that in the old French Market, where Twain once saw shellfish, a rainbow of fruit in pyramids, and "everything imaginable in the vegetable line," produce is now limited to a couple of stalls with bins of bananas, yams, onions, and watermelons. For every lemon there are ten cell-phone chargers; for every paper sack of fried peanuts, a dozen rainbow-reflector sunglasses. The real heir to the French Market of Twain's day is the Crescent City Farmers Market, which moves between the Warehouse and Garden districts two days a week.

This being early July, it's not the market's prime season; there are only about half as many vendors in the small warehouse (they're expecting rain) as there will be during the late-summer peak. But even now customers wander in the summer heat through baskets of okra, cymblins, and yellow squash, and watermelons piled high in a pickup. There are figs, cakes, towering basil plants, blueberries, peaches, Louisiana eggplants ("almost extinct"), and Creole tomatoes (Mr. B's Bistro serves a perfect salad: three meaty slices, Vidalia onion, vinaigrette, and that's it). There's pesto and chèvre and Creole cream cheese, mushrooms and tamales and New Orleans French bread.

And shrimp. Man, does this place have shrimp. It's not so much the volume; there are only two stands, both selling shrimp from coolers along with soft-shell crabs on ice and beautiful black drum fillets. But those stands are run by small, independent shrimpers and instantly raise my personal bar for what "fresh" means; the shrimp were swimming yesterday, the day before at the absolute outside, and they gleam. "Plump" is no longer a metaphor; these shrimp are chubby. When stand owner Clara Gerica drags one gloved hand through a bucket, she draws them up by long antennae (a sign of perfect freshness, I later learn—freezing causes the antennae to break off easily). They're so big that sixteen will make up a pound, which she sells for a jaw-droppingly cheap five dollars.

"These markets are a lifesaver for us," she says during a brief pause between customers. "Wholesale, we'd be getting maybe two dollars, so this is better than twice as good. And retail would be six, so the customer saves a buck there, too. We only ever sell at the farmers' markets—it just makes more sense for us, lets us keep on doing what we're doing." It sounds like a throwaway line, but the truth is that saying it lets the Gericas keep on doing what they're doing is saying something enormous. The fact that Clara's husband, Pete, is shrimping at all now is a bit of a miracle.

All the people I meet in New Orleans—all of them—date their lives by Katrina's landfall on August 29, 2005. Everything is *since Katrina* or *two years before Katrina, before the storm* or *after the storm, pre-K* or *post-K*. It's the city's B.C. and A.D., and everyone has personal stories of dread, flight, and loss. But Clara's is among the most hair-raising I hear: She was in her East New Orleans home near Bayou Sauvage, waiting out the storm with her husband and eighty-one-year-old mother-in-law, when the house came apart around them. "The roof went, and I was thinking, *Well, that's it*," she says with a laugh. "Then the walls went down. Then we were in the water." Pete managed to get into his skiff and came to pull his mother and Clara out. But Clara, a large woman who cheerfully describes herself as being in terrible shape, couldn't get in until a floating chair gave her enough leverage to claw her way over the gunwale. As they rowed to higher ground, they were lucky enough to find their household safe floating by.

Bayou Sauvage, Clara says, is paradise—home to egrets, alligators, raccoons, and otters, all within the New Orleans city limits. But it's also close to the MRGO, or Mississippi River–Gulf Outlet. The MRGO (often pronounced "Mr. Go") is a fantastically wrongheaded Army Corps of Engineers shortcut to the Gulf; fifty feet wide when first dug, the canal later eroded to two hundred feet across, swallowing and killing tens of thousands of acres of marsh. During Katrina the storm surge up the MRGO was a big reason that the levees failed (it's since been sealed off, closing one backdoor to the city). And at the same moment that they were being flooded from their home, Pete and Clara's three boats were sinking. It was a year before Pete got back on the water, and even then it was on the boats of generous friends.

One great thing about small shrimpers like the Gericas is that they can sell a single fish at market. Far less goes to waste than with massive factory trawlers, which can have ten-thousand-horsepower engines and are interested in nothing but shrimp. In unregulated fisheries such boats can end up discarding as much as *fifteen times* as many pounds of bycatch as they do shrimp. And put aside the clinical word "bycatch" for a moment—we're talking about rockfish, red snapper, sea horses, turtles, whatever life the fine-meshed nets sweep up. Just thinking about trading fifteen pounds of dead ocean life for a pound of shrimp gives me a migraine, and makes the small, fresh black drum fillets that Clara sells seem both decently human-scaled and even more appealing.

Using bycatch instead of tossing it over the side is one reason that Clara knows the taste of croaker as well as she does (Poppy Tooker, author of the *Crescent City Farmers Market Cookbook,* told me that locals most often use the fish for cat food). "Oh, that is excellent. It's bony, but real sweet," Clara says. She loves the fillets, which even people who eat croaker rarely taste—it's too small and bony for most people to bother cutting off the meat before eating. But Clara's gotten great at boning out fish. "Not by choice," she says.

Tooker's certainly right that croakers are almost determinedly modest. In 2004 a political fight erupted in Matagorda, Texas, over using croakers as trout bait; some guides worried that croakers made such appealing bait that the speckled trout population would be decimated. And croakers are less often sought for their own sake than used to substitute for more elevated fish, as when Rima and Richard Collin's *The New Orleans Cookbook* suggests, a bit ironically, that they make a decent replacement for speckled trout. When you do see a croaker-specific recipe, it invariably calls for frying, going all the way back to Lafcadio Hearn's 1885 *Creole Cook Book;* fried fish is terrific—done well, it's as good a meal as there is. But frying isn't usually the go-to cooking method for expensive or upscale species.

A platter of small fried croakers makes a delicious, crunchy meal; the Collins suggest frying the center bones and tail as an extra delicacy. Hearn is frustratingly vague, saying only to serve with "any sauce or catsup desired," but was probably thinking of one of his several butter or butter-and-lemon sauces, variations on a simple meunière. However it's served, croaker is a fish to be eaten in quantity—I imagine Twain, straight off the steamboat, ravenous after a long shift, sitting down with friends around a platter piled high and golden.

With sheepshead he'd have had many more options; many Creole cooks loved the fish. *Creole* cooks, I say again—unless he ate a home-cooked meal in the backcountry, Twain may never have eaten Cajun food in his life.

The distinction between Creole and Cajun cooking is sometimes lost, which is understandable; Louisiana's food comes from a fantastic blend of people and place you'll find nowhere else in the world. But Cajun food, though influenced by both Native Americans and people of African descent, is really the food of Acadians. Exiled from Nova Scotia in 1755 by the new English rulers of Canada, French-speaking

Acadians eventually found a home along the bayous of southern Louisiana, where their name was quickly corrupted as "Cajun." So Cajun food is country food, often one-pot food; think jambalaya, dirty rice, and the wonderful rich corn stew called maque choux. There's also a lot more pork, including fantastic roasted suckling pig, or cochon de lait. The distinctive charcuterie, from boudin to chaurice to hogshead cheese, is that of people making the necessity of butchering into a total delight.

Creole food, on the other hand, is the food of the several groups who call themselves Creoles. It's the food of the city, with roots among wealthy French and Spanish planters and—crucially—the black cooks they first enslaved and later employed in their city homes and on extensive country plantations. It tends to be less spicy, and somewhat more codified, than Cajun. Its gumbos use less sausage and Choctaw filé powder but more seafood and okra. It uses the classic sauces, such as meunière butter sauce over deep-fried trout or hollandaise over the artichokes and creamed spinach of eggs Sardou. Instead of hearty stews, there are delicate soups, such as turtle soup and crawfish bisque. And Creole dishes are much more likely than Cajun to be traceable to a single restaurant or cook, such as oysters Rockefeller and pompano en papillote (both invented at the still-thriving Antoine's). Creole food also has more pastries and baked goods, things like beignets and king cake. It was the food of restaurants, of full-time cooks, and it was what Twain ate while in town.

Using gumbo to tease out the intertwined roots of Louisiana cooking is a cliché, but it's a cliché because it's fun. So, briefly: Filé gumbo has roots on three continents, made in both Creole and Cajun variants (the original is Creole). The name *filé* is French and refers to the strings left by Choctaw-made sassafras powder; *gombo* is the Bantu word for okra. Gumbo begins with a French-derived roux, frying flour in fat until it's as brown as the cook likes (using the fat left after browning chicken is awesomely good). But as the name suggests, its original roots are in long-simmered African meat-and-vegetable relishes served over rice. Gumbo can include almost anything taken from the bayou, ocean, gardens, and smokehouses of Louisiana; but while Creole gumbo is usually a relatively delicate brew built around seafood and thickened with African okra, Cajun generally ends by stirring Choctaw filé into a pot of sausage with chicken or oysters.

Whether you're talking about Cajun or Creole food, you don't often hear about sheepshead and croaker. That's probably in part because they get lost among the riches—New Orleans easily has more beloved traditional dishes than any other American city. Barbecue shrimp, shrimp étoufée, beignets, calas, daube glacé, po'boys, muffulettas, trout meunière, trout amandine, boiled crawfish, soft-shell crabs, red beans and rice, pain perdu, pecan pie, bananas Foster, bread pudding with whiskey sauce . . . The temptation here is to fill several pages and then go eat, but the point is just that once you're talking about sheepshead and croaker you're pretty deep into the weeds.

But in the nineteenth century, sheepsheads were popular and often inexpensive. In 1885, twenty-five years after Twain left the river, you could still buy one broiled for thirty-five cents. The 1901 *Picayune's Creole Cook Book* called sheepshead "the most to be commended for household use, being susceptible of a far greater variety of modes of preparation" than any other Gulf fish. The fact that it was somewhat less rich than pompano and mackerel was, the writer thought, actually a virtue; it could be used every day "without injury to the stomach."

Sheepshead did sometimes appear on the city's best, and most expensive, Creole tables, as when Twain splurged on a ten-dollar "French" dinner (the word "Creole" wasn't commonly used to describe city cooking until several decades later). His sheepsheads were cooked with mushrooms, which may mean something like the *Picayune's* formula for garnishing a sheepshead "baked" on the stovetop with oysters, shrimp, and a tomato-and-mushroom gravy. Or it could have been like the sheepshead à la normande of a man said to know which fish were best in the markets and "the mode in which New Orleans chefs can best cook them": he poached the fish, then blended the liquid with butter, Calvados, and heavy cream. Sheepsheads were everyday fish, but they could be elevated by the right hand.

Today they're making a comeback on New Orleans tables, sometimes under the more appetizing name "sea bream" (there's a lot of wiggle room in the names of fish—twenty years ago you would have ordered Patagonian toothfish instead of Chilean sea bass, slimehead instead of orange roughy). When Pete catches a few sheepsheads in the summer months, Clara is happy enough to sell them at the stall. But unlike croakers, sheepsheads are worth pursuing for their own sake, especially in the autumn, just before the season for small white shrimp closes near Christmas.

"I'll be coming back in, see the school on the surface, and just change out nets," Pete says. "The shrimp trawl nets have a real fine mesh, so they push water in front of them. But the fish trawl is way more open, which lets the water pass through and the fish come in. You can get a good haul that way." It's nothing like a windfall; sheepsheads are bony fish, yielding as little as a five-to-one cut, meaning that about 20 percent of the fish's total weight is usable meat. Still, as the year ends, the white shrimp getting smaller and smaller until it takes a hundred to make up a pound, sheepsheads can be a real boon— they're one more thing that lets the Gericas keep on doing what they're doing.

Twain loved fish from the lake, bayou, and open Gulf, whether roasted with essence of mushroom or fried crisply and drizzled with browned butter. But the heart of New Orleans, for him, was the river. The river was why the city existed; the river was what carried him there. The fish he loved grew in its wetland nurseries, thriving on the nutrients it brought downstream.

Twain couldn't know that all that was slowly ending—that the great, muddy conveyor of life could stop.

There is an art in knowing how to fry fish properly. Perhaps there is no other method of cooking which is more commonly used, and no other which is more generally abused. There are few people who really know how to fry fish properly. The following general rule will give

THE SECRET OF GOOD FRYING

The secret of good frying lies in having the lard heated just to the proper point. If the fish is placed in the boiling lard, it is liable to burn quickly without being cooked through and through. If placed simply in the well-heated lard, it absorbs the fat and is delicate and tender and there is no tax upon the digestive organs. Always have sufficient lard in the pan to fry all the fish that is on hand and never add a lump of cold lard to the heated substance. This checks the cooking of the fish and spoils the taste. If the lard spits and crackles, that is no evidence of boiling. It only means that the lard is throwing off drops of moisture that have crept in. Boiling lard is perfectly still until it begins to smoke, and then it is in danger of burning and must be removed from the fire. To test the lard, drop in a piece of bread. If it begins to color, the lard is ready for frying. When all the fish is fried, skim it out, draining off all the fat. Butter is never used in frying fish, as it burns quickly.

Croakers are fried and served with garnish of parsley or lemon.

—*The Picayune's Creole Cook Book*, 1901

Rain falling on nearly half of California eventually drains into the San Francisco Bay. But the Mississippi River drains almost half the land of the *entire continental United States:* 41 percent of it, from New York to Montana and from West Virginia to Colorado. After the Amazon and the Nile, it's the third-largest drainage basin in the world. Twain believed that rain falling in part of twenty-eight states ended in the river.

You'd think that such an imposing flow would have carved itself a permanent bed, fixed and immutable as the walls of the Grand Canyon. But the Mississippi flows through some of the flattest land on earth, dropping a miserly three inches for every mile it runs. And though near Twain's Missouri hometown it usually remained between rocky walls, in the flat, silty country below Cairo, Illinois, it was free: the lower river ran wild. There, when the river wanted to slip its banks—carving out a new course through old woodlands, over a farm, or through a well-established town—there was nothing in the world to stop it. When René-Robert de La Salle explored the river, Twain believed, he had traveled an entirely different flow; the old bed was dry, forgotten. A shift in the river could bless tiny settlements with commerce or abandon thriving market towns to die. The Mississippi drowned what it wanted to drown.

In flood times the river turned surreal. The wedding-cake paddle wheelers would grope along backcountry chutes, through ancient forests and swamps, past forlorn families gathered on the roofs of sunken farmhouses. At such times land and water bled together. "We'll creep through cracks where you've always thought was solid land," Bixby told Twain. "We'll dart through the woods and leave twenty-five miles of river to one side; we'll see the hind-side of every island between New Orleans and Cairo." In the cracks they'd hang out torches to aid in steering past the "swinging grape-vines[,] flowering creepers waving their red blossoms from the tops of dead trunks, and all the spendthrift riches of the forest foliage" that overhung the narrow banks. During high floods they might lose track of the river's channel entirely—especially when piles of sugarcane refuse, or bagasse, were burning inland, leaving the world

gray, indistinct, and filled with a smoke "like Satan's own kitchen." Piloting could seem a dreamtime; even the river's fish were bizarre, prehistoric
species like the giant paddlefish, blue catfish, and alligator gar. In Twain's
youth the Mississippi was a beautiful, dangerous, defiant world.

So upon his return in 1882, it was exceptionally painful for Twain
to find the once thriving, once wild river tamed. At the St. Louis wharf,
once jammed by a "solid mile" of steamboats, a scant half dozen now
waited quietly for cargo; seeing what rails had done to the vibrant port
made Twain feel very old. "Mississippi steamboating was born about
1812," he reflected. "At the end of thirty years, it had grown to mighty
proportions; and in less than thirty more, it was dead! A strangely short
life for so majestic a creature."

What was more, the United States River Commission (predecessor
of the Army Corps of Engineers) had been hard at work. And though
Twain didn't know what the results of their labor would be, he was clearly
disturbed. Wing dams guided the current; dikes constrained it; the shoreline was shaved of timber, loaded down with stone ballast and wooden
pilings. "One who knows the Mississippi," Twain said, "will promptly
aver—not aloud, but to himself—that ten thousand River Commissions,
with the mines of the world at their back, cannot tame that lawless
stream, cannot curb it or confine it, cannot say to it, Go here, or Go there,
and make it obey; cannot save a shore which it has sentenced; cannot bar
its path with an obstruction which it will not tear down, dance over, and
laugh at." Were it not for the recently completed jetties at the river's
mouth, he'd think that "the Commission might as well bully the comets
in their courses and undertake to try to make them behave, as try to bully
the Mississippi into right and reasonable conduct."

He didn't know what the tamed river would do; still, he felt the
change in his blood. He saw snag boats "pulling the river's teeth" and
government beacons that made the dark flow into a "two-thousand-
mile torch-light procession." To Twain's eyes so many navigational aids
sterilized the river. "This thing," he reflected about the network of
lights, "has knocked the romance out of piloting, to a large extent."

One thing, at least, seemed the same—the mud. The Mississippi had always been famously muddy; in *Huckleberry Finn,* Twain's river men joked about being able to grow corn in the stomach of a man who drank enough of the water. "Here was a thing which had not changed," he wrote now. "A score of years had not affected this water's mulatto complexion in the least; a score of centuries would succeed no better, perhaps. It comes out of the turbulent, bank-caving Missouri, and every tumblerful of it holds nearly an acre of land in solution. . . . If you will let your glass stand half an hour, you can separate the land from the water as easy as Genesis; and then you will find them both good: the one good to eat, the other good to drink." But although Twain didn't know it, changes to the Mississippi's mud were the most momentous of all.

Certainly change seemed unlikely; there was probably more sediment in the river during Twain's piloting years than ever before, as plows loosed soil from tightly woven prairie-grass roots. Every year the Mississippi had carried some 400 million *tons* of dissolved earth to Louisiana. Much of it never went as far as New Orleans; before the river reached the city, it branched off into the Atchafalaya and other distributaries, spreading mud and sediment throughout the state's bayous. Both there and at the river's shifting, unsteady mouth, this sediment eventually settled, slowly extending the land; Twain wrote that Louisiana's coast was "much the youthfulest batch of country that lies around there anywhere." For seven thousand years, residue from Montanan turf, New York mud, Wisconsin sod, and Arkansan clay had built the swamps and wetlands; Illinois's and Iowa's losses were Louisiana's gain. The state was literally built from half of America.

But as Twain steamed toward New Orleans, all that was coming to an end. If you're like me, you may have heard about the state's disappearing wetlands and assumed that development was most to blame: tidal ponds filled in to make lawns, swamps drained for golf courses, that kind of thing. But the truth is that, in Louisiana, *the land is melting away.* And it's happening almost fast enough to be visible to the naked eye—a football field's worth of land vanishes every forty-five minutes. The equivalent of Manhattan disappears every ten months. This land is underwater; it's gone.

The reason, as Mike Tidwell says in his fascinating, deeply disturbing *Bayou Farewell,* is that during the 1880s—the very moment that Twain returned to the river—the ancient accrual of land stopped. Dams upstream trapped so much mud and sand that even as agricultural erosion increased, the lower Mississippi's sediment load fell. Instead of building Louisianan wetlands, the earth from midwestern prairies became sunken river sludge. Meanwhile, the Army Corps of Engineers' dikes and levees held back the floods that had once spread earth for miles alongside the Mississippi's banks, earth that had once countered erosion and subsidence (the natural tendency of wetlands to sink as sediments compact and organic elements rot away). Then, after the Great Flood of 1927 killed over a thousand people in Louisiana, Alabama, and Mississippi, the corps determined to stop the river from ever jumping its levees again. It was an understandable decision, but now there were no more annual floods at all, no more yearly renewals of the land. This in itself was a danger, though one that was harder to see.

Then there were the jetties at the river mouth. They greatly impressed Twain, keeping the river mouth open, making navigation much safer and easier. But they also channeled the Mississippi's mud into a massive flume, shooting it over the edge of the continental shelf into one of the deepest parts of the Gulf. Now, instead of spreading gently down the coast, all that land-building, life-giving mud was gone forever. And the Gulf Coast, it soon developed, hates a steady state: if the land isn't building up, then it's eroding away.

In one sense Twain was wrong: the corps has, in fact, channeled the river, tamed its lawless stream, saved shores it had sentenced. But he was deadly right that you can't bully the Mississippi without consequence. When the engineers cut off its natural course, the river took the land it carried with it; it let the sea begin stealing the shore. Meanwhile, the century-old grid of oil-company canals—thousands of miles of them—accelerate erosion and the coast's disappearance. Remember that the MRGO channel grew from fifty feet to two hundred in a few decades; wave action can double a canal's width in fourteen years, making what were once nearly portages into rivers in their own right.

Now, Tidwell says, the cemeteries of some Cajun communities are under feet of water; old baseball fields are fishing grounds. He watched the GPS of one shrimping boat as it cruised easily over what should have been solid ground—the electronic map, the captain explained, was seven years out of date.

In the long term, all this means catastrophe for Louisiana's critically important fisheries, which rely almost entirely on wetland breeding grounds and provide about a third of the nation's catch. But for now the effects aren't easy to see; ironically, grass that decays on sinking land causes great explosions of plankton, and fish, crab, and shrimp thrive in the kinds of edge habitats created when a solid bank of wetland breaks up. It's much like what happened to prairie chickens, which thrived on a temporary blend of corn and grass: there were more of the birds than ever before in history, and then they were gone. If the wetlands disappear, something like that is absolutely guaranteed to happen to Louisiana's fisheries. Sheepshead, crab, shrimp—they'll all appear in fine condition until, seemingly at once, they vanish.

In human terms this will mean the loss of unique American coastal cultures; the evacuation of Cajuns and their neighbors might be slower than during a hurricane, but it will be no less real. And every day that the wetlands shrink is a day that New Orleans is more vulnerable to the next major storm. Every 2.7 miles of coastal wetland can absorb a foot of storm surge; where New Orleans used to have 50 miles of buffer, it now has 20 and falling. There isn't a levee system in the world that can make up for that.

The solution, it increasingly seems, is to help the river go where it wants to go anyway. The proposed Third Delta Conveyance Channel would divert two hundred thousand cubic feet per second of muddy

Mississippi River water into the Atchafalaya Basin. As it poured through the wetlands into the Gulf, it could begin halting, then reversing, the damage done by long, slow erosion. Admittedly, it's unnerving to think of yet *another* cut through the wetlands, even one meant to heal. But the Atchafalaya River is the one major distributary that still carries mud and muck in something like a natural pattern; as a direct result, the Atchafalaya's outlet is the one place that the land actually grows, by two thousand acres a year. When Mike Tidwell traveled the Atchafalaya, he became a true believer in the river's restorative powers and the necessity for the channel; at the mouth "myriad small islands and sandbars dot the water, new ones popping up all the time, every few months, like mushrooms after a rainstorm." All through the new land, he writes, there's a "rich scent not found elsewhere in Louisiana, a smell like mud and musk and seaweed and salt water and hope all mixed together."

The project could cost $2 billion, or much more. But the alternative is landscapes like the one at the Mississippi's mouth. To get there you drive mile after mile along a highway tucked snugly between levees that extend like a copper pipe into the Gulf. The river is between the levees, too; it's a river in the ocean, maintained only to protect the navigational channel, its banks clustered with helipads and industrial facilities. And at the end, the loss of the coastland is glaringly, horribly obvious: skeletal oaks stand dead a half mile offshore, set firmly in sunken land.

In August 2005, bored enough to read up on Eight Easy Fashion Tips that I never intended to use, I spent part of a flight home from Boston leafing through *Men's Health*. One of the magazine's features was a list of endangered American places to visit, among which was New Orleans—it had a huge termite problem, the author explained, and besides, much of the city was gradually sinking, and the system of levees was old and ill maintained. Hurricane Katrina landed less than two weeks later. And there was President Bush, saying, "I don't think anyone anticipated the breach of the levees"—except (he neglected to add) for the crack team of hydraulic engineers employed by *Men's Health*.

We know what the problem is. We have at least a good idea of how to fix it and how much that might cost (it's a lot; it's also a lot less than the cost of doing nothing). And if the wetlands go, if New Orleans becomes a coastal city, if a hurricane then strikes dead-on, this time let's at least not act surprised.

As he steamed toward New Orleans for the first time in more than twenty years, Twain overheard two "scoundrels" talking about their businesses: one was an oleomargarine manufacturer, the other a counterfeiter of olive oil. Slashing a knife into his "ostensible butter," the oleomargarine maker declared that "you are going to see the day, pretty soon, when you can't find an ounce of butter to bless yourself with, in any hotel in the Mississippi and Ohio valleys, outside of the biggest cities. . . . We can sell it so dirt-cheap that the whole country has *got* to take it. Butter's had its *day*—and from this [day] out, butter goes to the wall."

One well-placed pistol shot would have made Twain a national culinary hero. Instead he listened to the man's companion describe the process for removing the "one little wee speck . . . in a gallon of cotton-seed oil, that gives it a smell, or a flavor." The oil could then be bottled, marked with an imported label, and sold as olive oil. "Maybe you'll butter everybody's bread pretty soon," the man gloated, "but we'll cotton-seed his salad for him from the Gulf to Canada, that's a dead-certain thing."

Twain was appalled. But, he found in the city, not every change was bad. There was ice in New Orleans—ice! There were even ice *factories*: the city that had once needed to ship ice from the distant Sierras now pumped it out in August. Twain visited one "to see what the polar regions might look like when lugged into the edge of the tropics." He didn't understand the process, but he was impressed by the large ice blocks, meant as centerpieces to decorate and cool a room, that held bouquets and French dolls frozen as behind plate glass.

And in New Orleans he could eat the food he loved best. He rode with his friends to the hotels beside Lake Pontchartrain and had dinner on a veranda over the water. "The chief dish," he said, "was the renowned fish called the pompano, delicious as the less criminal forms of sin." Even better, perhaps, was the pompano at a city club, where the fish "was in his last possible perfection . . . and justified his fame." Along with the pompano was "a tall pyramid of scarlet cray-fish—large ones; as large as one's thumb; delicate, palatable, appetizing. Also deviled whitebait, also shrimps of choice quality, and a platter of soft-shell crabs of a most superior breed. The other dishes," he mused, "were what one might get at Delmonico's, or Buckingham Palace; those I have spoken of can be had in similar perfection in New Orleans only, I suppose."

As the river changed, so did the life along it; and changes along the river changed the food of the South. Though Twain's menu included Southern-style light bread, wheat bread, and egg bread, in his youth none of these were as common as his corn bread, corn pone, and hoecake. But as the plow moved west into the mixed prairies of Kansas and Nebraska, wheat had ceased to be a luxury in the South. The opening of the Midwest's great flour mills meant that biscuits made with white flour would be far more common on Southern tables in the twentieth century than in Twain's childhood; his offhand comment that many steamboat pilots had left the river "to grind at the mill" had some truth in it.

But the biggest change in New Orleans cooking was emancipation. Though some remained as employees, black Creoles were no longer inextricably bound to the kitchens of slave owners. Many white Creoles either had to hire new cooks or learn their own way around a kitchen. Some tried to preserve recipes and techniques they'd once taken for granted, a point that *Creole Cookery* made directly and offensively: "In this time, glorious with the general diffusion of learning, it is befitting that the occult science of the gumbo should cease to be the hereditary lore of our negro mammies, and should be allowed its proper place in the gastronomical world."

Both *Creole Cookery* and *La Cuisine Creole* appeared in 1885; the first two Creole cookbooks, they give a picture of the city's cooking just two years after Twain's visit. The books have many surprises, such as a beef-based "gombo." But there are also dozens of dishes that could easily be served today—fried eggplant, stewed okra, ten styles of oyster, fifteen ways to cook fish. Meanwhile, Hearn wrote, peddlers walked the streets selling chickens, lemons, apples, and strawberries; many poked their heads through open windows, crying their wares. Twain himself marveled at the sheepshead, red snapper, and Spanish mackerel sold in "a very choice market for fish." Much on the river had changed, but these things at least were still there. Probably Twain thought they always would be.

CROAKERS AND MULLETS FRIED

Have them perfectly cleaned; trim the fins, wipe the fish with a clean cloth, salt and pepper each one, and roll it in flour or fine corn meal, and then drop it into a pot of boiling lard and bacon grease mixed. When brown, pile up on a hot dish and serve, with any desired sauce or catsup.

—LAFCADIO HEARN, *La Cuisine Creole,* 1885

I'm a ruthless wedding hors d'oeuvre grazer; before waving hello to the bride, I'll scope out the best bottleneck to snatch tidbits from passing trays. Servers will eye me warily, smile stiffly as they spin out of reach, even head for the back entrance.

Cruising the tables of the Louisiana Foodservice EXPO feels like crashing the world's largest wedding. Every vendor offers samples—it's only right—and so there's andouille and fresh Gulf shrimp and tasso and smoked, shredded Berkshire pork and a dozen cuts of beefsteak and lobster bisque and seafood gumbo, and there are crab cakes and smoked duck and *freaking foie gras,* which I never ever get to eat. I miss the last of the paddlefish caviar by seconds. There's also a great number of fine-looking vegetables and a few fruits, but in this kind of context I'm a carnivore (with, admittedly, frequent exceptions for pastries and the free and plentiful beer). There are also a tremendous number of seafood poppers and fried things various and sundry: some look bad and many are, and a few I can't even identify, but I taste all of them anyway because, hey, you never can tell.

This is after a few days of eating way, way too much. I'd been surprisingly on edge before coming—stomach literally clenched, having trouble sleeping, the whole deal. New Orleans is, far and away, my favorite American city, and I'd felt as if I were going back to see a relative I'd neglected for too long. Of course this is completely self-absorbed—I know that the city didn't care one way or the other about my arrival. Still, that's how I felt, and it wasn't until I sat down to a couple dozen charbroiled oysters with my friends Dora and Paul and Reilly that I could start to relax. Drago's is a New Orleans institution, even if it's a couple miles out of town, and walking in there felt good. Seeing the bar crammed three deep on a Thursday night felt even better. And working through the oysters—the wood fire had melted the butter, garlic, and Parmesan and Romano cheeses on each into a perfectly smoky, crusty cap—while washing them down with a beer or three was nigh on to blissful.

I don't want to overstate this, but the return—the survival—of places like the old-school hangout Drago's means something. It means people going out with friends for things they've been eating for years;

it means sitting at a familiar table, taking a bite and raising a drink. It means just knowing that the place is crammed midweek, that people are lining up at the bar, that the wood fire is roaring. It's not everything; it's something. "Everything was just so emotional when we started coming back," Dora says. "This restaurant, that restaurant, the first Saints game. It was all loaded. Highs and lows."

Which was all the permission I needed to treat eating in New Orleans as akin to a patriotic duty. The city's restaurants needed my help; I would help them until I could not see.

So already this week I've had charbroiled oysters and shrimp with fried eggplant and something, God help me, called the "Shuckee Duckee" (blackened duck breast and oysters in cream sauce over fettuccine). I've had fried rabbit liver on pepper-jelly toast, hogshead cheese, hen-and-andouille gumbo, barbecue shrimp, and shrimp and grits. I've had Creole tomato salad, fried-potato omelet, and a Ferdi Special po'boy filled with roast beef, ham, gravy, and debris (the blackened yummy bits from the roasting pan). I've had spearmint sno-balls and nectar sno-balls, fried oysters and fried shrimp and fries. I haven't had much green, but I've had pecan waffles with bacon, and I've inserted beignets and café au lait between meals with the regularity of an Old Testament prophet chanting "begat."

After a while I've begun to honestly fear I might die.

Now I'm at the expo; and appearances notwithstanding, I'm not there to embarrass myself. I'm there because it hosts the Great American Seafood Cook-Off, which an announcer dramatizes as having begun with "a single eight-by-ten piece of white paper" on which Louisiana governor Bobby Jindal inscribed a challenge—in blood, we are left to assume—to the nation's other sitting governors. But the truth is that the National Oceanic and Atmospheric Administration started the event six years ago to promote the nation's sustainable seafood stocks. The cook-off is tucked along the back edge of what seems like a square country mile of vendors promoting their wares; it's a promotional event within a promotional event. There's nothing spontaneous about it—it's a performance, not a festival—and when six masked, befeathered samba dancers arrive, drumming and marching to announce the event's beginning, they serve less to attract revelers than to leave three small alligators in a glass tank looking moderately surprised.

But, spontaneous or not, it's an event with a serious purpose; fish are the only wild foods that Americans still eat with regularity. We still know the difference between salmon and swordfish, just as people once distinguished between mallards and canvasbacks and wood ducks. But as Twain's menu shows, such things can be lost fast; already, Louisiana's beloved speckled trout and redfish are limited to a sports fishery, appearing in restaurants only when farmed or brought in from Alabama. We don't *have* to eat sustainably, but if we don't, the nonnegotiable fact is that our menus are going to get a lot less interesting. Today there are fifteen chefs here to promote their states' fish (and, not to be naïve about it, themselves); each qualified by winning a state cook-off, or else by being tapped by their respective governor.

Among them is Tory McPhail. Tory is executive chef at Commander's Palace in New Orleans's Garden District; Paul Prudhomme and Emeril Lagasse each held the same job, in a restaurant that opened in 1880. Along with Antoine's, Arnaud's, and Galatoire's, Commander's is one of the grand Creole restaurants—the old guard, in a city that takes its old guard very, very seriously. The reopening of Commander's after Katrina was one of the great post-storm reliefs, making the national news as a sign of the city's recovery.

Tory is thus the obvious local favorite. He's also an enormously friendly and welcoming guy, raised in a small town on the Puget Sound, with an obviously genuine love for Louisiana's seafood—right down to the humble sheepshead. He loves sheepshead so much, in fact, that when we spoke on the phone, he decided on the spot to prepare it for the cook-off.

"Sheepshead—oh, my goodness, that is just out-of-this-world good," he said. "It's fun to catch, too, under trestles or next to pilings, wherever you have some good structure, especially in brackish water. It eats mostly crab, and that's the scoop on its name—it has these big front teeth it uses to crunch through the shells and make it look kind of like a sheep." Its diet, he says, is what makes it so delicious. "It's clean, light, white, flaky meat, with nuances of fresh crab. In fact, if you steam it, flake it off, and serve it just with light salt and pepper, it's sometimes called poor man's crabmeat—it even *looks* like jumbo lump crab."

Sheepshead is getting more popular, but it still isn't often actively sought out by diners. At Commander's, though, Tory says, "we buy absolutely as much as we can get—forty pounds, eighty pounds, whatever the Fish House has that day. We print our menu up to five times daily, so we can use what we want, then turn to another fish real quick when we run out. And we have a great relationship with the Fish House—we use about eighty thousand pounds of fish a year, so they'll really try to help us out with what we need. I've had those guys leave their kids' soccer games when we're running low on oysters."

That relationship is why he has sheepshead today to work with at all. Sheepsheads aren't widely available until they school in the late autumn, right around the time that Pete Gerica starts taking them to pad out the end of the waning white-shrimp harvest. So Tory called Cliff Hall at the New Orleans Fish House, telling him he needed sheepshead for his cook-off entry.

"Wednesday, nothing," Cliff tells me. "Thursday, nothing. I'm sweating bullets. I call a guy I know spearfishes, tell him I need the fish. I tell him I'll give him two dollars a pound; he's saying, 'Man, I wouldn't do that to you.' I'm saying, 'Look, no problem, two dollars a pound, I just need the fish.' He calls me Friday noon, telling me Lake Pontchartrain is mud. I say, 'No, wrong answer. You gotta find clear water.' Finally he does, right there under the Fort Pike Bridge. He calls me and says he's got the fish—biggest relief of my week. Tory calls from the airport a half hour later, just in from California. I tell him no problem." Cliff laughs loudly. "He couldn't believe the product. I'm thinking, yeah, well, it was swimming about three hours ago. But the prep cooks were asking why all the fish had holes in their heads."

When Cliff fled the city during Katrina, he and his partners left behind some $2 million worth of fish. In the late summer. Without power. When they came back, they came with hip waders and heavily armed—shotguns, two pistols each—and started clearing out the rot as Black Hawk helicopters roared overhead and the occasional National Guard boat went patrolling by on the flooded street. I can't get my head around what it must have been like, hauling nearly seven hundred pallets with hand trucks to dumpsters just outside the loading door. And once the fish was in the dumpsters, of course, there were no trucks to haul them away. For *months*. It wasn't the worst tragedy of Katrina, not by a long shot, but it must have been a complete horror show, and it helps me to understand a little just how totally the city shut down.

The signs of Katrina are everywhere—rumpled pavement, lawns with three-foot-high grass, even the new wood in the walls of an Irish pub. But when I visited the New Orleans Fish House, I had to take Cliff's word for how bad it got. Everything there was clean, fast, fresh, and cold. Knives flashed, gutting out fish; water splashed over cutting tables; hoses sprayed the fish clean. Cutters washed down their boards after every fish—and there were a *lot* of fish. Black drum fillets piled up; cutters broke down red snapper, mahi-mahi, pompano, and flounder. I shivered; it was New Orleans in July, but it seemed a minor wonder that the floor wasn't a skating rink—I thought, inevitably, of Twain's polar regions at the edge of the tropics. A man introducing himself as George W., who said that sheepshead is the best eating fish in the house, was filleting skipjack; the flesh was red as beef, fresh as though hauled from the Gulf a minute before. In the New Orleans Fish House, the cliché that a cook is only as good as his ingredients rang true. The fish there demanded respect.

The Fish House works on what seems an almost impossibly tight schedule. "Our clients have until nine A.M. to get their orders in," Cliff says. "That's for an eleven-o'clock delivery. They call at nine, we've got two hours to pull anything from the freezer they need, then sort, cut, and pack the fresh product. I don't know any other city that has that kind of timing—usually it's something like call by four o'clock the day before. And, man, our customers'll let us know it if we're five minutes late. We just can't ever be wrong." What sets Louisiana apart, Cliff says, what makes it so addicted to perfectly fresh fish, is its marriage of land and water. "Alabama, Florida, and them, they've all turned their wetlands over to mostly recreational use, beaches and such. But as long as our wetlands last, we've still got a perfect breeding ground out there."

The cook-off starts are staggered to allow the judges to taste over the course of two hours; many of the cooks are already hard at work. It's wonderful, especially if you imagine eating each dish in a chef's own restaurant, close to the fish's source: there's Alaskan king salmon with low-bush cranberries, an Illinois fish stew with walleye, a curried striped bass from New Jersey served with crab-filled modak dumplings, and Mississippi shrimp and grits. John Varanese from Kentucky, Lord love him, cooks the ancient and seldom-eaten paddlefish. As a promotional event, it's devilishly effective; if this were a restaurant, I'd live in it.

I'm an unabashed fan of *Deadliest Catch*, the documentary series about the Alaskan king and opilio crab fisheries. The fishermen will work for forty hours straight in freezing, murderous seas; when I watch it, I eat popcorn, then sleep really well. So it's a minor thrill that one of the cook-off's emcees is Sig Hansen, captain of the *Northwestern*, who on the show appears to be both incredibly competent and an awful boss. Now, in his role as emcee, Sig's instincts kick in; he says literally nothing that would be out of place on the crab boat. "Gotta work fast here," he'll say. "They're under the gun, so they gotta work fast. But they gotta do it *right*. Doing it fast and getting it all wrong just won't do 'em any good." He chides the chefs to do it right, asks them if they know what they're doing, tells them to watch their fingers. But you have to be a smart guy to run a fishing boat, and when it comes to promoting sustainable seafood, he's calmer and more comfortable. "Wild American seafood draws a premium price, sure," he says. "But it's a premium product. Some wild-caught fish is just more flavorful. Salmon, farmed salmon—well, it's okay. But wild fish, that's the real thing. Nothing in the world like it."

Tory's workspace is covered with vegetables and spices. There's sea salt and kosher salt and salt he smoked for twelve hours, infusing it with hickory. There are four kinds of corn—red, white, yellow, and baby. There's bacon fat, which bodes well. There are shallots and jalapeños and tomatoes and milk, thyme and cayenne and a Cajun spice blend. There are gigantic shrimp—for a moment I wonder if Jonathan, a line cook at Commander's and today Tory's assistant, raided the Maine cooler for lobster—and lump crab. And, of course, there are the sheepshead fillets: visibly firm, less than a day from the water, their dark red blood lines glistening.

In a nod to the recession, Tory fills the two minutes before starting by talking to Sig about how economical sheepshead can be; you should be able to cook what he's about to for less than the price of a burger. If you can find it wholesale, the fish can be about $4.50 a pound. But his mind is already on the contest—he's starting to flush. He confesses to getting butterflies. At last he picks up a knife.

The other chefs began working slowly, some in an almost show-offishly leisurely way—there's been a pause after the starting three count that I don't think the several announcers are happy about. But at "*Three . . . two . . . one . . . Go!*" Tory plunges in, snatching up an onion and, in the best possible sense, annihilating it. Just to Tory's left, Jonathan strips ears of corn with long, sure strokes of his knife.

I'm a dedicated home cook, but I've never worked in a restaurant; my only exposure to watching a skilled chef work at high speed is from *Iron Chef*, or *Top Chef*, or some other show about chefs. But any sports fan knows that television can diminish and dull the skills on display. Watching Tory in the act makes me realize that the same is true for cooking. Even after absorbing hundreds of cooking shows, seeing him dissect a tomato—and cutting it concasse, a fine dice without skin or seeds—is frankly intimidating. I think of playing an instrument, speaking a language, of other things that need tens of thousands of hours of practice: life seems short.

Jonathan roasts tomatoes with a handheld torch. Tory seasons the fish, sprinkling a dozen spices liberally over the fillets. Then he drenches them with fresh bacon fat, which strikes me as awesome. He's working hard, sweating even before he starts working the grill, going red as steam bathes his face and neck. The crowd is six deep, pressed right up to the rope line; I didn't expect how much these particular Louisianans at least would want the win. When the crisp, brown fillets come off, Tory pours over *more* bacon fat; this, I feel, falls somewhere between genius and cheating.

Tory grills the shrimpzilla as lump crab simmers in champagne butter. Then he assembles the plates. There's a bed of mixed corn and sliced Creole tomatoes, then a mighty grilled shrimp, then a sheepshead fillet, and then another shrimp. Tory surrounds the tilting tower with lump crabmeat; he finishes the plate with greens, basil oil, and more cream. The combination is somehow both businesslike and literally fantastic, like a carnival mask hoisted on a pitchfork.

At the judges' table, Jonathan holds up a partially filleted sheepshead as Tory offers a mini-lecture, pointing out that sheepshead is economical, underused, and sustainable (the latter point one he cares about a good deal; he refuses to serve bluefin tuna and other threatened stocks at Commander's). The big challenge when cooking it, he points out, is dealing with the low yield. It's rare that more than 40 percent of the weight is usable meat (which may be, I suspect, why it's often steamed and flaked off—it's much easier to get the meat off that way than by filleting the bony fish raw).

While the judges confer, Tory hands out tastes in small paper cups. He called it "poor man's crab," and, in fact, I can't distinguish between crab and sheepshead; I couldn't even swear in court that there's sheepshead in there. It's all like lump crabmeat, fresh and sweet and bathed in a creamy pepper sauce, and it's exactly as good as it sounds—good enough that offering small tastes in paper cups verges on callous. I consider bribing Jonathan in a bid for a full plate.

There are a lot of serious chefs at the cook-off; they're cooking the best their states have to offer. But Tory wins.

SHEEPSHEAD À LA CRÉOLE
Casburgot à la Créole

Prepare the Sheepshead as for boiling. . . . When quite done, take out of the water and flake off all the flesh from the bones. Have ready a quart of boiled cream or milk. Beat the yolks of four eggs and mix with the cream. Chop one large onion, a bunch of parsley, a sprig each of thyme and bay leaf, and add to the cream and eggs. Let it boil up once, and while boiling, throw in three tablespoonfuls of flour, rubbed perfectly smooth, in a little cream, and about two tablespoonfuls of butter. Remove from the fire. Have ready a deep dish, well buttered, and put in a layer of fish and then a layer of the sauce, until the dish is full. Sprinkle over with bread crumbs. Place in the oven and bake about a half hour, or until brown. This is a very delightful method of preparing Sheepshead.

—*The Picayune's Creole Cook Book,* 1901

Though Twain's return to the Mississippi began as a joyful reminiscence, seeing so many changes often left him despondent. But the thing that brought him to tears was the most seemingly humble: the mud of Hannibal, Missouri. "Alas!" he wrote. "Everything was changed in Hannibal—but when I reached third or fourth [streets] the tears burst forth, for I recognized the mud. *It,* at least, was the same—the same old mud." By the trip's end, he seemed near true depression, writing to Livy, "That world which I knew in its blossoming youth is old and bowed and melancholy, now; its soft cheeks are leathery & wrinkled, the fire is gone out in its eyes, & the spring from its step. It will be dust and ashes when I come again."

Twain remembered an ever-changing river, a kaleidoscope of muddy water. Now it ran flat as though between walls. Now his home was Hartford.

Seven

IT IS *MY* THANKSGIVING DAY

Cranberries

TWAIN WAS NEVER ONE FOR SELF-RESTRAINT, especially in his fantasies—his ideal breakfast of porterhouse steak, biscuits, and coffee was to be delivered by "an angel suddenly sweeping down out of a better land." So when faced with "roast chicken, as tasteless as paper" in European hotels, his imagination went large; he thought of "a vast roast turkey, stretched out on the broad of his back, with his heels in the air and the rich juices oozing from his fat sides." But this, even he had to admit, was asking a lot, and he ended resignedly: "I might as well stop there, for they would not know how to cook him. They can't even cook a chicken respectably; and as for carving it, they do that with a hatchet."

It's true that turkeys can be daunting. They're big birds; trying to roast one that doesn't end up either raw or dried out is the biggest challenge many home cooks face in a year. There's a reason there are holiday turkey hotlines.

But you only have to brine a turkey once to realize that the days of devising intricate Thanksgiving Day roasting strategies, of planning your day around flipping and basting, are done. The debate is over; the code has been cracked. You submerge the bird overnight in a salt-and-sugar solution, with whole garlic cloves and plenty of fresh thyme. In the morning you dry it and smear the breast with butter. You roast it in a hot oven until it's as bronze as an ancient hoard. Salivating desperately, you force yourself to let it rest while the juices distribute. At last you cut through the skin and find that brining has turned the turkey into a loving bird, a forgiving bird—moist, flavorful, and full of compassion for cooks with aunts and uncles who should really have stayed in Boca Raton or Pismo Beach or Scottsdale but instead are *walking up the front steps right now.* On Thanksgiving brining is a cook's best friend.

Historically, that distinction has probably gone more often to cranberry sauce. My grandmother spent decades trying to roast a good, moist bird. Still, her turkeys were dry enough that after carving one you had to dust the mantel; cranberry sauce was less a condiment than a survival tactic. In using the sauce to dress birds that sometimes seemed made of pasteboard, Gran stood athwart a venerable American tradition—as far back as 1821, a visiting Frenchman complained about using the "most villainous sauce" to cover the sins of "half boiled meat, clammy puddings, and ill-concocted hash." This, he believed, left Americans "insensible to the advantages of . . . various rich [French] sauces" and doomed forever to bathe meat in crimson sugar.

But then again, a man who complains about New England boiled dinner and red flannel hash is only worth taking so seriously. And though cranberry sauce can be stultifyingly sweet, cranberries themselves are bitter; several of their Native American names, like the Wampanoag *sasemineash,* simply mean "bitter (or 'sour') berry." That's probably one reason that cranberries with roast turkey are tied to Thanksgiving on a nearly genetic level; a balanced, bright, acidic cranberry sauce is the perfect foil for a rich bird with buttery stuffing and potatoes.

Cranberries are a truly traditional American food, gathered by Native Americans as far west as Minnesota, and one of the few North American berries ever cultivated commercially (the others are blueberries and Concord grapes). The story of that cultivation is unusually specific: they were first grown by Henry Hall, in 1816, near Kiah Pond in the Cape Cod town of Dennis. Compared with crops like potatoes, which were first grown somewhere in the Andean highlands sometime around 5,000 B.C., that's truly pinpoint accuracy; and because the history is so recent, we know that the cranberries we eat today are often virtually identical to those first pulled from wild bogs and cultivated nearly two centuries ago.

Hall's major innovation was sanding. A schooner captain, he started a saltworks on the Cape, heaping up sand alongside adjacent bogs as he went. When sand blew over the bogs' cranberry vines, Hall expected it to smother them. Instead they thrived, their roots and uprights growing notably stronger. Sanding, whether done on winter ice or rails or even using barges, is still one of the most important techniques in the cranberry grower's arsenal; it protects against frost and disease while also helping bog leaf litter to decompose and release nitrogen. Hall's simple observation changed cranberries from something foraged into something farmed.

For decades, growing cranberries blurred the line between cultivation and wild harvest. Growers transplanted vines, sanded the bogs, and weeded out the competition, but their cranberries were often a single generation removed from those that had grown alongside cinnamon fern, white water lilies, and carnivorous pitcher plants. Even today, when the UMass Cranberry Station research center in Amherst has developed ultra-high-yielding hybrids, some of the most common varieties remain those carefully dug from wild bogs over a century ago. The Howes found in 1843, Early Blacks in 1852, and McFarlins in 1874 are still three of the most important cranberries and were probably the kinds eaten by Twain's family.

As Thanksgiving changed from a largely religious occasion to a national feast, cranberries would change as well—one of the most recently wild food crops would become one of the most frequently processed, almost always encountered as canned sauce or as an ingredient in a blend of sweetened juices. But in Twain's day, widespread processing was still a half century away; cranberries were still less a flavor than a fruit.

TO STUFF AND ROAST A TURKEY, OR FOWL

One pound soft wheat bread, 3 ounces beef suet, 3 eggs, a little sweet thyme, sweet marjoram, pepper and salt, and some add a gill of wine; fill the bird therewith and sew up, hand down to a steady solid fire, basting frequently with salt and water, and roast until a steam emits from the breast, put one third of a pound of butter into the gravy, dust flour over the bird and baste with the gravy; serve up with boiled onions and cramberry-sauce [sic], mangoes, pickles or celery.

—AMELIA SIMMONS, American Cookery, 1796

In November 1868, Twain had written a letter to his dear friend Mary Fairbanks on "*Thanksgiving* Day." "It is MY Thanksgiving Day," he'd said, "above all other days that ever shone on earth." Livy had agreed to marry him, and he was ecstatic; he swore off drink and resolved to become a Christian. He thought they might live in Cleveland. But now, in 1885, after nearly twenty years of marriage, he was in his house on Hartford's Nook Farm, and here he was well and truly home.

Though he often regretted that his free days of wandering had passed, the seventeen years that Twain lived in the house on Farmington Avenue were among the happiest of his life. He raised his daughters there (a third, Jean, had been born in 1880); it became a gathering place for friends as well as family, with neighbors and guests coming for lavish banquets or simply Friday-night billiards and beer. From the Viennese music box that played during dinner to the library where he'd read to the children, to the bed with its headboard of carved cherubs, the entire house gave Twain a palpable, "all-pervading spirit of peace & serenity & deep contentment." For him it was "the loveliest home that ever was."

The Victorian era idealized domestic life; one of a household's major showcases was the dinner table, where elegant hospitality and efficient household management melded into a (hopefully) seamless whole. Sideboards, the grandest and most representative furnishings of the era, were often designed to suggest Gothic cathedrals. When serving dinner to guests—many Nook Farm neighbors were also writers and artists—Livy displayed her skills as a mother and a wife; Twain's status as an upper-middle-class Victorian gentleman was at stake.

So dinners were often self-consciously lavish. Katy Leary, the family's maid for some thirty years, later recalled that most were built around canvasback ducks or a fillet of beef:

> We had soup first, of course, and then the beef or ducks, . . . and then we'd have wine with our cigars, and we'd have sherry, claret, and champagne, maybe . . . we'd always have crème de menthe and most always charlotte russe, too. Then we'd sometimes have Nesselrode pudding and very often ice cream for the most elegant dinners. No, never plain ordinary ice cream—we always had our ice cream put up in some wonderful shapes—like flowers or cherubs, little angels—all different kinds and different shapes and flavors, and colors—oh! Everything lovely!

Afterward the men stayed at the table with champagne while the ladies went to the drawing room for coffee.

From the roast to the champagne to the molded ice cream, it was all an extravagant, luscious display. Even the enormous quantities of butter reflected the host's ability to pay for a considerable amount of refrigeration, while also (in my view at least) reflecting a reassuringly right-thinking attitude toward cooking. The table itself was strikingly beautiful; Louisiana author Grace King recalled a gorgeous display of cut glass, twisted silver candlesticks, and an "exquisite cut glass bowl . . . filled with daisies, ferns and grasses," while every setting included a bunch of white roses. The night of King's visit, they ate fresh salmon with white-wine sauce, sweetbreads in cream, broiled chicken, green peas, and new potatoes, followed by strawberries and powdered sugar along with the charlotte russe. "Never in [New Orleans]," she wrote, "have I seen such beautiful dishes, or such exquisite flavoring," a compliment that would have gone straight to Twain's heart.

But such banquets were exceptions. Leary certainly remembered them as special occasions, often prompted by Twain's suggesting, "Well, I think it would be nice maybe if we give a dinner party" (these are Leary's words; it's a bit hard imagining her employer being so tentative). More usually, Twain and Livy would sit to a simple lunch of boiled chicken or potatoes hashed with cream. Such a lunch might be the first meal of their day, eaten soon after they made their way downstairs at around eleven-thirty (the girls ate several hours earlier).

Then there were holidays. "Thanksgiving," Leary remembered, "was most as wonderful as Christmas." That was saying something—Christmases on Nook Farm were epic, with Livy beginning to prepare weeks or even months in advance. She'd assemble fifty baskets in the billiards room, filling each with "a big turkey and cans of peas and tomatoes and vegetables," along with nuts, raisins, a bottle of wine, and a box of candy. If there was snow on Christmas morning, Twain would put on a white-collared fur coat that made him "look just like Santa Claus," and load the baskets into the family sleigh. Then he and the girls would ride around town giving their gifts before returning home for their own celebration.

On Nook Farm, Leary said, the family celebrated Thanksgiving with a "great dinner" for "people that wasn't very well off, poor people—not [Livy's] own friends specially." Later the family gathered at the Twichell house for yet *another* great dinner, before returning for a massive game of charades (Livy always made sure the children could easily reach ten quickly emptied bowls of candy).

The Thanksgiving dinners themselves were probably much like what most Americans eat today: Twain's 1879 menu lists "Roast turkey, Thanksgiving style," cranberry sauce, and celery before moving on to roast wild turkey. Twain was right to list wild birds separately; they'd been mostly hunted out of New England's forests by 1850. Still, Victorian families saw them as deeply rooted in the region's colonial history, and they were becoming the holiday's standard centerpiece—though now driven to the slaughterhouse in domesticated flocks or shot on Thanksgiving morning in organized "hunts" of farmed birds. Cranberries, meanwhile, had been paired with turkey for centuries (one of the very first mentions of them by name, in 1689, said that "an excellent sauce is made of them for venison, turkeys and other great fowl") and, as a wild plant, could also be plausibly linked to early colonists. Celery didn't have the same historical pedigree. Still, being best when left in the ground well into the cold winter, it enjoyed a central place as the season's single fresh green vegetable, often kept crisp in ice water, then set out in special celery glasses. Twain's Thanksgiving dinner was a meal that New Englanders could easily believe was rooted in their cherished history—with the addition of some elegant, if less storied, foods.

But the meal actually had little in common with the gathering usually called the first Thanksgiving. In fact, if you want your next Thanksgiving dinner to rigorously reflect what we *know,* for absolute certain, was served at the 1621 Plymouth harvest celebration, here's your menu:

Venison.

Birds (various).

Missing from the list, of course, is everything we now associate with Thanksgiving, from cranberries and turkey to mashed potatoes and pumpkin pie. And the first time the 1621 celebration was actually described as the first Thanksgiving seems to have been in 1841. In a *footnote.* The Thanksgiving holiday didn't spring into being all at once. Thanksgiving—the story of its origins, the ways we celebrate it, and of course its menu—had to be invented.

CRANBERRY SAUCE

Wash a quart of ripe cranberries, and put them into a pan with about a wine-glass of water. Stew them slowly, and stir them frequently, particularly after they begin to burst. They require a great deal of stewing, and should be like a marmalade when done. Just before you take them from the fire, stir in a pound of brown sugar.

When they are thoroughly done, put them into a deep dish, and set them away to get cold.

You may strain the pulp through a cullender or sieve into a mould, and when it is in a firm shape send it to table on a glass dish. Taste it when it is cold, and if not sweet enough, add more sugar. Cranberries require more sugar than any other fruit, except plums.

Cranberry sauce is eaten with roast turkey, roast fowls, and roast ducks.

—ELIZA LESLIE, *Directions for Cookery, in Its Various Branches,* 1840

Jannette Vanderhoop once walked around Martha's Vineyard. It took her three September days, and she didn't do it for fun; she could feel the coming autumn—could feel even the distant winter leaning in—and she suddenly wanted to walk. The Vineyard's shore is sliding sand and cobblestone, left behind during the island's glacial genesis. Both make for uncertain footing. "I don't think people are meant to walk for twelve hours a day," Jannette says now. "Especially with one foot lower than the other the whole time. I love the island, but it can get constraining." At night she camped on the beaches; as she walked, she watched the sea, as though she were pacing a pen.

Jannette, a member of the island's Aquinnah Wampanoag tribe, has enough energy that I'm entirely unsurprised by her walk. She writes poetry; she makes dolls, traditional clothing, wampum necklaces, leather pouches, and natural and recycled art. She's putting the final touches on a modern fable. She's thinking about a curatorial degree; she's considering a cross-country road trip with her cat. When I arrive on the Vineyard in mid-October, it's clear that much of it closes down after Columbus Day; signs read LAST DAY—THANK YOU! or SEE YOU NEXT YEAR. To fill the time, Jannette—a few years out of college, with a tied-back bundle of blond dreadlocks—goes to puppet shows, takes the tour of old haunted houses, whatever, and, at least that once, the island's nonnegotiable borders had her walking the edge of the ocean.

Her first children's book ("The first of many," she says) is called *Cranberry Day*. Cranberry Day is why I'm on the Vineyard; it's a holiday for the island's Wampanoag, most of whom live near the westernmost promontory of Aquinnah (it, and the dramatic gray, red, and orange Aquinnah cliffs, were called Gay Head until the tribe restored the original name). On Cranberry Day many Aquinnah Wampanoag go out to the tribe's common lands, where they gather cranberries and beach plums and wild cherries that grow in low bogs amid the sand dunes. It's one of the year's last harvests and also a time of homecoming; the tribe has more than a thousand members, many of whom return each year to join the three hundred or so still living on the island (the Wampanoag name is Noepe, or "dry land").

Jannette's book follows Chris Hawksler, a Wampanoag fifth-grader, as he interviews a tribal elder to learn more about the history of Cranberry Day and how it has changed through the generations. "Never assume that a native child knows his culture—or the history behind it, at least," Jannette says. "That's just a stereotype." Before Chris interviews an elder, he knows only that on Cranberry Day (a school holiday for the tribe's children) he goes out to the common lands with his family, where they gather fruit, share food with family and neighbors, and gather for drumming that lets him feel, in his feet, what the drummers say is the heartbeat of Mother Earth.

The cranberry harvest once lasted from three days to as long as a week, with many families riding oxcarts to the common lands and camping among the surrounding dunes. It was particularly important for the tribe's poor; in 1842, when crooked land deals had reduced Wampanoag ownership to Aquinnah, Christiantown, and Chappaquid-dick, the cranberries were said to provide "a Staple means of support through the winter" for "the most Indigent of the Women and Children." That year the Aquinnah Wampanoag asked the state legislature to take action against the "thoughtless White Neighbors" who had been gathering berries without permission, thus harming the tribe's "means of a living and supporting [its] poor." Within a few years, the tribe was levying fines on any nonmembers who took cranberries before the season had been open for ten days.

Back then much of the common lands consisted of a single huge bog among the dunes. Cranberries do best in acidic, wet—but not constantly soaked—soil; peat moss is ideal, and the main bog had plenty of it. Sand from the dunes blew over the vines, strengthening their roots; there was enough water for the moss to decompose and release its nutrients, but not usually so much as to stunt fruiting. With such good conditions, it's no wonder that Aquinnah Wampanoag made the cranberry harvest a mainstay of their year. What's more, the nutritious berries kept well; stored in cool, dry pits, they were a comforting check against winter hunger and disease. When it was time to cook, they could be mixed with cornmeal to form cakes, which were then boiled in water or wrapped in corn husks and baked in the ashes.

But in 1938 a huge hurricane ripped out root systems, shifted dunes, and dumped sand and soil over much of the peat. There was nothing unnatural about the storm, of course. It was simply a particularly severe natural event, one that transformed already slowly shifting lands. But it cut the acres of good cranberry bog enormously, leading to a certain dilemma: The tribe's elders care intensely about maintaining the common lands as a natural habitat. But they also want the berries to thrive. Soon after the tribe finally attained federal recognition in 1987, elder Gladys Widdiss said she hoped that Cranberry Day would only become a stronger tradition, a nearly official day of tribal homecoming.

When Bret Stearns, head of the tribe's Natural Resources Division, drives me out to the common lands, the ocean beyond the dunes is silvered and glassy, the road quiet save for the occasional locals pulling out their boats from a nearby marina before the weather truly turns. The undulations of the common lands make them at once wide open and constrained, expansive even as most sight lines end in a nearby sandy dune or thicket of coastal vegetation. Today few if any Wampanoag live in the gray, shingle-sided, broad-windowed homes—many of them on three acres of land, costing $2 million each—that loom at the edge of the five hundred acres of dunes.

At first I see only shades of brown in the bogs; under the gray sky they seem faded, in a going-to-winter kind of way. Between the dunes three-sided grass spreads out like a minuscule prairie. Ferns stand motionless, waiting for breeze; there are thick, determined patches of bayberry and wild cherry and oak. More bracken flanks the bogs; where an oak does stand alone, it grows low and sprawling, forever clutching the sand against ocean wind. The common lands are dunes and pothole bogs, vines and twisted trees, vegetation wrestling over lobes of sand, and sloping, sandy soil, and flats of peat. And after a while, the colors begin to seem quietly insistent. The reds are like ocher and rust, the browns those of leather and wave-wet sand. The most brilliant are the greens: brush as dark as ivy, vivid bunchgrasses brighter than the day should allow. These aren't the crimsons or scarlets or tanager yellows of the New England forest autumn. But as we wander the bogs between the dunes, even the ocean quiet, I realize that this is one of the loveliest places I've been.

The lack of wind turns out to be lucky. I've worn sneakers to the bog, which is as ill-considered as it sounds; the first time I step on what seems like a firm tussock, I smoosh down, ankle-deep, into an instant watery hole in the peat moss (later, in the Martha's Vineyard Museum, I'll see a horse's old bog shoes—broad wooden disks nailed to the bottoms of standard iron horseshoes). "We do most of our work here in the winter," Bret says. "Lots of people hunt out there before then, going for deer and waterfowl—some rabbits, though those are pretty spare—and we want to leave them in peace until the season's over. Besides, our main work is cutting out the other plants, giving the vines air and light." He pushes grass aside, revealing a patch of cranberry. Cranberry vines grow flat on the ground, budding thickly into four-inch stolons, or uprights, that look something like sprigs of giant, dark green thyme. When the plants bloom, the blossoms droop like a crane's neck—their English name may be a corruption of "craneberry." But now the blossoms are gone, and some have been replaced by bright red fruit, distinct as small holes in a tent.

"The easiest time to cut is when the bog is frozen," Bret goes on. "Then we can just come in with a tractor, push mowers, and some hand tools and cut straight down to the level of the ice. Give the berries space and they really thrive." Because of the surrounding dunes and hard winter winds, there's not even any need to add sand—more than enough will blow over the vines before spring.

Bret started working the overbrush hard about five years ago—just long enough to be able to see some results, since it takes around four years for a new sprout to bear fruit. He gestures at a small bog, cupped cozily between dunes and high ground thick with oaks. "All this is on the chopping block for winter," he says. But after they tear out invasives like catbrier and spotted knapweed, hauling off the debris to burn, what will be left will still be visibly wild landscape. Dense beds of cranberries will grow alongside bayberries, beach plums, highbush blueberries, and wild cherries; marsh hawks and bobwhites and toads will live in and on and under the thickets. The tribe harvests from the bog but also protects it, consciously and constantly, as a habitat.

Historically, gathering one plant might have helped others to thrive. Kristine Keese, an organic grower who also consults on bog restoration for the Vineyard Open Land Foundation, says that one of the most common weeds on her Plymouth acreage is wild bean, also called groundnut—an important traditional Wampanoag food. "And it's more than the wild bean," Kristine told me. "Once I made a list of all our worst weeds and cross-referenced it with a book about traditional medicines. Almost all were medicinals of one kind or another—St. John's wort, goldenrod, joe-pye weed, boneset, all of them" (she uses the goldenrod to hold down her own ragweed allergy).

As Linda Coombs, an Aquinnah Wampanoag and director of the Wampanoag Center for Bicultural History at Plimoth Plantation, puts it, that sounds like one-stop shopping—gathering groundnuts for food or joe-pye weed for medicine could also have helped to clear away the cranberries' competition. Meanwhile, controlled winter burns could have cleared brush right down to the level of the ice, leaving the vines safely frozen below. It wouldn't have been farming as it's usually understood—certainly nothing like the all-important cultivation of the Three Sisters of maize, beans, and squash that the Wampanoag agricultural year revolved around. But it would have been a kind of farming nonetheless, tending and encouraging the cranberries based on long years of watching the bogs.* Henry Hall's status as the first cranberry farmer may be only a distinction of degree.

---

*Not all bog plants are valuable as either food or medicine, of course—poison ivy, another woody vine, openly competes with cranberry, helping to cement its reputation as the Plant from Hell.

Much of the peat here was covered by the storms of '38 and '45; when he wants to open up a new area, Bret grades it down with a tractor, letting water flood in over the newly exposed moss. But he also leaves higher hummocks and woody areas to diversify the landscape, shelter the bogs, support wildlife, and—vitally—maintain strong root systems along the dunes. The area has already been transformed by hurricanes; now Bret is careful to maintain the roots, protecting against another major shift when the next big storm hits.

"What I'd like to do is double the available growing area," he says. But he's talking about the vines themselves, not necessarily about fruit. A good harvest depends on more factors than anyone can control, especially given the desire of tribal elders to maintain the bogs as a basically natural landscape. There's no pumping or water control; they're reluctant to burn. Still, the goal might well be met—there are about twenty acres of good cranberry ground now, about 60 percent more than just five years back (though that's still well less than half of what there was before the storms).

A commitment to mostly letting things be makes for a huge gap between good and bad harvests. "Last year everyone spent the whole morning working one pothole bog," Bret says, shaking his head a bit. But this year there's no chance of that; though my eyes have grown a bit more educated—an open space flanked by a stand of dense, green growth suggests cranberries, sometimes thick as moss—we see hardly any fruit. In fact, in more than an hour of looking, we see multiple berries only once—five dark red balls lying glistening amid the vines.

"Look over there." A truck towing an eighteen-foot boat is stopping at the intersection of Lobsterville Road. When it pulls away, water streams from the boat's bilge. "That's a big part of the runoff problem, too," Bret says. "We consider this a sustenance-food area. But that's pretty dirty water, and it all runs off into the bogs, along with the hydrocarbons and such in the roadway itself." Now he's using a federal grant to install catch basins, stopping much of the storm water;

filtration units will catch about 80 percent of toxins before they reach the bog.

This constant balance between tradition and recent changes is what Jannette wanted to capture in *Cranberry Day;* she wrote the book, in part, to fight stubborn stereotypes. Some of these are startling— when reading to fifth-grade classes, she says, she's had children ask where her horse is. "I'm like, 'Kid! Look, I drive a Ford Escape. It's 2009!'" she says. "I'll bring along some buckskin clothing, but I make it clear that it's really just for special occasions—and it's clothing, *not* a costume. I really want to give them a sense of what it means to be a native person in the contemporary world."

Her own sense of what the cranberry harvest means changed and deepened during the writing process. "I learned just like the kid does," she says. "I only knew it was something we do every year—that's the thing about culture, it's just what you do without thinking about it. Maybe you eat matzo, but you don't know much about matzo until you start looking into it." That's why her character Chris starts from a position of ignorance, knowing almost as little about Cranberry Day as someone reading about it in Florida. The book insists that culture is something passed on, something learned; traditions can only offer a still place in a changing world if they're taught, observed, and tended to.

The harvest itself is only for tribe members. That night, though, there's an open gathering and potluck at the tribal headquarters, a wood-framed building that suggests more a grand home than a community center. Kids run and tumble on a slope outside, their parents streaming past with trays and covered bowls. Within, a hundred people join hands. Elder Gladys Widdiss, who remembers harvesting in the days of oxcarts, delivers a blessing; she asks the Great Spirit for guidance and offers thanks for the next generation. There aren't always so many energetic young people, she says, and they need everyone working, all the time. There are too many challenges to wait.

The two long potluck tables are packed. There's baked ham and roasted turkey; the Three Sisters appear in a sweet casserole, a soup, and a savory dish with broccoli. There are four different corn breads, pigs in blankets, venison chili, and a coleslaw made with striped bass from just off the island. There are noodle casseroles with cheese and corn; there are cookies, coffee cake, toffee, and fudge (my small contribution; I don't have a kitchen here). Notably, though, I don't see any cranberries; ordinarily they'd appear as sauce, or chutney, or in a fantastic crisp (the recipe is in Jannette's book), but this year there just weren't enough to prepare for such a large group.

Given climate change, I ask Jannette, is Cranberry Day at risk? The question leaves her uncharacteristically quiet. "I don't want to be the voice of doom," she finally says. "But I think everything's at risk. The berries are down so low, right by sea level. If the ocean rises . . ." She trails off.

In a good year, members of the tribe harvest with the kind of toothed wooden scoops used since at least World War I. Today there weren't enough berries to take the trouble; instead they picked with their fingers. It rained all morning. But the serving trays are emptying; the room is full. And now seven drummers sing, each beat thrumming through the floor, their firm voices raised high and clear. One by one, dancers assemble, shaping a circle, forming a ring. It's a thanksgiving.

TO MAKE CRANBERRY TARTS

To one pound of flour three quarters of a pound of butter, then stew your cranberry's [sic] to a jelly, putting good brown sugar in to sweeten them, strain the cranberry's and then put them in your patty pans for baking in a moderate oven for half an hour.

—HANNAH GLASSE, *The Art of Cookery Made Plain and Easy*, 1805

For many Americans, New England is almost the default setting when imagining an inviting holiday landscape: snowy Christmases, Halloween under bright fall foliage, Fourth of July on the beach. So it's worth remembering how threatening—how utterly alien—it felt to the English who settled on the site of the plague-decimated Wampanoag village of Patuxet in 1620, building the town that would enter American lore as the Plymouth of the first Thanksgiving. Some of the English later produced boosterish prose, as when Edward Winslow wrote in the 1622 *Mourt's Relation* that "the country wanteth only industrious men to employ, for it would grieve your hearts if, as I, you had seen so many miles together by goodly rivers uninhabited." But they also had to admit that it was a country whose boughs and bushes "tore [their] very armor in pieces." To the English it was a place of howling wolves, one where "two lions roaring exceedingly for a long time together" left them witlessly terrified.

But the worst thing may have been signs of the plague recently brought by coastal traders and fishermen from Europe; in the weeks after landing at Patuxet, the English saw it as a country of ghosts. Sometimes the plague had struck with such speed and force that the Wampanoag had been unable to bury one another, "their skulls and bones . . . found in many places lying still above the ground where their houses and dwellings had been, a very sad spectacle to behold." The new arrivals could tell that "thousands of men ha[d] lived" at Patuxet, and "had died in a great plague not long since"; it was a pity, they said, "to see so many goodly fields, and so well seated, without men to dress and manure the same." Several times they dug into what turned out to be graves, hacking through the icy ground with swords; they hoped to find baskets full of corn, like those they'd already stolen from a Wampanoag winter-storage cache.

Having arrived in December, the English struggled to build enough houses. Even so, half died before spring; it might have been even worse without the stolen maize. Stealing the winter provisions of people already devastated by plague was a dire theft (the English did eventually repay the corn, though long after it might have been needed). But, fortunately for the newcomers, the local sagamore leader, Massasoit, was badly in need of a political alliance and willing to overlook the offense.

Linda Coombs thinks that the biggest misconception about the 1621 gathering is that it was motivated by pure friendship. "This wasn't because they were great friends," she says. "People think it was the first celebration in a long series. It was a onetime thing, and it only happened because Massasoit was between a rock and a hard place, being pressed between the English to the east and the Narragansett to the west." The latter hadn't yet been struck as hard by disease, and Massasoit "had to choose what was best for his people. So he took a gamble, trying to avoid subjection to the Narragansett."

In the months before the harvest, the English became heavily dependent on the Wampanoag man Tisquantum, or "Squanto," to the point that other Native Americans sometimes viewed him as a collaborator (at one point, having learned that Tisquantum was demanding tribute in return for supposedly restraining European disease, Massasoit unsuccessfully demanded his head). Tisquantum was from Patuxet and had survived the plague only because he'd been in Spain and London when it struck. Now he taught the English to plant, fish, and hunt; in one famous episode, he told them that unless they used alewife fish from the local brook as fertilizer, the maize crop "in these old grounds . . . would come to nothing." On another occasion he went fishing for "fat and sweet" eels that he "trod out with his feet," returning at last "with as many as he could well lift in one hand." Other Wampanoag fed the settlers a corn bread called *maizium,* along with "spawn of shads," boiled acorns, bass, roasted crab, oysters, and "other dried shell fish." The English planted in the fields of Patuxet; little by little, and with plenty of help, they learned to feed themselves from ocean and forest and marsh.

But the truly fearsome time was winter, and the newcomers would survive a second one only with a robust harvest. When it exceeded their hopes, they naturally celebrated with an event in the English "harvest home" tradition, feasting after bringing in the final crops. The only eyewitness account of the occasion is blink-and-you-miss-it short:

> Our harvest being gotten in, our governor sent four men on fowling, that we might after a special manner rejoice after we had gathered the fruit of our labors. The four in one day killed as much fowl as, with a little help beside, served the company almost a week. At which time, amongst other recreations, we exercised our arms, many of the Indians coming amongst us, and among the rest their greatest king Massasoit, with some ninety men, whom for three days we entertained and feasted, and they went out and killed five deer, which they brought to the plantation and bestowed on our governor, and upon the captain and others.

That's it; that's everything written at the time about the event that spawned a thousand pageants performed by kids in buckled hats. And, unsurprisingly, those pageants—showing a lot of prayerful English hosting a few Native American guests with a meal of turkey and pumpkin pie—have rarely gotten much right.

The 1621 harvest prompted a three-day gathering. About two of every three people there were Wampanoag; given the small size of the few houses, nearly everyone must have cooked and eaten outside, where there were various games and competitions (considering the politics of the moment, the fact that the English "exercised [their] arms," or had target practice, seems less than casual). Along with venison, the main food was probably migrating waterfowl like ducks and geese, which were plentiful in autumn; Governor William Bradford does mention taking turkeys that year, but not in connection to the harvest celebration.

Since there were at least ninety Wampanoag and only fifty English, the gathering must have been shaped largely by the former's ideas about what a harvest celebration should look like. Nancy Eldredge, a

Nauset Wampanoag, writes that offering thanks was "woven into every aspect of Wampanoag life." When harvesting a plant, netting a bird, or catching a fish, "acknowledgment and gratitude were given for the lives that were taken." Winslow, on the other hand, never mentions either prayer or offering thanks. It's a particularly striking omission, because when the English Separatists wanted to offer thanks to God, they said so: Winslow wrote in 1623 of a "solemn day . . . set apart and appointed . . . wherein we returned glory, honor and praise, with all thankfulness, to our good God" after the end of a particularly dire drought. Surely the English were grateful for the harvest, but as an expression of communal thanksgiving the feast was probably more in the Wampanoag tradition.

Whether anyone offered thanks over Wampanoag-style food depends on who exactly Massasoit brought with him; the gathering was, after all, a political event, cementing the alliance between him and the English, and the one account specifically mentions only "some ninety men." But, as food historians Kathleen Curtin and Sandy Oliver point out, those men are said to have come "among the rest." If "the rest" included women—something Linda thinks possible enough that she's included Massasoit's wives in several exhibits—then the feast is more likely to have included such dishes as sobaheg, a stewed mix of corn, roots, beans, squash, and various meats.

Though we only know about venison and fowl for certain, this was, after all, a harvest celebration, and the English may have cooked many things they'd been wanting since leaving Europe a year before. Along with the vital corn, squash, and beans, crops grown in the first year may have included pumpkins (pies wouldn't appear for at least another generation), onions, turnips, greens from spinach to chard, and dozens more. Still, the harvest festival was built around deer, and birds, and very possibly clams, lobsters, cod, eels, and other fish and game. Twain's Thanksgiving dinners were domestic meals with wild roots; this was a wild meal with some domestic foods.

If anyone at the gathering ate cranberries, it definitely wasn't as a sweet sauce. The Wampanoag often ate the berries raw, or else in boiled or ash-roasted corn cakes (other tribes pounded the berries with dried meat or fish, making long-lasting pemmican, a preparation Linda says the Wampanoag didn't share). The English would probably have used them the way they did barberries—as one element in a wine- or gravy-based sauce, which added an acidic, cleansing edge (an updated recipe for roasted duck with cranberries and wine in Curtin and Oliver's *Giving Thanks* was enough to convince me that English cooking has been getting a bad rap for centuries). Sweet sauce would have to wait for a regular supply of cane or maple sugar; the first mention of such a thing comes from John Josselyn in 1672, who wrote that "the *Indians* and *English* use them much, boyling them with Sugar for Sauce to eat with their Meat."

Josselyn suggested that the sauce was particularly good with mutton; it was also paired with game such as venison. But increasingly the meat seems to have been turkey. In the very first American cookbook, the 1796 *American Cookery,* Amelia Simmons suggested that roasted turkey should be accompanied by "cramberry-sauce," along with boiled onions, pickles, mangoes, and celery. By the time the first actual sauce recipe appeared a few decades later, turkey was becoming the default meat for Thanksgiving dinner—and the dinner itself was becoming, for the first time, the heart of the holiday.

Throughout the colonial era, says historian and *Thanksgiving* author James Baker, the true New England Thanksgiving had been "an officially declared weekday event marked by a day of religious meetings and pious gratitude for God's favorable providence." Until the late 1700s, Thanksgiving remained a mostly regional celebration, a day of prayer declared annually by various state governors (the Continental Congress declared the first genuinely national Thanksgiving in 1777; George Washington followed in 1789 and '95). Many families attended church twice; the meal was an afterthought, a break between services. For over a century, the holiday was more like the 1623 day of end-of-drought worship than the 1621 harvest celebration.

When dinner did become the day's focal point, it was usually built around New England foods—or at least a particular idea of what New England foods had once been. For many New Englanders, the Thanksgiving feast was as much an aspirational meal as were the Victorian banquets at Nook Farm: a chance for families who normally ate salted beef, beans, peas, cornmeal mush, apples, and brown bread to enjoy a "gentry-style meal of roasted and boiled meat, vegetables, and pies." Still, it took Americans a while to settle on a standard menu; the wildly popular 1877 *Buckeye Cookery,* for instance, suggested oyster soup, boiled cod, corned beef, and roasted goose as good Thanksgiving choices, accompanied by brown bread, pork and beans, "delicate cabbage," doughnuts, "superior biscuit," ginger cakes, and an array of fruits. Chicken pies were a particular favorite and seem to have been served nearly as often as turkey (usually as an additional dish rather than a substitute).

Just as Thanksgiving was becoming something we'd recognize today—a day with less church and substantially more food—cranberries were systematically cultivated for the first time; the fruit and the holiday were a perfect match. In 1820 Hall shipped thirty barrels from his "cranberry yards" to New York; a decade later, cultivated berries were being shipped as far off as New Orleans and even to Europe. Wild berries did remain common for decades, and city markets often mixed them with farmed fruit; in 1830 Bostonian Lydia Child wrote in *The Frugal Housewife* that it was better for children to "pick cranberries from the meadow, to be carried to market" than to "romp away their existence" (other approved anti-romping measures included making patchwork, braiding straw, and knitting garters, suspenders, and stockings). But the trend was all toward cultivated fruit, and thus toward more widespread use. Cranberries were a genuine New England food, one that Victorians liked to think had been eaten by the earliest English settlers, but they also shipped well, especially when packed into straw or brine. The fruit and the holiday would be partnered for centuries.

Then, as now, the ideal Thanksgiving dinner was immense. In her

1827 novel *Northwood,* Sarah Josepha Hale described a mind-blowing feast:

> The roasted turkey took precedence on this occasion, being placed
> at the head of the table; and well did it become its lordly station,
> sending forth the rich odor of its savory stuffing, and finely cov-
> ered with the froth of its basting. At the foot of the board, a sirloin
> of beef, flanked on either side by a leg of pork and loin of mutton,
> seemed placed as a bastion to defend the innumerable bowls of
> gravy and plates of vegetables disposed in that quarter. A goose
> and pair of ducklings occupied side stations on the table; the
> middle being graced, as it always is on such occasions, by the rich
> burgomaster of the provisions, called a chicken pie. This pie,
> which is wholly formed of the choicest parts of fowls, enriched
> and seasoned with a profusion of butter and pepper, and covered
> with an excellent puff paste, is, like the celebrated pumpkin pie,
> an indispensable part of a good and true Yankee Thanksgiving;
> the size of the pie usually denoting the gratitude of the party who
> prepares the feast. The one now displayed could never have had
> many peers. . . .

There were also pickles, preserves, plum pudding, custards, cakes, sweetmeats, and more pies—pumpkin occupied "the most distinguished niche"—as well as cider, currant wine, and ginger beer. By 1827 the grand Thanksgiving dinner was coming into shape. The only thing missing was the Pilgrims.

Because, amazingly, there's no evidence that *anyone* called the Plymouth harvest celebration the first Thanksgiving until 1841, when the Unitarian reverend Alexander Young published *Chronicles of the Pilgrim Forefathers.* Winslow's description of the celebration had been left out of previous editions of *Mourt's Relation;* after it was rediscovered in an old pamphlet in Philadelphia, Young reprinted it, adding the footnote that "this was the first Thanksgiving, the harvest festival of

New England." It was terrific timing—as the holiday changed from a religious observance to an annual family feast, calling the Plymouth celebration the first Thanksgiving made intuitive sense. But it was many years before most people assumed the connection; the first image Baker has found connecting Plymouth to Thanksgiving is an 1870 *Harper's* woodcut. Thanksgiving dinner wasn't the continuation of an old Pilgrim tradition, or even modeled after it; instead the Pilgrim story was used to explain a holiday dinner that more and more people were eating anyway.

Hale, who was also the editor of *Godey's Lady's Book,* had a lot to do with making the meal a national, rather than regional New England, custom. Starting in 1837, she wrote a letter to every governor, every member of Congress, and the president; she editorialized tirelessly in her magazine. In 1863 her campaign finally succeeded; Lincoln, having decided that a national Thanksgiving could be a unifying event, declared it the last Thursday in November.*

It was, it turned out, only partially unifying; in 1863 a New England holiday established by Lincoln wasn't likely to be universally beloved south of Washington, D.C. (after the Civil War, many white Southerners scheduled their own Thanksgivings or ignored the holiday altogether, while images of African-American families preparing their holiday dinners became magazine mainstays). And the usual connection between Thanksgiving and early colonial history was, and remains, loaded: in 1970 the censorship of a speech by a Wampanoag teacher named Frank James prompted American Indian activists to declare Thanksgiving Day in Plymouth to be their National Day of Mourning, a protest that continues every year.

Celebrated or challenged, Thanksgiving and the (largely invented) story of its origins were finally totally ingrained in the American consciousness. At least partially as a result, cranberries changed from

---

*It became the fourth Thursday of the month in 1941, a change made to lengthen the Christmas-shopping season.

being an occasionally foraged fruit into one of the major crops of both Massachusetts and New Jersey. More than a traditional New England food, cranberries were local to Plymouth itself—by 1915, Plymouth County produced 61 percent of the state's crop, which was often sold with images of Native Americans on the label. The berries were set on the holiday table as reflexively as salt and pepper, harvested as systematically as maize.

Still, like any agriculture, cranberry cultivation can be contentious. And for a good reason: debates about how best to grow cranberries are really about how best to treat the land.

CHICKEN PIE FOR THANKSGIVING

Two chickens, three pints of cream, one pound of butter, flour enough to make a stiff crust. Cut the chicken at the joints, and cook in boiling salted water till tender.

Crust.—Three pints of cream, one heaping teaspoonful of salt, and flour to mix it hard enough to roll out easily.

Line a deep earthen dish having flaring sides with a thin layer of paste. . . . Fill the centre with the parboiled chicken. Take out some of the larger bones. Season the chicken liquor with salt and pepper, and pour it over the chicken; use enough to nearly cover. Cut the remaining quarter of butter into pieces the size of a chestnut, and put them over the meat. Roll the remainder of the crust to fit the top. Make a curving cut in the crust and turn it back, that the steam may escape. Bake three hours in a brick oven. If baked in a stove oven, put on only two rims of crust and bake two hours. —Miss A. M. Towne

—MARY JOHNSON LINCOLN, *Mrs. Lincoln's Boston Cook Book,* 1884

When I arrive at Cranberry Hill Farm in Plymouth, Kristine Keese greets me in a soft Polish accent: "I'm afraid you've arrived at a small crisis." Just last night someone vandalized equipment and set a fire beside the bogs she farms with her husband, Robert. On top of being the kind of thing that makes you despair at humanity—vandalizing an *organic cranberry bog?*—this strikes me as severely ill considered. Robert's eyes are friendly above his crazed, salt-and-pepper beard; still, you can sense how quickly they might go cold and flat. Between tasks he smokes the stub of a foul-smelling cigar that leaves him in a permanent fog; he has anchors tattooed on his shoulders. There are *scorpions* on his *fists.* If I were breaking the windows out of an excavator, stealing the gas can, and spilling the gas beside a cranberry bog and setting it afire, Robert ranks high on the list of people I wouldn't want to see coming down the forested dirt road.

The cranberry wet harvest, when workers flood the bogs and use water-reel harvesters to flail berries from the vines, is one of the most beautiful harvests in the world. On a cloudless New England October day, the floating cranberries—swept by floating booms into a dense mat—make a study in color, standing out against the blue water as clearly as a clutch of eggs on sunlit grass. In aerial shots they seem solid enough to tiptoe across. What's more, protecting a cranberry bog's watershed requires three or four acres of forest for every one cultivated; at harvest time the pines are stubbornly green, the elms and maples orange and yellow and a vibrant red that mirrors the fruit gathered on the flood.

But that isn't how they harvest at Cranberry Hill. Which is, of course, one reason that I'm there: Twain never ate a wet-harvested cranberry. Neither have you, at least in the literal sense of cooking or eating whole berries; cranberries have to be thoroughly dry to be packed and shipped, which wet harvesting obviously doesn't permit. Berries scooped up during wet harvest—over 90 percent of the crop—are all destined for quick processing into sauce, chutney, and of course into juice. But in 1879, when Twain wrote "cranberry sauce" on his menu, canned sauce was still nine years away from being invented in Maine; all his cranberry sauce came from berries picked with fingers or scoops.

The other (and, it turns out, related) reason for my visit is that Cranberry Hill is entirely organic. Kristine and Robert aren't altogether happy about the fact that their fruit is dry-harvested, then sold fresh and direct to the customer—wet harvesting is easier, more economical, and recovers a higher percentage of the berries. But the major distribution chains (especially the giant Ocean Spray and Northland cooperatives) are set up to handle conventionally grown fruit: typically, conventional growers turn to middleman handlers to process the crop, which is then sold through the co-ops. A handler who processes conventional berries has to clean off all his equipment before working with organic fruit—an impossibly slow process, given how fast wet-harvested berries will rot. So, though there's undoubtedly demand for organic sauce and juice, the distribution chain just isn't there. Growing organic means that the Keeses have to sell the berries themselves, as whole fruit, and selling whole fruit means dry harvesting.

Even if the Keeses didn't dry-harvest, I'd be curious about how they've managed to succeed. Cranberry cultivation has become incredibly productive; in 2002 the Wisconsin growers averaged over two hundred hundred-pound barrels per acre of bog, as opposed to fifteen per acre a century before. But it's also, historically, been hugely dependent on chemical pesticides and herbicides (they are, after all, growing in bogs). I'm not always reflexively opposed to the use of conventional farming methods, and I take the views of conventional growers—several of whom outright rejected the notion of abandoning herbicides—seriously. Still, cranberries often grow on land sensitive enough that it reverts into protected wetland if left fallow for even five years; this seems like a case where you'd want to limit chemicals as much as possible. What, I wonder, stops people from making the transition to organic? And what's at stake when they try?

When cranberry farming began in the 1820s, the bogs of southeastern Massachusetts were valued mostly for their iron. Bog iron is formed by bacteria that cause the natural iron in water to settle out; decades of dredging for the deposits (used, among other things, to make cannonballs) left the area with hundreds of shallow, irregular quadrangles cut into the marshes. When the market for cranberries began expanding in the 1830s, a sea captain who had a regular crew and some extra capital was in a perfect position to buy bog land on the cheap; many of the first cranberry growers were sailors. The connection was so strong that after the Civil War, when the advent of railroads and steel-hulled steamers left captains of the old wooden schooners casting about for new careers, cranberries "may have provided the economic salvation" of heavily nautical Cape Cod. Some older bogs are still divided into one-sixty-fourth ownership shares, mirroring the division of nineteenth-century ships.

Robert and Kristine fit comfortably into the tradition. When they bought the property in 1988, Robert worked as a scalloper; cranberry farming was a hobby that let the couple maintain the bogs on their beautiful Plymouth land. Just a few years later, the Massachusetts scallop fishery collapsed—scallops scarce, fishing grounds closed—which seemed to put an end to the Keeses' cranberrying entirely. They loaded their boat on a trailer and hauled it all the way to Alaska, hoping for better fishing. But the Alaskan seas were too high for their boat; from then on, Kristine and Robert were cranberry farmers.

Now Robert is happy to talk about how the language of sailors survives in the bogs—coming out of a bog is called "going ashore"— and how whaling vessels once carried cranberries against the scurvy.* But even if the bogs are talked about as bodies of water, even if hundreds of postcards show cranberries bobbing merrily during harvest, cranberry vines have to be dry for a good portion of the year. Too much

---

*The whaling story is a great one but may be apocryphal; Sandra Oliver, author of *Saltwater Foodways,* says she's never seen cranberries included as a substantial part of a ship's lading. And at least one frequently quoted bit of evidence linking berries and whaling, a supposed passage from *Moby-Dick* about how Ahab refused to carry them against the scurvy, is definitely made up (Ahab was many things, but he wasn't an incompetent).

water, like this year's heavy spring rains, can hurt the all-important pollinators—the Keeses just lost two of their three beehives. And, even worse, too much water makes weeds go wild.

"People always think the big problems with growing organically are going to be pests," Kristine says. "But pests aren't so bad. I saw a presentation once where an entomologist wrote the names of four major pests up on a board, then crossed three of them out. She said we wouldn't have to worry about those, since without spraying we have enough natural predators to take care of them for us." *Sparganothis* fruitworm, for example, attracts birds and other predators, which is why the Cranberry Hill bogs are surrounded by birdhouses for nesting swallows (as well as bug zappers the size of bedsprings). They'll also flood the bogs in spring, "holding early water" for longer than conventional growers to limit the spread of cranberry fruitworm larvae.

But the main problem, Kristine says, is "weeds—weeds and yields." Even in a good year, weeding by hand is a long, laborious, exhausting job. It's also an expensive one; the labor costs would be prohibitive if it weren't for what Kristine calls the "woofers." World Wide Opportunities on Organic Farms (or WWOOF—"woof") is an organization that matches young travelers interested in organic farming with local producers who need cheap labor. Cranberry Hill provides room and board and experience; the woofers weed. It's a huge savings of labor costs and helps the Keeses to continue growing without herbicides, maintaining the bog as a vibrant ecosystem.

"We bought the bog from a conventional grower, and he was saying, 'Oh, you gotta spray, you gotta spray,'" Kristine says. "Robert asked him, 'But what about all the crayfish in the ditches?' He said, 'Oh, don't worry about that, it'll kill 'em all!'" She laughs. "When we started, we thought organic was the wave of the future. And it's true, people are willing to pay a premium for healthy food, grown without chemicals. But that's not why we do it. People are always finding clever ways of killing each other—we mostly wanted to maintain the land and keep it healthy." Of course, healthy land and productive cranberry land aren't always the same thing. "A few years ago, we had an entomologist come out—when she lifted up some of the vines, she jumped back and said, 'This is *alive*—I'm not used to that!'"

Down on the bogs, Robert runs a picker over the vines (the fire, fortunately, remained on the far side of the watery ditch, which is intended in part to protect against forest fires). Dry pickers are built like push lawn mowers, but instead of a hidden, spinning blade, the teeth of a steel comb sweeps berries up and into a series of trays, which empty into a wooden box under the handle. Robert leans backward, restraining the picker as though holding back an ox, slowing the machine's progress to allow the teeth more rotations. A cool breeze blows through the pine trees and yellowing elms; the bog has a warm, reddish tint, as if the grass had begun to blush.

In the steep, inaccessible ditches, a worker named Amanda harvests with a scoop (Robert buys them for about $250 in antique shops; a new one is twice as much). "If it's hard, you're doing it wrong," he coaches her. When I try scooping berries, I realize at once that I must be doing it wrong—it's hard. The scoop is rounded on the bottom, and getting the lower berries takes a particular rocking motion, working the teeth through the vines inch by gradual inch, letting the berries tip back into the pocket. I never succeed in doing more than "scalping," taking off the top layers of fruit, leaving those closer to the ground. In the old days, a line of harvesters (many from Finland or Cape Verde) would work their way across the field, scooping from right to left, always training the vines.

With all the built-in checks on growing organically—labor costs, lack of processing facilities, the relative inefficiency of dry harvest— the good news is that organic berries command around three times the price of conventional fruit. That's especially important since cranberries are one crop where organic yields simply can't compete with conventional. The Keeses feel great when they get sixty barrels of Early Blacks per acre, while conventional growers get up to two hundred. Still, it's worth remembering that the Keeses are doing way better than *anybody* was in 1900, when the national average hovered around fifteen. Sanding, mechanical harvest, and near-religious weeding give them a yield that old-time growers would have killed for; coupled with the premium many are willing to pay for their product, it's been enough to keep them going for nearly twenty years.

The Keeses' converted garage has fishing rods in the rafters, a dartboard, an old iron stove, a pool table covered with plywood to create a workspace—and a pair of cranberry separators from the 1930s. Made of beautiful, polished wood, the separators consist of a series of downward-angled shelves; good, ripe cranberries are hard enough to bounce off all seven and onto a conveyor belt for packaging, while soft fruit slips down below to be discarded. The bounce method, the story goes, was invented by a New Jersey grower known—appropriately—as Peg Leg John Webb; Peg Leg John evidently tired of carrying cranberries down stairs for packing and so started simply rolling them down the stairs. Today it's the last step before the berries go into half-pound packs for individual shipments all over the country.

Though what Robert and Kristine do here is enormously appealing, there are clearly at least a few things that might stop more growers from converting to organic. There's the price of weeding, which would be astronomical on larger bogs (though "larger" here is relative—the average grower for the dominant Ocean Spray cooperative has less than twenty acres of bogs, compared to the Keeses' six), and there aren't ever going to be enough woofers to go around. There are the much lower yields, which must be unnerving for a conventional grower to accept. And, most important, there's the fact that the entire cranberry distribution system is structured toward selling conventional fruit. Between weeding, dry harvesting, and selling all the product, organic farming is just much more work.

But, tempting as it might be to lionize organic agriculture, when I talk to Hilary Sandler, project manager of integrated pest management at the Cranberry Station research center, she immediately explodes my clean mental dichotomy. Before 1983, it's true, growers would simply spray broad-band pesticides, wiping out all insect life. Most sprayed based on the calendar instead of observation, applying their chemicals without regard for what was actually happening in the bogs. And that's a hard habit to break; as Kristine put it, some third-generation growers "get real nervous when May fifteenth comes around and they're not putting anything on the crop."

But spraying by the calendar is exactly what integrated pest management, or IPM, is designed to stop. "Ultimately, it's a philosophy," Hilary says. "The idea is to consider both the environmental and social effects of what we're doing." The most important part of that philosophy is probably the willingness to absorb a certain amount of loss, to give up the idea that everything has to be controlled from the start. Instead of trying to destroy all pests before they can do any damage at all to vines or fruit, IPM growers spray only after a given pest rises above a certain level. They monitor their bogs rigorously, doing periodic "sweep sets" with muslin nets and counting the pests to determine when it's time to apply an insecticide. And when they do spray, the chemicals are far more targeted than what Hilary calls the old sledgehammers of malathion and parathion, meant to kill everything that so much as thought of crawling across a cranberry vine.

Considering the social effects of farming, Hilary says, is more important as the suburbs spread. "You have people moving out by the bogs because it's beautiful, then realizing that they didn't know much about the reality of living beside a working farm." Massachusetts is the nation's third most densely populated state. And all that surrounding, supporting woodland is powerfully attractive to developers, its sandy soil being as well suited for septic systems as it is for cranberry vines (A. D. Makepeace, the biggest cranberry grower in the world, has begun developing housing on some of its land—Hilary says it's now just a company, rather than a cranberry-growing company).

So though in my perfect world I'd love for all cranberries to be grown organically, the reality is that in southern Massachusetts the choice may not be between organic and conventional cranberry farming, but rather between housing developments and any cranberry farming at all. It's not that cranberries would ever disappear from the country entirely; Wisconsin, unconstrained by small, irregular, ex-bog-iron bogs, is now the nation's largest producer. But it's a crop with deep historical and cultural roots in Massachusetts. Cranberry bogs aren't just something worth keeping—they're something worth keeping *here*. And, I realize, it doesn't much matter to me how that's done, especially given the strides IPM growers have made in reducing their chemical loads.

Talking to Hilary is frankly not very different from talking to Kristine; both obviously care deeply about the land and how best to care for it. What separates them is more the old question of purity versus pragmatism—do you effect better change by living the ideal or by trying to move the greatest number of people in a good direction? On the latter point, IPM has been hugely successful, with more than 80 percent of conventional growers giving up the old calendar-spraying system.

The Keeses have been successful, too; they're a model for others who want to farm with as small an environmental footprint as possible. What's more, the methods of pest and weed control developed by organic growers like them help to make IPM possible—there is, Hilary says, a constant and ongoing dialogue. But successful or not, it's a wearing, wearying life; Robert and Kristine are thinking of putting their land on the market.

AFTER THANKSGIVING DINNER

A most excellent hash may be made thus: Pick meat off turkey bones, shred it in small bits, add dressing and pieces of light biscuit cut up fine, mix together and put into dripping-pan, pour over any gravy that was left, add water to thoroughly moisten

but not enough to make it sloppy, place in a hot oven for twenty
minutes, and, when eaten, all will agree that the turkey is better
this time than it was at first; or warm the remnants of the turkey
over after the style of escaloped oysters (first a layer of bread-
crumbs, then minced turkey, and so on); or add an egg or two
and make nice breakfast croquettes. . . . All such dishes should
be served hot with some sort of tart jelly. Always save a can of
currant juice (after filling jelly cups and glasses), from which to
make jelly in the winter, and it will taste as fresh and delicious
as when made in its season.

—ESTELLE WOODS WILCOX, *Buckeye Cookery and Practical
Housekeeping*, 1877

As a boy, Twain often went hunting with his cousins and his Uncle
John, stalking squirrels, geese, and deer in the forests and prairies beyond the farm. Perhaps their favorite quarry were the wild turkeys that
gathered at dawn in great flocks; Quarles, Twain later remembered,
imitated a turkey call "by sucking the air through the leg bone of a
turkey which had previously answered a call like that and lived only just
long enough to regret it."

He himself wasn't nearly as wily a hunter. Once, lugging a massive
shotgun, he followed an "ostensibly lame turkey over a considerable
part of the United States" because he "believed in her and could not
think she would deceive a mere boy, and one who was trusting her and
considering her honest." Having lured him miles from her brood, she
flew off into the woods.

Twain was humiliated—and lost—but as he searched for his uncle
and cousins, he came across an abandoned log cabin. The old, weedy
garden was full of perfectly ripe tomatoes. "I ate them ravenously," he
wrote, "though I had never liked them before. Not more than two or

three times since have I tasted anything that was so delicious as those tomatoes." He gorged until even the sight of a tomato was too much for him; still, he had the turkey to thank for what he remembered as "one of the best meals that there in my life-days I have eaten."

Twain hunted wild turkey and came back with tomatoes; he went into the woods and found a garden. Writing his menu, he'd make a show of wanting all his favorite foods assembled from the corners of the United States. But if that angel could actually appear with steak and biscuits, with roast turkey and Tahoe trout and New Orleans croakers, each might lose something essential—the inborn qualities that fixed them on the land, and in Twain's life and memory. Sometimes it's good not to get exactly what you want, whenever you want it; sometimes it's better to be open to what a season has to offer, to celebrate what's already there.

Eight

TWILIGHT

Maple Syrup

To have to give up your home," Twain wrote in 1875 to his friend David Gray, "is only next in hardship to having to give up your babies." Gray, deep in debt, was being forced to sell his home, and Twain was painfully sympathetic. "Ten days ago I had a great tree cut down," he wrote, "which stood within five steps of the house, because I thought it was dead; & it turned out that it was all perfectly sound except one big branch near the top. A stranger would not think we had not trees enough, still; but I find myself keeping away from the windows on that side because that stump is such a reproach to me. That maple was *part of our home*, you see; & it is gone."

It was an awful loss; Twain's love of maples and their sugar was as old as he was. Thinking back to his childhood days on John Quarles's farm, he could still see "the woods in their autumn dress, the oaks purple, the hickories washed with gold, the maples and the sumachs luminous with crimson fires." He could remember "the taste of maple sap, and when to gather it, and how to arrange the troughs and the delivery tubes, and how to boil down the juice, and how to hook the sugar after it is made, also how much better hooked sugar tastes than any that is honestly come by, let bigots say what they will."

Maples are long-lived trees; Twain's might have been centuries old. Sugar maples were an integral part of the New England woods that once covered his Connecticut land and which had stunned early settlers from wood-hungry England. In England most old-growth forests had been cut down as early as the thirteenth century; when crossing the Atlantic, many settlers reported smelling the forests of New England before they could see the shore. "Here is good living for those who love good Fires," one wrote.

But even people who saw trees primarily as firewood, construction material, or an impediment to farming were astonished by sugar maples. Maples were grand, their canopies a hundred feet high; their seeds had wings, spreading on the wind. Their autumn foliage was among New England's most spectacular, ranging from a burning red to what seemed liquid gold. Sometimes their seedlings sprouted thickly between burned trunks (New England's forests as much shaped by Native American burning as the prairies and western mountains); larger trees had healed gashes from stone axes, signs of earlier sugaring seasons. Even today it's possible—if only barely—that New England sugar makers still tap the same trees the Plymouth settlers did, drilling their holes beside the buried scars of axes and augers.

It's amazing to think that maple syrup, which seems so intensely domestic and originates in one of the homiest of trees, remains a largely wild food. The trees can be planted, of course. But it takes some forty years for a tree to grow big enough to tap; actually planting a maple is an act almost entirely for the future, like a brandy maker distilling spirits that he knows won't mature until after he dies. Most makers rely on the wild groves—some with hundreds or thousands of trees—known as sugar bushes. Tending a wild sugar bush by clearing out underbrush and thinning trees to let in air and light means entering into a quiet, centuries-long conversation. It means continuing phrases begun before the Revolution, and tasting sugar from trees once reached only on horseback.

Given how long it takes to make, it seems right that of all the foods of Twain's feast, maple syrup is the one that lasts longest. In a sense it's as much a seasonal food as asparagus, or butter beans, or anything on the menu; making it requires the delicate ebb and flow of frosts and thaws, the hesitant, stop-and-start beginning of spring in New England. But once boiled down to its sweet, unmistakable core, syrup has enough sugar to deter bacteria; sealed in glass, it can keep for years. Maple syrup can travel slowly. It lasts.

I can't be judicious when I praise maple syrup: my love for syrup is pure. All three of my sisters prefer artificial syrup, but on this score my sisters—intelligent, down-to-earth native New Englanders—are insane. My own devotion was cemented early, when I watched sap boil in my Connecticut nursery school's modest sugarhouse, waiting in the steamy wooden lean-to as the ladle passed between small hands. We'd spent the morning walking through the snow from tree to tree, emptying the metal pails into big plastic buckets and ferrying them back to the modest, waist-high iron evaporator. When I finally took a sip, it was one of those straight-to-the-brain-stem experiences, a perfect blend of flavor and place and moment that I'll have for the rest of my life. To a four-year-old, it was magic: the trees whose leaves we'd collected in fall, whose limbs were still bare and frosted—those trees gave us *this*?

I'm lucky. Those early memories are of a food that's still plentiful, that travels easily and well. But I can't deny the poignancy of thinking of that morning, and of my eagerness as I waited for a taste. Syrup is a food of childhood kitchens. It's a food of the sugar moon—the first full moon of April or May, when the Iroquois danced in thankfulness for what the forest gave. It's a food of the year's turning. Making it takes readiness, and care, but most of all it takes steady observation—understanding the pulse of one small piece of the world, as the years roll on and on.

And now it's a food that makes me think, unavoidably, of Twain. Of Twain the boy, of course, as he gathered sap and hooked finished sugar in Missouri. But also of Twain the man, avoiding the windows in his beloved home—wanting never to see the stump of the tree he'd ordered felled, wanting never to give things up before their time.

A RECEIPT TO MAKE MAPLE SUGAR

Make an incision in a number of maple trees, at the same time, about the middle of February, and receive the juice of them in wooden or earthen vessels. Strain this juice (after it is drawn from the sediment) and boil it in a wide mouthed kettle. Place the kettle directly over the fire, in such a manner that the flame shall not play upon its sides. Skim the liquor when it is boiling. When it is reduced to a thick syrup and cooled, strain it again, and let it settle for two or three days, in which time it will be fit for granulating. This operation is performed by filling the kettle half full of syrup, and boiling it a second time. To prevent its boiling over, add to it a piece of fresh butter or fat of the size of a walnut. You may easily determine when it is sufficiently boiled to granulate, by cooling a little of it. It must then be put into bags or baskets, through which the water will drain. This sugar, if refined by the usual process, may be made into as good single or double refined loaves, as were ever made from the sugar obtained from the juice of the West India cane.

—Susannah Carter, *The Frugal Housewife,* 1803

Mark Twain was a man who loved flavor and hated its lack. He loved fresh radishes, oily possum, and Southern corn bread; he detested watery cream, exhausted fruit, and the "sham" of unsalted butter.

So why on earth did he ask for "clear" maple syrup? The clearest syrup is Grade A Extra Fancy, usually from the year's first good run of sap. Its color (the only basis for grading) has been compared to ginger ale; it's the slightest, most subtly flavored of the syrups. Though it's great in its own right, I'll never understand why, if you want maple syrup, you wouldn't go for the darkest, mapliest syrup you can get.

The answer could simply be that Twain was a man of his times. Back then, strangely enough, the most common complaint about maple syrup or sugar was that you could taste it. Officials at the 1844 New York State Agricultural Fair awarded first prize to a maple sugar whose "whole coloring matter [had been] extracted . . . leaving the sugar fully equal to the double refined cane loaf sugar." Like most contemporaries, they didn't want *maple* sugar, with its rich, distinctive blend of flavors—its notes of butter or vanilla or marshmallows or smoke or grass. They simply wanted *sugar,* white cane sugar from the West Indies, which tasted nothing but sweet and could be used in Twain's "American mince pie" and "all sorts of American pastry" without making them taste much like maple. There was no hiding the presence of strong, dark, assertive sugar, which may have been best in a pot of his "Boston bacon and beans."

True, an 1893 letter in *Garden and Forest* magazine claimed that most city people did "not want the kind of pure maple-sugar that is white," preferring the true flavor of maple. But by then white sugar was much cheaper than it had been in previous decades, and cooks had begun to judge maple on its own terms, rather than as a substitute sweetener. When people wanted sugar for everyday use, there's no question that most thought lighter was better.

Even Grade A Extra Fancy, if a bit less robust than I like, is genuinely layered; it can suggest cream, salt, hay, or dozens of other flavors. Twain was always an instinctive critic, his judgments as passionate as they were sometimes imprecise: Did a thing have flavor? Did it please nose, stomach, tongue? Then it was good. And clear maple syrup, light and clear, was good.

But by 1896, Twain could feel the color bleaching from the world around him—the flavor of life going watery and pale. He had often been haunted by despondency, even depression. Sometimes he made what sounded like jokes about longing for death, like the time he remembered the people who saved him from drowning in the Mississippi. "I can't feel very kindly or forgivingly toward either that good apprentice boy or that good slave woman," he wrote in the *Autobiography* he began in earnest in 1906, "for they saved my life." Writing entries for Pudd'nhead Wilson's calendar, he included the question "Why is it that we rejoice at a birth and grieve at a funeral?" and answered that "it is because we are not the person involved." "It is sad to go to pieces like this," he reflected, "but we all have to do it."

But as he aged, Twain increasingly dropped the wryly joking tone. Life, he said, was a succession of "labor and sweat and struggle . . . [and] aching grief," until at last men vanished "from a world where they were of no consequence." Only death, he wrote, brought peace; only in death would he truly speak freely. When his brother Orion died, Twain wrote that the "release from the captivity of a long and troubled and pathetic and unprofitable life had been swift and painless." In a prolonged, inevitable progression, friend after old friend passed away; it may have been worse because he had described so many of them, vividly and repeatedly, as children with their whole lives before them. More and more often, he echoed his daughter Susy's plaintive question, "What is it all for?"

He had good reason to wonder; the early loss of his younger brother, Henry, seemed only a hint of those he suffered through in his last years. Perhaps the worst came in 1896. By that year a series of horrendous investment decisions (especially the famous disaster of the Paige typesetting machine, which cost him what would be millions of today's dollars) left him bankrupt. Desperate to pay off his debts, he left on a round-the-world lecture and writing tour.

Then, while still in England, he received word that Susy—by all accounts his favorite child—was desperately ill with spinal meningitis. She died before he could return home. "It is one of the mysteries of our nature," he later wrote, "that a man, all unprepared, can receive a thunder-stroke like that and live."

MAPLE SUGAR FROSTING

1 lb. soft maple sugar.
1/2 cup boiling water.
Whites 2 eggs.

Break sugar in small pieces, put in saucepan with boiling water, and stir occasionally until sugar is dissolved. Boil without stirring until syrup will thread when dropped from tip of spoon. Pour syrup gradually on beaten whites, beating mixture constantly, and continue beating until of right consistency to spread.

—FANNIE MERRITT FARMER, *The Boston Cooking-School Cook Book,* 1896

When Erik and I reach Jim Dina's house in Windsor, he already has a fire going. Windsor is just north of Hartford, on the Connecticut River's far bank, and Jim and his wife live in the kind of old New England house I'd want to live in myself if I'd stayed in the state: a weathered, even beaten old building, probably once a farmhouse, probably a bit drafty on cold nights, but well loved and lived in for more than three decades. The only thing that makes the house stand out is the fact that the fire isn't in a fireplace—it's burning between a pair of snow-covered wigwams toward the rear of a wide backyard.

Jim is tall and thin, with long, graying hair pulled back into a ponytail. He has the air of an enthusiastic art teacher who could easily fall into a project and happily stay there all day, and, in fact, he does teach classical guitar, though he has an engineering degree from MIT. We follow him into his workroom, the one place his wife lets him fill to the ceiling with his music and crafts and projects; along with his guitars are a pair of homemade lutes, a set of recorders, panpipes, and a music stand holding a classical arrangement of "Here Comes the Sun."

But most of the room is given over to what Jim calls, with a disarming mix of guilelessness and self-deprecation, "playing Indian." By this he means experimenting with technologies reflected in the New England archaeological record. He chips arrowheads and spearheads and harpoons from flint, sets knives in deer-horn handles, sews beaver-skin pouches, folds birch bark and seals it with pitch to make *mocuck* baskets. He decorates home-fired pottery by pressing homemade cords into the still-wet clay. Jim bow-hunts deer, turkey, and pheasant; the pelts of fisher cats and otters hang on the wall.

I know before I arrive that Jim takes all this very seriously; some twenty years ago, he told me, he built himself a birch-bark canoe and paddled it up the Connecticut River to Canada. He grows the traditional Three Sisters on two separate plots; in a few years, he'll know whether corn, squash, and beans grow better on dry bluffs or on bottomland annually fertilized by Connecticut River silt (he's nailed a deer skull to a tree near his lower garden to mark the last flood's highwater). But it's when he shows me a buckskin he tanned using the brains of a deer he killed with a homemade bow and arrow that I realize how serious he really is. The room speaks to a questing curiosity, a real, searching need to know with the hands as well as with the mind.

Getting Erik out of the house isn't easy—Jim is generous about letting him handle anything not immediately dangerous (though, between the flint points and the self-assembled black-powder muskets, there's a fair amount of that), and there's plenty there to fire his imagination for a week. But we're here to see Jim tap maples the way people might have done before white settlers arrived, as he does every year at the Institute for Native American Studies in Litchfield.

We follow him through a snowy stand of backyard trees, finally pausing before a sugar maple. "I think the way people first found out how to sugar was probably just seeing a broken branch," Jim says. He snaps off the end of a twig; a bead of sap gathers shining on the broken tip. It's surprisingly clear and fluid, crystal without the slightest cloudiness, and thin as water—totally unlike the kind of oozing sap that can petrify into amber. When it falls to the snow, a second droplet gathers, gleaming. I touch the twig to my tongue, then to Erik's. If there's sweetness, it's only a suggestion, a bare hint that there's more here than water; before boiling, maple sap is only 2 percent sugar, the taste so dilute as to be nearly undetectable.

Talk to any maple-sugar maker and within a few minutes you're likely to hear the magical ratio of forty to one. This is usually said quickly, almost as one staccato word (*fortytoone*), and refers to the daunting, stubborn fact that it takes an average of forty gallons of sap to make one of syrup. Sap is so dilute that white settlers called it maple water, or sugar water; it's not at all obvious to the eye or the tongue that what runs from these uniquely North American trees might be gathered and boiled into syrup or heavy brown sugar. One story says that the Iroquois leader Woksis killed a deer, meaning to cook it the next day; before he went to sleep, he stuck his ax into a nearby maple, which dripped sap all night into a cooking pot below. After his wife simmered venison in it for a day, the stew was sweet. An Ottawa and Chippewa story, on the other hand, says that the hero Ne-naw-bo-zhoo came upon a seemingly abandoned village; the people were lying under maples, mouths agape as they drank syrup straight from the trees. Ne-naw-bo-zhoo filled the trees with a lake's worth of water, diluting the syrup, forcing the people to work for their sugar so they wouldn't become slothful.

But when Jim hacks into the wood, it's easy to imagine how the discovery happened. At the first blow of his homemade basalt ax, the lightly gashed wood begins to bleed. Soon it's as wet as though freshly splashed. Jim cleans the edges with a knife, then a flint awl. Next he takes out a sap guide, a two-foot-long forsythia twig he's split and scraped into a thin gutter. When he fixes the guide into place with pitch, sap flows down it, dripping into the *mocuck*. The run is quick and unwavering; I'd guess that anyone who saw such a flow, or the sap icicles that can form from broken branches, would be moved to taste and cook with it. Why not?

Plus, I remind myself, my modern palate has been pretty well shot by a lifetime of easy access to white sugar, brown sugar, sugar-in-the-raw, turbinado sugar, beet sugar, honey, and way, way too much corn syrup (not to mention, to the extent I've been unable to avoid them, an abominable array of NutraSweets and Splendas). Native Americans had honey and the tart sweetness of ripe berries, but other than that, sweet flavors were rare before someone first boiled down sap into its essence. That spare 2 percent of sugar, touched to the tongue, might have seemed a gift.

That's certainly how many of the northern nations understood it. Like the booming of prairie chickens, the run of maple sap was a signal of spring, and of the rebirth of the nurturing world. The Abenaki named April's first full moon Sogalikas, or the sugar maker's moon. Others called it, simply, the sugar moon—the time when they knew to watch for flowing sap. Once the sugar was made, it could be mixed with crushed corn, then simmered into a nutritious pottage. It might also be mixed with water and drunk, blended with bear fat to make a sauce for strips of venison, even eaten straight. Some whites thought that many Native Americans used it more often than salt to season meat, and many acquired the habit themselves, buying golden *mocucks*—birch-bark baskets filled with sugar—from local tribes. Others embraced dishes like Boston baked beans, probably adapted from the Native American method of burying a pot of maple-flavored beans in an ember-filled pit.

But maples, however useful and beloved in the North, didn't run with sap everywhere; for sap to flow, the seasons had to have the proper shape. "There is a sumptuous variety about the New England weather," Twain once declared, "that compels the stranger's admiration—and regret. . . . [The weather is] always getting up new designs and trying them on the people to see how they will go. But it gets through more business in spring than any other season. In the spring I have counted one hundred and thirty-six different kinds of weather inside of four-and-twenty hours." Every year, he said, New Englanders killed a good number of poets for daring to use the phrase "beautiful spring." Describing the New England spring, Twain was also unknowingly describing a perfect sugaring season—the long, northern springtime, when sap runs freely.

During the year's first thaw, the sapwood begins releasing carbon dioxide; soon pressure builds up in the tree, pushing sap from any cut or hole. Then, when the temperature falls at night, conditions reverse; now the tree draws water in through the roots, replenishing its sap. Without the indecisive New England spring, wavering between beautiful days and frigid nights, the sap would flow only once; there might be a run for a day or two, but no real sugar *season* at all. People used to talk about sap "rising" from the roots in preparation for spring—and it's lovely to think of walking over all that waiting sap in the wintertime—but the truth is that thick sapwood runs all through a maple. That makes for an enormous amount of sap; sugar makers take only 2 or 3 percent of a tree's total.

Simmering all that down to make sugar (it required forty gallons to make eight pounds) would have taken days, especially for people without iron pots. Low-fired earthenwares were best suited for slowly cooking grains or stews; if the contents were brought to a high boil, the clay would eventually crack and crumble. "That's a big loss, this time of year," Jim says. "It's tough to dig out the clay to burn more pots until after the final thaws." No iron, and earthenware didn't work well: that left boiling stones.

Beside the fire, Jim dumps a gallon of water into a six-by-fifteen-inch trough carved from a thick chestnut log, then starts fishing hot river stones from the embers with a pair of sapling tongs. When the first stone hits the water, it steams; the second raises a furious boil.

"You think it'd make a low simmer, steam coming off the surface," Jim says. "But it's this quite amazing, pyrotechnic boiling—if this was real sap, you'd smell the maple sugar already. You'd see it thickening around the rocks." Erik actually stumbles back, less in alarm than delight, falling backward over a low fence of untrimmed branches and yelling, "The steam is coming *at* me!" Jim adds five more stones. Within two minutes nearly all of the gallon has boiled away, leaving a bare, hot film.

The boiling stones are incredibly effective; Jim thinks that using them means that sugaring would have had to be group work. "You'd have families coming together, working to gather the sap," he says, "throwing in the stones, pouring in more sap as the first sap reduced and thickened." Freezing the sap overnight might have sped the process somewhat—ice could have been lifted off the top, leaving behind sweeter, more concentrated sap. "When I'm doing this for real, I'll keep pouring in fresh sap all day," Jim goes on. "Finally it'll be thick enough to finish at a simmer in a clay pot. You end with a real thick, dark sugar, perfect for traveling."

"Dark" sugar is right; the soot from even seven stones has left the little water at the bottom gray and cloudy. A whole day of adding sap and stones might leave as much ash as sugar. "There's no way to avoid it, really," Jim says. "You're putting the sap into immediate contact with the heating element." That, he thinks, is why early Quebecois Jesuits reported that Indian sugar tasted more burned than the French product, with one opining in 1724 that "the French make it better than the Indian women, from whom they have learned how to do it."

Jim's sugar making follows almost exactly the process described by a Kickapoo man in 1835 after someone suggested to him that whites invented maple sugaring. He was understandably taken aback and described "the art of excavating the trees in order to make troughs of them, of placing the sap in these, of heating the stones and throwing them into the sap so as to cause it to boil, and by this means reducing it to sugar." But Jim's first few tries didn't go smoothly.

"The first time I did this in public, I felt like the biggest fraud," he says. "It was so muddy—I mean, am I conning these people? I brought the syrup home to my wife, and after the first taste neither of us would touch it. But the next morning it had settled out, and you could skim off the top and simmer it to sugar. It's great energy, that way—I brought a lot of it with me when I paddled up to Canada." Jim smiles at the memory; he says he closed the circle.

AUNT TOP'S NUT TAFFY

Two pints maple sugar, half pint water, or just enough to dissolve sugar; boil until it becomes brittle by dropping in cold water; just before pouring out add a table-spoon vinegar; having prepared the hickory-nut meats, in halves if possible, butter well the pans, line with the meats, and pour the taffy over them.
—Estelle and Hattie Hush

—ESTELLE WOODS WILCOX, *Buckeye Cookery and Practical Housekeeping*, 1877

After cutting down his maple, Twain had written that "I comprehend & realize one little fraction of what it is to part with *all* of one's home." But by 1904 the house at Nook Farm had been sold; he and Livy had been unable to bring themselves to live there after Susy's death. Once, after a rare return to the home before it was sold, he wrote to Livy that he'd looked up the stairs, and "it seemed as if I had burst awake out of a hellish dream, & had never been away, & that you would come drifting down out of those dainty upper regions with the little children tagging after you."

Now Livy was sick, and weakening; they sought medical care in Florence. As she faded, doctors consigned her to her room, with instructions that her husband was to see her for only two minutes a day. They'd been married for thirty-four years, and of course they cheated—passing note after note under the door, scrawling a final few words. Soon Livy died. "She was my riches, and I am a pauper," Twain wrote.

Twain's home was gone; he'd lost half his family. He could feel the world starting to slip.

———————

"No more knowledge is necessary for making this sugar," the abolitionist Benjamin Rush wrote in 1792, "than is required to make soap, cyder, beer, sour crout, etc., and yet one or all of these are made in most of the farm houses of the United States." I love that Rush could assume such homey competence on the part of Americans—these days saying that making sugar is as simple as making sauerkraut is like saying it's as easy as unicycling. But what surprises me more is that Rush thought it necessary to promote maple sugar at all. Americans used to make a lot more maple sugar and syrup than they do today; peak production came in 1860 with 8.2 million gallons, while today it hovers around 1.6 million in a good year. But Rush, it turns out, had a good reason for promoting maple sugar—and for wanting to see it replace white sugar completely and forever. Maple sugar, he believed, could deal a fatal blow to West Indian slavery.

In 1794 Rush wrote a letter describing sugar maples to Thomas Jefferson, who was then the secretary of state and, just as important for Rush's purposes, vice president of the American Philosophical Society. Maple sugar, Rush wrote, was cleaner than the West Indian product and at least equally strong (one of Rush's taste testers was Alexander Hamilton, himself born on the sugar-growing West Indian island of Nevis). The trees also provided molasses, vinegar, and the basis for a pleasant summer beer. There was much profit in it; there was reason to believe it might guard against the plague.

Then Rush began to bear down. Maple sugar, he argued, might sometimes be needed as medicine or food "by persons who refuse to be benefited even indirectly by the labour of slaves" but who enjoyed the produce of the "innocent" maple. He ended with his true hope, that maple sugar might be "the happy means of rendering the commerce and slavery of our African brethren, in the sugar Islands as unnecessary, as it has always been inhuman and unjust."

Other abolitionists agreed. Robert B. Thomas wrote in the 1803 *Farmer's Almanack* that maple sugar was "more pleasant and patriotic than that ground by the hand of slavery, and boiled down by the heat of misery." In 1840 *Walton's Vermont Register and Farmer's Almanac* observed that "sugar made at home must possess a sweeter flavor to an independent American of the north, than that which is mingled with the groans and tears of slavery." Writer after writer declared maple syrup to be free of the sweat, tears, and blood of slaves.

If abolitionists had succeeded in cutting deeply into the cane-sugar market, it would have been a true triumph. It's easy to forget, given how completely the United States was shaped by African slavery, but the country was actually a (relatively speaking) minor importer of slaves— some 15 percent of all enslaved Africans came here, with most of the rest going to sugar plantations in Brazil and the West Indies. Unfortunately, maple sugar never managed to displace cane in anything like the volume hoped by Rush, and the sheer deadliness of sugarcane plantations meant a constant stream of newly kidnapped Africans up until the end of the illicit Brazilian and Cuban trades in the 1860s.

But every bit of maple sugar made did mean less slave-grown sugar bought; when a long run of sap meant a man could "make enough maple sugar to last all the year, for common every day," that much at least did not come from slave plantations. But in the end maple syrup failed as a plantation crop on the kind of scale that might threaten sugarcane; efforts to transplant sugar maples to Germany, Russia, and even Virginia all failed (Jefferson's trees at Monticello survived but never yielded sap). Maple syrup remained a fundamentally local food, one that might be shipped but could be made only under particular, nonnegotiable conditions.

As Rush said, private families were best equipped to make sugar because of "the scattered situation of the trees, the difficulty of carrying the sap to a great distance, . . . and the many expenses which must accrue from supporting labourers and horses in the woods in a season in which nature affords no sustenance to man or beast." Such smallholders often used most of what they made, selling off surplus only in unusually good years. When she was sixty years old, Laura Ingalls Wilder remembered her father bursting into their Wisconsin cabin with the news that the cold snap was a sugar snow (she snuck to the door and secretly licked a bit from a nearby drift to see if it was sweet). The late, unexpected cold lengthened the spring, meaning a longer sugar season—and, for her grandfather, a welcome surplus of sugar the whole year round. It was a great occasion all through the woods, celebrated by a great communal feast and a rare dance; most of the sugar seems to have been eaten personally, and by friends and family, instead of sold.

Wilder's grandfather was lucky, living in a section of woods where "the trees grew closer together and larger" (she may have misremembered the spacing—the best sugar bushes have well-spaced trees with high, massive crowns). Other farmers had to travel through the forest to the best groves, remaining in distant sugar camps for as long as the season lasted. They augered holes in maples, hauling sap with buckets yoked over their shoulders or on sleds drawn by horses and huffing oxen. Then they boiled the sap in kettles set over curved stone bases, or "arches" (a term still used for the rectangular iron bases of modern evaporators). Some makers used a single pot, but that could result in burned-tasting, dirty syrup; the best used a row of kettles, ladling the sap into smaller, cooler ones as it thickened. When it boiled over, the fat in a dollop of milk or cream might settle the foam; less appetizingly, a piece of salt pork hung over the kettle would slowly render into it all day long.

It was hard, heavy work. Very often the only shelter was a simple cabin or lean-to. Once boiling began, it didn't end until the sugar was done, so someone had to be awake through the night: pouring sap, throwing on wood, pouring graining sugar into shallow pans to cool into loaves. Most of the work was outdoors, the fire roaring as it boiled off the five hundred gallons of sap needed to make a mere twelve of syrup (or, more commonly, a hundred pounds of hard sugar).

Whether sugar was made indoors or out, in a single kettle or in a diligently tended row, it took skill to judge when syrup was actually done. *Boil until thick,* instructions might read. *Until sweet. Until dark. Boil as long as you can without burning.* Sugaring was a skill gained through experience, by boiling season after season until one knew what "thick" meant, or "sweet," or "dark." A sugar maker might drizzle syrup on a snowball, watching to see if it filtered through; another might dip in a loop of twig, drawing it from the kettle to see how far the ribbon stretched. A third would drip syrup onto a cold ax head to see if it turned brittle. They were boiling sugar in the woods, over a fire miles from home; they had little special gear except for their kettles. Instead they used what lay on the forest floor, what grew from it, and what they'd used to cut wood.

There were farms throughout New England, but they were farms hewn from the forest, and the forest was waiting to come back. It was a land for those who loved good fires.

TO MAKE MAPLE BEER

To every four gallons of water when boiling, add one quart of maple molasses. When the liquor is cooled to blood heat, put in as much yeast as is necessary to ferment it. Malt or bran may be added to this beer, when agreeable. If a tablespoonful of the essence of spruce be added to the above quantities of water and molasses, it makes a most delicious and wholesome drink.

—SUSANNAH CARTER, *The Frugal Housewife,* 1803

When you talk to sugar makers in Connecticut today, you're likely to hear about a conversion moment—the day a maker decided to go out to his or her own backyard maples and see what the trees had to give. Small Connecticut makers tend to have started from scratch. It's different in Vermont, where a single operation might run a hundred thousand taps; Vermont maple syrup is big business, a brand defended by inspectors who travel the state judging purity and imposing fines for improper grading. That's admirable, and obviously important—by far the majority of American maple sugar comes from Vermont, which makes about 5.5 percent of the world's total, and it should be made and sold correctly. Still, I love the fact that sugar makers from Connecticut often come to sugaring relatively late. For them it's a new direction—an abandonment of one life, an adoption of another.

Which brings me to Bill and Amy Proulx. Before starting to sugar, Bill was a cop, serving on the Hartford K-9 unit for about twenty years. His best dog, Bruno, helped in some eleven hundred arrests, seven hundred of them felony convictions. They also did rescue work—there's a picture of Bill and Bruno at Ground Zero on 9/12. Once, Bruno's barking told Bill that there was still a fugitive hiding in a marsh they'd already pulled six guys out of—even surrounded by police and arrestees and diesel fire trucks, Bruno could smell the apocrine sweat a stressed man releases. Bill describes police work as 98 percent boredom and 2 percent sheer terror, which his unaffected stories graphically bear out.

Bill started sugaring after visiting his friend Armand Barrett one night during a good run. Armand is descended from French Canadians—

Quebec, with apologies to Vermont, is the true center of the sugaring world, producing some 85 percent of the world's total—and his own backyard sugarhouse is made of wood salvaged from an ancient and collapsing one down the road. "I walked in there," Bill says, "and I don't know, it was night, and the smoke was going, the evaporator was boiling. . . . It just gets in your blood. We started sugaring not long after that." But it was only a hobby at first, guided by Armand and a book called *Backyard Sugaring*. "We had twenty taps going straight into buckets. Our evaporator was this big commercial lasagna pan, probably two feet long by twenty inches, set over a fire we'd built in an old oil drum with the side cut out. There had to be a constant stream of sap into the pan—we could boil down maybe four gallons of sap an hour, forty or fifty gallons a day, and that'd give us a gallon of syrup. The system we've got now, we can go through five hundred gallons an hour. Five thousand gallons on a good day."

But before the boiling comes tapping the trees, which is something like blackjack—Bill and Amy have a certain amount of information, but at the end of the day they're still playing the odds. A tapped tree starts healing right away; a given hole will run with sap for five or six weeks at the absolute most. A sugar maker who taps in early February to ensure catching the first, most valuable run risks missing the whole second half of the syrup season. When Bill and Amy were hobbyists, they could simply have waited for the weather to turn before setting their twenty spouts (usually called spiles). Now, with some three thousand holes to drill, they have to try to anticipate the run. But if they're too early, they can't retap; putting too many spiles into a single tree leaves it vulnerable to disease.

On the other hand, if they wait too long, they might have only a few weeks before the maples bud; after that the sap will only make "buddy" syrup,* which one maker compared to burned bacon and is

---

*It's also called the "frog run," because the screaming of the peeper frogs used to signal the season's end.

mostly used as an additive in chewing tobacco and other products. So when Bill and Amy tap, they're betting that the best run will be in the next four or five weeks. A too-long spell of cold weather after they tap would kill their season, allowing them to gather only half of what they might otherwise. "A couple of times recently, you're sitting there in January and there's birds out," Bill says. "You're going, 'Man, we should be tapping *now.*' [The year] 2000 was a total disaster, we got like five percent of our normal crop. It's better when it's cold to start— when it's warm, you need the weather to swing twice, to cold and then to warm again. When it's cold, you just need it to warm up."

This year their timing looks to have been perfect. They tapped most of their trees a week or two back, avoiding a bitterly cold February that left a lot of sugar shacks that tapped earlier in bad shape for the year. Now there are only a few taps to go; we climb into Bill's pickup and head off toward a local Scout camp.

Drivers of passing cars honk or wave; the four-hundred-gallon white plastic tank in the pickup's bed makes Bill as identifiable as an ice-cream man. At one stoplight a car pulls up beside us, the driver shaking a jar as she calls, "Will you taste my syrup?" Bill obliges in the parking lot of a nearby fire station, declaring that the effort, which is her first attempt at sugaring in between teaching neuromusicology courses at UConn, has good flavor and great consistency. She beams—you can tell that her kitchen is going to be steamy this year.

Bill has the same kind of deal with the Scouts that he does with all the landowners who let him tap their trees, trading a percentage of finished syrup or its cash value for sap (the Scouts, wisely in my opinion, take syrup). Most of the trees to be tapped are spaced evenly along the road, maybe ten feet between each trunk. Bill thinks they were planted as part of a farmstead, possibly that of one Lieutenant Colonel Thomas Knowlton. Knowlton was the founder of Knowlton's Rangers, the precursor to the U.S. Army's intelligence service; he fought at Bunker Hill and died on September 16, 1776, at the Battle of Harlem Heights (his son survived the fight). Probably Knowlton never got to enjoy his trees, either for their sugar or merely as grand ornaments along the lane. But we can enjoy them now, over two hundred years later, on a snowy March morning. And if Knowlton sugared, his scar wood might still be here in the old, wild maples, not to be exposed until the trees fall and are cut open. Then someone might see his old auger holes in cross section, buried under more than two hundred new rings of growth.

In 1832 the appropriately named Ethan Greenwood wrote to the *New England Farmer,* asking, "Why should men delay to plant all sorts of good trees because they may not live to see them fully grown? What can a man do better on the face of the earth than to cultivate and beautify it? While ever ready to depart, the lover of beautiful trees should act as though he expected to live a thousand years." Greenwood understood the wonder and generosity of planting trees, the way it both concedes mortality and comforts. But tending is beautiful and creative in its own way. If Bill owned this land, he'd tend the sugar bush, trimming back the understory and the weaker maples to give the best trees more light. Trees on open ground would crown lower and wider than those crowded in the forest, spreading up to eighty feet across. The light would touch more leaves, the trees make more sap, the sap perhaps run sweeter.

All Bill can do now is gather from the trees as they stand; he drills two inches into the nearest trunk. When he clears the wood, the hole wells with sap—it reminds me of sticking a finger into wet sand, the depression quickly filling with ocean water. As sap streaks from the hole, Bill hammers in a blue plastic spile, tapping just hard enough to create a good seal; the sap flows down the attached clear plastic line, dropping with tiny thumps into the bottom of a white bucket. He lets us do the next few. I drill, then Erik taps in the spiles, almost shuddering with excitement as sap fills the lines.

It's beautiful. And it's fun—but that's because most of the work was done last week. At its height, sugaring is no more restful than any harvest. Tapping, cleaning, prepping, hauling, boiling—the urgent rhythms are more reminiscent of a fisherman hauling nets of schooling sardines than the quiet roadside stands you see in a Vermont autumn. What you see then is a sugar maker's dormant period; the trees have made their summer starch and are yellowing, reddening, readying to sleep.

It's all very benign; what we're doing isn't really much different from what the Iroquois or Algonquin would have done, cutting into the sapwood and letting a container fill. Even the switch to plastic buckets by everyone but hobbyists and Mennonites has something to recommend it, since lead can leach into sap from traditional galvanized pails. The path from stone ax, sap guide, and *mocuck* to power drill, plastic line, and bucket is a simple and direct one.

But our next stop, farther up the mountain, is something different. Beyond an ice-edged brook crossed by a single board, a spiderweb of black and white tubing winds from the back of a simple wooden shack and out of sight into the woods. Bill and Amy have hundreds of miles of line, all suspended four feet off the forest floor; most of their taps drain through the lines and into the shack's vacuum system, one of the major innovations in modern sugaring.

It's not that warm a day, maybe forty degrees at most, and last night it was in the single digits—exactly the kind of frustrating combination that freezes sap solid in the trees, without enough daytime heat to thaw it and let it flow. Still, the sap seems to want to run. Gravity alone has filled the long tubes—hundreds of yards in some cases—so that some has trickled through the pump and into the seven-hundred-gallon roadside holding tank it feeds. "It's a real good sign for tomorrow, as long as tonight doesn't get too cold," Bill says. "We better kick this on for a bit, clear the lines." The vacuum engine is loud in the shack; I cup my hands over Erik's ears. But after a few moments, sap dumps into the catch tank, five gallons at a time, less than ten seconds between each broad spray. Erik gets fist-pumpingly excited, beaming, shouting with every burst.

"This'll at least double your flows," Bill says. "People think it's sucking the sap from the trees, but that's not really right. What makes the sap flow usually is a pressure differential between the tree's interior and the open air, made by the shift from warm to cold and back to warm again. The sap just wants to go where there's less pressure, so we lower the pressure with the vacuum. Each tree, individually, is just drip . . . drip . . . drip. But look here—you couldn't get more flow than that with a water nozzle opened wide up."

The system does mask the character of the individual trees, with those giving eight gallons a day pouring into the same lines as the poor ones that should probably be thinned out. And Bill loves the look of buckets hanging on trees; losing that is probably his biggest regret about putting in the lines. Still, if you try to imagine running three thousand buckets back to the car from maybe twenty-one hundred trees scattered all over the Connecticut countryside, it's easy to see why he put in the system. Of course, the lines don't eliminate work; just stringing them was a major undertaking in itself. Now they need regular flushing with boiling water. Squirrels and fisher cats (like minks on steroids, Bill says) will gnaw through for the sap, sending him and Amy out to bind and splice and fix it all.

"When the temperature's in the twenties at night, we all celebrate," he says. "Then it hits the forties the next day, and, man, you've got a gusher going. It gets so we can't keep up, running back and forth to the holding tanks with the truck. It gets real hectic around here around tapping, and once the flow starts, it's usually a good eighteen- or twenty-hour day. But you can't cry about it—if you've got a good run going, you can make twenty thousand dollars' worth of syrup in a day, enough to carry you through all the down months. There's no tomorrow during a good run; you just have to be ready to go."

Erik and I are staying at a bed-and-breakfast, a 1740s farmhouse with a long hill behind it. The owners let us use their toboggan. Erik is new to snow; after his first run, he tosses handful after handful into the air. "I throw it up to see it sparkle!" he yells. "To celebrate!" I throw a handful; it sprinkles over his face. "How do you get it so high?"

In his *Autobiography*, Twain wrote that he didn't fear annihilation; before he was born, he'd spent all of eternity in that condition. That's an overwhelming but oddly comforting thought—trying to remember the years before you were born is like a Zen koan. But it's sad to think that Twain often went further, not only coming to terms with his mortality but seeing in it a great blessing; in one agonizing passage, he declared that he would not restore a single friend or family member to life. "The most precious of all gifts," he declared, "that which makes all other gifts mean and poor," is that of death. He'd sustained terrible losses; they must have been made more unbearable by his rich memory, by a life spent looking back and back and back.

Still, I'm selfish enough to want the joyful Twain, the vibrant Twain, smoking his cigar and munching on boiled eggs in a stagecoach descending through the mountains or feeling "sweet to all the world" as he feasted on fresh milk and berries. I'm selfish enough to want the Twain a friend watched chasing driftwood beside a river—throwing up his hands ecstatically, yelling when the wood went over the falls—and who later said he hadn't been so excited in three months. I'm selfish enough to wish that he hadn't sunk into despair, not only for his sake but for mine. I wish he'd found some kind of peace in his final days, something that he felt could sustain him. Because even from this great distance, it's purely heartbreaking to think of Twain's final years—of how a man who took so much joy in life could be so wounded by it.

By 1909 he was living near Redding, Connecticut, in the house he named Stormfield after the captain who'd brought him from San Francisco in the far-off days of 1866. In "Captain Stormfield's Visit to Heaven," Twain imagined the old mariner racing comets through space and finding Halley's too slow to test him; the captain glimpsed it only as "a flash and a vanish" as he hurtled onward, away from the world.

Twain had been born during Halley's comet's last visit. Now, he said, "it will be the greatest disappointment of my life if I don't go out with Halley's Comet. The Almighty has said, no doubt: 'Now here are these two unaccountable freaks; they came in together, they must go out together.'"

He waited; the comet would return in a year.

MAPLE-SUGAR SAUCE

Break half a pound of maple-sugar in small bits, put it into a thick saucepan with half a gill of cold water; set the saucepan over the fire, and melt the sugar until it forms a clear sirup; then remove it from the fire, and stir in two heaping tablespoonfuls of butter cut in small bits. Serve the sauce hot with any fruit-pudding.

—JULIET CORSON, *Practical American Cookery and Household Management*, 1886

Steam puffs gently from the wings on the sugarhouse cupola, wafting across the spread Bill and Amy and their kids share with their horses, beehives, and pack of dogs. On cold mornings the steam can billow a hundred feet into the air; neighbors have been known to come jolting down the dirt road in pickups to see if the place is on fire. Today is too warm for such a false alarm; it's the beginning of what will probably be a good run—even a banner run, Bill hopes, with temperatures for the next few days looking ideal.

The boiling room is dominated by the evaporator, a divided pan ten feet long and four across (it's been quite a while since Bill and Amy gave up their lasagna pan). Every compartment is full of furiously boiling sap; the rafters are fogged almost from sight, gray light shining in through the steam. The smell isn't as rich as finished syrup—most of the steam, after all, is coming from something more like dense sap than what you'd find on a breakfast table. But it's somehow all the more appealing for that, a sweetness I think I could breathe until nightfall and after without finding it cloying.

When Bill and Amy used a single pan, they were making syrup much as with boiling stones—adding sap continuously to a single vessel, with a last-minute transfer to a cooler pot for finishing. Now Bill pours sap into the evaporator's main chamber; each addition pushes the already boiled, thicker sap further along, until it reaches the last and smallest compartment. When it does, this syrup will be medium amber. Sweet, first-run sap needs relatively little boiling, thus making lighter syrup; late in the season, lower-sugar sap will need more boiling, darkening and intensifying it.

"I need a special kind of wood. It's called *free*," Bill says with a grin. And he needs plenty of it—the broad rear entryway behind the evaporator opens onto wood stacked a neat eight feet high. Bill pulls on thick, nearly elbow-length work gloves; the firebox is blasting like a forge. He throws in four big logs, slams the door shut, and flips the fan back on, stoking the fire. When the syrup foams, threatening to spill from the pan, Bill drips in a precise five drops of a tasteless vegetable-oil emulsion, the modern version of salt pork or cream in the days of outdoor kettles. I've rarely seen any product work as well; it takes perhaps three seconds for the foam to vanish into the darkening sap.

A last innovation used by the Proulxs is a big reason old-timers sometimes call their product "technosyrup." When Amy pulls up outside, the pickup riding low under the weight of the tank's four hundred gallons of sap, Bill leads us down a steep staircase into the cellar. Over a gigantic steel tank, a fine-meshed bag is cinched around the end of a pipe; suddenly a waterfall of thin, clear sap pours through, filtered of any flecks of wood or bark or dirt as it splashes into the tank. But the really modern change is what's between the tank and the evaporator— the reverse-osmosis system, which Amy and Bill call the RO. The RO pushes the sap against a semipermeable membrane that will allow only water to pass through, removing some 75 percent of the water before boiling even begins. This cuts the forty-to-one ratio down to about ten to one, a huge savings of time and firewood.

Finally, finally, it's time to taste. Bill twists a spigot, pouring a smooth amber stream of syrup, filling paper cups. We blow and sip, and it's exactly as good as you'd expect hot syrup to be when you've seen the trees it came from, when you've learned a little about the slow roll of seasons coming around brightly. It's sweet and rich; it's vanilla and toasted marshmallows and caramel. Chemically, the sugar from maple and cane and beets is nearly identical, but the extra compounds in cane and beets taste awful and have to be refined out. With maple they're the whole point—they're what make it *maple*. Erik drinks cup after cup; it's going to be hard to convince him that we should ever drink anything else.

In his 1886 *Signs and Seasons,* the naturalist John Burroughs said that well-made maple syrup has "a wild delicacy that no other sweet can match." In the Old World, he reflected, "in simple and more imaginative times, how such an occupation as this would have got into literature, and how many legends and associations would have clustered around it!" In fact, Virgil did fantasize about something like maple syrup, dreaming of a golden age when grapes would grow from briars and "stubborn oaks sweat honey-dew." It really is miraculous, and entirely natural; though Bill and Amy don't bother to certify their syrup as organic, no cattle graze in the forest, no pesticides or fertilizers are added to the land. It's forever a thing of place, a food of brief hours and long years.

Old-timers may call what the Proulxs make technosyrup, but it's the innovations that let Bill and Amy do the work they love—that let them make it a life. And every innovation has its old analogue: drills instead of augers, plastic buckets instead of galvanized pails, reverse osmosis instead of freezing, an evaporator pan instead of kettles or a hollowed-out log. Even the filter in the cellar reminds me of Wilder's grandfather, out in the woods with his kettle and ladle, constantly skimming. . . .

Then it hits me. Burroughs thought that maple sugar was too often "made in large quantities and indifferently," thus ending dark and coarse, unlike sugar made from "properly treated" early sap. Boiling outside meant dirty snowmelt from branches overhead; it meant twigs, dead leaves, cinders, all ending up in the kettle. I grin—I almost laugh. I should have known better than to doubt Twain. Maybe he didn't want it *clear* as in *light;* maybe he wanted it *clear* as in, simply, *clean.* As in *pure.* There were no inspectors back then, nobody checking whether sugar makers were filtering sap through mats of hemlock and spruce bark, no one ensuring that there was more sugar than cinder. Maybe Twain did like his syrup dark. Dark and clear.

Of course, I'll never know for sure. But I like thinking that that's the case, that Twain loved the flavor of dark syrup as he did the Mississippi's dangerous currents or a deckhand's artful curse. I throw a mental apology back a century. And standing in the sugarhouse, the firebox roaring, Erik gathering wood, Bill preparing to pour off another batch of syrup, I include a short, heartfelt thanks.

———

Livy, Twain remembered, "always worked herself down with her Christmas preparations." On his last Christmas Eve, his daughter Jean did the same; she decorated the house, readied a tree, and littered the parlor with so many presents that Twain was reminded of the nursery when his children were young. But that night Twain was awoken by a servant's cry for help: Jean was dead, drowned in her bath after an epileptic seizure. He'd outlived his wife and three of his four children. "Seventy-four years old yesterday," he wrote. "Who can estimate my age today?"

Twain was already failing; he died at Stormfield, in April. Overhead, Halley's comet burned as it had the night of his birth, half a continent away, in what was then a very different country. Now, as the comet sailed silently through the darkness, it shared a sky with the sugar moon.

EPILOGUE

A BIG BOWL OF HOMEMADE FRIED CHICKEN, waiting in the middle of a table, is one of life's great satisfactions. It's also among the best meals to share with family and friends; you sit around talking, and drinking lemonade or beer, as the bowl gradually empties and the afternoon goes slowly dim and mellow. Besides, as long as you leave yourself enough time, frying chicken is easy, while still seeming complicated enough to impress.

Twain, of course, would have said that I'm being grossly superstitious when I claim that I, a Connecticut Yankee in California, can fry chicken; I may as well season the bird with salt tossed over my shoulder or use a horseshoe to hook each piece from the pan.

Well, I can't make myself Southern. But I can brine the chicken for twelve hours. I can soak it in buttermilk and hot sauce overnight. To make the frying fat, I can clarify butter, and melt the butter into lard, and season the butter and lard with a heavy slice of good country ham (not faux-smoked Safeway hock, but a real, salty-enough-to-roll-your-eyes-back, Gwaltney country shoulder, simmered until the fat tastes softly smoky). I can start cooking at nine in the morning, giving myself enough time to pan-fry the chicken in small batches. And I can invite right-thinking friends, who will get why all this has to be done.

The chicken may still end up a mockery, but it won't be for lack of care.

—❧—

For Twain, life without variety, life without change, was literally not worth living. He once wrote that he'd happily die to escape the torture of a monotonous song (the singer, appropriately, later disappeared into the "white oblivion" of a snowstorm). He believed that "no land with an unvarying climate can be very beautiful" and that "*change* is the handmaiden Nature requires to do her miracles with." He spent much of his life searching out the "certain something" that made things worth tasting, and returning to, and remembering.

He was a lucky man: his own life was full of change, of exploration and discovery. As a child he woke early on a cold prairie morning and heard, even through the cabin walls, that the prairie chickens were booming; he knew that spring had come. He hunted raccoon and turkey and possum in forests full of sumac and hickory and oak; he climbed from the deserts of Washoe and, with alkali dust still on his boots, fished for trout longer than his arm. He navigated the shoals of a river full of catfish and black bass, tasted the terrapin championed by three different cities, and ate the oysters beloved in a hundred more.

All of it seemed so natural, so rooted, that most Americans imagined it couldn't ever be lost. The prairies were as vast and daunting as oceans—oceans of big bluestem and purple coneflower, where herds of bison took the place of pods of whales. The Mississippi seemed untamable, its muddy currents building the birthplace of a carnival of seafood. The water nearest Washington had reefs of oysters that could stop ships. Passenger pigeons could turn afternoon to midnight; at the Quarles farm, the birds were so numerous that they were hunted only with clubs, their millions enough to "cover the trees and by their weight break down the branches." Few people had the foresight of the terrapin trader who feared the loss of ducks, and game, and so many of "the other things that are worth living for." Few thought that the pigeons could vanish from the sky, that the oyster reefs could be mined out, that the teeming crabs and salmon runs could fail.

In Twain's day wild things were at the heart of American cooking; they took pride of place alongside garden tomatoes, apple cider, and fresh corn. But that would be true only until people turned their faces from the things they loved—until they let them slip.

As Twain said, "The way that the things were cooked was perhaps the main splendor." I drop four wings into the hot fat; while frying in lard and clarified butter, chicken smells purely luxurious. Fifteen minutes later the first batch is cooling on a rack. Tasting the first wing is a cook's prerogative, as unassailable as taking a giant spoonful of cake batter, and my first bite is impatient enough that I singe the tip of my tongue. But after a brief wince, I don't regret the hurry. The skin and dredge have melded into a crunchy, subtly smoky shell; the chicken is savory with buttermilk, with just enough hot-sauce bite to give it authority.

Twain may have thought that only Southerners could cook fried chicken. And, granted, I'm using the technique laid out by Edna Lewis and Scott Peacock, Southerners both, in their *Gift of Southern Cooking*. Still, Twain can stuff it; I made this, and this is *good*.

While the next batch of chicken cooks, I clean six pounds of greens. Eli steals a moment from watching Mio to chop garlic. Collards, chard, kale, turnip greens, mustard greens: I put each bunch into a giant bowl of water, waiting for the dirt to loosen and fall easily away. When it does, I chop the leaves coarsely, the resulting pile soon overflowing our biggest stockpot. Twain said *bacon* and greens. But we have more of the good country ham I used to flavor the fryer—and country ham, if less veined with fat than Virginia bacon, tastes as layered and smoky and rich as any.

Greens don't need to be tough and bitter; good, young ones need only a quarter hour of simmering. But even greens that start tough can be terrific. Their toughness is even a virtue—growing hardy, robust greens, fit for cooking with pork, isn't like raising baby lettuce. Chard will volunteer wherever it's thrown down (our old yard sported an uninvited, and seemingly invincible, five-foot specimen); if you couldn't eat kale, you'd call it a weed. The fact that many greens are as vigorous as they are nutritious has made them the salvation of generations of Americans with a spare spot in the yard, or who know what to look for in meadows and ditches: De Voe enjoyed shepherd sprouts, pigweed ("much used by country people"), dandelion, milkweed, and evening primrose gathered from roadsides and pastures.

Whatever their source, when cooked in real, homemade stock, greens bloom with flavor. One kind is good. But when you have four or five—collards forming a foundation, kale adding body, mustard lending its peppery sparkle—each green becomes the others' best sauce. Even those that start bitter end as something layered and complex: different yet wonderfully familiar, always new and always the same.

For me the glory of Twain's feast is in its inclusiveness, in how it honors forest and farm, prairie and orchard, wetland and dairy. All of Twain's foods came from distinct American places; all were, in some way, the essence of their sources. When Twain ate roe from shad netted in the Connecticut River, a Missouri partridge, a possum fattened on persimmons from the orchard it was trapped in, or mussels gathered off rocks at low tide, his meal depended on a wholly American place. The same thing was true when he ate butter beans, peas, sweet potatoes, and radishes from the garden—or blackberries and wild grapes from the forest's edge, or hickory nuts from well within the woods. It was true when he drank coffee with fresh cream on a cliff above the ocean, or spread butter on hot wheat bread on a cold morning, or cut himself a piece of peach cobbler made with backyard-orchard fruit.

Saying that food is the essence of place can seem like a sentimental throwback, or like something we've totally lost. But here's the thing: it's still always true. It's true whether you're eating a grilled sardine, or a tomato selected for perfectly voluptuous freshness, or a Whopper. Behind the sardine there's a rock-rimmed bay, thick with drifting kelp; behind the tomato there's a farm, and a farmer who chose the fruit for flavor instead of rubbery durability. And the Whopper—flat, gray, salty, and otherwise tasteless—represents wholly and without deviation the sprawling but cruelly confined pens that produce fast-food cattle. A McNugget has as much *terroir* as an oyster; it's just not the *terroir* of a place you want to be.

Twain would have recognized the false abundance of fast food at once. "The number of dishes is sufficient," he wrote in Europe. "But then it is such a monotonous variety of *unstriking* dishes. It is an inane dead level of 'fair-to-middling.'" He wanted food that had body and heft—that he could call mighty, rich, and ample. He wanted sputtering, smoking, fragrant, frothy, even clotted food, food that had vibrancy and energy and life, food straightforward enough about what it was to be called genuine, honest, and real. When we insist on uniformity—on having plenty of *something* instead of a jumbled, various, magnificent plenitude—one inevitable result is food that Twain would describe as monotonous, tiresome, and feeble, as a base counterfeit and sham. Bad food, he'd have known, comes from hurt and shrunken places.

When Twain was born, the bond between food and place was more obvious; wild foods were knit tightly into the fabric even of city cooking. Baltimore perch and canvasback ducks, Philadelphia terrapins, San Francisco mussels, New Orleans croakers and sheepsheads, even Boston beans flavored with maple—every one relied on wild lands beyond the city lines. As Twain's life passed, more and more foods disappeared from American tables; choosing mining over fisheries, pulp mills over oysters, even corn over prairie and cantaloupe over trout, changed American food—and the American landscape—forever. Twain was born in a country of woodcock and died in one of Coca-Cola.

Today, of course, how we treat the land and water still determines what foods we eat. But just as often, choices about what we eat help to determine which American landscapes survive and thrive. There are enormous economic and political pressures to define food as, ultimately, a calorie-production system, the end product of a basically mechanized and mechanical process. But our choices aren't inevitable.

And our choices matter. We can choose to support Massachusetts cranberry growers as suburban development pushes up against their bogs, and we can buy from people raising oysters in the nation's cleanest bays. We can help to keep shrimpers on the water after they lose their boats in a hurricane; we can work in community gardens and help with a local clambake, fish fry, or even a coon supper. We can eat seafood from low on the food chain, preserving the ocean life that's the one remaining wild thing most Americans ever see on their tables. We can support local bakers, restaurants, farmers, grocers—all the people whose work with food helps to make communities better, richer, more entirely themselves. And, maybe most important of all, we can recognize the scandal of food deserts—urban neighborhoods with as much as a twenty-to-one ratio of liquor stores to greengrocers—and work to ensure that everyone has at least the opportunity to choose good, healthy food, that everyone can access the true, varied abundance that farmers can produce on the American land.

All this helps make food what it was to Twain, whose best-loved meals gained savor from the parts they played in his life: a human project.

Next up is chess pie. Chess pie is an old Southern dessert of uncertain origin; the only thing I'm sure of is that it's impossible to bake a better pie. It's made of eggs, buttermilk, butter, and sugar. Lemon chess pies have lemon; chocolate have chocolate. Of course there's a crust. That's about it—but a good chess pie is sweet and moist and custardy, like the platonic ideal of cookie dough.

The one Erik and I like to make is also one of the world's great kid-friendly recipes—there's no sifting dry parts, or mixing wet parts, or beating whites until they form soft peaks, or any of that foofaraw. You just add the ingredients, one at a time, and wait for the kid to do as he will with a whisk.

I put the eggs in a big bowl; Erik beats the holy hell out of them.

"You measure, I mix!" he says.

"Right," I say, and pour in the sugar; he beats it until eggs and sugar are pale as cream. Butter, buttermilk, lemon juice, vanilla—after each addition Erik goes to town, whisking until it's vanished, the filling always getting richer, sweeter, better. My only concern will be washing the walls; this pie's gonna be smooth.

"I know the stain of blackberry hulls," Twain wrote. "I know how a prize watermelon looks when it is sunning its fat rotundity among pumpkin vines." He could still hear the cracking as a melon split below the carving knife, could still see "the rich red meat and the black seeds, and the heart standing up, a luxury fit for the elect." He knew how to choose ripe apples, peaches, and pears; he knew how to roast apples and walnuts before washing them down with cider. He knew the taste of fresh corn, butter beans, asparagus, and squash—knew them well enough that he'd call out poor produce with all the scorn he had, which was a lot.

It takes work to know food. It always has: the first market guides appeared in America in the eighteenth century, though the culinary world they described was of course very different from ours. An 1805 edition of Hannah Glasse's *The Art of Cookery* declared that April was the time for young geese, January for hen turkeys, and that smelts were good until after Christmas. Glasse knew how to choose lobsters by weight, herring by their full eyes and the "lively shining redness" of their gills, and how to test an egg by touching the bigger end to her tongue ("if it feels warm, be sure it is new"). Bull beef, she said, was "tough in pinching," while with cow beef "the dent you make with your finger will rise again in a little time." Such market guides could assume physical access to food, an ability to engage with it using all the senses. True, part of the reason that they insisted on that access was that some butchers and fishmongers and dairymen were cheats (a personal connection doesn't guarantee an honest person). Still, the result was something worth holding on to: a complete sensory experience before cooking ever began, looking and smelling and touching and even tasting to find what was good.

Knowing food takes attention and deciding to know something about the things in our kitchens: When and where apples grow. How to choose fish. How to store mushrooms; how chopping and slicing and crushing change garlic. It takes repetition, making a soup again and again and again, each time honing the seasoning, adjusting the broth. It can mean growing a pot of thyme and rosemary, or eating all the kinds of briny or lemony or coppery oysters you can get your hands on. It means experiencing flavors with full attention.

It also means sharing them. Twain grumbled about hotels that "pass the sliced meat around on a dish . . . so you are perfectly calm about it, it does not stir you in the least." But he had a suggestion: "perhaps if the roast of mutton or of beef,—a big generous one,—were brought on the table and carved in full view," it might give "the right sense of earnestness and reality to the thing." Even carving at the table could transform a meal, making the eaters participants, turning the experience into something communal and worth remembering. That, I think, is what he'd recently encountered in a private Venetian home; "if one could always [eat] with private families, when traveling," he reflected, "Europe would have a charm which it now lacks."

Cooking at home isn't always easy (or even possible). It takes time, and planning, and sometimes (not always) more money than ordering takeout or heating up something frozen. But even if what you're making is nothing much—five cloves of garlic, a half cup of olive oil, a pound of spaghetti—cooking can be a full, rounded event, an evening of experience instead of routine. Garlic sizzles; salt wells up in water; windows cloud with steam. A kitchen can give a home a center and mark it as a place. When people think of home, the kitchen is often the first place they think of; when they come home, it's often the first place they go.

The last thing's the corn bread. Not sweet—I know enough to know that that's exactly the mistake Twain would expect me to make. Corn bread isn't cake. Corn bread is *corn bread*. It shouldn't just melt away in your mouth; if your teeth aren't fully involved, something's wrong. To get a good crust, I plan to use my cast-iron skillet (known, in our house, as the World's Greatest Pan). I'll heat the skillet in the oven, drop in a knob of butter, then blend the melted butter into a bowl of buttermilk and cornmeal and salt.

When I pour the batter back into the hot, slick skillet, the edges will immediately form up; in the oven it'll make a good, chewy crust. When it's done, I can turn the golden circle out onto a platter. But I'll do all that at the last minute, so the bread will be hot and ready for more butter.

Right now the chicken is finished; the bowl waits to be filled. Chess pie cools on a rack. The greens simmer, sending up their steam; the kitchen is heady with smoked pork. There's time for me to take a deep breath before our friends arrive.

But the instant I'm out of the kitchen, my plan for a quiet moment evaporates. Erik's in the mood for tag; Eli chases him around the living room, balancing Mio in the crook of one arm, motioning for me to intercept. I zoom in to cut Erik off. He jukes past, shooting out the front door, down the steps, and along the edge of the massive juniper bush that runs from the sidewalk to our front wall. I'm a step behind. The bay's morning fog has burned away, the sky washed clear; and as I catch Erik, sweeping him up, swinging him over the juniper's edge, part of me suddenly sees the bush as a tremendous waste of sunlit ground.

Twain started with radishes; this spring it's time to think about a garden.

ACKNOWLEDGMENTS

Many people shared their work and knowledge during the writing of this book. I'm particularly grateful to the following: Frank and Judy Oberle, John and Linda Cover, Frank and Helen Wolfe, Robert Eagle, Rena Obernolte, Bud Abbott, Marguerite Whilden, Tory McPhail, Cliff Hall, Jannette Vanderhoop, Bret Stearns, Kristine and Robert Keese, Jim Dina, and Bill and Amy Proulx. Thanks also to Dianne Jacob, Scott Simpson, Terry Esker, Vernon Kleen, Ronald Westemeier, Jay Miller, Sumadu Welaratna, Marilyn Latta, Hilary Sandler, Linda Coombs, Patti Phillippon, Lydia Matthias, Lisa Monachelli, Kay Carroll, Craig Borges, Nancy Rabelais, Kevin Craig, Ray and Kay Brandhurt, Pete and Clara Gerica, Poppy Tooker, Barbara Brennessel, Darra Goldstein, Sandra Oliver, and Cameron Monroe.

The staff at the Mark Twain Project, headed up by Robert Hirst at Berkeley's Bancroft Library, deserves special mention: Neda Salem, Vic Fischer, Michael Frank, and Lin Salamo were all welcoming and enormously helpful from the first day I came knocking. I'm grateful for their dedication to sharing their remarkable depth of knowledge about Twain, as well as for their infectious enthusiasm.

Paula Marcoux and Pret Woodburn, Terry and Lynn Myers, Bill and Chris Merritt, and Dora, Paul, and Reilly Cullen were all terrific hosts, and often sources in their own right—I hope to be able to return the hospitality to each of you soon. Thanks also to Cameron, Stephanie,

Angela, Miranda, Ryan, Dave, Karin, Brio, Nathan, and Natalie, for the steady support (and for sharing a last celebratory lunch).

I'm tremendously fortunate in my agent, Emma Sweeney, and my editor, Laura Stickney. Emma's enthusiasm, encouragement, and guidance continued long after she found the book its best possible home. Laura has been a constantly insightful, focused, and dedicated presence; I'm very grateful for her sharp eye, steady hand, and sure instincts.

I can never thank my family enough for their help and support during the writing of a book that overlapped, in large measure, with my daughter's first year. Eli, Erik, and Mio were terrific cheerleaders, research partners, and occasional travel companions; when I did go without them, the best part was always coming home.

Finally, I have to acknowledge my great gratitude to Samuel Clemens for his lifetime of inspiring work. His words are as full of life as when he wrote them; the world is a better place for having had him in it.

NOTES

vii   "If I have a talent"   Mark Twain, *Mark Twain's Notebooks & Journals*, vol. 2 (1877–1883), Frederick Anderson, Lin Salamo, and Bernard L. Stein, eds. (Berkeley: University of California Press, 1975), 204.

INTRODUCTION

1   "as tasteless as paper"   Mark Twain, *A Tramp Abroad* (1880; New York: Modern Library, 2003), 291.

1   monotonous, a hollow sham   Ibid., 289–91.

2   "suddenly sweeping down"   Ibid., 291.

3   hung in a cool, dry spot   Harold McGee, *On Food and Cooking: The Science and Lore of the Kitchen* (New York: Scribner, 2004), 143–45.

4   a simple, imperious "try it"   John Hammond Moore, *The Confederate Housewife* (Columbia, SC: Summerhouse Press, 1997).

5   Recipe for German Coffee   Twain, *A Tramp Abroad*, 294.

5   diluting single cans   Twain, *Notebooks & Journals*, vol. 2, 104.

5   "maybe they *can't* give good milk"   Ibid.

5   a temperature as high as 171 degrees   McGee, *On Food and Cooking*, 22.

6   "so rich and thick that you could hardly have strained it"   Mark Twain, "Early Rising, as Regards Excursions to the Cliff House," first appeared in the *Golden Era*, July 3, 1864; reprinted in *The Washoe Giant in San Francisco: Being Heretofore Uncollected Sketches by Mark Twain Published in the Golden Era in the Sixties,* Frank Walker, ed. (San Francisco: George Fields, 1938), 87.

6   "This tea isn't good"   Twain, *Notebooks & Journals*, vol. 2, 87.

7   1840, reputedly when   Alan Davidson, *The Penguin Companion to Food* (New York: Penguin, 1999), 1022.

8   "Radishes. Baked apples, with cream"   Twain, *A Tramp Abroad*, 292–93.

10   "earnest" and "generous," "genuine" and "real"   Ibid., 290–93.

11   "insipid" or "decayed"   Ibid., 292.

11   "perfection only in New Orleans"   Mark Twain, *Life on the Mississippi* (1883; New York: Oxford University Press, 1996), 446.

11   "It makes me cry to think of them"   Mark Twain, *The Autobiography of Mark Twain*, Charles Neider, ed. (1956; New York: HarperCollins, 1990), 5.

12   "use a club, and avoid"   Twain, *A Tramp Abroad*, 294.

12   "the way that the things were cooked"   Twain, *Autobiography*, 14.

12   "Open air sleeping"   Mark Twain, *The Adventures of Tom Sawyer* (1876; Berkeley: University of California Press, 1980), 108.

12   "nothing helps scenery like ham and eggs"   Mark Twain, *Roughing It,* Harriet Elinor Smith and Edgar Marquess Branch, eds. (1872; Berkeley: University of California Press, 1993), 121.

12   the invention of Saratoga potatoes   Ron Powers, *Mark Twain: A Life* (New York: Free Press, 2005), 64.

13   "As a nation, their food is heavy"   James Fenimore Cooper, *The American Democrat* (Cooperstown, NY: H. & E. Finney, 1838), 164.

13   "Cooper's eye was splendidly inaccurate"   Mark Twain, "Fenimore Cooper's Literary Offenses," in *Mark Twain: Collected Tales, Sketches, Speeches, and Essays, 1891–1910* (essay first published 1895; New York: Library of America, 1992), 184.

1. IT MAKES ME CRY TO THINK OF THEM: PRAIRIE-HENS, FROM ILLINOIS

16   "The fountains of the deep have broken up"   Samuel Langhorne Clemens (SLC) to William Bowen, Feb. 6, 1870, Buffalo, NY, in *Mark Twain's Letters, 1870–1871*, Victor Fischer, Michael B. Frank, and Lin Salamo, eds. Mark Twain Project Online (Berkeley: University of California Press, 1995, 2007), www.marktwainproject.org/xtf/view?docId=letters/UCCL02464.xml;style=letter;brand=mtp, accessed Oct. 20, 2009.

16   "a level great prairie"   Twain, *Autobiography*, 13.

16   Ducks and geese, wild turkeys   Ibid., 5.

16   "I can call back the prairie"   Ibid., 16.

17   "I remember . . . how we turned out"   Ibid., 19–20.

18   Prairie Chickens   Estelle Woods Wilcox, *Buckeye Cookery and Practical Housekeeping* (1877; Bedford, MA: Applewood Books, 2002), 143.

20   filled with their own gravy   James M. Sanderson, "Above All Other Birds," in *American Food Writing: An Anthology with Classic Recipes*, Molly O'Neill, ed. (New York: Penguin Putnam, 2007), 38.

22   "Some morning in the month of April"   T. A. Bereman, "The Boom of the Prairie Chicken," *Science*, n.s. 22, no. 546 (1893), 22–23.

22   among the wildest of animals   Frances Hamerstrom, *Strictly for the Chickens* (Ames: Iowa State University Press, 1980).

23   Charles Ranhofer of New York's   Charles Ranhofer, *The Epicurean* (New York: Charles Ranhofer, 1894), 643.

23   "only tolerable in point of flavor"   *The Journals of the Expedition Under the Command of Capts. Lewis and Clark*, Nicholas Biddle, ed. (New York: Heritage Press, 1962), 398.

23   resented having to stuff their skins   Hamerstrom, *Strictly for the Chickens*, 65.

24   one 1887 dinner at Twain's house   Evelyn L. Beilenson, *Early American Cooking: Recipes from America's Historic Sites* (White Plains, NY: Peter Pauper Press, 1985), 38.

25   words like "ocean" and "sea"   John Madson, *Where the Sky Began: Land of the Tallgrass Prairie* (Iowa City: University of Iowa Press, 1982), 14.

25   calls such land "food deserts"   Michael Pollan, *The Omnivore's Dilemma: A Natural History of Four Meals* (New York: Penguin, 2006), 34.

25   230 species   Janine Benyus, *Biomimicry: Innovation Inspired by Nature* (New York: Harper Perennial, 1997), 25.

25   French or Belgian name   Madson, *Where the Sky Began*, 5.

26   periodic burns and occasional grazing   Personal communications, Scott Simpson, Dec. 22, 2006, and Terry Esker, Apr. 6, 2007.

26   "Beyond the road"   Twain, *Autobiography*, 13.

27   In 1836 an eight-mile-wide blaze   *Prairie Establishment and Landscaping* (Springfield: Illinois Division of Natural Heritage, Natural Heritage Technical Publications, no. 2, 1997), 3.

27   the same word, *sce-tay*   Madson, *Where the Sky Began*, 48.

27   "a Cloudy morning & Smokey all Day"   William Clark and Meriwether Lewis, *Journals*, Mar. 6, 1805.

28   Each hen typically spends five days   Hamerstrom, *Strictly for the Chickens*, 94.

29   Prairie Chickens Stewed Whole   Juliet Corson, *Practical American Cookery and Household Management* (New York: Dodd, Mead, 1886), 227.

29   "permanent ambition"   Twain, *Life on the Mississippi*, 62–63.

29   *14 million* of the birds   Scott Simpson, "Prairie Chickens: Promoting a Population 'Boom,'" *Illinois Steward* 10, no. 1 (Spring 2001), 21.

30   the Nantucketer "lives on the sea"   Herman Melville, *Moby-Dick* (1851; New York: Everyman's Library, Alfred A. Knopf, 1988), 85.

30   "the land was rolling"   Twain, *Roughing It*, 6.

30   Prairie Chicken clan   Gilbert L. Wilson, *Buffalo Bird Woman's Garden: Agriculture of the Hidatsa Indians* (1917; St. Paul: Minnesota Historical Society Press, 1987), xix.

30   "soft and easy to work"   Ibid., 9.

30   "a great part [of northern Illinois]"   Quoted in Madson, *Where the Sky Began*, 30.

30   fourteen oxen pulling a hundred-pound   Ibid., 206.

31   more than a hundred daily trains   John F. Stover, "Railroads," in *The Reader's Companion to American History*, Eric Foner and John A. Garraty, eds. (Boston: Houghton Mifflin, 1991), 906–10.

32   author Ann Vileisis   Ann Vileisis, *Kitchen Literacy: How We Lost Knowledge of Where Food Comes From and Why We Need to Get It Back* (Washington, D.C.: Island Press/Shearwater Books, 2008), 15.

32   converted cotton plantations   Ibid., 38.

32   spectacular price of five dollars   Thomas F. De Voe, *The Market Assistant* (New York: Hurd and Houghton, 1867), 160.

32   the quickly vanishing Long Island grouse   Vileisis, *Kitchen Literacy*, 60.

32   measured them by the cord and ton   Ronald L. Westemeier, "The History of Prairie-Chickens and Their Management in Illinois," in *Selected Papers in Illinois History, 1983*, Robert McCluggage, ed. (Springfield: Illinois State Historical Society, 1985), 20.

33   had fallen to fifty cents   De Voe, *The Market Assistant*, 161.

33   insulated shipping barrels   Westemeier, "The History of Prairie-Chickens," 20.

33   "chicken hunting culture"   Ross H. Hier, "History and Hunting the Greater Prairie Chicken: A Rich Tradition," in *The Greater Prairie Chicken: A National Look*, W. Daniel Svedarsky, Ross H. Hier, and Nova J. Silvy, eds. (Minneapolis: University of Minnesota, 1999), 163–67.

33   the *Prairie-Chicken*   Westemeier, "The History of Prairie-Chickens," 21.

33   killed and shipped to market   Bereman, "The Boom of the Prairie-Chicken," 32.

33   "a Christmas present of prairie chickens"   SLC to Critchell, Dec. 26–31, 1879, Hartford, CT, www.marktwainproject.org/xtf/view?docId=letters/UCCL12963.xml;style=letter;brand=mtp accessed July 30, 2009.

33   Prairie Chickens   *"Aunt Babette's" Cook Book* (Cincinnati: Block, 1889), 90.

35   applying ammonium nitrate   Pollan, *The Omnivore's Dilemma*, 41–44.

35   cultivated redtop grass   Scott Simpson, personal communication, Dec. 22, 2006. See also Simpson, "Prairie Chickens: Promoting a Population 'Boom,'" 22.

35   land going "corn sick"   Betty Fussell, *The Story of Corn* (Albuquerque: University of New Mexico Press, 1992), 154–64.

36   "differences betwixt clear-water rivers"   Mark Twain, *The Adventures of Huckleberry Finn* (1885; Berkeley: University of California Press, 1985 and 2001), 112–13.

36   "her hurricane deck would be worth"   Twain, *Life on the Mississippi*, 258.

36   six bushels of earth for every bushel of corn   Benyus, *Biomimicry*, 15.

37   modern monocultures still shadow   Madson, *Where the Sky Began*, 20.

37   ordered a roasted prairie chicken   Mark Twain, "Sociable Jimmy," *New York Times*, Nov. 29, 1874; reprinted in Shelley Fisher Fishkin, *Was Huck Black? Mark Twain and African-American Voices* (New York: Oxford University Press, 1993), 20.

37   the first seeds of Huckleberry Finn's   Ibid., entire volume.

38   "divine place for wading"   Twain, *Autobiography*, 7.

38   To Choose a Young   Mary Newton Foote Henderson, *Practical Cooking and Dinner Giving* (New York: Harper & Brothers, 1877), 184.

43   Prairie-Chicken or Grouse   Ibid.

45   the Eiffel Tower had been built   Mark Twain, "'Was the World Made for Man?'" in *Collected Tales, 1891–1910*, 576.

2. A BARREL OF ODDS AND ENDS: POSSUM AND RACCOON

51   In 1625, a muster   James Deetz, *Flowerdew Hundred: The Archaeology of a Virginia Plantation, 1619–1864* (Charlottesville: University Press of Virginia, 1993), 22–23.

52   *Joy of Cooking*   Irma S. Rombauer and Marion Rombauer Becker, *Joy of Cooking*, 4th ed. (London: J. M. Dent & Sons, 1963), 454.

52   "just as tasty as squirrel"   Angus Cameron and Judith Jones, *The L.L. Bean Game and Fish Cookbook* (New York: Random House, 1983), 123.

53   "I remember the 'coon and 'possum hunts"   Twain, *Autobiography*, 19.

53   "hungry, thirsty, tired"   De Voe, *The Market Assistant*, 127.

54   their Algonquin name, *aroughcun*   Dorcas MacClintock, *A Natural History of Raccoons* (Caldwell, NJ: Blackburn Press, 2002), 1.

54   the skin on its paws softens   Ibid., 14.

54   A tapetum lucidum   Ibid., 18.

54   tagged one blind raccoon with a radio   Ibid., 20.

54   one two-hundred-pound hunter   Ibid., 30.

55   *twenty times* as many raccoons   Humane Society Web site, www.hsus.org, accessed Jan. 18, 2009.

56   knew more about growing rice   Judith A. Carney, *Black Rice: The African Origins of Rice Cultivation in the Americas* (Cambridge, MA: Harvard University Press, 2001). See also Karen Hess, *The Carolina Rice Kitchen: The African Connection* (Columbia: University of South Carolina Press, 1992).

56   The farmers pierced each earthwork   Carney, *Black Rice*, 17–19, 87–89.

56   "growing their crops on the riverain deposits"   Ibid., 18.

56   French ships carried seed rice   Gwendolyn Midlo Hall, *Africans in Colonial Louisiana: The Development of Afro-Creole Culture in the Eighteenth Century* (Baton Rouge: Louisiana State University Press, 1992), 59.

56   "accustomed to the planting of rice"   Robert L. Hall, "Food Crops, Medicinal Plants, and the Atlantic Slave Trade," in *African American Foodways: Explorations of History and Culture*, Anne L. Bower, ed. (Urbana: University of Illinois Press, 2007), 23.

57   white farmers from slaveholding states like Virginia   R. Douglas Hurt, *Agriculture and Slavery in Missouri's Little Dixie* (Columbia: University of Missouri Press, 1992), xii–6.

58   "a faithful and affectionate good friend"   Twain, *Autobiography*, 7–8.

58   "all the negroes were friends of ours"   Ibid., 7.

58   "entered a dense wood"   Twain, *The Adventures of Tom Sawyer*, 63.

58   "as well as anyone"   Ibid., 204.

58   vitally important mental maps   Rhys Isaac, *The Transformation of Virginia, 1740–1790* (Chapel Hill: University of North Carolina Press, 1982), 52–53.

59   "blacks understood the advantage"   Maria Franklin, "The Archaeological and Symbolic Dimensions of Soul Food: Race, Culture and Afro-Virginian Identity," in *Race and the Archaeology of Identity*, Charles Orser, ed. (Salt Lake City: University of Utah Press, 2001), 96.

59   a reputation among some whites   Ibid., 99.

59   the few unwatched hours they had   Jessica Harris, *The Welcome Table: African-American Heritage Cookery* (New York: Simon & Schuster, 1995), 26.

59   "procure supplies of such things"   Charles Bell, *Slavery in the United States: A Narrative of the Life and Adventures of Charles Bell, a Black Man* (New York: John S. Taylor, 1837), 261–80.

60   profusion of "rackoon"   C. B. [Frederick] Marryat, *Second Series of a Diary in America, with Remarks on Its Institutions* (1839; Philadelphia: T. K. & P. G. Collins, 1840), 36.

60   "both alive and dead"   De Voe, *The Market Assistant,* 127.

60   Virginia's Rich Neck Plantation   Franklin, "The Archaeological and Symbolic Dimensions of Soul Food," 100; for a Louisiana example, see Elizabeth Scott, "Some Thoughts on African-American Foodways," *Newsletter of the African-American Archaeological Network*, no. 22, Fall 1998.

60   "there is scarce anything [the people] do not eat"   Anne Yentsch, *A Chesapeake Family and Their Slaves* (Cambridge: Cambridge University Press, 1994), 198.

60   obvious raccoon analogue called the grasscutter   J. C. Monroe, personal communication, Jan. 15, 2009.

60   throughout the African diaspora   John Martin Taylor, *Hoppin' John's Lowcountry Cooking* (New York: Houghton Mifflin, 1992), 144.

60   "Oh! I was fond of 'possums"   Franklin, "The Archaeological and Symbolic Dimensions of Soul Food," 102.

60   "Sometimes de boys would go down in the woods"   Ibid., 99.

61   Possum Roasted   Martha McCulloch-Williams, *Dishes & Beverages of the Old South* (New York: McBride, Nast, 1913), 175.

64   Cutting up meat with an ax   James Deetz, *In Small Things Forgotten: An Archaeology of Early American Life,* 2nd ed. (New York: Doubleday/Anchor, 1996), 171.

65   Homaro Cantu at Chicago's Moto restaurant   Megan Twohey, "Raccoon Dinner: Who's Game?" *Chicago Tribune*, Jan. 18, 2008.

66   250 carcasses   Ibid.

66   the Soulard Farmer's Market in St. Louis   Chad Garrison, "Eat More Beaver," *Riverfront Times,* Jan. 5, 2005.

66   a volume of essays   *Gillett, Arkansas: Celebrating 100 Years,* John Cover, ed. (Gillett Centennial Cel-
       ebration Committee, 2006).

67   "Arkansas' outstanding ceremonial feast"   "The Possum Club of Polk County, Arkansas," in *The Food
       of a Younger Land,* Mark Kurlansky, ed. (New York: Riverhead Books, 2009), 151.

68   Stuffing for a Suckling Pig   Rufus Estes, *Good Things to Eat, as Suggested by Rufus* (Chicago: Rufus
       Estes, 1911), 43.

69   "The way that the things were cooked"   Twain, *Autobiography,* 5.

69   "big broad, open, but roofed"   Twain, *Huckleberry Finn,* 276.

70   widely dispersed customs   Yentsch, *A Chesapeake Family and Their Slaves,* 210.

71   West Africans made vegetable relishes   Leland Ferguson, *Uncommon Ground: Archaeology and Early
       African America, 1650–1800* (Washington, D.C.: Smithsonian Institution Press, 1992), 94.

71   corn, as on the Gold Coast, or yams,   Yentsch, *A Chesapeake Family and Their Slaves,* 197.

71   shared six major cooking techniques   Harris, *The Welcome Table,* 21.

71   African banjos   Deetz, *In Small Things Forgotten,* 178.

71   Yoruba *to-gun*   J. Michael Vlach, "Shotgun Houses," *Natural History* 87, no. 2 (1977), 50–57; cited in
       Deetz, *In Small Things Forgotten,* 215.

72   the chicken was so familiar to many Africans   Franklin, "The Archaeological and Symbolic Dimen-
       sions of Soul Food," 104. See also Yentsch, *A Chesapeake Family and Their Slaves,* 203.

72   replacing the dried shrimp   Harris, cited in Yentsch, *A Chesapeake Family and Their Slaves,* 202.

72   maize was well known in regions   Hall, "Food Crops, Medicinal Plants, and the Atlantic Slave Trade," 27.

72   increasingly offered poor cuts   Yentsch, *A Chesapeake Family and Their Slaves,* 234.

72   Guinea hens, the African fowl   Edna Lewis, *The Taste of Country Cooking* (New York: Alfred A.
       Knopf, 2006), 159.

72   the Kongo word *nguba*   Hall, "Food Crops, Medicinal Plants, and the Atlantic Slave Trade," 32.

73   "Sometimes I've set right down and eat *with* him"   Twain, *Tom Sawyer,* 200.

73   "barrel of odds and ends"   Twain, *Huckleberry Finn,* 2.

73   colonoware pots made by some slaves   Ferguson, *Uncommon Ground,* 18–32.

74   "I hadn't had a bite to eat since yesterday"   Twain, *Huckleberry Finn,* 154–55.

74   now a cotton plantation   Twain, *Autobiography,* 5.

75   "scalded like a pig"   De Voe, *The Market Assistant,* 129.

75   "Ef dey's anyt'ing dat riles me"   Paul Laurence Dunbar, "Possum," first appeared in *Howdy Honey
       Howdy* (New York: Dodd & Mead, 1905); quoted in O'Neill, *American Food Writing,* 132–33.

79   "hardly to be discerned"   Edward Winslow, *Mourt's Relation: A Journey of the Pilgrims at Plymouth*
       (1622; Bedford, MA: Applewood Books, 1963), 43.

79   "Bear I abominate"   Marryat, *A Diary in America,* 37.

3. MASTERPIECE OF THE UNIVERSE: TROUT AT LAKE TAHOE

83   "balloon voyages"   Twain, *Roughing It,* 153.

84   "[We] toiled laboriously up a mountain"   Ibid., 147–48.

84   "too much dish-rag"   Ibid., 24.

85   "winging about in the emptiness"   Ibid., 154.

85   "As the great darkness closed down"   Ibid., 148.

85   a slave murdered on a whim   Powers, *Mark Twain,* 37–38.

85   He'd spied on his own father's autopsy   Ibid., 43.

85   given matches to a drunken tramp   Twain, *Life on the Mississippi,* 548.

86   he told the story in letters   Powers, *Mark Twain,* 89.

86   "incapacitated by fatigue"   Twain, *Autobiography,* 134.

86   accidentally gunning down a civilian   Mark Twain, "The Private History of a Campaign That Failed,"
       in *Mark Twain: Collected Tales, Sketches, Speeches, and Essays, 1852–1890* (story first published 1885;
       New York: Library of America, 1992), 879.

86   "it never rains here, and the dew never falls"   SLC to Jane Lampton Clemens, Oct. 26, 1861, Carson City,
       NV, *Mark Twain's Letters, 1853–1866,* Edgar Marguess Branch, Michael B. Frank, Kenneth M. Sanderson,
       Harriet Elinor Smith, Lin Salamo, and Richard Bucci, eds. Mark Twain Project Online, www.marktwain
       project.org/xtf/view?docId=letters/UCCL00031.xml;style=letter;brand=mtp, accessed Mar. 18, 2009.

87   "I wish I was back there piloting"   SLC to Jane Clampton Clemens, Jan. 20, 1866, San Francisco,

Mark Twain's Letters, 1853–1866, Mark Twain Project Online, www.marktwainproject.org/xtf/
view?docId=letters/UCCL00094.xml;style=letter;brand=mtp, accessed Nov. 9, 2009.

87   **eighteen great boats**   R. Kent Rasmussen, *Mark Twain A–Z* (New York: Oxford University Press,
1995), 440.

87   **Fried Trout**   Corson, *Practical American Cookery,* 217.

88   **prospectors spread rainbow trout**   Details on transfers from Ralph Cutter, *Sierra Trout Guide* (Portland, OR: Frank Amato Publications, 1991), 21–25.

88   **from the crest of the Rockies**   John Merwin, *The New American Trout Fishing* (New York: Macmillan,
1994), 75.

88   **Europe's eleven historically recognized species**   Cutter, *Sierra Trout Guide,* 23.

89   **a writer for *American Angler***   Merwin, *New American Trout Fishing,* 76.

89   **"They fried the fish with the bacon"**   Twain, *The Adventures of Tom Sawyer,* 100.

89   **"one of the largest brook trout"**   De Voe, *The Market Assistant,* 237.

89   **"roaring demon"**   Twain, *Life on the Mississippi,* 33.

89   **the nation's first fishing**   Susan Williams, *Food in the United States, 1820s–1890* (Westport, CT: Greenwood Press, 2006), 133.

90   **"supposed the gas-works"**   De Voe, *The Market Assistant,* 241.

90   **Light bends when it enters water**   Thomas C. Grubb, *The Mind of the Trout: A Cognitive Biology for
Biologists and Anglers* (Madison: Univeristy of Wisconsin Press, 2003), 10.

90   **the eyes of trout continue to grow**   Ibid., 15.

90   **beer, cheese, and mustard**   Powers, *Mark Twain,* 114.

90   **ten thousand tents**   George Williams III, *Mark Twain: His Life in Virginia City, Nevada* (Carson City,
NV: Tree by the River Publishing Trust, 1986), 38.

90   **"'papered' inside with flour-sacks"**   SLC to Pamela A. Moffett and Jane Lampton Clemens, Oct. 25, 1861,
Carson City, NV, *Mark Twain's Letters, 1853–1866,* Mark Twain Project Online, www.marktwainproject
.org/xtf/view?docId=letters/UCCL00030.xml;style=letter;brand=mtp, accessed Jan. 12, 2010.

91   **"their own bacon and beans"**   Twain, *Roughing It,* 392.

91   **butter could take nearly a year**   Williams, *Food in the United States,* 141.

91   **"for breakfast, hot biscuit, fried bacon"**   Annie Tallent, "Bill of Fare on the Plains," in O'Neill, *American Food Writing,* 119.

91   **booms in the canning industry**   Vileisis, *Kitchen Literacy,* 75.

91   **lack of air that sterilized**   Ibid., 78.

91   **Twain did get used to trail food**   Twain, *Roughing It,* 182.

92   **"water in a high place"**   Robert Stewart, "Sam Clemens and the Wildland Fire at Lake Tahoe," *Nevada
Historical Society Quarterly* 51, no. 2 (Summer 2008), 103.

92   **"If there is any life that is happier"**   Twain, *Roughing It,* 152.

93   **"When we come to speak of beauty"**   Mark Twain, *The Innocents Abroad* (1869; New York: Penguin,
2002), 380.

94   **"is agreeably struck"**   Jean Anthelme Brillat-Savarin, *The Physiology of Taste; or, Meditations on Transcendental Gastronomy,* M.F.K. Fisher, trans. (1825; New York: Harcourt Brace Jovanovich, 1949), 40.

94   **"prim, hideous, straight-up-and-down"**   Twain, *A Tramp Abroad,* 169–70.

95   **Cream Trout**   Eliza Leslie, *The Lady's Receipt-Book* (Philadelphia: Carey and Hart, 1847), 23.

96   **"not prepared in the ineffectual goblet"**   Twain, *A Tramp Abroad,* 293.

96   **"*iced* water"**   Twain, *Autobiography,* 6.

96   **"merely give you a tumbler"**   Twain, *A Tramp Abroad,* 154.

96   **"pure and limpid ice-water"**   Ibid., 270.

96   **"How do they know?"**   Ibid., 154.

96   **"I think that there is but a single specialty"**   Mark Twain, "What Paul Bourget Thinks of Us," in *Collected Tales, 1891–1910,* 172.

97   **By 1842 railroads**   Williams, *Food in the United States,* 86–87.

97   **fresh milk to cities from the countryside**   Vileisis, *Kitchen Literacy,* 38.

97   **large-scale brewing of beer**   Williams, *Food in the United States,* 87.

97   **after Gustavus Swift built a line of icehouses**   Vileisis, *Kitchen Literacy,* 68.

97   **"Sierra ice"**   Joanne Meschery, *Truckee: An Illustrated History of the Town and Its Surroundings*
(Truckee, CA: Rocking Stone Press, 1978), 48.

98   How to Mix Absinthe   Lafcadio Hearn, *Lafcadio Hearn's Creole Cook Book* (1885; Gretna, LA: Pelican Publishing, 1990), 249.

98   pathogens from newly introduced   Cutter, *Sierra Trout Guide*, 15.

98   UC Davis Tahoe Research   "Lahontan Cutthroat Trout Stand Little Chance in Lake Tahoe," UC Davis Tahoe Research Group, July 18, 2003, www.universityofcalifornia.edu/news/article/5595, accessed Nov. 20, 2008.

98   "purest, . . . most unadulterated"   SLC to Pamela A. Moffett and Jane Lampton Clemens, Oct. 25, 1861, Carson City, NV, *Mark Twain's Letters, 1853–1866*, Mark Twain Project Online, www.marktwainproject .org/xtf/view?docId=letters/UCCL00030.xml;style=letter;brand=mtp, accessed Jan. 12, 2010.

98   *tomoo agai*   Patrick Trotter, *Cutthroat: Native Trout of the West* (Berkeley: University of California Press, 2002), 159.

99   only to spawn   Ibid., 162.

100   "so villainously rapid and crooked"   Oct. 25, 1861, *Mark Twain's Letters, 1853–1866*, Mark Twain Project Online, www.marktwainproject.org/xtf/view?docId=letters/UCCL00031.xml;style=letter;brand=mtp, accessed Mar. 18, 2009.

101   originated along the Pacific coast   Cutter, *Sierra Trout Guide*, 13.

101   Sixty-thousand-year-old fossils   Robert J. Behnke, *Trout and Salmon of North America* (New York: Free Press, 2002), 211.

101   feed on the tui-chub   Trotter, *Cutthroat*, 163.

102   magnolia and polecat   Oct. 25, 1861, *Mark Twain's Letters, 1853–1866*, Mark Twain Project Online, www.marktwainproject.org/xtf/view?docId=letters/UCCL00031.xml;style=letter;brand=mtp, accessed Mar. 18, 2009.

102   "the meanest compound"   Twain, *Roughing It*, 182.

102   "superior, in fact, to that of any other fish"   Trotter, *Cutthroat*, 148.

102   particularly rich   Cutter, *Sierra Trout Guide*, 15.

103   a genetic memory   Ibid., 13.

103   two hundred thousand pounds   Ibid., 15.

104   Fulton Fish Market   Merwin, *New American Trout Fishing*, 9.

104   quarter million acre-feet of water a year   Trotter, *Cutthroat*, 154.

104   "fish have no rights in water law"   Quoted in Behnke, *Trout and Salmon*, 215.

104   "Pyramid Lake exists"   Ibid.

105   seventy thousand pounds of fish were caught   Trotter, *Cutthroat*, 169–70.

105   collected in Summit Lake   Pyramid Lake Paiute Tribe Fisheries Department, *Natural Resources Report of Pyramid Lake Fisheries*, (1, no. 2) Spring 2008, 2.

105   Paiute John Skimmerhorn   Trotter, *Cutthroat*, 149.

106   below subspecies level   Behnke, *Trout and Salmon*, 4.

106   in 2004 over thirteen thousand fish   Craig Springer, "The Return of a Lake-Dwelling Giant," *Endangered Species Bulletin* 32, no. 1 (February 2007), 10–11.

106   "twenty years down the road"   Ibid.

108   market fisherman Seth Green   Merwin, *New American Trout Fishing*, 8.

108   Trout Pie   Susannah Carter, *The Frugal Housewife* (New York: G. & R. Waite, 1803), 141.

109   "galloping all over the premises"   Twain, *Roughing It*, 155–56.

109   "the mountains seem to be"   Quoted in Stewart, "Sam Clemens," 111.

109   during spring's first thaws   Harold Biswell, *Prescribed Burning in California Wildlands Management* (Berkeley: University of California Press, 1989), 48.

109   "the Indians always kept"   Ibid.

109   seventeen hundred strikes per year   Ibid., 45.

109   "within half an hour"   Twain, *Roughing It*, 156.

110   "*lava* men"   Sept. 18, 1861, *Mark Twain's Letters, 1853–1866*, Mark Twain Project Online, www.marktwainproject.org/xtf/view?docId=letters/UCCL00029.xml;style=letter;brand=mtp, accessed Jan. 12, 2010.

110   near Stateline Point, on Tahoe's northern edge   David C. Antonucci, "Mark Twain's Route to Lake Tahoe," *Nevada Historical Society Quarterly* 51, no. 2 (Summer 2008), 116–26.

110   favored by ponderosa pines   Biswell, *Prescribed Burning in California Wildlands Management*, 33.

109   "deeply carpeted"   Twain, *Roughing It*, 154.

111   "standard-bearers"   SLC to Jane Lampton Clemens, Sept. 18–21, 1861, Carson City, NV, *Mark Twain's*

Letters, 1853–1866, Mark Twain Project Online, www.marktwainproject.org/xtf/view?docId=letters/
UCCL00029.xml;style=letter;brand=mtp, accessed Dec. 3, 2009.

111 **dead and extremely dry growth**   Stewart, "Sam Clemens," 108.

111 **"dense growth of manzanita"**   Twain, *Roughing It,* 156.

111 **"he was paying me ten dollars"**   Ibid., 237.

111 **a long, familiar**   Ibid., 81.

4. HEAVEN ON THE HALF SHELL: OYSTERS AND MUSSELS IN SAN FRANCISCO

114 **thriving business in seabird eggs**   Susan Casey, *The Devil's Teeth* (New York: Owl Books, 2005), 79–85.

114 **"When I was a boy"**   Joseph Mitchell, "Old Mr. Flood," in *Up in the Old Hotel and Other Stories* (story first published 1944; New York: Vintage Books, 1993), 377.

115 **Oyster Omelet**   Wilcox, *Buckeye Cookery,* 262.

116 **"I began to get tired"**   Twain, *Roughing It,* 376.

116 **"Sir, you are a stranger to me"**   Ibid., 276.

117 **Laird refused to pay**   Powers, *Mark Twain,* 139–41.

117 **"the most cordial and sociable"**   Twain, *Roughing It,* 396.

117 **an early San Franciscan bohemia**   Doris Muscatine, *Old San Francisco: The Biography of a City from Early Days to the Earthquake* (New York: Putnam's, 1975), 171.

118 **"a huge double bed"**   Dan De Quille, *Golden Era,* Dec. 6, 1863.

118 **"Mark and I agreed well as room-mates"**   De Quille, *Golden Era,* Dec. 6, 1863.

118 **dozens of restaurants**   Muscatine, *Old San Francisco,* 129–34.

118 **197,639,000 pounds**   Elinore M. Barrett, "The California Oyster Industry," in Scripps Institution of Oceanography Library, *Fish Bulletin* 123, Mar. 1, 1963, p. 6, http://repositories.cdlib.org/sio/lib/fb.123, accessed June 3, 2009.

119 **"To a Christian who has toiled months and months in Washoe"**   Twain, "In the Metropolis," in *The Washoe Giant in San Francisco* (originally in *Virginia City Territorial Enterprise,* June 17, 1864), 74.

119 **the Occidental served quails at 6:00 A.M.**   Mark Twain, *Clemens of the Call: Mark Twain in San Francisco* (first appeared in *Morning Call,* Sept. 16, 1864), Edgar Marquess Branch, ed. (Berkeley: University of California Press, 1969), 64.

120 **slow the metabolism**   Barrett, "The California Oyster Industry," 13.

120 **"Oysters in the shell"**   Wilcox, *Buckeye Cookery,* 258.

120 **an Indiana cook to declare a sauce**   A. M. Collins, *The Great Western Cookbook, or Table Receipts, Adapted to Western Housewifery* (New York: A. S. Barnes, 1857), 36.

120 **"a more used-up, hungrier"**   Powers, *Mark Twain,* 363.

121 **"this delicious article of food"**   Barrett, "The California Oyster Industry," 21.

121 **champagne and pickled-oyster stew**   Twain, *Autobiography,* 136.

122 **to bail out prostitutes**   Muscatine, *Old San Francisco,* 131.

122 **"people who are unaccustomed"**   Mitchell, "Old Mr. Flood," 388.

123 **Oyster Loaves**   Jane Cunningham Croly, *Jennie June's American Cookery Book* (New York: American News, 1870), 76.

123 **"as the Americans assert"**   Marryat, *A Diary in America,* 36.

123 **"the Northern oyster has"**   De Voe, *The Market Assistant,* 306.

124 **"balances the saltiness"**   Jaimarie Pomo, *The Hog Island Oyster Lover's Cookbook* (Berkeley, CA: Ten Speed Press, 2007), 35.

124 **"no relation at all to the taste, if there is one"**   Eleanor Clarke, *The Oysters of Locmariaquer* (New York: Pantheon, 1966), 6.

125 **24 billion gallons**   John Hart, *San Francisco Bay: Portrait of an Estuary* (Berkeley: University of California Press, 2003), 1.

125 **a new North Beach bathing house**   *Mark Twain: San Francisco Correspondent,* Henry Nash Smith and Frederick Anderson, eds. (San Francisco: Book Club of California, 1957), 55.

126 **a cruise to Oakland, or San Leandro, or Alameda**   SLC to Pamela A. Moffett, May 18?, 1863, San Francisco, *Mark Twain's Letters, 1853–1866,* Mark Twain Project Online, www.marktwainproject.org/xtf/view?docId=letters/UCCL00065.xml;style=letter;brand=mtp, accessed Dec. 15, 2008.

126 trawlers, feluccas Muscatine, *Old San Francisco*, 224.

126 oyster omelets Clarence E. Edwords, *Bohemian San Francisco: Its Restaurants and Their Most Famous Recipes* (1914; San Francisco: Silhouette Press, 1973), 60.

126 Ed Ricketts Edward F. Ricketts and Jack Calvin, *Between Pacific Tides* (Stanford, CA: Stanford University Press, 1939), 253.

126 "the small-shelled oysters" Wilcox, *Buckeye Cookery*, 258.

127 six hundred bushels Barrett, "The California Oyster Industry," 22.

127 huge floods flushed the bay Ibid.

127 "far superior to the poor" *Mark Twain: San Francisco Correspondent*, 85.

127 a sailboat could arrive from Washington Ibid.

128 "in San Francisco you earn" W. Mackay Laffan, "Canvas-Back and Terrapin," *Scribner's Monthly* 15, no. 1 (Nov. 1877), 1.

128 "the slightly coppery taste" Edwords, *Bohemian San Francisco*, 60.

129 "had abused the Scoofy oysters" *Mark Twain: San Francisco Correspondent*, 84.

129 Roast Oysters in the Shell Fanny Lemira Gillette, *White House Cook Book* (Chicago: R. S. Peale, 1887), 63.

130 "After a few months' acquaintance" Twain, *A Tramp Abroad*, 3.

131 "we could scarcely see" Twain, *The Washoe Giant in San Francisco*, 87–88.

132 look pretty monotonous Anne Wertheim Rosenfeld, *The Intertidal Wilderness: A Photographic Journey Through Pacific Coast Tidepools* (Berkeley: University of California Press, 2002), 36; see also Ricketts and Calvin, *Between Pacific Tides*, 396.

133 To Stew Oysters Carter, *The Frugal Housewife*, 91.

133 Four hundred such shell mounds Hart, *San Francisco Bay*, 17–20.

134 A day's haul Edwords, *Bohemian San Francisco*, 76–77.

134 fishermen never used ice Muscatine, *Old San Francisco*, 227.

134 some fifty large anchovies Myrtle Elizabeth Johnson and Harry James Snook, *Seashore Animals of the Pacific Coast* (New York: Dover, 1955), 427.

134 venison, bear Muscatine, *Old San Francisco*, 132; see also Andrew Neal Cohen, *An Introduction to the Ecology of the San Francisco Bay*, 2nd ed. (Save San Francisco Bay Association, San Francisco Estuary Project, June 1991), 8.

135 nearly eight hundred ships in the cove Muscatine, *Old San Francisco*, 109.

135 One of the town's first Italian restaurants Ibid., 110.

136 Much of the Gold Rush consisted Walton Bean and James J. Rawls, *California: An Interpretive History*, 4th ed. (New York: McGraw Hill, 1983), 92–93; see also S. T. Harding, *Water in California* (Palo Alto, CA: N-P Publications, 1960), 62–65.

136 some 1.5 *billion* Ibid.

137 an 1884 lawsuit Harding, *Water in California*, 57.

137 train-car loads Barrett, "The California Oyster Industry," 27.

137 2.5 million pounds of oyster meat Fred S. Conte, "California Oyster Culture," in *California Aquaculture* (UC Davis Department of Animal Science, 1996), 1–3.

138 "Mr. Taft's beds" Jack London, "A Raid on the Oyster Pirates," in *Tales of the Fish Patrol* (Berkeley, CA: Heyday Books, 2005), 27–40.

138 two hundred thousand fish Cohen, *An Introduction to the Ecology of the San Francisco Bay*, 2.

138 The bay fishery for crabs Hart, *San Francisco Bay*, 120.

139 some fisheries do survive Ibid., 12.

139 Oyster Soup Mary Randolph, *The Virginia Housewife* (Baltimore: Plaskitt, Fite, 1838), 16.

140 earliest oyster pens Christine Sculati, "Still Hanging On: The Bay's Native Oysters," *Bay Nature*, Oct. 2004.

142 "Methinks a toddy, piping hot" Twain, *The Washoe Giant in San Francisco*, 50.

143 "repackage" some of the nutrients Ibid.

144 describing oyster beds under the heading Mark Twain, "How I Edited an Agricultural Paper Once," in *Collected Tales, 1852–1890*, 412–17.

144 To Boil a Shoulder Esther Allen Howland, *The New England Economical Housekeeper* (Cincinnati: H. W. Derby, 1845), 57.

5. DINNER WAS LEISURELY SERVED: PHILADELPHIA TERRAPIN

148   Canadians used the crustaceans   Farley Mowat, *Sea of Slaughter* (Toronto: Bantam, 1984), 200.

148   "signs of poverty"   Ibid.

148   the first lobsters sent from New York   Williams, *Food in the United States*, 28.

149   two average lobsters   Mowat, *Sea of Slaughter,* 201.

150   "laying claim to being a pretentious affair"   "A Talk About Terrapins: How Maryland's Favorite Delicacy Is Obtained and Stewed," *New York Times,* Dec. 5, 1880 (repr. *Washington Post*), p. 9.

150   Terrapin Clear Soup   Corson, *Practical American Cookery,* 192.

151   Diamondback terrapins rule   Barbara Brennessel, *Diamonds in the Marsh: A Natural History of the Diamondback Terrapin* (Hanover, NH: University Press of New England, 2006), 3–42.

151   "Terrapin" is a corruption   Brennessel, *Diamonds in the Marsh*, 137.

151   North Carolinians tracked   "Hunting for Terrapin: A Profitable Industry Along the Chesapeake," *New York Times,* Nov. 20, 1892, p. 9.

152   Chesapeake tribes such as the Delaware   Brennessel, *Diamonds in the Marsh*, 137.

152   "an art about making terrapin"   "A Talk About Terrapins," *New York Times,* Dec. 5, 1880.

152   "original bandana-crowned"   "Hints for the Household: Miss Corson's Lecture on the Cooking of Terrapin," *New York Times,* Mar. 13, 1881, p. 9.

152   "require[d] the native born culinary genius of the African"   Ward McAllister, "Success in Entertaining," from *Society as I Have Found It,* excerpted in O'Neill, *American Food Writing*, 99.

152   "raised their voices in loud complaint"   "Terrapin Season Begun," *New York Times,* Nov. 6, 1898 (repr. *Baltimore Sun*), p. 6.

153   Lafayette's love for the dish   Evan Jones, *American Food: The Gastronomic Story* (Woodstock, NY: Overlook Press, 1990), 53.

153   "Turttle, and every other Thing"   John Adams, Journal entry for Sept. 22, 1774, online at www.masshist.org/digitaladams/aea/diary, accessed Dec. 27, 2008.

153   "precious cordial"   "Hints for the Household," *New York Times*.

153   Stewed Terrapin   Gillette, *White House Cook Book*, 58.

155   "something more than a human"   Quoted in Powers, *Mark Twain*, 213.

155   artists, social reformers, and writers   Ibid., 251.

155   "The Facts Concerning"   Everett Emerson, *Mark Twain: A Literary Life* (Philadelphia: University of Pennsylvania Press, 2000), 105–6.

155   under the name Sam Clemens   Ibid.

155   "row of venerable and still active"   From autobiographical dictations in Jan. 1906, quoted in *Mark Twain: Plymouth Rock and the Pilgrims and Other Speeches,* Charles Neider, ed. (New York: Cooper Square Press, 2000), 56.

156   the evening's menu   *Boston Daily Globe,* Dec. 18, 1877. Online at http://etext.virginia.edu/railton/onstage/whitnews.html.

158   ice-cream knives and fish cutters   Susan Williams, *Savory Suppers and Fashionable Feasts: Dining in Victorian America* (New York: Pantheon, 1985), 87–90.

158   "Mr. Emerson was a seedy little bit of a chap, red-headed"   Mark Twain, "Whittier Birthday Speech," in *Plymouth Rock and the Pilgrims,* 51.

158   "I didn't know enough to give it up"   From autobiographical dictations in Jan. 1906, 57.

159   "Bishop was away up"   Twain, "Whittier Birthday Speech," 57.

160   "high-flavored Nevada delirium"   Powers, *Mark Twain,* 411.

160   "I feel my misfortune"   Emerson, *Mark Twain: A Literary Life,* 110.

160   Maryland Terrapins   Carrie V. Shuman, *Favorite Dishes* (Chicago: R. R. Donnelley & Sons, 1893), 43.

161   "been agitated for thirty years"   Quoted in O'Neill, *American Food Writing*, 101.

161   Colonel John Forney   John Forney, "Terrapin," in *The Epicure,* quoted in Williams, *Food in the United States,* 119.

161   met before an impartial jury   Jones, *American Food,* 53.

161   "contained the meat, hearts and livers"   Joseph Mitchell, "The Same as Monkey Glands," in *Up in the Old Hotel,* 322.

162   Amelia Simmons had begun   Amelia Simmons, *American Cookery* (Hartford, CT: Hudson and Goodwin, 1796); facsimile in *The First American Cookbook* (New York: Oxford University Press, 1958), 20–22.

162   "no longer used in cooking"   Gillette, *White House Cook Book,* 57.

162   Baltimore's Hotel Rennert   Michael W. Fincham, "The Men Who Would Be Kings: How Grand Plans for the Terrapin Went Somewhat Awry," *Chesapeake Quarterly*, Dec. 2008. Online at www.mdsg.umd.edu/cq/v07n4/main2/.

162   "very small raw oysters"   SLC to Olivia L. Clemens, Nov. 18,1885, *Microfilm Edition of Mark Twain's Manuscript Letters Now in the Mark Twain Papers*, Mark Twain Project, Bancroft Library, University of California, Berkeley, CA.

163   "There is no need to prepare"   Laffan, "Canvas-back and Terrapin," 10.

163   "as national a dish as canvasback"   Quoted in O'Neill, *American Food Writing*, 99.

163   "the great delicacies in America"   Marryat, *A Diary in America*, 36.

163   "necessary to a very swell dinner"   "Canvas-Back Duck Trust: No Monopoly in Terrapin Possible," *New York Times*, Feb. 5, 1888, p. 10.

163   baby mushrooms   Mitchell, "The Same as Monkey Glands," 322.

163   A recent *Baltimore Sun* article   Arthur Hirsch, "These Terrapin Aren't So Popular," *Baltimore Sun*, Mar. 26, 2003, p. 1F.

164   "if there was a better way of taking away her life"   "Hints for the Household," *New York Times*, p. 9.

164   "be careful not to cut off their heads"   Shuman, *Favorite Dishes*, 43.

165   "Even a pinprick of gall"   "A Talk About Terrapins," *New York Times*.

165   "Here was your terrapin"   "Hints for the Household," *New York Times*.

165   "A little gall does not impair"   Jones, *American Food*, 53.

165   the ideal Maryland winter dinner   "A Talk About Terrapins," *New York Times*.

165   "after his second spoonful"   "Hints for the Household," *New York Times*.

166   "One feels so cowed, at home"   Twain, *Notebooks & Journals*, vol. 2, 56.

166   "It will not do for me to find merit"   Twain, *A Tramp Abroad*, 275–76.

166   "There are artists in Arkansas"   Twain, *Notebooks & Journals*, vol. 2, 191.

166   "a luxury which very seldom"   Twain, *A Tramp Abroad*, 290.

167   "made a rare & valuable"   Twain, *Notebooks & Journals*, vol. 2, 192.

167   Rhine wine from vinegar   Twain, *A Tramp Abroad*, 64.

167   "we bought a bottle or so of beer"   Ibid., 196.

167   Emmentaler cheese   Twain, *Notebooks & Journals*, vol. 2, 195.

167   green, egg-size plums   Twain, *A Tramp Abroad*, 58.

167   German pears, cherries   Twain, *Notebooks & Journals*, vol. 2, 273.

167   "we had such a beautiful day"   Twain, *A Tramp Abroad*, 171.

168   "There is no pleasanter place"   Ibid., 64.

168   "poor cheap 2d hand meats"   Twain, *Notebooks & Journals*, vol. 2, 315.

168   "Short visits to Europe"   Twain, *A Tramp Abroad*, 297.

168   "Ah for a hot biscuit"   Twain, *Notebooks & Journals*, vol. 2, 272.

169   Calf's Head   Fannie Merritt Farmer, *The Boston Cooking-School Cook Book* (Boston: Little, Brown, 1896), 187.

171   "there are whole banks of them"   Robert A. Hedeen, *The Oyster: The Life and Lore of the Celebrated Bivalve* (Centreville, MD: Tidewater Publishers, 1986), 6.

171   a female can store sperm   Brennessel, *Diamonds in the Marsh*, 80.

173   "one may commit murder, steal a horse"   *Washington Post*, Nov. 1902, quoted in Eugene Meyer, "Easy Come, Easy Go," *Chesapeake Bay Magazine*, Apr. 2005. Online at www.terrapininstitute.org/turtleking%20text.htm.

175   Italy's Queen Margaret   "Maryland Dishes for Rome," *New York Times*, Dec. 3, 1897, p. 1.

175   list of their individual characteristics   Brennessel, *Diamonds in the Marsh*, 11.

176   "only flesh known"   "Terrapin Culture," *New York Times*, Dec. 26, 1897 (repr. *Baltimore Sun*), p. 9.

176   commanded ninety dollars a dozen   "Chesapeake Bay Terrapin," *New York Times*, Apr. 1, 1894, p. 21.

176   The official 1891 harvest   Meyer, "Easy Come, Easy Go."

176   Baltimore's Hotel Rennert   Fincham, "The Men Who Would Be Kings."

176   well-known Baltimore gourmet   "Chesapeake Bay Terrapin," *New York Times*.

176   "a delusion and a snare"   "Canvas-Back Duck Trust," *New York Times*, Feb. 5, 1888.

176   no more than fifteen thousand   "Terrapin Season Begun," *New York Times*.

176   "there ain't nobody in a hundred"   Ibid.

177   "I am constantly surprised"   "Chesapeake Bay Terrapin," *New York Times*.

178   Genuine bluepoint oysters   Vileisis, *Kitchen Literacy,* 62–63.
178   some of the many substitutions   Ibid., 60–63.
181   "tangled, inextricable confusion"   Twain, *Autobiography,* 232.
181   a culture that treats foods as medicines   Pollan, *The Omnivore's Dilemma,* 1–3.
181   "it is a pity"   Twain, *Autobiography,* 6.
182   "Dear Mrs. H—"   Twain, *Notebooks & Journals,* vol. 2, 204.

6. THE MOST ABSORBING STORY IN THE WORLD: SHEEP-HEAD AND CROAKERS, FROM NEW ORLEANS

183   "told an astonishing tale of *coca*"   Mark Twain, "'The Turning Point of My Life,'" in *Collected Tales, 1891–1910,* 932.
183   "the concentrated bread & meat of the tribes"   Unpublished sketch, quoted in Emerson, *Mark Twain: A Literary Life,* 9.
183   "discovered that there weren't any"   Twain, *Autobiography,* 128.
184   the nine or ten   Twain, *Life on the Mississippi,* 79.
184   "I thought I had seen all kinds"   SLC to Ann E. Taylor, June 1, 1857, New Orleans, *Mark Twain's Letters, 1853–1866,* Mark Twain Project Online, www.marktwainproject.org/xtf/view?docId=letters/UCCL00013.xml;style=letter;brand=mtp, accessed May 5, 2009.
185   some two hundred steamers   Details on steamboating from Rasmussen, *Mark Twain A–Z,* 440–42.
185   "the only unfettered"   Twain, *Life on the Mississippi,* 166.
185   "a wonderful book"   Ibid., 118.
186   "My nightmares, to this day"   Twain, *Notebooks & Journals,* vol. 2, 449–50.
186   nearly a thousand boats   Powers, *Mark Twain,* 79.
186   Ten of the fifteen   Ibid.
186   back into the New Orleans levee   Ibid., 94.
187   "A broad expanse of the river"   Twain, *Life on the Mississippi,* 119.
188   "Yesterday I had many things to do"   SLC to Orion Clemens, Sept. 29, 1860, New Orleans, *Mark Twain's Letters, 1853–1866,* Mark Twain Project Online, www.marktwainproject.org/xtf/view?docId=letters/UCCL00025.xml;style=letter;brand=mtp, accessed May 5, 2009.
188   if all of Louisiana's shrimp survived   Mike Tidwell, *Bayou Farewell: The Rich Life and Tragic Death of Louisiana's Cajun Coast* (New York: Vintage Departures, 2003), 143.
188   "I think that I may say that an American"   SLC to Pamela A. Moffett, March 9 and 11, 1859, New Orleans, *Mark Twain's Letters, 1853–1866,* Mark Twain Project Online, www.marktwainproject.org/xtf/view?docId=letters/UCCL00019.xml;style=letter;brand=mtp, accessed May 5, 2009.
189   Baked Sheepshead   *The Picayune's Creole Cook Book* (New Orleans: Picayune, 1901; repr. Mineola, NY: Dover, 2002), 42.
192   *fifteen times*   Monterey Bay Aquarium Seafood Watch Factsheet, online at www.montereybayaquarium.org/cr/SeafoodWatch/web/sfw_factsheet.aspx?fid=245.
193   replacement for speckled trout   Rima and Richard Collin, *The New Orleans Cookbook* (New York: Alfred A. Knopf, 1994), 83.
193   frying the center bones   Ibid., 89.
193   "any sauce or catsup"   Hearn, *Creole Cook Book,* 23–24.
195   buy one broiled for thirty-five cents   William Head Coleman, *Historical Sketchbook & Guide to New Orleans* (New York: W. H. Coleman, 1885), 86.
195   "the most to be commended"   *Picayune's Creole Cook Book,* 42.
196   "the mode in which New Orleans"   Quoted in Coleman, *Historical Sketchbook,* 85.
197   The Secret of Good Frying   *Picayune's Creole Cook Book,* 41.
198   rain falling in part of twenty-eight states   Twain, *Life on the Mississippi,* 22.
198   a miserly three inches   John M. Berry, *Rising Tide: The Great Mississippi Flood of 1927 and How It Changed America* (New York: Simon & Schuster, 1997), 7.
198   René-Robert de La Salle   Twain, *Life on the Mississippi,* 25.
198   "We'll creep through cracks"   Ibid., 125.
198   "swinging grape-vines"   Ibid., 134.
198   "like Satan's own kitchen"   Ibid., 136–38.
199   "solid mile"   Ibid., 254.

199   "One who knows the Mississippi"   Ibid., 302.
199   "pulling the river's teeth"   Ibid., 300.
199   "two-thousand-mile torch-light procession"   Ibid., 295.
200   "Here was a thing which had not changed"   Ibid., 252.
200   "much the youthfulest batch"   Ibid., 23.
200   For seven thousand years   Gay Gomez, *The Louisiana Coast: Guide to an American Wetland* (College Station: Texas A&M University Press, 2008), 19–21.
201   The equivalent of Manhattan   Ibid., 26.
201   during the 1880s   Tidwell, *Bayou Farewell,* 129.
201   Army Corps of Engineers' dikes   Ibid., 31; for more details on the era's engineering of the river, see Berry, *Rising Tide.*
201   century-old grid of oil-company   Christopher Hallowell, *Holding Back the Sea: The Struggle on the Gulf Coast to Save America* (New York: Harper Perennial, 2001), 17.
202   the GPS of one shrimping boat   Tidwell, *Bayou Farewell,* 178.
202   fish, crab, and shrimp thrive   Ibid., 140, 265–67.
202   Every 2.7 miles   Ibid., 57; see also Hallowell, *Holding Back the Sea.*
202   Third Delta Conveyance Channel   Ibid., 183–89.
203   "myriad small islands"   Ibid., 313.
204   "scoundrels"   Twain, *Life on the Mississippi,* 412–14.
204   "to see what the polar regions"   Ibid., 409.
205   "The chief dish"   Ibid., 445–46.
205   wheat had ceased to be a luxury in the South   Joe Gray Taylor, "Foodways," in *The Encyclopedia of Southern Culture,* vol. 2: *Ethnic Life-Law,* Charles Reagan Wilson and William Ferris, eds. (New York: Anchor, 1989), 362.
206   "glorious with the general diffusion"   Christian Women's Exchange, *Creole Cookery* (1885; Gretna, LA: Pelican Publishing, 2005), iii.
206   peddlers walked the streets   Hearn, *Creole Cook Book,* unnumbered preface.
206   "a very choice market for fish"   Twain, *Notebooks & Journals,* vol. 2, 554.
206   Croakers and Mullets Fried   Hearn, *Creole Cook Book,* 23.
215   Sheepshead à la Créole   *Picayune's Creole Cook Book,* 43.
215   "Everything was changed in Hannibal"   Twain, *Notebooks & Journals,* vol. 2, 479.
216   "That world which I knew"   Emerson, *Mark Twain: A Literary Life,* 138.

7. IT IS MY THANKSGIVING DAY: CRANBERRIES

217   "a vast roast turkey"   Twain, *A Tramp Abroad,* 292.
218   "most villainous sauce"   Anonymous, "Memoir on the Consumption of Cranberry Sauce," in William Tudor, *Miscellanies* (Boston: Wells and Lilly, 1821), 19–21.
219   Henry Hall   Christy Lowrance, "From Swamps to Yards," in *Cranberry Harvest: A History of Cranberry Growing in Massachusetts,* Joseph D. Thomas, ed. (New Bedford, MA: Spinner Publications, 1990), 14.
219   the Andean highlands   Jonathan Roberts, *The Origins of Fruits and Vegetables* (New York: Universe Publishing, 2001), 187.
219   Sanding, whether done on   Carolyn DeMoranville and Hilary Sandler, "Best Management Practices Guide: Sanding," Cranberry Experiment Station Publication, 2000, www.umass.edu/cranberry/services/bmp/sanding.shtml.
219   carefully dug from wild bogs   Paul Eck, *The American Cranberry* (New Brunswick and London: Rutgers University Press, 1990), 69–71.
220   To Stuff and Roast a Turkey   Simmons, *American Cookery,* 18.
220   *"Thanksgiving* Day"   SLC to Mary Mason Fairbanks, Nov. 26–27, 1868, Elmira, NY, in *Mark Twain's Letters, 1867–1868.* Harriet Elinor Smith, Richard Bucci, and Lin Salamo, eds. Mark Twain Project Online (Berkeley: University of California Press, 2007), www.marktwainproject.org/xtf/view?docId=letters/UCCL02767.xml;style=letter;brand=mtp, accessed Nov. 27, 2009.
221   Friday-night billiards   Mary Lawton, *A Lifetime with Mark Twain: The Memories of Katy Leary, for Thirty Years His Faithful and Devoted Servant* (New York: Harcourt, Brace, 1925), 70.
221   "all-pervading spirit"   Powers, *Mark Twain,* 563.

221 **Sideboards, the grandest** Williams, *Food in the United States,* 67.

221 **"We had soup first"** Lawton, *A Lifetime with Mark Twain,* 18–20.

222 **enormous quantities of butter** Unless noted, details on the Twain household's dining style are from Patti Phillippon, head curator at the Mark Twain House and Museum, personal communication, Sept. 29, 2009.

222 **"exquisite cut glass bowl"** Grace King Papers, Mss 1282, Louisiana and Lower Mississippi Valley Collections, LSU Libraries, Baton Rouge.

222 **"Thanksgiving," Leary remembered** Lawton, *A Lifetime with Mark Twain,* 70–72.

223 **driven to the slaughterhouse** James W. Baker, *Thanksgiving: The Biography of an American Holiday* (Durham: University of New Hampshire Press, 2009), 47–49.

223 **"an excellent sauce is made of them"** Constance Crosby, "'The Indians and English use them much,'" in *Cranberry Harvest,* 19.

223 **the season's single fresh green** Baker, *Thanksgiving,* 55–56.

223 **crisp in ice water** Kathleen Curtin, Sandra Oliver, and Plimoth Plantation, *Giving Thanks: Thanksgiving Recipes and History, from Pilgrims to Pumpkin Pie* (New York: Clarkson Potter, 2005), 32.

224 **Cranberry Sauce** Eliza Leslie, *Directions for Cookery, in Its Various Branches'* (Philadelphia: E. L. Carey & Hart, 1840), 169.

225 *Cranberry Day* Jannette Vanderhoop, *Cranberry Day: A Wampanoag Harvest Celebration* (Aquinnah, MA: Wampanoag Tribe of Gay Head Education Department, 2002).

226 **"a Staple means of support"** Crosby, "'The Indians and English use them much,'" 23.

226 **peat moss is ideal** Jennifer Trehane, *Blueberries, Cranberries and Other Vacciniums* (Portland, OR: Timber Press, 2004) 38–39.

227 **mixed with cornmeal** Linda Coombs, personal communication, Oct. 30, 2009.

227 **elder Gladys Widdiss** Quoted in Crosby, "'The Indians and English use them much,'" 25.

229 **invasives like catbrier** Mark Alan Lovewell, "Bonanza Cranberry Harvest Has Island Growers Seeing Good Red," *Vineyard Gazette,* Oct. 31, 2008.

232 **To Make Cranberry Tarts** Hannah Glasse, *The Art of Cookery Made Plain and Easy* (1805; Bedford, MA: Applewood Books, 1997), 138.

233 **"the country wanteth only industrious men"** Winslow, *Mourt's Relation,* 83.

233 **"two lions roaring exceedingly"** Ibid., 46.

233 **"their skulls and bones"** William Bradford, *Of Plymouth Plantation, 1620–1647* (New York: Modern Library, 1981), 97.

234 **"in these old grounds"** Ibid., 95.

234 **"fat and sweet" eels** Winslow, *Mourt's Relation,* 59.

235 **English "harvest home" tradition** James Deetz and Patricia Scott Deetz, *The Times of Their Lives: Life, Love, and Death in the Plymouth Colony* (New York: W. H. Freeman, 2000), 6.

235 **"Our harvest being gotten in"** Winslow, *Mourt's Relation,* 82.

236 **"every aspect of Wampanoag life"** Nancy Eldredge, "Wampanoag Traditions of Giving Thanks," in Curtin and Oliver, *Giving Thanks,* 14.

236 **"solemn day . . . set apart and appointed"** Edward Winslow, *Good Newes from New England: A True Relation of Things Very Remarkable at the Plantation of Plimoth in New England* (1624; Bedford, MA: Applewood Books, 1996), 56.

236 **"among the rest"** Curtin and Oliver, *Giving Thanks,* 22–24.

236 **crops grown in the first year** Ibid., 20.

237 **the way they did barberries** Ibid., 21.

237 **"the *Indians* and *English*"** Crosby, "'The Indians and English use them much,'" 22.

237 **"cramberry-sauce"** Simmons, *American Cookery,* 18.

237 **"an officially declared weekday event"** Baker, *Thanksgiving,* 6, 34.

237 **the Continental Congress** Ibid., 33.

238 **"gentry-style meal"** Sandra Oliver, *Food in Colonial and Federal America* (Westport, CT: Greenwood Press, 2005), 157–58.

238 **oyster soup, boiled cod** Wilcox, *Buckeye Cookery,* 301.

238 **shipped thirty barrels** Lowrance, "From Swamps to Yards," 17.

238 **even to Europe** Eck, *The American Cranberry,* 6.

238 **"pick cranberries from the meadow"** Lydia Maria Francis Child, *The Frugal Housewife* (Boston: Carter and Hendee, 1830), 4.

239   "The roasted turkey took precedence"   Sarah Josepha Hale, *Northwood; or, Life North and South,* 5th ed. (New York: H. Long and Brother, 1852), 89–90.

239   Unitarian reverend Alexander Young   Baker, *Thanksgiving,* 12–13.

240   images of African-American families   Ibid., 90–92.

241   by 1915 Plymouth County produced   Robert Demanche, "The Early Cultivators," in *Cranberry Harvest,* 29.

241   Chicken Pie for Thanksgiving   Mary Johnson Lincoln, *Mrs. Lincoln's Boston Cook Book* (Boston: Roberts Brothers, 1884), 268.

242   over 90 percent of the crop   Hilary Sandler, personal communication, Nov. 17, 2009.

243   canned sauce   Trehane, *Blueberries, Cranberries and Other Vacciniums,* 71.

243   in 2002 the Wisconsin growers   National Agricultural Statistics Service, "Cranberry Yield, Acreage, and Production by State, 2000–2002," online at www.nass.usda.gov/nj/frtsum02cran.pdf.

244   "the economic salvation"   Lowrance, "From Swamps to Yards," 16.

244   one-sixty-fourth ownership shares   Eck, *The American Cranberry,* 7.

247   hovered around fifteen   Ibid., 36.

247   Peg Leg John   Trehane, *Blueberries, Cranberries and Other Vacciniums,* 32.

247   Before 1983   Hilary Sandler, "Challenges in Integrated Pest Management for Massachusetts Cranberry Production: A Historical Perspective to Inform the Future," in *Crop Protection Research Advances,* Earl N. Burton and Peter V. Williams, eds. (Hauppauge, NY: Nova Science Publications, 2008), 21–55.

248   suited for septic systems   Cornelia Dean, "A Tradition at Risk in the Northeastern Bogs," *New York Times,* Nov. 23, 2004.

249   After Thanksgiving Dinner   Wilcox, *Buckeye Cookery,* 301–2.

250   "by sucking the air"   Mark Twain, "Hunting the Deceitful Turkey," in *Collected Tales, 1891–1910,* 805–7.

8. TWILIGHT: MAPLE SYRUP

252   "To have to give up your home"   SLC to David Gray, Mar. 28, 1875, Hartford, CT, in *Mark Twain's Letters, 1874–1875.* Michael B. Frank and Harriet Elinor Smith, eds. Mark Twain Project Online (Berkeley: University of California Press, 2007) www.marktwainproject.org/xtf/view?docId=letters/UCCL11401.xml;style=letter;brand=mtp#an1, accessed Jan. 12, 2010.

252   "the woods in their autumn dress"   Twain, *Autobiography,* 16.

252   "the taste of maple sap"   Ibid., 17.

253   most old-growth forests   Keith Thomas, *Man and the Natural World* (New York: Oxford University Press, 1983), 193.

253   "Here is good living"   William Cronon, *Changes in the Land: Indians, Colonists, and the Ecology of New England* (New York: Hill and Wang, 1983), 25.

255   A Receipt to Make Maple Sugar   Carter, *The Frugal Housewife,* 209.

256   "whole coloring matter"   Helen Nearing and Scott Nearing, *The Maple Sugar Book,* (1950; White River Junction, VT: Chelsea Green, 2000), 62.

256   "the kind of pure maple-sugar that is white"   Ibid., 191.

257   "I can't feel very kindly or forgivingly"   Twain, *Autobiography,* 94.

257   "Why is it that we rejoice"   Mark Twain, *Pudd'nhead Wilson and Those Extraordinary Twins* (New York: Harper and Brothers, 1922), 69.

257   "It is sad"   Twain, *Autobiography,* 4.

257   "labor and sweat and struggle"   Ibid., 250.

257   Only death, he wrote   Ibid., 326.

257   "release from the captivity"   Ibid., 295.

257   "What is it all for?"   Ibid., 99.

258   "It is one of the mysteries of our nature"   Ibid., 422.

258   Maple Sugar Frosting   Farmer, *The Boston Cooking-School Cook Book,* 438.

259   paddled it up the Connecticut River   Jim Dina, *Voyage of the Ant* (Washington, CT: Birdstone Publishers, 1989).

260   called it maple water   Nearing and Nearing, *The Maple Sugar Book,* 14.

260   the Iroquois leader Woksis   Janet Eagleston and Rosemary Hasner, *The Maple Syrup Book* (Boston: Boston Mills Press, 2006), 12.

260   Ne-naw-bo-zhoo   Ibid.

261   mixed with crushed corn   Nearing and Nearing, *The Maple Sugar Book*, 33.

261   Native American method of burying   Williams, *Food in the United States*, 108.

261   "There is a sumptuous variety"   Mark Twain, "New England Weather," in *Plymouth Rock and the Pilgrims*, 40–41.

263   "the French make it"   Nearing and Nearing, *The Maple Sugar Book*, 25.

263   described by a Kickapoo man   Ibid., 23–24.

264   Aunt Top's Nut Taffy   Wilcox, *Buckeye Cookery*, 98.

264   "I comprehend & realize"   SLC to David Gray, Mar. 28, 1875, Mark Twain Project Online.

264   "it seemed as if I had burst"   Powers, *Mark Twain*, 564.

265   "She was my riches"   Twain, *Autobiography*, 449.

265   "No more knowledge is necessary"   Benjamin Rush, *Essays, Literary, Moral, and Philosophical*, 2nd ed. (Philadelphia: Thomas and William Bradford, 1806), 279.

265   peak production came in 1860   Nearing and Nearing, *The Maple Sugar Book*, 266.

265   Alexander Hamilton   Rush, *Essays, Literary, Moral, and Philosophical*, 280.

266   "by persons who refuse"   Ibid., 286.

266   "pleasant and patriotic"   Nearing and Nearing, *The Maple Sugar Book*, 19.

266   "sugar made at home"   Ibid.

266   "enough maple sugar to last all the year"   Laura Ingalls Wilder, *Little House in the Big Woods*, rev. ed. (New York: Harper and Brothers, 1953), 127.

266   Jefferson's trees   Eagleston and Hasner, *The Maple Syrup Book*, 27.

267   "the scattered situation of the trees"   Rush, *Essays Literary, Moral, and Philosophical*, 278.

267   Laura Ingalls Wilder remembered   Wilder, *Little House in the Big Woods*, 126.

267   the only shelter   Nearing and Nearing, *The Maple Sugar Book*, 48–50.

268   *Boil until thick*   Details on tests, ibid., 58–59.

268   To Make Maple Beer   Carter, *The Frugal Housewife*, 210.

269   5.5 percent of the world's total   Eagleston and Hasner, *The Maple Syrup Book*, 33.

272   "Why should men delay"   Nearing and Nearing, *The Maple Sugar Book*, 76.

275   "The most precious of all gifts"   Twain, *Autobiography*, 494.

275   chasing driftwood beside a river   Twain, *Notebooks & Journals*, vol. 2, 143.

275   "a flash and a vanish"   Mark Twain, "Extract from Captain Stormfield's Visit to Heaven," in *Collected Tales, 1891–1910*, 826.

276   "'Now here are these two unaccountable'"   Albert Bigelow Paine, *Mark Twain: A Biography*, vol. 3 (New York: Harper and Brothers, 1912), 1511.

276   Maple-Sugar Sauce   Corson, *Practical American Cookery*, 464.

278   "a wild delicacy that no other sweet can match"   John Burroughs, *Signs and Seasons* (Boston: Houghton, Mifflin, 1886), 258.

278   a golden age   Nearing and Nearing, *The Maple Sugar Book*, 8.

278   "stubborn oaks sweat"   Virgil, *The Eclogues*, Eclogue 4, http://classics.mit.edu/Virgil/eclogue.4.iv.html.

279   "always worked herself down"   Twain, *Autobiography*, 489.

279   "Seventy-four years old"   Ibid., 488.

EPILOGUE

281   I can brine the chicken   Recipes described in epilogue are from Edna Lewis and Scott Peacock, *The Gift of Southern Cooking* (New York: Alfred A. Knopf, 2006).

282   the torture of a monotonous song   Twain, *Roughing It*, 209.

282   "no land with an unvarying climate"   Ibid., 386.

282   "cover the trees and by their weight"   Twain, *Autobiography*, 19.

284   "much used by country people"   De Voe, *The Market Assistant*, 341.

285   "The number of dishes is sufficient"   Twain, *A Tramp Abroad*, 291.

287   1805 edition   The first edition was written in England in 1747; the 1805 edition included many specifically American recipes.

287   April was the time for young geese   Glasse, *The Art of Cookery*, 3–13.

288   "pass the sliced meet around"   Twain, *A Tramp Abroad*, 291.

SELECTED BIBLIOGRAPHY

IN ADDITION TO THE following and the sources cited in the notes, two magnificent online resources were indispensable while writing this book: the Mark Twain Project Online (www.marktwainproject.org), an extensive—and constantly growing—archive of Twain's correspondence and work, and also the wonderful collection of vintage cookbooks made available by the Feeding America Project at the Michigan State University Library (http://digital.lib.msu.edu/projects/cookbooks/index.html).

Microfilm Edition of Mark Twain's Manuscript Letters Now in the Mark Twain Papers. Bancroft Library, University of California, Berkeley, 2001.

Baker, James W. *Thanksgiving: The Biography of an American Holiday.* Durham: University of New Hampshire Press, 2009.

Barrett, Elinore M. "The California Oyster Industry." Scripps Institution of Oceanography Library, *Fish Bulletin* 123, 1963.

Behnke, Robert J. *Trout and Salmon of North America.* New York: Free Press, 2002.

Benyus, Janine. *Biomimicry: Innovation Inspired by Nature.* New York: Harper Perennial, 1997.

Berry, John M. *Rising Tide: The Great Mississippi Flood of 1927 and How It Changed America.* New York: Simon & Schuster, 1997.

Bower, Anne L., ed. *African American Foodways: Explorations of History and Culture.* Urbana: University of Illinois Press, 2007.

Brennessel, Barbara. *Diamonds in the Marsh: A Naural History of the Diamondback Terrapin.* Hanover, NH: University Press of New England, 2006.

Brillat-Savarin, Jean Anthelme. *The Physiology of Taste; or, Meditations on Transcendental Gastronomy.* M.F.K. Fisher, trans. New York: Harcourt Brace Jovanovich, 1949 (1825).

Burk, John, and Marjorie Holland. *Stone Walls and Sugar Maples: An Ecology for Northeasterners.* Boston: Appalachian Mountain Club, 1979.

Carney, Judith A. *Black Rice: The African Origins of Rice Cultivation in the Americas.* Cambridge, MA: Harvard University Press, 2001.

Carter, Susannah. *The Frugal Housewife.* New York: G. & R. Waite, 1803.

Child, Lydia Maria Francis. *The Frugal Housewife.* Boston: Carter and Hendee, 1830.

Corson, Juliet. *Practical American Cookery and Household Management.* New York: Dodd, Mead, 1886.

Curtin, Kathleen, Sandra Oliver, and Plimoth Plantation. *Giving Thanks: Thanksgiving Recipes and History, from Pilgrims to Pumpkin Pie.* New York: Clarkson Potter, 2005.

Cutter, Ralph. *Sierra Trout Guide.* Portland, OR: Frank Amato Publications, 1991.

Davidson, Alan. *The Penguin Companion to Food.* New York: Penguin, 1999.

Deetz, James. *Flowerdew Hundred: The Archaeology of a Virginia Plantation, 1619–1864.* Charlottesville: University Press of Virginia, 1993.

———. *In Small Things Forgotten: An Archaeology of Early American Life,* 2nd ed. New York: Doubleday/ Anchor, 1996.

———, and Patricia Scott Deetz. *The Times of Their Lives: Life, Love, and Death in the Plymouth Colony.* New York: W. H. Freeman, 2000.

Eagleston, Janet, and Rosemary Hasner. *The Maple Syrup Book.* Boston: Boston Mills Press, 2006.

Eck, Paul. *The American Cranberry.* New Brunswick and London: Rutgers University Press, 1990.

Edwords, Clarence E. *Bohemian San Francisco: Its Restaurants and Their Most Famous Recipes.* San Francisco: Silhouette Press, 1973 (1914).

Emerson, Everett. *Mark Twain: A Literary Life.* Philadelphia: University of Pennsylvania Press, 2000.

Ferguson, Leland. *Uncommon Ground: Archaeology and Early African America, 1650–1800.* Washington, D.C.: Smithsonian Institution Press, 1992.

Fishkin, Shelley Fisher. *Was Huck Black? Mark Twain and African-American Voices.* New York: Oxford University Press, 1993.

Franklin, Maria. "The Archaeological and Symbolic Dimensions of Soul Food: Race, Culture and Afro-Virginian Identity." In *Race and the Archaeology of Identity,* Charles Orser, ed. Salt Lake City: University of Utah Press, 2001, 88–107.

Gomez, Gay. *The Louisiana Coast: Guide to an American Wetland.* College Station: Texas A&M University Press, 2008.

Hall, Gwendolyn Midlo. *Africans in Colonial Louisiana: The Development of Afro-Creole Culture in the Eighteenth Century.* Baton Rouge and London: Louisiana State University Press, 1992.

Hall, Robert L. "Food Crops, Medicinal Plants, and the Atlantic Slave Trade." In *African American Foodways: Explorations of History and Culture,* Anne L. Bower, ed. Urbana: University of Illinois Press, 2007, 17–44.

Hallowell, Christopher. *Holding Back the Sea: The Struggle on the Gulf Coast to Save America.* New York: Harper Perennial, 2001.

Hamerstrom, Frances. *Strictly for the Chickens.* Ames: Iowa State University Press, 1980.

Harran, Mark. "Edible Traditions: Return of a Sugarbush Native." In *Edible Nutmeg,* Winter 2006, 22–27.

Harris, Jessica. *The Welcome Table: African-American Heritage Cookery.* New York: Simon & Schuster, 1995.

Hart, John. *San Francisco Bay: Portrait of an Estuary.* Berkeley: University of California Press, 2003.

Hess, Karen. *The Carolina Rice Kitchen: The African Connection.* Columbia: University of South Carolina Press, 1992.

Hurt, R. Douglas. *Agriculture and Slavery in Missouri's Little Dixie.* Columbia: University of Missouri Press, 1992.

Jones, Evan. *American Food: The Gastronomic Story.* Woodstock, NY: Overlook Press, 1990.

Jones, Stephen R. *The Last Prairie: A Sandhills Journal.* Lincoln: University of Nebraska Press, 2006.

Kaplan, Justin. *Mr. Clemens and Mark Twain.* New York: Simon & Schuster, 1966.

Kurlansky, Mark. *The Big Oyster: New York on the Half Shell.* New York: Ballantine Books, 2006.

———, ed. *The Food of a Younger Land.* New York: Riverhead Books, 2009.

Lawton, Mary. *A Lifetime with Mark Twain: The Memories of Katy Leary, for Thirty Years His Faithful and Devoted Servant.* New York: Harcourt, Brace, 1925.

Leslie, Eliza. *Directions for Cookery, in Its Various Branches.* Philadelphia: E. L. Carey & Hart, 1840.

———. *The Lady's Receipt-Book.* Philadelphia: Carey and Hart, 1847.

Lewis, Edna. *The Taste of Country Cooking*. New York: Alfred A. Knopf, 2006.

MacClintock, Dorcas. *A Natural History of Raccoons*. Caldwell, NJ: Blackburn Press, 2002.

McGee, Harold. *On Food and Cooking: The Science and Lore of the Kitchen*. New York: Scribner, 2004.

Madson, John. *Where the Sky Began: Land of the Tallgrass Prairie*. Iowa City: University of Iowa Press, 1982.

Mariani, John. *The Dictionary of American Food and Drink*. New York: Ticknor & Fields, 1983.

Marryat, C. B. [Frederick]. *Second Series of a Diary in America, with Remarks on Its Institutions*. Philadelphia: T. K. & P. G. Collins, 1840 (1839).

Merwin, John. *The New American Trout Fishing*. New York: Macmillan, 1994.

Muscatine, Doris. *Old San Francisco: The Biography of a City from Early Days to the Earthquake*. New York: Putnam's, 1975.

Nearing, Helen, and Scott Nearing. *The Maple Sugar Book*. White River Junction, VT: Chelsea Green, 2000 (1950).

Oliver, Sandra. *Food in Colonial and Federal America*. Westport, CT: Greenwood Press, 2005.

O'Neill, Molly, ed. *American Food Writing: An Anthology with Classic Recipes*. New York: Penguin Putnam, 2007.

Pollan, Michael. *The Omnivore's Dilemma: A Natural History of Four Meals*. New York: Penguin, 2006.

Powers, Ron. *Mark Twain: A Life*. New York: Free Press, 2005.

Ranhofer, Charles. *The Epicurean*. New York: Charles Ranhofer, 1894.

Rasmussen, R. Kent. *Mark Twain A–Z*. New York: Oxford University Press, 1995.

Roahen, Sara. *Gumbo Tales: Finding My Place at the New Orleans Table*. New York: Norton, 2008.

Sandler, Hilary. "Challenges in Integrated Pest Management for Massachusetts Cranberry Production: A Historical Perspective to Inform the Future." In *Crop Protection Research Advances,* Earl N. Burton and Peter V. Williams, eds. Hauppauge, NY: Nova Science Publications, 2008, 21–55.

Schlosser, Eric. *Fast Food Nation: The Dark Side of the All-American Meal*. Boston: Houghton Mifflin, 2001.

Simmons, Amelia. *American Cookery*. Hartford, CT: Hudson and Goodwin, 1796. Facsimile as *The First American Cookbook*. New York: Oxford University Press, 1958; repr. New York: Dover, 1984.

Thomas, Joseph D., ed. *Cranberry Harvest: A History of Cranberry Growing in Massachusetts*. New Bedford, MA: Spinner Publications, 1990.

Tidwell, Mike. *Bayou Farewell: The Rich Life and Tragic Death of Louisiana's Cajun Coast*. New York: Vintage Departures, 2003.

Townsend, Charles H. "Report of Observations Respecting the Oyster Resources and Oyster Fishery of the Pacific Coast of the United States." In *Report of U.S. Fish Commission, 1889–91*. Washington, D.C.: 1893, 343–72.

Trehane, Jennifer. *Blueberries, Cranberries and Other Vacciniums*. Portland, OR: Timber Press, 2004.

Trotter, Patrick. *Cutthroat: Native Trout of the West*. Berkeley: University of California Press, 2002.

Twain, Mark. *The Adventures of Huckleberry Finn*. Berkeley: University of California Press, 1985, 2001 (1885).

———. *The Adventures of Tom Sawyer*. Berkeley: University of California Press, 1980 (1876).

———. *The Autobiography of Mark Twain*. Charles Neider, ed. New York: HarperCollins, 1990 (1956).

———. *Clemens of the Call: Mark Twain in San Francisco*. Edgar Marquess Branch, ed. Berkeley: University of California Press, 1969.

———. *The Innocents Abroad*. New York: Penguin, 2002 (1869).

———. *Life on the Mississippi*. New York: Oxford University Press, 1996 (1883).

———. *Mark Twain: Collected Tales, Sketches, Speeches, and Essays, 1852–1890*. New York: Library of America, 1992.

———. *Mark Twain: Collected Tales, Sketches, Speeches, and Essays, 1891–1910*. New York: Library of America, 1992.

———. *Mark Twain: Plymouth Rock and the Pilgrims and Other Speeches*. Charles Neider, ed. NewYork: Cooper Square Press, 2000.

———. *Mark Twain: San Francisco Correspondent*. Henry Nash Smith and Frederick Anderson, eds. San Francisco: Book Club of California, 1957.

———. *Mark Twain's Letters, 1853–1866*. Edgar Marquess Branch, Michael B. Frank, Kenneth M. Sanderson, Harriet Elinor Smith, Lin Salamo, and Richard Bucci, eds. Mark Twain Project Online, www.marktwainproject.org. Berkeley: University of California Press, 1988, 2007.

————. *Mark Twain's Letters, 1867–1868*. Harriet Elinor Smith, Richard Bucci, and Lin Salamo, eds. Mark Twain Project Online, www.marktwainproject.org. Berkeley: University of California Press, 2007.

————. *Mark Twain's Letters, 1870–1871*. Victor Fischer, Michael B. Frank, and Lin Salamo, eds. Mark Twain Project Online, www.marktwainproject.org. Berkeley: University of California Press, 1995, 2007.

————. *Mark Twain's Letters, 1874–1875*. Michael B. Frank and Harriet Elinor Smith, eds. Berkeley: University of California Press, 2007.

————. *Mark Twain's Notebooks & Journals*, vol. 2 (1877–1883). Frederick Anderson, Lin Salamo, and Bernard L. Stein, eds. Berkeley: University of California Press, 1975.

————. *Pudd'nhead Wilson and Those Extraordinary Twins*. New York: Harper and Brothers, 1922.

————. *Roughing It*. Harriet Elinor Smith and Edgar Marquess Branch, eds. Berkeley: University of California Press, 1993 (1872).

————. *A Tramp Abroad*. New York: Modern Library, 2003 (1880).

————. *The Washoe Giant in San Francisco: Being Heretofore Uncollected Sketches by Mark Twain Published in the Golden Era in the Sixties*. Frank Walker, ed. San Francisco: George Fields, 1938.

Vileisis, Ann. *Kitchen Literacy: How We Lost Knowledge of Where Food Comes From and Why We Need to Get It Back*. Washington, D.C.: Island Press/Shearwater Books, 2008.

Westemeier, Ronald L. "The History of Prairie-Chickens and Their Management in Illinois." In *Selected Papers in Illinois History, 1983*. Robert McCluggage, ed. Springfield: Illinois State Historical Society, 1985, 17–27.

Wilcox, Estelle Woods. *Buckeye Cookery and Practical Housekeeping*. Bedford, MA: Applewood Books, 2002 (1877).

Williams, Jacqueline. *Wagon Wheel Kitchens: Food on the Oregon Trail*. Lawrence: University Press of Kansas, 1993.

Williams, Susan. *Food in the United States, 1820s–1890*. Westport, CT: Greenwood Press, 2006.

————. *Savory Suppers and Fashionable Feasts: Dining in Victorian America*. New York: Pantheon, 1985.

Yentsch, Anne. *A Chesapeake Family and Their Slaves*. Cambridge: Cambridge University Press, 1994.

INDEX

abalone, 178–79
Abbott, Bud, 141, 144, 145–46
Abenaki Indians, 261
absinthe, 98
Academy Awards, 170
Acadians, 193–94
Adams, John, 153, 170
A. D. Makepeace (cranberry grower), 248
"Adventure of the Blue Carbuncle, The"
    (Doyle), 2
Adventures of Huckleberry Finn (Twain), 3,
    6, 35–36, 73, 74, 85, 200
Adventures of Tom Sawyer, The (Twain), 3,
    12, 85, 155
    cooking in, 73–74
    trout in, 89
African Americans, 60, 240
    see also slaves, slavery
Agriculture Department, U.S., 42
Aleck, Ben, 99–101, 104–5
Algonquin Indians, 273
Amanda (farm worker), 246
American Angler, 89
American Cookery (Simmons), 220, 237
American Philosophical Society, 265
Amigo (Twain's friend), 129
ammonium nitrate, 35
Antoine's (restaurant), 194, 209
Aquinnah Wampanoags, *see* Wampanoag
    Indians
Arbogast's California oyster omelet, 128
Arkansas Game & Fish Commission, 66
Armoricaine oysters, 124
Army Corps of Engineers, 100, 192, 199, 201

Arnaud's (restaurant), 209
Art of Cooking Made Plain and Easy, The
    (Glasse), 232, 287–88
Atchafalaya River, 203
Atlantic Monthly, 155, 156, 160
"Aunt Babette's" Cook Book, 33–34
Autobiography (Twain), 58, 86, 181, 257, 275
Aythya valisineria, see canvasback duck

Backyard Sugaring, 270
Baker, James, 237, 240
"balloon voyages," 83
Baltimore Sun, 163
Barrett, Armand, 269–70
Batali, Mario, 95
Bayou Farewell (Tidwell), 201
Bayou Sauvage, 192
Bazzurro, Giuseppe, 135n
Beahrs, Eli, 15, 22–23, 50, 52, 114–15, 170,
    283, 289
Beahrs, Erik, 114–15, 170, 171, 179–80,
    258–59, 272, 274, 278, 279, 287, 289–90
Beahrs, Mio, 170, 171, 283, 289–90
Beebe, Mike, 80
beef, 97
    grass-fed, 8
Bell, Alison, 50
Bell, Charles, 59
Benin (Whydah), 56, 60
Bereman, T. A., 22
Bermuda, 155
Berry, Marion, 79
Bigler, John, 92n
biscuits, 3–4, 7, 205

Bishop (dinner speaker), 159–60
Bixby, Horace, 185, 188, 198
black drum (fish), 191, 192, 211
Blackfoot Indians, 27
Blindman, Kia, 105, 107–8
Bluepoint oysters, 178
Bob (park guide), 20–21
bog iron, 243–44
Bohemian San Francisco (Edwords), 126
boiling stones, 263, 277
Boston Cooking-School Cook Book, The
    (Farmer), 169, 258
Boston Daily Globe, 156
Bowen, Will, 16
Bradford, William, 235
Brazil, 183, 266
"Breakfast" (Steinbeck), 2
Brillat-Savarin, Jean Anthelme, 94
brining, 218
brook trout, 14, 84, 88, 89
brown trout, 88, 108
*Buckeye Cookery and Practical
    Housekeeping* (Wilcox), 19, 115, 120,
    126, 238, 250, 264
buckwheat cakes, 4, 7
buddy syrup, 270
Buffalo Bird Woman, 30
Bumpers, Dale, 55, 68
Bunker Hill, Battle of, 271
Bureau of Land Management, 99
Bureau of Reclamation, 104
Burroughs, John, 278, 279
Bush, George W., 203–4
butter, 204
bycatch, 192

Cahokia (mound city), 27, 30
Cajun cooking, 188, 193–95
    origins of, 193
California Current, 132
Calvino, Italo, 2
Canada, 193
Cannery Row (Steinbeck), 126
Cantu, Homaro, 65–66
canvasback duck (*Aythya valisineria*), 20,
    177–78, 209, 285
    in terrapin soup, 162–63, 165
"Captain Stormfield's Visit to Heaven"
    (Twain), 275
Carson River, 100

Carter, Susannah, 108, 133, 255, 269
"Celebrated Jumping Frog of Calaveras
    County, The" (Twain), 154
celery, 223
chess pie, 286–87
Cheyenne Indians, 27
chicken pie, recipe for, 241
Child, Lydia, 238
China, 179
Chippewa Indians, 260
Chitimacha Indians, 184
Choctaw Indians, 184
Chris (Amish teen), 44–45
Chronicles of the Pilgrim Forefathers
    (Young), 239–40
Chuck, Preacher, 79
Civil War, U.S., 32, 86, 91, 240, 244
Clare, Ada, 117
Clark, William, 23, 25, 27
Clarke, Eleanor, 124
Clemens, Clara, 155, 166
Clemens, Henry, 86, 257
Clemens, Jean, 221, 279
Clemens, Olivia Langdon (Livy), 155, 162,
    166, 182, 215–16, 220–23, 264–65, 279
Clemens, Orion, 86, 188, 257
Clemens, Samuel, *see* Twain, Mark
Clemens, Susy, 155, 166, 257–58, 264
Clinton, Bill, 55, 57, 67–68
Cobweb Palace, 126
cocaine, 183–84
coffee, 4–5, 7, 132, 168
    European, 130–31
    French-pressed, 5
    ideal cup of, 131
Collect Pond, 89–90
Collins, Richard, 193
Collins, Rima, 193
Columbian Exposition (1893), 164
Commander's Palace, 209–10, 213
Comstock Lode, 116
Confederate Housewife, The, 4
Congress, U.S., 240
Conservation Reserve Program (CRP), 42
Continental Congress, 237
Coombs, Linda, 229, 234, 236–37
Cooper, James Fenimore, 13
Corson, Juliet, 29, 87, 151, 153, 164, 165, 276
Cosentino-Manning, Natalie, 141
Cover, John, 66, 78, 81

Cover, Linda, 66
cranberries, 217–51
    bog iron and, 243–44
    dry harvest of, 243, 246
    first growers of, 244–45
    housing development and, 248–49
    as major crop, 240–41
    Native American cultivation of, 219
    Native American names for, 218
    organic cultivation of, 243, 245–46
    pesticides and, 243, 245–48
    recipe for, 232
    sanding technique and, 219
    Thanksgiving and, 218–19, 223, 238,
      240–41
    turkey and, 223
    varieties of, 219–20
    in Wampanoag's diet, 236–37
    Wampanoag's harvesting of, 225–29, 231
    wet harvest of, 242–43
Cranberry Day (Vanderhoop), 225, 231
Cranberry Hill Farm, 242–43
cranberry sauce, 218
    canned, 242–43
    recipe for, 224
Crassostrea virginica (oyster), 123
Creole Cook Book (Hearn), 193
Creole cooking, 188, 193–95, 205–6
Crescent City Farmers Market, 190
Crescent City Farmers Market Cookbook
    (Tooker), 192
croaker (fish), 192–93, 195, 196, 285
    recipe for, 206
Croly, Jane Cunningham, 123
Cuisine Creole, La (Hearn), 98, 206
cui-ui (suckerfish), 100–101
Curtin, Kathleen, 236–37
cutthroat trout, 88–89, 90, 100–101, 105
    see also Lahontan cutthroat trout

Dan'l, Uncle (slave), 58
D'Arcy's Pint, 34
Dawson, Anthony, 60–61
Deadliest Catch (television show), 212
de Broca, P., 121
Deere, John, 31
Deetz, Jim, 50–51, 59
Delaware Indians, 152, 164–65
Delmonico's (restaurant), 23–24, 178, 205
De Quille, Dan, 118, 142

Derby Dam, 104, 105
De Voe, Thomas, 32, 53, 60, 75, 89, 90,
    123, 284
diamondback terrapin, 282, 285
    with canvasback duck, 162–63, 165
    of Chesapeake Bay, 175–76
    cooking, 151–52
    development and, 172, 179
    eggs of, 171–72, 179–80
    farming of, 173–74
    habitat of, 151, 170
    killing, 163–65
    long-distance shipping of, 165, 175
    meat of, 163
    name of, 151
    poaching of, 173–75, 179
    preparation of, 165
    Prohibition and, 170, 179
    recipes for, 150–51, 153–54, 160–61,
      169, 180
    salt gland of, 151
    scarcity of, 175–77
    Southern style of, 161–62
    species of, 175–76
    substitutions for, 177–79
    taste of, 163
    in transition from common to elite food,
      149–53
Diary in America, A (Marryat), 59–60
Dina, Jim, 258–60, 263–64
Directions for Cookery, in Its Various
    Branches (Leslie), 224
Dishes & Beverages of the Old South
    (McCulloch-Williams), 61–62
Dora (author's friend), 207–8
Drago's (restaurant), 207
Drake's Bay Oyster Farm, 141
Dunbar, Paul Lawrence, 75

Eagle, Robert, 103, 106
Early Black cranberries, 219–20
echinacea (purple coneflower), 25
Edwords, Clarence, 126, 128
Eldredge, Nancy, 235–36
Emerson, Ralph Waldo, 155, 158
English, Phil, 79, 81
Environ, 141
Eric (cook), 51–52, 79
Erie Canal, 32
Estes, Rufus, 68

"Facts Concerning the Recent Carnival of Crime in Connecticut, The" (Twain), 155
Farallon Islands, 114
Farmer, Fannie Merritt, 169, 258
Farmer's Almanack, 266
fast food, 285
Favorite Dishes (Shuman), 161
Fish and Wildlife Service, U.S., 106
Fish Commission, U.S., 108
Fisherman's Wharf, 134
Fishkin, Shelley Fisher, 37–38, 73
Flood, Mr., 114, 122
Florida, Mo., 16, 38
Flowerdew Hundred Plantation, 50–52
food:
    American, 8–11
    fast, 285
    lost from American table, 285–86
    of Louisiana, 193–94
    market guides for, 287–88
    place and, 284–85
    of slaves, 70–71, 72
    Southern, 61, 69–74, 205
    substitutions and, 177–79
    transportation of, 31–32
    Twain's enthusiasm for, 10–14
    of West Africa, 60, 70–72
    of Western trails, 91
food deserts, 25, 286
foodsheds, 32
Forest Service, 109
Forney, John, 161
France, 121, 123
Franklin, Benjamin, 181
Franklin, Maria, 59
Freetown, Va., 73
Frémont, John C., 102
French Market, 184–85, 190
French press, 5
Frugal Housewife, The (Carter), 108, 133, 255, 269
Frugal Housewife, The (Child), 238
fruitworm (*Sparganothis*), 245
Fulton Fish Market, 104

Galatoire's (restaurant), 209
Galaxy, 144
Garden and Forest, 256
Gerica, Clara, 191–93, 196

Gerica, Mike, 210
Gerica, Pete, 191–92, 196
Gift of Southern Cooking, The (Lewis and Peacock), 283
Gillett, Ark., 62, 65–68, 82
Gillett Coon Supper, 55–66, 67
    after party of, 81–82
    butchering and, 63–64
    communal hunt and, 63
    outdoor cookery and, 62–65, 76–78
    program of, 80
    protests against, 80–81
    smell of, 64–65
Gillette, Fanny Lemira, 130, 154
Gillett Farmers' and Businessmen's Club, 62, 65
Giving Thanks (Curtin and Oliver), 237
Glasse, Hannah, 232, 287–88
Godey's Lady's Book, 240
Gold Coast (Ghana), 72
Golden Era, 118
Gold Hill News, 129
Gold Rush, 91, 126, 146
    hydraulic mining and, 135, 136–37
Good Things to Eat, as Suggested by Rufus (Estes), 68
Goose Lake Prairie, 34
Grand Trunk Railroad, 97
grassland, *see* prairie
Gray, David, 252
Great American Seafood Cook-Off, 208, 212–15
Great Depression, 179
Great Flood of 1927, 201
Green, Seth, 108
Greenwood, Ethan, 272
Gridley, Reuel, 116–17
gumbo, 72, 194, 208

Haitian Revolution, 152
Hale, Sarah Josepha, 238–39, 240
Hall, Cliff, 210–12
Hall, Henry, 219, 229, 238
Halley's comet, 275–76, 279
Hamerstrom, Frances, 23
Hamilton, Alexander, 68, 265
Hangtown fry, 113–15
Hannah, Aunt (slave), 58
Hansen, Sig, 212–13
Harlem Heights, Battle of, 271

Harper's, 91, 240
Hearn, Lafcadio, 98, 193, 246
Heki, Lisa, 106
Hemingway, Ernest, 2, 118*n*
Henderson, Mary Newton Foote, 38, 43
Hidatsa Indians, 30
Hog Island Oyster Company, 124
Holmes, Oliver Wendell, 155, 158
hoppin' John (Southern dish), 72
horseshoe, 34–35
Hotel Rennert, 162, 176
hot toddies, 142
Houma Indians, 184
Howells, William Dean, 160
Howes cranberries, 219–20
Howland, Esther Allen, 145
Huckabee, Mike, 67, 68
Humane Society, 55

ice water, 96–98, 104, 158
Innocents Abroad (Twain), 154
Institute for Native American Studies, 259
intergrated pest management (IPM), 248–49
Iron Chef (television show), 213
Iroquois Indians, 254, 260, 273
Isleños, 184

jambalaya, 194
James, Frank, 240
Jefferson, Thomas, 30, 265, 266
Jennie June's American Cookery Book
      (Croly), 123
Jindal, Bobby, 208
Jolliet, Louis, 47
Jonathan (cook), 213, 214–15
Jones, Joe, 172
Josselyn, John, 237
Joy of Cooking (Rombauer), 52

Katrina, Hurricane, 191–92, 203–4, 209, 211
Keese, Kristine, 229, 242–47, 248, 249
Keese, Robert, 242–47, 249
Kellogg, John Harvey, 181
KFC Double Down Sandwich, 178
Kickapoo Indians, 263
King, Grace, 222
Kinney, John, 83–84, 85, 89, 109, 111
Kitchen Literacy (Vileisis), 178
Knowlton, Thomas, 271–72
Knowlton's Rangers, 271

Lady's Receipt-Book, The (Leslie), 96
Lafayette, Marquis de, 152–53
Lagasse, Emeril, 209
Lahontan, Lake, 99, 101
Lahontan cutthroat trout:
      hatchery maintanence process for, 102–8
      of Pyramid Lake, 98–99, 102, 106, 108
      size of, 105–6
      taste of, 102
Laird, James, 116–17
lake trout, 84, 88
Langdon, Olivia, *see* Clemens, Olivia Langdon
La Salle, René-Robert de, 198
Leary, Katy, 221–23
Least Heat-Moon, William, 2
Lee, Bessie, 64
Leslie, Eliza, 96, 181, 224
Lewis, Edna, 73, 283
Lewis, Meriwether, 25
Lewis, Rodney, 173
Life on the Mississippi (Twain), 4, 36
Lincoln, Abraham, 34, 161,
      Thanksgiving holiday and, 240
Lincoln, Mary Johnson, 241
Little Dixie, 57
L.L. Bean Game and Fish Cookbook, 52
lobster, 113–14, 148–49, 163–64, 179
London, Jack, 138
Long, Billy, 66, 75
Long, Heath, 65–67, 74–75, 78
Longfellow, Henry Wadsworth, 155, 158
Louisiana Foodservice EXPO, 207–8

McAllister, Ward, 152, 161, 163
McCulloch-Williams, Martha, 62
McFarlin cranberries, 219–20
McNuggets, 11, 285
McPhail, Tory, 209–15
Mann, Mary, 181
Manning's Oyster House, 121
maple syrup, 4, 7, 14
      Canadian production of, 269–70
      clarity of, 255–57
      evaporator for, 277–78
      grading of, 255–56
      as local food, 266–67
      making, 254, 262–74, 276–79
      Native Americans and, 261
      recipes for, 255, 258, 267, 268–69, 276
      slavery and, 265–66

maple syrup (*cont.*)
    sugar in, 260–61
    Twain's fondness for, 252–53
    vacuum system for, 273–74
    of Vermont, 269
    weather and, 261–62
maple trees:
    of New England woods, 253
    sap of, 260–61, 270–71, 274
    tapping of, 270–71
    wild groves of, 253
Mardi Gras, 188–89
Margaret, queen of Italy, 175
Marin Rod & Gun Club, 140, 141, 145
Market Assistant, The (De Voe), 32
Marryat, Frederick, 59–60, 79, 123, 128, 163
Martha's Vineyard, 225
Maryland Department of Natural Resources,
    170, 173
Maryland Watermen's Society, 174
Massasoit, 234–36
Mayer, Todd, 141
Melville, Herman, 30
Menken, Adah, 117
Men's Health, 203–4
mercury, 136–37, 138, 143
milk, 5–6
Miller, Joaquin, 109
Mississippi River, 85, 86, 87, 282
    alteration of, 199–203
    drainage basin of, 198
    fish of, 199
    flooding of, 198–99, 201
    in flux, 186–87
    Great Flood of 1927 of, 201
    sediment of, 200
    steamboating on, 185–86, 199
    wetlands and, 200–204
    see also New Orleans, La.
Mississippi River–Gulf Outlet (MRGO),
    192, 202
Missouri, 41–42
Mitchell, Joseph, 2, 161, 163
Moby-Dick (Melville), 30, 244n
Moffett, Pamela Clemens, 188
Monroe, Cameron, 70
Monroe, James, 30
Monterey Bay Aquarium, 23
Moore, Francis, 60
Moore, Michelle, 107

Mormon Battalion, 109
Morning Call, 119
Morrison Creek, 106
Moto (restaurant), 65
Mourt's Relation (Winslow), 233, 238
Mr. B's Bistro, 190
Mrs. Lincoln's Boston Cook Book
    (Lincoln), 241
muskrat, 52, 59
mussels, 14, 122, 285
    filter feeding by, 142
    marine life of, 132–33
    recipe for, 133
    steamed, 119–20, 130

Narragansett Indians, 234
Natchez Indians, 184
National Lahontan Fish Hatchery, 106
National Oceanic and Atmospheric
    Administration, 141, 208
Native Americans, 27, 30, 54, 71, 218,
    253, 261
    cranberry cultivation by, 219
    gumbo and, 194–95
    prairie and, 27, 30
    settlement of New England and, 233–35
    terrapins and, 151, 164–65
    Thanksgiving holiday and, 240
    see also specific tribes
Nevada Fish Commissioners, 104
Newell, Frederick, 104
New England:
    settlement of, 233–35
    weather of, 261–62
New England Farmer, 272
Newlands Project (1905), 104
New Orleans, La., 11, 96, 121, 183–208
    cuisine of, 184–85
    emancipation of slaves and effects on
        cooking, 205–6
    ethnic population of, 184–85
    farmers' market of, 190–91
    fish of, 188
    Foodservice EXPO of, 207–8
    French Market of, 184–85, 190
    geography of, 188
    Hurricane Katrina and, 191–92, 203–4
    Mardi Gras in, 188–89
    restaurants of, 207–8
    traditional dishes of, 195

Twain in, 183–84
wetlands of, 202
see also Cajun cooking; Creole cooking;
    Mississippi River
New Orleans Cookbook, The (Collins and
    Collins), 193
New Orleans Fish House, 210, 211–12
Newton, Ill., 19–20
New York City, 32–33
    Collect Pond of, 89–90
New Yorker, 161
New York State Agricultural Fair of
    1844, 256
New York Times, 151, 152, 163, 165, 176,
    177, 178
Norma's Restaurant, 113
Northland (cooperative), 243
Northwestern, 212
Northwood (Hale), 239

Oberle, Frank, 38–48
    controlled burn and, 44–48
    on prairies, 41–42, 47–48
Oberle, Judy, 39
Obernolte, Rena, 141, 143–46
Occidental Hotel, 117–19, 121
Ocean Spray (cooperative), 243, 247
Ohlone Indians, 133–34
okra, 194
"Old Times on the Mississippi" (Twain), 155
oleomargarine, 204
Oliver, Sandra, 236–37, 244*n*
Olympia oysters, 126–28, 129, 138
Omnivore's Dilemma, The (Pollan), 25
opossum, 50, 52, 75, 76, 282
    recipes for, 61–62, 68
    as slave food, 59
Ostrea conchaphila (oyster), 126
O. edulis (oyster), 123
Ottawa Indians, 260
oysters, 177, 188, 282, 286
    Armoricaine, 124
    Bluepoint, 178
    filter feeding by, 123–24, 142, 143
    in Hangtown fry, 113–15
    hydraulic mining and, 136–37
    Mexican, 127–28
    Olympia, 126–28, 129, 138
    poaching of, 137–38
    preparations of, 120–21

raw, 121–22
recipes for, 115, 123, 129–30, 133, 139,
    144–45
in salt roast, 121
of San Francisco Bay, 126–27
Save the Bay project and, 140–44
shell mounds of, 133–34
silt and, 135–36
species of, 123
Sweetwater, 124
transportation of, 121–22
Twain's fondness for, 120–21
in Twain's ideal menu, 128–29

Paiute Indians, 98, 99–101, 102, 105, 108
passenger pigeon, 282–83
pasteurization process, 5
Paul (author's friend), 207
Peacock, Scott, 283
"Personal Habits of Siamese Twins, The"
    (Twain), 155
Pfaff's Cellar, 117–18
Physiology of Taste (Brillat-Savarin), 94
Picayune's Creole Cook Book, The, 190,
    195, 197
Pilot Peak, 106
Plaice, Scott, 63, 64, 75, 76
Polk County Possum Club, 67
Pollan, Michael, 25, 181
pompano, 205
Pontchartrain, Lake, 188
"Possum" (Dunbar), 75–76
*Practical American Cookery and Household
    Management* (Corson), 29, 87, 151, 276
Practical Cooking and Dinner Giving
    (Henderson), 38, 43
prairie:
    conservation of, 42–43
    corn farming and, 19, 25, 30–31, 35–37
    erosion of, 35–36
    fertilizer and, 35
    fire and, 26–28, 45–46
    as "food desert," 25
    grasses of, 25
    of Missouri, 41–42
    name of, 25–26
    Native Americans and, 27, 30
    Oberle on, 41–43, 47–48
    Oberle's controlled burn of, 44–48
    preservation of, 26

prairie (*cont.*)
  railways and, 31–32
  scale of, 25
  sod of, 30–31
  soil of, 17, 30–31, 57
  steel plow and, 31
  today, 26
  Twain's recollection of, 16–17, 26
Prairie-Chicken, 33
prairie chickens, 14, 15–48, 97, 133, 178, 282
  booming display of, 20–25, 28
  cooking, 23–24
  farming and, 30
  habitat loss and, 35
  hunting of, 17–18
  ideal habitat of, 30
  instructions for selecting, 38
  market hunting of, 32–33
  meat of, 23
  population of, 20, 29–30
  railways and, 31–33
  recipes for, 18–19, 29, 33–34, 43
Prairie Ridge State Natural Area, 19, 35
Prohibition, 170, 179
Proulx, Amy, 269–74, 276–79
Proulx, Bill, 269–74, 276–79
Prudhomme, Paul, 209
Pure Air Native Seed Company, 39
purple coneflower (echinacea), 25
Pyramid Lake, 98–105
  agricultural diversions from, 104
  alkaline water of, 102
  development and, 104–5
  fishery of, 103–4
  modern extent of, 99
  trout of, *see* Lahontan cutthroat trout

Quaker City, 154, 166
Quarles, John, 16, 32, 38, 57, 250
Quarles farm, 16, 32, 38, 74, 252, 282
  meals served at, 11, 17, 23–24
  slaves of, 53–54, 57, 61, 69–70
  Southern cooking and, 72–73

raccoon:
  in author's kitchen, 49–50
  Cantu's preparation of, 65–66
  eating, 59–61
  fat of, 65, 75–76
  fur of, 63

  hunting, 53, 66–67
  overview of, 54–55
  recipe for, 78–79
  as slave food, 59–60
  taste of, 52, 76, 79
  West African food and, 60
  see also Gillett Coon Supper
"Raid on the Oyster Pirates, A"
  (London), 138
rainbow trout, 88
Randolph, Mary, 139
Ranhofer, Charles, 23–24
recipes:
  for cranberries, 232
  for diamondback terrapin, 150–51, 153–54,
    160–61, 169, 180
  for German coffee, 5
  for maple syrup, 255, 258, 267, 268–69, 276
  for mussels, 133
  for oysters, 115, 123, 129–30, 133,
    139, 144–45
  for prairie hen, 18–19, 29, 33–34, 43
  for raccoon, 77–78
  for Thanksgiving, 249–50
  for trout, 95–96, 108
Red Cross, 116
redtop grass, 35
Reilly (author's friend), 207
rice, 56–57
Rich Neck Plantation, 60
Ricketts, Ed, 126
Roughing It (Twain), 86, 109–10, 116
Royal West Africa Company, 60
Rush, Benjamin, 265–67

salmon, 178, 179, 209, 213
  of San Francisco Bay, 145–46
Saltwater Foodways (Oliver), 244n
Samson, Steve, 105
Sandler, Hilary, 247–48, 249
San Francisco:
  fish abundance of, 134
  fog of, 132
  Occidental Hotel of, 117–19, 121
  offshore upwelling and, 132
  oyster houses of, 122
  Twain's flight to, 116–17
San Francisco Bay:
  filling in of, 134–37
  fisheries of, 138–39

oyster poaching in, 137–38
oysters of, 126–27
restoration of, 140–46
salmon of, 145–46
ship hulks in, 135
water flow of, 124–25
Sanitary Commission, 116
savanna, 47
Save the Bay project, 141
Sawyer, Tom, 125*n*
Science, 22, 33
Scoofy, Mr., 127, 129
Scotland, 72
Scribner's, 128
Sea of Galilee, 93–94
Sea Salt (restaurant), 128
Senegal Concession, 56
Separatists, 236
sheepshead (fish), 188, 193, 206, 211,
    214, 285
  catching of, 209–10
  cooking of, 195–96
  recipes for, 189–90, 215
  taste of, 210, 214–15
Shoalwater Bay, 126
Shoshone Indians, 27, 101
shrimp, 191–92
"Shuckee Duckee," 208
Shuman, Carrie V., 161
Sierra ice, 97
Signs and Seasons (Burroughs), 278
Simmons, Amelia, 162, 220, 237
Sioux Indians, 27
Skimmerhorn, John, 105
slaves, slavery:
  in colonial Virginia, 51
  foods of, 70–71, 72
  local environment and, 58–59
  maple syrup industry and, 265–66
  opossum as food of, 59
  on Quarles farm, 53–54, 57, 61, 69–70
  rice cultivation and, 56
  terrapin and, 151, 152, 164–65
  Twain's recollection of, 58–59
  West African foods and, 60
slumgullion, 84
Snell's window, 90
"Sociable Jimmy" (Twain), 37
Soulard Farmer's Market, 66
Soul Food Farm, 114

South Carolina, 56
Southern cooking, 61, 69–74, 205, 283
  African influence on, 70–72
  Twain on, 69, 72
Sparganothis (fruitworm), 245
speckled trout, 193, 209
Spenger's (restaurant), 133
spotted trout, 88
Springfield, Ill., 34–35
Squanto (Tisquantum), 234
steak:
  dry-aged, 3
  Twain's favorite, 1–2, 3
  wet-aged, 3, 6–7
steamboating, 185–86, 199
Stearns, Bret, 227, 228–29, 230
steel plow, 31
Steinbeck, John, 2, 126
Stormfield (Twain's house), 275
Stowe, Harriet Beecher, 155
suckerfish (cui-ui), 100–101
sugar, 256
  in maple syrup, 260–61
sugar bushes, 253
Summit Lake, 105
Sutherland, J. B., 97
Sweetwater oysters, 124
Swift, Gustavus, 97

Tahoe, Lake, 83
  name of, 91–92
  today, 95
  trout of, 84–85, 87–90
  Twain's forest fire at, 109–12
  water of, 83–85, 90
Tahoe Research Group, 98
Tales of the Fish Patrol (London), 138
Tallent, Annie, 91
taste:
  of diamondback terrapin, 163
  of Lahontan cutthroat trout, 102
  memory and, 94
  of oysters, 127
  of raccoon, 52, 76, 79
Taste of Country Cooking, The
    (Lewis), 73
Taylor, John Martin, 60
Taylor Shellfish, 128
technosyrup, 277–78
terrapin, *see* diamondback terrapin

Thanksgiving, 220
    cranberries and, 218–19, 238, 240–41
    first, 223–24, 233–36, 239–40
    ideal dinner for, 238–39
    as national custom, 240
    recipe for, 249–50
    standard menu for, 238
    turkey and, 237
    at Twain's Hartford home, 221–23
Thanksgiving (Baker), 237
Third Delta Conveyance Channel, 202–3
Thomas, Elizabeth, 105–6
Thomas, Robert B., 266
Tidwell, Mike, 201–2
Tisquantum (Squanto), 234
Tom Sawyer Abroad (Twain), 6
Tooker, Poppy, 192, 193
Top Chef (television show), 213
Tramp Abroad, A (Twain), 1–2, 94–95
transcontinental railroad, 137
trout, 215–16, 282
    brook, 14, 84, 88, 89
    brown, 88, 108
    cutthroat, 88–89, 90, 100–101, 105
    eyes of, 90
    ice and, 204–5
    Lahontan, *see* Lahontan cutthroat trout
    lake, 84, 88
    rainbow, 88
    recipes for, 87, 95–96, 108
    species and varieties of, 88–89
    speckled, 193, 209
    spotted, 88
    Twain's fondness of, 87–88
    water quality and, 89–90
    world record for, 105
turkey, 217–18, 282
    recipe for, 220
    Thanksgiving holiday and, 237
Twain, Mark:
    alias of, 118*n*
    bankruptcy of, 257
    Confederate service of, 86
    death of, 279
    and decision to go west, 86
    depression of, 256–58, 275
    in European and Middle Eastern tour,
        154–55, 166–68
    on European coffee, 130–31
    European food disliked by, 1–2, 12, 166–68
    fame of, 154
    final years of, 275
    in flight to San Francisco, 116–17
    food enthusiasm of, 10–12
    forest fire caused by, 109–12
    German coffee recipe of, 5
    Hartford home of, 220–21
    ice water liked by, 96–98
    ideal breakfast of, 217
    ideal menu of, 8–10, 242, 251,
        284–85
    ideal steak dinner of, 1–3
    at Lake Tahoe, 83–85, 90
    Livy's death and, 264–65
    maple syrup liked by, 252–53
    marriage of, 155
    on New England weather, 261–62
    New Orleans visited by, 183–84
    oyster menu of, 128–29
    prairie recollected by, 16–17, 26
    as public speaker, 156, 158
    in raccoon hunt, 53
    slaves in boyhood of, 58–59
    on Southern-style cooking, 69, 72
    as steamboat pilot, 183, 185–87
    Susy's death and, 257–58
    Thanksgiving celebrated by, 221–23
    turkey hunt and tomato garden,
        250–51
    Whittier dinner fiasco and, 155–61, 169
    youth recalled by, 15–17

UMass Cranberry Station, 219
United States River Commission, 199

Vallisneria americana (wild celery), 20
Vanderhoop, Jannette, 225–26, 231–32
Varanese, John, 212
Vermont, 269
Vertigo (film), 171
Vesuvius restaurant, 134
Vileisis, Ann, 32, 178
Vineyard Open Land Foundation, 229
Virgil, 278
Virginia & Truckee Railroad, 97, 104
Virginia City Territorial Enterprise, 92,
    111, 117
Virginia City Union, 117
Virginia colony, 51
Virginia Housewife, The (Randolph), 139

W., George, 211
*Walton's Vermont Register and Farmer's
   Almanac,* 266
Wampanoag Center for Bicultural
   History, 229
Wampanoag Indians:
   common lands of, 226–28
   cranberries in diet of, 236–37
   cranberry harvest of, 225–29, 231
   potluck dinner of, 231–32
   settlement of New England and, 233–35
Ward, Sam, 165
Warner, Abe, 126
Washington, George, 152–53
   Thanksgiving holiday and, 237
Washington Post, 150, 151–52, 165, 173–74
Washoe Indians, 109
Was Huck Black? (Fishkin), 73
Webb, Charles Henry, 117
Webb, Peg Leg John, 247
West Africa, 56, 60
   cooking techniques of, 71–72
Whilden, Marguerite, 170–74, 180

White House Cook Book (Gillette), 130,
   154, 162
Whitman, Walt, 117
Whittier, John Greenleaf, 155, 158
Whydah (Benin), 56, 60
Widdiss, Gladys, 227, 231
Wilcox, Estelle Woods, 19, 115, 250, 264
wild celery (*Vallisneria americana*), 20
Wilder, Laura Ingalls, 2, 267
Winslow, Edward, 233, 236, 239
Wisconsin, 249
Woksis (Iroquois leader), 260
Wolfe, Frank, 62–65, 67, 76
Worcestershire sauce, 7–8
World Wide Opportunities on Organic Farms
   (WWOOF), 245, 247

Yeardley, Temperance Flowerdew, 50
Yerba Linda Cove, 135
Yorktown, Battle of, 152–53
Young, Alexander, 239–40

Zillion Dollar Lobster Frittata, 113